Chaplaincy and the Soul
of Health and Social Care

by the same author

Spiritual Dimensions of Pastoral Care
Practical Theology in a
Multidisciplinary Context
Edited by David Willows and John Swinton
ISBN 978 1 85302 892 2
eISBN 978 1 84642 218 8

Spirituality and Mental Health Care
Rediscovering a 'Forgotten' Dimension
John Swinton
ISBN 978 1 85302 804 5
eISBN 978 1 84642 220 1

of related interest

**Chaplaincy and Spiritual Care
in Mental Health Settings**
Edited by Jean Fletcher
Foreword by Professor John Swinton
Afterword by Rev Canon Dr Margaret Whipp
ISBN 978 1 78592 571 9
eISBN 978 1 78450 981 1

Spiritual Care in Practice
Case Studies in Healthcare Chaplaincy
Edited by George Fitchett and Steve Nolan
Foreword by Christina Puchalski
Afterword by John Swinton
ISBN 978 1 84905 976 3
eISBN 978 0 85700 876 3

Evidence-Based Healthcare Chaplaincy
A Research Reader
*Edited by George Fitchett, Kelsey
B. White and Kathryn Lyndes*
ISBN 978 1 78592 820 8
eISBN 978 1 78450 923 1

Case Studies in Spiritual Care
Healthcare Chaplaincy Assessments,
Interventions and Outcomes
Edited by George Fitchett and Steve Nolan
ISBN 978 1 78592 783 6
eISBN 978 1 78450 705 3

Critical Care
Delivering Spiritual Care in Healthcare Contexts
*Edited by Jonathan Pye, Peter
Sedgwick and Andrew Todd*
ISBN 978 1 84905 497 3
eISBN 978 0 85700 901 2

**Ethical Questions in
Healthcare Chaplaincy**
Learning to Make Informed Decisions
Pia Matthews
ISBN 978 1 78592 421 7
eISBN 978 1 78450 788 6

Treating Body and Soul
A Clinicians' Guide to Supporting the Physical,
Mental and Spiritual Needs of Their Patients
Edited by Peter Wells
ISBN 978 1 78592 148 3
eISBN 978 1 78450 417 5

Spiritual Care in Common Terms
How Chaplains Can Effectively Describe the
Spiritual Needs of Patients in Medical Records
Gordon J. Hilsman, D.Min.
Foreword by James H. Gunn
ISBN 978 1 78592 724 9
eISBN 978 1 78450 369 7

**Talking About Spirituality in
Health Care Practice**
A Resource for the Multi-
Professional Health Care Team
Gillian White
ISBN 978 1 84310 305 9
eISBN 978 1 84642 493 9

Spiritual Care for Allied Health Practice
A Person-centered Approach
*Edited by Lindsay B. Carey, PhD
and Bernice A. Mathisen, PhD*
Foreword by Harold G. Koenig, RN, MD
ISBN 978 1 78592 220 6
eISBN 978 1 78450 501 1

Chaplaincy and the Soul of Health and Social Care

Fostering Spiritual Wellbeing in Emerging Paradigms of Care

Edited by
Ewan Kelly and **John Swinton**

Foreword by Stephen Pattison

Jessica Kingsley *Publishers*
London and Philadelphia

Table I.1 is adapted from Kelly, E. (2013) 'Policy, practice and strategic priorities and healthcare chaplaincy.' *Scottish Journal of Healthcare Chaplaincy* 16, 53–59. Copyright © Equinox Publishing Ltd, 2013.
The bullet list on page 40 is reprinted by permission from Springer Nature: *Journal of Religion and Health*, 'The spiritual and theological challenges of stillbirth for bereaved parents.' Nuzum, D., Meaney, S. and O'Donoghue, K. Copyright © 2017.
'St Julian and the Leper' on page 61 is reproduced from R. S. Thomas, *Selected Poems 1946–1968* (Bloodaxe Books, 1986). With permission of Bloodaxe Books www.bloodaxebooks.com.
Chapter 11 is an updated version of the following article: Swinton, J. (2003) 'A question of identity: What does it mean for chaplains to become healthcare professionals?' *Scottish Journal for Healthcare Chaplaincy* 6, 2, 2–7. Copyright © Equinox Publishing Ltd, 2003.
Figure 12.1 is reproduced from Murphy, P.E., Fitchett, G. and Canada, A.L. (2008) 'Adult Spirituality for Persons with Chronic Illness.' In V.B. Carson and H.G. Koenig (eds) *Spiritual Dimensions of Nursing Practice* (revised edition). West Conshohocken, PA: Templeton Foundation Press. With kind permission from Templeton Foundation Press.
Figure 12.2 is reproduced from Snowden, A., Telfer, I., Kelly, E., Bunniss, S. *et al.* (2013) 'The construction of the Lothian PROM.' *The Scottish Journal of Healthcare Chaplaincy* 16, 3–16. Copyright © Equinox Publishing Ltd, 2013.
'Visiting Hour' on page 289 is reproduced from Stewart Conn, *The Touch of Time: New & Selected Poems* (Bloodaxe Books, 2014). With permission of Bloodaxe Books www.bloodaxebooks.com.
The bullet list on page 312 is reproduced from UK Board of Healthcare Chaplaincy (2017) *Spiritual and Religious Care Capabilities and Competences for Healthcare Chaplains Bands 5, 6, 7 and 8*. Cambridge: UK Board of Healthcare Chaplaincy. With kind permission from UK Board of Healthcare Chaplaincy.
VBRP, NAVVY and the PROM are NES products and use of these products for educational and/or commercial purposes is only possible with written permission from NES.

First published in 2020
by Jessica Kingsley Publishers
73 Collier Street
London N1 9BE, UK
and
400 Market Street, Suite 400
Philadelphia, PA 19106, USA

www.jkp.com

Copyright © Jessica Kingsley Publishers 2020
Foreword copyright © Stephen Pattison 2020

Library of Congress Cataloging in Publication Data
A CIP catalog record for this book is available from the Library of Congress
British Library Cataloguing in Publication Data
A CIP catalogue record for this book is available from the British Library

ISBN 978 1 78592 224 4
eISBN 978 1 78450 498 4

Printed and bound in Great Britain

MIX
Paper from
responsible sources
FSC
www.fsc.org FSC® C013056

With thanks to those whose stories are shared, with permission, to illustrate what spiritual need feels like and ground this collaborative project in the reality of why it was conceived and sought publication.

Contents

Collaborators

Timothy P Bennison
Timothy P Bennison has a background in person-centred counselling and is Head of Spiritual Care at NHS Forth Valley in Scotland. He is involved in the development and governance of NHSScotland's Community Chaplaincy Listening (CCL) service as well as being a CCL listener and trainer.

Don Bryant
Don Bryant is an ex-service user at Mersey Care NHS Foundation Trust in England. He was on the board of the Mental Health Network and is presently involved in mental health research and development as well as being on the investigation panel for serious incidents occurring in the Trust.

Eva Buelens
Eva Buelens is a PhD student at the KU Leuven in Belgium, researching the outcomes and active underlying processes of hospital chaplaincy activities. Prior to this, she worked as a hospital chaplain for several years as well as conducting research on spiritual care delivered by volunteers, screening and patient-reported outcomes.

Kenneth J Donaldson
Kenneth J Donaldson is medical director at NHS Dumfries and Galloway, Scotland. He is also a consultant nephrologist. His main interests are in delivering true person-centred care and enhancing the experience of service users. Ken is also passionate about improving staff wellbeing.

Hans Evers
Hans Evers, MA, BCC, directs the Spiritual Care Service at the Leiden University Medical Center (the Netherlands). He teaches and publishes about healthcare chaplaincy in general and especially about pastoral and moral counselling.

George Fitchett
George Fitchett, DMin, PhD, is Professor and Director of Research, Department of Religion, Health, and Human Values, Rush University Medical Center, Chicago, Illinois. He is a certified chaplain (APC) and chaplain educator (ACPE). George holds a PhD in epidemiology and with Wendy Cadge co-directs the *Transforming Chaplaincy* project.

David W Fleenor
The Rev. David W Fleenor, STM, BCC, is Director of Education at the Center for Spirituality and Health at Mount Sinai in New York City. He is an ACPE-certified educator, a board-certified chaplain and an Episcopal priest who has served as a chaplaincy educator and clinician in oncology, psychiatric and medical settings, and as a parish priest.

Kevin Franz
Kevin Franz recently retired from his post as lead chaplain for Mental Healthcare in NHS Greater Glasgow and Clyde. Having studied history and theology at Edinburgh University, he completed a doctoral thesis on ethics and public policy. A frequent broadcaster, he is a member of the Religious Society of Friends.

Derek Fraser
Derek Fraser has served for the past 17 years as lead chaplain at Cambridge University Hospitals. He was also chair of the UK Board of Healthcare Chaplaincy from its inception until 2017. Derek has been a major figure in the development of chaplaincy in the UK and continues to teach and research the field in semi-retirement in Cambridge.

Daniel H Grossoehme
Daniel H Grossoehme, DMin, MS, is staff scientist in the Palliative Care Program at Akron Children's Hospital, Ohio, USA. Prior to this, he was a paediatric hospital chaplain for 26 years as well as conducting research on spirituality and health behaviours. He is an associate member of the Society of Ordained Scientists.

George F Handzo
The Rev. George F Handzo, APBCC, BCC, CSSBB, is director of health services research and quality at HealthCare Chaplaincy Network and president of Handzo Consulting. He is regarded as one of the foremost authorities on the deployment and practice of professional healthcare chaplaincy.

Cheryl Holmes

Cheryl Holmes, OAM (BAppSc, DipPastMin, Grad Cert, MAppSocSc), is the chief executive officer for Spiritual Health Victoria in Australia. Her professional experience and publications focus on spiritual care in health, organisational change and leadership. Cheryl commenced a PhD in 2016 exploring the narratives shaping spiritual care in public hospitals.

Ewan Kelly

Ewan Kelly is Spiritual Care Lead for NHS Dumfries and Galloway, Scotland and has for many years been involved in promoting collaborative innovation in spiritual care practice, research, education and strategic development.

Jo Kennedy

Jo Kennedy is a facilitator, consultant and coach who works across the faith, health and social care sectors in Scotland supporting them to provide more meaningful support to those who use them.

Carlo Leget

Carlo Leget is full professor of care ethics at the University of Humanistic Studies in Utrecht, the Netherlands. At the same university he holds an endowed chair in ethics and spirituality in palliative care, established by the Netherlands Comprehensive Cancer Organisation and the Association Hospice Care Netherlands.

Steve Nolan

Steve Nolan, PhD, is chaplain at Princess Alice Hospice and a Visiting Research Fellow at the University of Winchester, England. A dual-qualified chaplain and BACP-accredited counsellor/therapist, his publications include *Spiritual Care at the End of Life: The Chaplain as a 'Hopeful Presence'* and two volumes of chaplains' case studies co-edited with George Fitchett.

Daniel Robert Nuzum

Daniel Robert Nuzum is an Anglican priest, healthcare chaplain and Clinical Pastoral Education supervisor at Cork University Hospital, Ireland, and a lecturer and member of the Pregnancy Loss Research Group at the College of Medicine and Health, University College Cork.

Madeleine Parkes

Madeleine Parkes is a spiritual care practitioner within a large hospital chaplaincy team in Birmingham, UK. She specialises in pastoral and spiritual care for non-religious patients and has a special interest in psychiatric and mental health chaplaincy. She is studying for a PhD in Divinity at the University of Aberdeen.

Neil Pembroke

Neil Pembroke is associate professor of Practical Theology in the School of Historical and Philosophical Inquiry at the University of Queensland, Brisbane, Australia. He received his PhD from New College, University of Edinburgh. His latest book is *Foundations of Pastoral Counselling* (SCM Press).

Julian Raffay

Julian Raffay is specialist chaplain (Research, Education and Development) at Mersey Care NHS Foundation Trust, England. He is currently researching the ethics of co-production and the relationship between mental health services and faith communities.

Raymond Reddicliffe

Raymond Reddicliffe, PhD, is an honorary research fellow (Studies in Religion) in the School of Historical and Philosophical Inquiry within the University of Queensland, Brisbane, Australia. He is also a minister of the Uniting Church in Australia, with extensive experience as a church leader, healthcare chaplain and clinical pastoral educator.

Austyn Snowden

Austyn Snowden is professor in Mental Health at Edinburgh Napier University, and visiting professor at Leuven University, Belgium, where he is lead researcher of the European Research Institute for Chaplains in Healthcare. He is co-author of the Scottish PROM, the first validated measure of the impact of chaplain interventions.

Ian Stirling

Ian Stirling's recent thesis, *Deep Silences: A Spiritual Autoethnography – Reclaiming Inner Space and Silence as a Locus of the Sacred*, reflects his decade of involvement within hospice chaplaincy and the wider spiritual care landscape of Scotland. Ian has now returned to his roots in parish ministry.

Mark Stobert

Mark Stobert is lead chaplain at Cambridge University Hospitals NHS Foundation Trust. He has 23 years of experience as a healthcare chaplain and is chair of the UK Board of Healthcare Chaplaincy. Mark is currently studying for a doctorate in Practical Theology using critical reflection to critique his practice of creating Safe Space for Slow Questions.

John Swinton

John Swinton is professor in Practical Theology and Pastoral Care in the School of Divinity, Religious Studies and Philosophy at the University of Aberdeen. He has a background in nursing and healthcare chaplaincy and has researched and published extensively within the areas of practical theology, mental health, spirituality and human wellbeing and the theology of disability.

Iain Telfer

From a background in Church of Scotland parish ministry, Iain Telfer worked for 18 years as a healthcare chaplain in the Royal Infirmary of Edinburgh. With Austyn Snowden, Iain has developed the first validated, internationally recognised Patient Reported Outcome Measure for spiritual care.

Anne Vandenhoeck

Anne Vandenhoeck is an assistant professor in the Faculty of Theology and Religious Studies at the KU Leuven in Belgium. Anne has years of experience as a chaplain. She was the coordinator of the European Network of Healthcare Chaplaincy (2010–2016) and is the director of the European Research Institute for Chaplains in Healthcare.

Foreword

Stephen Pattison

During an address to a congregation at the Anglican Cathedral in Cairo in 1944, Field Marshall Bernard Montgomery alluded to the fact that for him going into battle without his chaplains would be as significant as doing so without his artillery. A clergyman's child, Montgomery was living in what proved to be the dying days of Christendom at a time when an established church unquestioningly provided religious support to state institutions and their members, most of whom would have been brought up as at least nominally Christian. The fighting power that was enhanced by chaplains was not specified by Montgomery. Did he think they were valuable because they communicated with the divine by their prayers, provided pastoral support, created friendships, enhanced morale, oiled the organisational machine, dealt with death ritually, created moral legitimacy or just represented aspects of normal civilian reality amidst the chaos of war? Maybe all these things, and more. The point is that neither chaplains nor their employers had to articulate, understand or question a role that was taken to be integral in the forces as in other contexts like hospitals. Chaplaincy had an accepted, uncontroversial role, was undoubtedly worthy, and, also, perhaps a little dull. It did not require much in the way of reflection, research, justification or critique.

Things could not be more different today, in all types of chaplaincy across the Western world, and in the health and social care sphere in particular. Within the Christendom paradigm, health and social care chaplaincy was mainly a matter of delivering overtly Christian religious services while being present to, and accompanying, individuals within a medicalised environment focused on disease and deficit. As this fascinating collection of writings shows, that model has been blown out of the water. Most health and social care users are not Christians, spiritual care for all, rather than religious care for a few, prevails, chaplains are employed by and accountable to public institutions rather than sending churches, and the whole health and care system is re-orienting itself towards patient empowerment, community prevention, promoting wellbeing, identifying individual and social assets, and resilience, all against a background of financial austerity and the quest for ever-greater effectiveness and efficiency.

With all this uncomfortable, maybe unwelcome, contextual change in which its nature, role, legitimacy and value is being challenged, chaplaincy is fundamentally re-orienting itself as it begins to articulate new modes of understanding, working and being. Thus, unsought crisis is midwifing professional and intellectual creativity. Nowhere is this creativity being seen more clearly than in Scotland, the native land of this volume's editors and of many of its contributors. Chaplaincy is in many ways in a liminal, confused, creative and malleable state as it seeks to respond more effectively and appropriately to its changing context and environment. This book, written by some of the most interesting players on the scene from around the world, provides a unique ringside seat for understanding what is going on and listening in to important discussions and debates.

Ewan Kelly and John Swinton are to be congratulated on putting together such a strong collection of chapters that cover so many both fascinating and disputed areas of concern emerging in the crucible of contemporary health and social care chaplaincy. Here are just a few of the valuable things I have taken from this book. First, the authorship is international, bringing together leading thinkers on the nature and future of chaplaincy from a number of different countries and showing how chaplaincy ideas and practices are now being shared worldwide. While the book is rooted in experience in Scotland and the UK, it is not parochial in its focus. Second, these thinkers, all of whom are clear, passionate and erudite, are allowed to disagree within and between chapters, sometimes directly with each other, on issues such as the importance of outcomes or of research. Readers are taken directly into debate and deliberation; there is no attempt at homogenisation or finding a party line. And the topics covered in the book do much to update and illuminate key concepts and issues in chaplaincy, providing basic information and critical discussion on issues such as the nature of professionalisation, training, education, evidence-based practice, asset-based work, co-production, values, spirituality, spiritual assessment, leadership and strategy.

Chaplaincy and the Soul of Health and Social Care will, I believe, prove to be an indispensable, timely, stimulating and enjoyable resource and companion for contemporary health and social care chaplaincy as it continues to explore its identity and future. Like any good book, it raises more questions than it answers and opens up many questions in the reader's mind, not least because of its (properly) very porous and partial nature. I wonder, for example, if there might be a distinctive role for women's perspectives in chaplaincy; would they be different from those of the men who wrote most of the chapters in this volume? And what of the place and needs of the many lay volunteers working in the professionalising health and social care environment of the new chaplains? Similarly, while there are parts of the world which are fairly religiously monochrome and perhaps almost entirely non-religious, in many parts of the Western world there are minorities for whom religion rather than spirituality is primary. What then of multi-faith religious chaplaincy in and for these groups in publicly funded institutions? In the same vein, is there any real continuing role and value beyond a kind of nostalgia for Christian tradition and theology as a resource for chaplaincy in non-religious institutions? Or does this have to be relegated to the past in the interests of fitting in with the interests of secular institutions powered by utilitarian ratio-instrumental ideologies and practices? Such questions might also contribute to seeking the soul of health and social care, and, indeed, the soul of chaplaincy. So perhaps the editors or interested others might like to compile another volume which broadens understanding and debate even further?

For chaplains and all those who care about their work, theoretically or practically, this is going to be such a useful, interesting book. I hope its many readers will enjoy and gain as much from reading it as I have.

Stephen Pattison
Formerly of the University of Birmingham, UK

Introduction

Ewan Kelly and John Swinton

The dogmas of the quiet past are inadequate to the stormy present.
The occasion is piled high with difficulty, and we must rise to the
occasion. As our case is new, so we must think anew and act anew

Abraham Lincoln
(address to Congress, 1862, cited by Lyon 2013, p.3)

Current global socio-political and healthcare context

We consider the most worthwhile introductions to books which seek to
aid reflection on the correlation between practice and theory to not only
set out the purpose and content of that book, but also to model something
of the approach towards which its contributors point. In *Pastoral Care and
Liberation Theology*, Stephen Pattison (1997) emphasises the significance
of first analysing a socio-political context in order to develop meaningful
practice in that context which promotes the wellbeing of people. Chaplaincy,
like any other healthcare profession, has been guilty of shoehorning models
of practice into contexts rather than developing practice which is fit for
purpose in particular times and places. Hence, this book begins with a brief
analysis of the post-industrial world and its attitudes towards health and care,
in which chaplains and the people they work with currently inhabit.

Andrew Lyon's (2013) use of words from Abraham Lincoln's address
to the American Congress during a time of great transition and challenge
is highly apt for people designing and delivering health and care services,
including chaplains, in the current era. This edited book has been co-
constructed during a period of rapid flux in global financial, political and
demographic realms. Socio-politically, worldwide, we are indeed in a time of
transition, uncertainty and insecurity; or as the title of a 2018 exhibition of

the German photographer Ursula Schulz-Dornburg at the Stradel Museum (Frankfurt) puts it, we are dwelling in *The Land in Between*.

Such liminality has a significant impact on the wellbeing of people where the collaborators of this book live and work. Chaplaincy also is betwixt and between what has been and the rapidly emerging what may be, even as chaplains function in the shifting sands of what is. How chaplaincy as a profession chooses to respond in a manner that is contextually relevant is crucial for its future.

At present, some of the most challenging issues which threaten individual and collective wellbeing and confront healthcare systems and those who shape and work in them include:

- financial austerity

- rapid demographic changes

- increasing number, and financial cost, of people living with comorbidity (and associated loss of function, role and identity)

- healthcare inequalities/poverty

- societal loneliness and isolation

- staff and care provider stress (and associated recruitment and retention issues)

- increased expectations of quality and quantity of life by the general population.

To tackle such a complexity of issues, honest and bold conversations about healthcare provision are required globally at political, inter-professional and intra-professional levels. Within a Scottish context, the Auditor General for NHSScotland (2018, p.5) has sought to stimulate such conversations by publicly stating in her latest annual report:

> To meet people's health and care needs, the NHS urgently needs to move away from short-term fire-fighting to long-term fundamental change. The types of services it offers, and the demand for those services, have changed significantly over the 70 years since the NHS was created. The challenges now presented by an ageing population means further and faster change is essential to secure the future of the NHS in Scotland… The NHS in Scotland is not in a financially sustainable position.

This leads her to conclude that 'the current healthcare delivery model is not sustainable' (p.7).

Stephen Platt (2015, p.49), writing within a British chaplaincy context, concurs and lays out the challenges that lie ahead:

There is a crisis in contemporary healthcare; a service that began with the noble intention of providing care, free at the point of delivery, for all finds itself facing unprecedented challenges. A chaplaincy service that is able to respond to the changing context of healthcare and facilitate staff and patients in engaging with the spiritual dimension of health and illness is needed more than ever.

In such a climate, the philosophical and ideological underpinnings of healthcare in the post-industrial world are changing. There are various paradigm shifts occurring in this area which affect the way healthcare design and delivery are being envisioned, whatever their means of being funded (Table I.1).

Table I.1 Paradigm shifts influencing health and care planning and delivery

Current focus in healthcare	Moving towards
Treating ill health	Promoting wellbeing
Working with what is broken and needs to be fixed	Identifying and fostering individual and communal assets
Professional prescribing	Enabling self-management
Professional expertise	Co-production of wellbeing
Acute, institutional care	Enhancing and developing primary and community care
Individuals	Supporting communal resilience and meaning-making

Adapted from Kelly (2013)

In 1997 McKnight (p.76), with a consideration for North American healthcare, described the need to move from a medically dominated or modernist understanding of health, in which disease is sought to be overcome and illness cured, towards a vision of collectively promoting assets-based wellbeing as a basis for public health.

The raw material of community is capacity. The raw material of medicine is deficiency. In this harsh reality is a competition for resources based upon an ideological struggle. The community-building interest is in an antidiagnostic ethos focused on gifts to be manifested. The medical interest is in a prodiagnostic ethos focused upon brokenness to be fixed. Each approach is a worldview that shapes how power and resources are allocated and which values are affirmed and legitimised. Each approach creates a map of community that guides community residents, local groups, major institutions and governments towards competing visions of healthful communities.

The deficits-based model which McKnight (1997, p.76) alludes to focuses on the deficiencies in communities such as material deprivation, illness and health-damaging behaviours. Healthcare interventions are designed to fill in the gaps or fix that which is broken. This in turn disempowers individuals and communities who become passive recipients rather than active participants in dealing with their health and wellbeing.

Significantly, from a US chaplaincy perspective in an article entitled 'The medical captivity of religion and health', Fitchett (1991, p.280) suggests that 'the church once again needs a revisioning of health which is based on theological notions of the church as sustaining community and a school for empowerment'. There is, however, at this time, no exploration of a change in practice to suggest chaplains be an active part of that revisioning process and its enactment.

Until now chaplains have majored in supporting individuals in ill health within structures and systems dominated by a medical model which prioritises the fixing or curing of individuals in crisis or deficit within institutional settings. What might it be like to work otherwise, with an 'antidiagnostic ethos' outwith healthcare facilities, collaboratively enabling and supporting communities to work with and share their strengths and find shared meaning, purpose and hope in doing so? What does it mean exactly to work towards promoting wellbeing rather than seeking to support individuals whilst they are experiencing ill health?

Thinking about wellbeing

Wellbeing is concerned with far more than the absence of ill health (World Health Organization 1946). To have individual or communal health is only a part of what wellbeing is. Wellbeing necessitates:

- a holistic approach to health

- having individual and shared meaning and purpose

- positive relationships in life

- communities which promote engagement and enablement

- access to nature and attention to environmental issues

- security: basic human needs, stable employment, sufficient finances and personal safety.

(based on Kreitzer 2012)

At this point it is important to note the relationship between living well as an individual and living well in community. Wallace (2019, p.7) cites the example of the work of the New Economics Foundation and its 'Five ways to wellbeing' work to illustrate the focus of personal wellbeing and its primary weakness:

> 'Five ways to wellbeing' work…aimed to provide people with a basic guide to personal wellbeing: connect, be active, take notice, keep learning and give. While these activities are strongly correlated with personal wellbeing, they take no account of the structural factors at play that allow people to live a good life.

Living well together, for example in the Aristotelian tradition, has shared human flourishing as its goal. As Wallace (2019, p.7) continues: 'To flourish is understood as having a purpose in life, participating in society, having a community around oneself.' Corporate flourishing is thus both spiritually informed and values driven. In order to enhance personal flourishing, individuals also need to seek the good of the community they inhabit (McGregor and Pouw 2016). In short, wellbeing is to have a good life, lived well in community.

Wellbeing, not just health, is now a high priority for governments and social policymakers worldwide. Politicians and policymakers are increasingly interested in the governance and measurement of flourishing or wellbeing initiatives. The approach taken is evolving from a 'command and control' approach to a more outcomes focused one in which collaboration and participation are key to engagement, and the local service-level interventions or initiatives developed are becoming more preventative rather than crisis driven (Wallace 2019). An example of such an approach is the Scottish government's National Performance Framework (2018) whose purpose is 'to focus on creating a more successful country with opportunities for all of Scotland to flourish through increased wellbeing and sustainable and inclusive economic growth'.

One final dimension of complexity within healthcare culture which chaplains have to navigate relates to the dance – at times *clash* – between the two predominant epistemologies which influence healthcare theory, design and delivery:

- The still dominant positivistic or modern epistemological understanding of healthcare which emphasises understanding knowledge in terms of empiricism, that is, the belief that the only things that are true are those which fall upon the retina of the eye – things you can *see*, *feel*, *touch* and *measure*.

- Interpretive epistemologies that emphasise the constructed and interpretative nature of reality, that is, the idea that truth and knowledge is emergent, contextual and interpretative rather than propositionally universal and only accessible via empirical methods.

In the former, science is king, evidence is assumed to be quantitative and education is competency or skills based to support the performing of tasks safely and consistently. The outcomes which are focused on are clinical. However, the natural inclination of chaplaincy is towards interpretive epistemology. Chaplains are sympathetic to perceiving healthcare as an art, considering stories as evidence, thinking about education as formation and outcomes which relate to quality of life. Pragmatically, if chaplaincy is to develop and have influence as a profession, it requires to be equipped to inhabit and crucially understand this world, as well as to be able to speak the language of both. Chaplains therefore must become bilingual – fluent in the language of the empirical and the language of the interpretative. Stories and randomised control trials must be held in critical tension.

Such is the complexity of the context in which this book has been written. An overview of the volume's content and the core argument made, for what purpose and for whom, now follows.

Overview of content

Chaplaincy is an important and increasingly integral aspect of health and social care provision within the post-industrialised world. With changes in legislation and policy, the significance of spiritual care is being recognised across disciplines as never before. Chaplaincy has been at the forefront of this movement in terms of conceptualising and resourcing the spiritual dimension within health and care systems. In the United States there is a burgeoning literature exploring the relationship between spirituality and health. It now seems reasonably clear that, contrary to many common misconceptions, religion and spirituality can play a positive and arguably necessary role in the provision of healthcare and in promoting health and wellbeing. Within Europe, spirituality has developed in a more generic and secular mode. Here spirituality has come to relate to issues of meaning, purpose, hope, value and, for some, God. Chaplaincy has developed in similar but subtly different ways within these two contexts as it has striven to meet the spiritual needs of service users and care providers, and enhance spiritual wellbeing in individuals and communities.

To date there has been relatively little work done on the nature of chaplaincy and what its current status is within the ever-changing machinations of contemporary health and care systems. This book seeks to fill this gap by providing a range of perspectives on health and care chaplaincy as it is working itself out across the globe. This edited book gathers together the reflections and vision of experienced practitioners, academics, educators, researchers and strategic leaders from around the world to explore, from a spiritual and theological perspective, a range of issues vital to the future of spiritual care within the health and wellbeing agenda in the twenty-first century.

The book is, therefore, for active chaplaincy practitioners, educators, researchers and leaders as well as chaplaincy students and pastoral carers. It will also be of interest to health and care managers and leaders, and anyone else who recognises the centrality of spirituality for wellbeing and wishes to see what that might look like.

Core aims

The core aims of this book are to:

- explore the nature and purpose of health and social care chaplaincy, and to lay out in detail something of its history, its present state and what it might become

- facilitate readers' engagement with crucial yet challenging questions about the current and future practice of chaplains.

This book does not offer ready-made answers or contextual solutions, but shares innovative practice, raises important questions and points towards possible futures. The book is designed to aid reflective practice and help chaplains working at different levels of healthcare activity to revisit and question 'chaplaincy lore' – the 'taken as given', normative approaches and current ways of working.

Arguing for new models of chaplaincy

In our current era, the content and form of health and social care is rapidly changing. The underlying premise of this book is that the present prevalent model of healthcare chaplaincy – one-to-one acute crisis intervention in institutional settings – may no longer be the most effective way of specialist spiritual care providers promoting individual and corporate spiritual wellbeing. This book points to, in response to the already outlined paradigm shifts, in the theoretical underpinning of health and social care delivery, chaplains working as spiritual agents of transformation collaboratively with other health and social care disciplines and agencies, including faith communities, to help others utilise their assets to promote individual and collective wellbeing. Several contributors explore the significance of chaplains working as spiritual leaders or enablers of transformation (a concept based on the work of Paterson and Clegg 2013) at different levels of healthcare activity:

- *micro* (individual) level

- *meso* (team, department, community or locality/institution with a healthcare system or organisation) level

- *meta* (organisational, systems, national or international) level.

Another paradigm shift currently gathering momentum within the global chaplaincy community is a movement from a strongly influenced Rogerian psychotherapeutic approach to an evidence-based outcomes-focused one. Such a move is part of the overall professionalisation of chaplaincy and the need, like any other health or care profession, to promote best practice which enhances quality of life in a person-centred manner. *Chaplaincy and the Soul of Health and Social Care* intends to stimulate reflection on this and other significant changes as well as the innovative and collaborative approaches that are emerging amidst such transition, by sharing examples of groundbreaking and meaningful work in research, practice, education and strategic engagement.

Soul work

Part of the prophetic challenge that chaplaincy brings to public health and care practices is that it reminds leaders and practitioners of the nature of wholeness. The use of the word 'soul' within the Christian tradition also points to this: '[Soul]…denotes not part of a person that relates to God but rather the whole person in relationship to the living God, whether in life or death. "A person is a soul. A soul is a person"' (Cole 2010, p.178). We are our bodies as we are our souls. In a context where specialisms tend to fragment systems and individuals, part of the task of this book is to remind all of us that true health and wellbeing can only be found through a holistic approach. Such an approach is increasingly being urgently called for in contemporary healthcare in the post-industrial world, for example to help people live well with comorbidity: 'I am not just my conditions. Take time to understand me and my life' (The Health and Social Care Alliance Scotland, n.d., p.3). That is a potential gift that chaplaincy brings to the table of healthcare.

Yet within contemporary secular parlance the term 'soul' has another meaning which is also significant. This is illustrated in Iain Banks' (2013) novel *Complicity* which explores issues of justice and retribution. Near the end of the novel the main protagonist, journalist Cameron Colley, seeks to find the motivation of a serial killer. The murderer has intentionally chosen wealthy and powerful victims who, in his opinion, have been the cause of countless others' pain, poverty and misery. Cameron confronts him on this (p.295):

' …But is a sick response to a sick system really the best we can do? You think you're fighting it but you're just joining in. They've poisoned you, man. They've taken the hope out of your soul and put some of their own greedy hate in its place.'

'"Soul," did you say, Cameron?' He smiles at me. 'You getting religion?'

'No, I just mean the core of you, the essence of who you are; they've infected it with despair, and I'm sorry you can't see any better response than to kill people.'

This is part of the challenge that chaplaincy faces in promoting and embedding their 'soul work' in healthcare systems: moving from being perceived as peripheral or being seen as a 'fluffy extra' or 'icing on the cake' of care, which can be done without in times of financial austerity, to being understood as a core essential to individual and communal wellbeing for all, not just the religious.

Threads

The reader will discern several threads or themes, which are interwoven throughout and across various sections, contributing to the pattern of the book. These threads defy the necessary structure of the book yet help to hold it together and, we believe, contribute to the cohesion of the patchwork formed. These threads include:

- the debate about chaplaincy as an evidence-based profession and what sort of evidence is required

- the role of outcomes in chaplaincy

- how chaplaincy navigates, works with and challenges the predominant epistemologies which underpin healthcare, for the benefit of the people with whom chaplains work

- a tartan thread. (This book is co-edited by two Scots, and part of the story of the recent development of Scottish chaplaincy is woven throughout it.)

Structure and signposting: orientating the reader

Part 1, 'The Essence of Healthcare Chaplaincy: What Does Spiritual Need Feel Like?', explores the lived experience of illness, loss and transition, and what spiritual need feels like. Chaplaincy deals first and foremost with human experience. It is true that that experience is named in different ways across the disciplines. However, chaplaincy may be the one healthcare discipline that begins by allowing people to name their experience and remains with that definition throughout. Whilst diagnosis shifts the experience into a different realm and places it under a certain set of healthcare disciplines, chaplaincy always keeps open the possibility of a different interpretation of the person's story: a spiritual rather than a medical one. In Part 1 we begin by allowing people to tell their own stories (with the support of a chaplain) quite apart from the various interpretations into which such stories are baptised within the healthcare system. This is the starting point for genuinely person-centred chaplaincy.

In Chapter 1, through interviewing, recording and transcribing the anonymised story of a woman living with a long-term chronic condition and her reflections on what having a chaplain journey with her means, chaplain and researcher Eva Buelens enables that narrative to be told and heard.

In Chapter 2, chaplain, researcher and educationalist Daniel Robert Nuzum shares some of the findings of his qualitative research which gives voice to the experience of parents living with perinatal loss, as an example of what people may live through in acute hospital settings.

The story of one woman's experience of living with ongoing severe mental illness is anonymously told in Chapter 3, in collaboration with Madeleine Parkes. How a chaplain helped to meet some of her spiritual and religious needs along with the spiritual support of a psychiatrist is part of her story.

Following from the suggestion that chaplaincy is a narrative-based discipline, in the sense that it begins with the patient's story and tries to stick with that throughout, Part 2, 'Is Chaplaincy an Art or a Science?', wrestles with the question as to whether chaplaincy is an art or a science: Does it belong to the realm of the sciences or is it an aspect of the humanities? How chaplaincy answers this question will determine its methods, approaches, practices and precisely what body of evidence it should choose to validate its practices.

In Chapter 4, through prose and poetry, Mark Stobert, a leader in UK chaplaincy, explores in depth the role of reflective practice both as paradigm and process, in informing the embodiment of professional artistry as a creative and countercultural (to healthcare) model of chaplaincy.

In Chapter 5, utilising insights from public health and the arts, Kevin Franz reflects on his experience as a mental health chaplain in institutional and community settings to explore the significance of learning in, and from, liminality for individual practitioners and the chaplaincy profession as a whole.

In Chapter 6, through reflecting on the narratives and meta-narrative that have informed his faith and practice, chaplain and researcher Daniel H Grossoehme explores the significance of science for chaplaincy practice, and that which underpins and guides it.

In Chapter 7, George F Handzo, a chaplaincy advocate and educationalist, and Steve Nolan, a chaplain and researcher, engage in a creative trans-Atlantic conversation about the benefits and dangers of an outcomes-focused approach to chaplaincy, including research.

In Part 3, 'What Kind of Professionals Are Chaplains – Healthcare Professionals?', we begin to lay out the nature of chaplaincy as a profession. What does it mean to say that chaplains are healthcare professionals? What body of literature underpins their practices? What specialist training defines their profession? This section wrestles with the unique contribution of chaplaincy to healthcare and how and why chaplains might wish to become formally one of the healthcare professions.

In Chapter 8, Derek Fraser, who has made a significant contribution to the development of the professionalisation of chaplaincy in the UK in recent years, outlines the aspects of chaplaincy development which have been important in that journey.

Anne Vandenhoeck has had a key role in promoting knowledge exchange and sharing of best practices between, and research by, chaplains in Europe. In Chapter 9, she describes the development of chaplaincy in Europe within its range of cultural and religious contexts and the importance of research for chaplaincy to become more professional and sustainable.

In Chapter 10, Hans Evers, a chaplain and educator, describes the evolution of chaplaincy models from modern to post-modern times and proposes ways in which chaplaincy can become more fully integrated and professionally credible within healthcare systems.

John Swinton concludes Part 3 with Chapter 11 by exploring what shapes professional identity and informs professional confidence in order to effect meaningful collaboration and inter-professional dialogue within health and care settings.

In order to become and sustain the status of a healthcare professional, there is a necessity to prove your case, that is, to provide rigorous evidence that will explain and sustain your status within a healthcare context which requires that chaplaincy be 'seen to be believed'. The way that chaplaincy comes to be 'seen' is not simply through presence, but also via evidence that that presence is worthwhile, both in terms of economics and therapy. The chapters in Part 4, 'Researching Chaplaincy: What Kind of Evidence Base Do Chaplains Actually Need?', explore what kind of evidence chaplaincy might require to be perceived as valid, rigorous and economically viable, and how such evidence can be attained.

Reflecting on his experience as a researcher and research advocate as well as research educator within healthcare chaplaincy globally, George Fitchett outlines his perspectives, in Chapter 12, on the advancement of chaplaincy research, how that might be done and who needs to be involved.

In Chapter 13, Austyn Snowden, a quantitative researcher, and Iain Telfer, a former practising chaplain, describe their research journey in developing a spiritual care Patient Related Outcome Measure and the global collaborative research opportunities that have subsequently emerged.

In Part 5, 'Creative Engagements', we open up the developing understanding of chaplaincy to the wider healthcare community. How do chaplains engage with the institution in ways that have integrity and are at the same time deeply spiritual? How can chaplains creatively support others in their provision of person-centred and spiritual care? How can chaplains help to influence the culture of teams and organisations to promote their wellbeing? These questions help to orientate chaplaincy in a healthcare space which takes seriously the role of other disciplines but is not dictated by them.

In Chapter 14, underpinned by covenantal theology and organisational cultural theory and informed by qualitative research, Australian practical theologians Neil Pembroke and Raymond Reddicliffe explore the role of chaplaincy in influencing the corporate spirituality of a healthcare organisation.

Kenneth J Donaldson, a consultant nephrologist and medical leader, and Ewan Kelly then describe the influence of Values Based Reflective Practice, developed and embedded in NHSScotland by healthcare chaplains, on Scottish healthcare culture. Their Chapter 15 explores what collaboratively transforming culture might involve and significantly includes a case study exploring Ken's clinical decision-making as a powerful example of the impact such chaplaincy work may have.

Carlo Leget, an academic with an interest in the spiritual and the ethical, concludes Part 5 with Chapter 16 by describing the creative utilisation of a reframed medieval approach to dying, *ars moriendi*, to enable spiritual issues to be consistently explored with terminally ill patients and their carers. The potential benefits to holistic end-of-life care and to chaplaincy are also outlined.

In Part 6, 'Caring Well, Caring Spiritually', we look at the actual practice of caring. What does it mean to care well? How can chaplains care counterculturally to reduce codependency and promote individual and collective wellbeing? To do so means to risk being innovative, collaborative and enabling others to identify and utilise their assets.

In Chapter 17, Timothy P Bennison outlines the development and national embedding of assets-based Chaplaincy Listening Services within community contexts by Scottish chaplaincy. His is a strategic as well as practice-based story.

Jo Kennedy, with a background in community development, and Ian Stirling, a palliative care chaplain and parish minister, then reflect, in Chapter 18, on their innovative work exploring the possibilities of the impact healthcare chaplains can make on communal spiritual wellbeing. From such experience they offer a framework to inform future practice and its possible outcomes.

Situated within mental health, and modelling their subject matter, chaplain and researcher Julian Raffay and service user Don Bryant share their reflections on co-production in Chapter 19. This includes work in Liverpool to co-produce research design and development as well as their vision to co-produce mental health services.

Part 7 is titled 'Educating Chaplains: What Do Chaplains Need to Learn to Work in and Influence Twenty-First Century Healthcare Systems?'

In Chapter 20, by reiterating the significance of spiritual, psychological and character formation for promoting practical wisdom in chaplaincy work, Ewan Kelly, out of his experience as chaplain, educator and strategic leader, emphasises the necessity of formation as the foundation for transformative learning and practice at all levels of healthcare activity.

The process of co-constructing Chapter 21 is as important as the content itself, as David W Fleenor, chaplain and educator, and Ewan Kelly collaborate to propose a utilisation of the strengths of approaches to chaplaincy education on either side of the Atlantic to equip chaplains to act as spiritual agents of transformation within rapidly changing healthcare contexts.

Part 8, 'Shaping the Future', focuses on the ways in which chaplaincy can, may and should develop for the future. It includes reflections on some of the challenges and tensions within and outside of chaplaincy based on the types of evidence and perspectives laid out in the previous chapters. Here we ask questions which we hope will inform conversations globally about envisioning the future of chaplaincy.

First, in Chapter 22, out of Australian and Scottish contexts Cheryl Holmes and Ewan Kelly explore the significance of transformative strategic leadership for the future of healthcare chaplaincy, utilising case studies from their work to ground and illustrate their arguments.

Then, Chapter 23 (the final chapter), by the co-editors, points to future directions informed by the range of contributions to this book. Central to such directions is having the courage and honesty within the chaplaincy profession and in engagement with health and care systems to ask, and live with, often difficult questions. From such questions, we believe, will emerge new visionary prophetic, yet fit for purpose, models of health and care chaplaincy which will contextually promote individual and communal spiritual wellbeing across the globe.

References

Auditor General (2018) *NHS in Scotland 2018*. Edinburgh: Audit Scotland.

Banks, I. (2013) *Complicity*. London: Abacus.

Cole, A. (2010) 'What makes care pastoral?' *Pastoral Psychology 59*, 711–723.

Fitchett, G. (1991) 'The medical captivity of religion and health.' *The Journal of Pastoral Care XLV*, 3, 280–287.

Kelly, E. (2013) 'Policy, practice and strategic priorities and healthcare chaplaincy.' *Scottish Journal of Healthcare Chaplaincy 16*, 53–59.

Kreitzer, M.J. (2012) 'Spirituality and wellbeing: focussing on what matters.' *Western Journal of Nursing Research 34*, 6, 707–711.

Lyon, A. (2013) 'Foreword.' In S. Gray and A. Strong (eds) *Health and Social Care in Scotland: Integration or Transformation?* Glasgow: Health and Social Care Alliance Scotland.

McGregor, J.A. and Pouw, N. (2016) 'Towards an economics of wellbeing.' *Cambridge Journal of Economics 41*, 4, 1123–1142.

McKnight, J. (1997) *The Careless Society: Community and its Counterfeits*. New York, NY: Basic Books.

Paterson, M. and Clegg, C. (2013) *Education, Training and Formation for Healthcare Chaplains: Report of an NHS Review*. Edinburgh: NHS Education for Scotland.

Pattison, S. (1997) *Pastoral Care and Liberation Theology*. London: SPCK.

Platt, S. (2015) 'Making Use of Models of Healthcare Chaplaincy.' In J. Pye, P. Sedgwick and A. Todd (eds) *Critical Care: Delivering Spiritual Care in Healthcare Contexts*. London: Jessica Kingsley Publishers.

Schulz-Dornburg, U. (2018) *The Land in Between*. Stradel Museum, Frankfurt. Accessed on 14/12/2018 at www.staedelmuseum.de/en/ursula-schulz-dornburg.

Scottish Government (2018) *National Performance Framework*. Accessed on 13/12/2018 at https://nationalperformance.gov.scot.

The Health and Social Care Alliance Scotland (n.d.) *Many Conditions, One Life: Living Well with Multiple Conditions*. Glasgow: The Health and Social Care Alliance Scotland.

Wallace, J. (2019) *Wellbeing and Devolution: Reframing the Role of Government in Scotland, Wales and Northern Ireland*. Cham, Switzerland: Palgrave Macmillan. Accessed on 01/07/19 at www.dtni.org.uk/sites/default/files/2019_Book_WellbeingAndDevolution.pdf.

World Health Organization (1946) 'Preamble to the constitution of the World Health Organization as adopted by the International Health Conference, New York.' *Official Records of the World Health Organization 2*, 100.

Part 1

The Essence of Healthcare Chaplaincy

What Does Spiritual Need Feel Like?

Life –
scattered and gathered
fragments.

Broken,
ragged and jagged
pieces.

Not
rounded, whole or
complete
stories.

Beauty and meaning
are there.

– Ewan Kelly

Chapter 1

Living with a Chronic Long-Term Condition

'I Can Reflect with Chaplains About Things I Cannot Share with Others'

Eva Buelens

Introduction

This is the story of a young Belgian woman who has lived with a debilitating chronic illness for many years. During her first weeks in hospital for investigation and treatment, she was visited by a female chaplain of approximately the same age. What started as a casual meet and greet flourished into a significant caring relationship. When this chaplain left the hospital, another female chaplain began journeying with this woman. This is a story that illustrates the impact that living with a chronic long-term illness and associated spiritual suffering may have on a person's quality of life and wellbeing. In addition, it shows the significance of chaplaincy care in response. The patient's story was gathered by recorded interview with a chaplain. The interview was transcribed and then read by the patient to verify its accuracy.

Can you describe the impact of your chronic illness on your life and wellbeing?

My identical twin sister had type-1 diabetes. Ten years after her diagnosis, I was diagnosed with the same disease; therefore, I knew what to expect. I realised immediately that I would be ill for the rest of my life. This irrevocability is extremely difficult. I didn't know how to communicate this to family, friends and colleagues. Being chronically ill has had an enormous impact on my life.

During the first years of my illness, I felt a need to hide it from my colleagues and friends. Only my parents, sisters and some family members were informed. I felt so ashamed. I didn't dare say that I needed to follow a diet when out together with friends or colleagues. I would be in a situation where I would have dinner in a restaurant and drank too much soda. I didn't want others to know I was sick. I also played competitive volleyball at that time and didn't tell the team about my illness. One time I became really ill during a game because of low blood sugar. Instead of just telling others what was wrong, I pretended I needed to use the bathroom urgently and left the field.

I don't know where the shame came from. Maybe I did not want to acknowledge that I was becoming more ill as time passed. The fact that my partner left me because I was diabetic was such a negative experience that I feared others would react in the same hurtful way. Not telling most people what was happening to me complicated the process of integrating my illness in a major way. When I look back now, maybe I would have handled it differently.

During the years that followed, my hospital stays became longer and the loneliness greater. At first friends came to visit me, but as time went by, they too stayed away. The distance that they had to travel to come see me in the university hospital was too far and I was there for so long every time. Maybe I am partly to blame for their waning interest as I often didn't tell them I was admitted to the hospital again. I did not only lose a lot of friends but also my colleagues. My doctor advised me to resign from my position as a gym teacher in a high school. It became impossible to continue my profession. I did not have a lot of contact with fellow patients because I found it very hard to talk about my illness. Consequently, I was only in touch with staff in the hospital: doctors, nurses, dieticians, physiotherapists and the chaplains. I experienced my illness as very isolating. Luckily, I did have the ongoing support of my family.

The challenges I had to endure were not only social, but physical also. A lot of surgery, a lot of tests, a pancreatic transplantation and all the scars that I have as a result. I often had to stay for months on end in the hospital, a few times a year. (At least I don't get lost in this big hospital any more!) There were so many treatments that were unsuccessful. Because of that, new surgeries and therapies were always stressful. I felt a lot of anxiety that they too would not work. The uncertainty was horrible to endure.

A lot has changed on a financial level too since I have been ill. My financial situation has become more and more difficult, and I find that debilitating and destructive. I used to travel a lot, but I can't afford to do that any more. Just like my illness, my financial limitations will be there for the rest of my life. I cannot change anything about that.

Therefore, my illness has had a major negative impact on the quality of my life. If I hadn't become ill, at least I would have had friends and colleagues. Sometimes I notice that other patients discover a positive meaning in their chronic illness. I cannot seem to do that.

What are your resources? What is important and meaningful?

The connectedness with my twin sister is extremely important to me. I had, despite the difficulties associated with a chronic illness, a very strong bond with her. Unfortunately, she died some time ago. I visit her grave regularly.

The connectedness with my parents is strong. I moved back into their house after my mum developed cancer. By doing so I could make sure, together with my dad, that she didn't need to go into hospital as we could take care of her at home. My mum was grateful for that. It was very hard on me, including physically. Yet I find it very meaningful that I was able to do that for her. This way I was able to give something back for all the care she gave me over all these years. After she passed away, I stayed in the house to take care of my dad. The opportunity to take care of him is very important to me at this point. I also know my mum would have wanted me to do so. It is because of him that I carry on, but other than that I don't have much to live for.

I had a dog for 10 years. We had a very special bond. He was very faithful and I loved him very much. It really was devastating when he died. Luckily, I still know some people with dogs from the time we went to the dog-training school together. The contacts remain and I try to join them for dog walking once a week, which I enjoy.

Small things are very meaningful to me: going away, taking beautiful pictures, being in nature, praying with others, visiting the graves of my twin sister and mum.

How did you experience the contact with the chaplains?

A chaplain came to visit me when I was admitted for the first time in the university hospital. I didn't ask for a chaplain at that point, but maybe I would have later on. We hit it off immediately. When the first chaplain left the hospital after 10 years, she introduced me to her colleague. I have a very good relationship with this chaplain too. They brought diversion during those long days and nights. I didn't receive any visitors during the week. At the weekend my family visited. Therefore, I really looked forward to the visits of the chaplains.

We talked about daily life and we explored what kept me going in all kinds of circumstances in relation to my illness and life. We also talked about faith. Sometimes the talks were very deep, other times they were entertaining and light; we could share funny stories and sometimes they helped me play practical jokes on the staff. I really needed these conversations and experienced them as very positive, enriching and supportive. I could, for example, share all my anxiety and uncertainty about the coming treatments with them. It relieved me of tension. I felt less anxious and I had the feeling I was not alone. The talks helped me to continue and to hang in there; a great bond between me and the chaplains grew. I could reflect on things with them that I could not share with doctors, nurses or my parents. I do have a good relationship with my doctor and with some of the nurses, but still the relationship with the chaplains is really different. Sometimes the chaplains would send their interns to me for a visit because they said I had more experience with chaplaincy visits than any other patient in the hospital. I enjoyed meeting with them and I would tell the trainees if I thought they would make good chaplains.

As well as talking with me, the chaplains also prayed and lit candles for me. If I was discharged, I regularly got a phone call which made me feel supported outside the hospital too.

A lot of meaningful assets in my life have gone in recent years: the passing away of my dog, my twin sister and my mum. Also, during these hard times, the chaplains supported me. I could share my grief and anxiety with them. They supported me in focusing on memories and the ongoing connectedness with my loved ones, and they helped me confirm what is important to me, like stressing the meaning I find in taking care of my dad. When my twin sister died, the chaplains, together with a head nurse, came to the funeral. I did not expect that. It meant so much to me that they came.

At this stage of my illness, now that I have to battle chronic kidney failure along with diabetes, the chaplains play an important role. I know that I will probably end up on dialysis. My sister was on dialysis for 3 years and then died. I think that the same destiny awaits me. Despite the emptiness I experience in my life, I would like to continue to live. But those harsh realities of the future can be shared with the chaplains, and that is a major support to me. They create a space alongside my anxiety and grief which gives me hope and trust.

Chapter 2

Experience of Spiritual Distress in an Acute Setting

Living with Perinatal Loss

Daniel Robert Nuzum

Introduction

Pregnancy and childbirth are at the heart of human creation and existence. Both are profoundly relational experiences that touch at what it is to be human. Likewise, life is finite, so coping with death and loss is also an essential human experience. We call it grieving. In the normal course of life, we encounter loss as we grieve the death of grandparents and parents. However, it is a sad fact that death also occurs at the beginning of life, and when it does it disrupts the perceived 'normal order of events'. Uninvited and often unexpected, such a death enters our human narrative with lifelong impact.

Most parents, from the moment they discover that they are pregnant, enter a time of excitement, planning and anticipation as they await the birth of their baby. For some parents, pregnancy is a time of anxiety as perhaps this pregnancy was unplanned or unexpected. For all parents, the impending arrival of a new baby changes their world. As parents journey towards the birth of their baby, this time of waiting and expectation is for many a spiritually positive experience as new life is both experienced and anticipated during pregnancy. Although not an illness, pregnancy can bring with it complications and uncertainty; many parents receive bad news about the health of their baby during routine antenatal care. An antenatal diagnosis of a life-limiting condition presents parents with difficult choices, and in all of these cases parents have to come to terms with loss – of hopes, health or function, and the hoped-for future with their baby. While most pregnancies result in healthy babies and much joy for new parents, it is a sad reality that not all babies will survive pregnancy. Many parents will instead experience the heart-rending grief of the death of their baby during pregnancy or shortly after birth. In this experience, parents begin a lifelong journey of grief as they are set adrift from the joy of new life into the abyss of bereavement. The joy of new life is replaced with the spiritual low and distress of perinatal death.

The death of a baby is recognized as one of the most traumatic and enduring bereavements with multiple sequelae. Unlike other bereavements, perinatal grief is a 'prospective grief' that has a repeating cyclical pattern. It continues throughout the lives of the surviving bereaved parents, siblings and extended family. As future life events, significant milestones and family and community occasions take place, the absence of the baby who has died brings a fresh experience of grief and a profound sense of loss as each life moment is navigated. As these occasions and events arise, parents and family members grieve afresh. These experiences of grief are often framed by 'what if?' questions as families seek to locate their baby in the narrative of their family story.

Coupled with the personal and familial experience of bereavement is the reality for many parents that their grief is not publicly acknowledged or recognized (Kelley and Trinidad 2012). This 'silence' is in itself a further isolating experience for parents and contributes to a disenfranchisement of grief. Only in recent years has there been more public awareness and discourse about miscarriage, stillbirth and neonatal death both in society and in faith communities (Meaney *et al.* 2017; Nuzum, Meaney and O'Donoghue 2017, 2018b). The lack of public and religious ritual and resources is indicative of the experience of silence.

In this chapter the lived experiences of bereaved parents who participated in an in-depth qualitative study are explored to illustrate the impact of perinatal death as an experience of spiritual distress in an acute setting. The setting is Cork University Maternity Hospital, Ireland[1] – the broader context being one that is predominantly Christian, albeit with varying levels of commitment and practice. From a chaplaincy perspective, however, the expression of perinatal grief is one that transcends religious affiliation. In common with other forms of grief, perinatal death is a profoundly spiritual experience, and in the context of the stories presented here pastoral care encompasses both generic spiritual care and ritual alongside faith-specific ceremony. Highlighting these personal stories and experiences will help to reframe a pastoral response to this distinctive grief.

---

1   I acknowledge the contribution of Dr Keelin O'Donoghue, Consultant Obstetrician and Gynaecologist and Senior Lecturer, University College Cork and Cork University Maternity Hospital, Ireland, and Dr Sarah Meaney, National Perinatal Epidemiology Centre, University College Cork, Ireland, in the original research study from which this chapter is drawn. Qualitative methods are used to understand complex social processes, to capture essential aspects of a phenomenon from the perspective of participants.

The experiences of the parents of babies Aoife, Michael, Joan, Rory, Thomas, Samuel, Richard and James, each of whom died before birth, are given voice in this chapter. While the experiences are particular to the participants, they nonetheless highlight broader commonalities that can be applied to other parents and families who experience similar grief. This chapter is not an isolated enterprise and builds on previous work by chaplains Wretmark (1993), Pierce (2003), Kelly (2007) and Newitt (2015) to offer a broad pastoral response to perinatal loss and grief.

The spiritual impact of perinatal death is described here under six overarching themes. Each of these themes in turn can be used to shape a pastoral response both in hospital and community. These themes are:

- searching for meaning

- maintaining hope

- importance of personhood

- protective care

- suffering

- belief and relationships.

(Nuzum, Meaney and O'Donoghue 2017, 2018a)

The experience of grief is multidimensional, so while each theme highlighted is distinctive and presented separately here, they are all interconnected and are not experienced in isolation. In visual terms they might be described as various 'strands' of loss and hope that, when woven together, make up the varied textured experience of perinatal grief. The role of the chaplain is to recognize the varied dimensions of this particular loss and, through sensitive spiritual care, to accompany parents as they begin the weaving of their particular and unique experience and life story to create a pattern for meaningful expression of love, loss and hope.

Search for meaning

Searching for meaning is a fundamental human endeavour as we seek to make sense of life experience. The death of a baby is no exception. The move from a trajectory of expectation, hope, excitement and planning to one of grief, sadness, pain and death is one of extraordinary proportions and existential conflict. This fundamental change, often with no preparation or notice, is one that unsurprisingly raises existential questions about meaning and purpose. In an increasingly technological and scientific age, these questions take on further meaning as parents seek to understand what has happened and why their baby has died. Parents often revisit their experiences to try and attribute meaning to the 'why' as well as the 'what' of their baby's death. For some parents the search for meaning contributes to a sense of purpose in their baby's death. This can be expressed as a sense of 'being chosen' to bear this particular burden, although it also can bring an ambivalence as parents would naturally prefer not to be chosen for this. One mother whose daughter, Aoife, was diagnosed antenatally with a life-limiting condition and who died at 37 weeks of gestation described this sense of being chosen as follows:

> Aoife was a little angel and she needed to be born and she picked us to bring her into the world and that was our gift to her…to bring her into the world. She knew from the outset that she wasn't going to last longer than the pregnancy and she needed someone strong to be able to bring her into the world and she picked us.

Another mother, whose son Michael died unexpectedly during birth, described the ambivalence associated with being chosen as: '[People said] "Oh God, he's chosen you" and I remember saying, "I wish he had chosen me for something else, but in some ways I kind of treasure the fact that we were chosen."'

Parents who receive an antenatal diagnosis of a life-limiting condition that is likely to result in the death of their baby, and by implication have more time to prepare for their baby's death, can often find greater meaning during this time of anticipatory bereavement, whereas for other parents this 'waiting' can be experienced as a burden too painful to bear.

Central to a search for meaning following the death of a baby is the recognition of the value of a baby's life – that their baby mattered. The significance associated with the meaning of a baby's life is considerable and can be the lens through which parents view their experiences with healthcare professionals including chaplains. When parents have time to prepare for their baby's death, they often use this time to acknowledge and honour the life of their baby. This is done in a myriad of ways, unique to each family but most frequently in the creation of mementos and memories. Although tinged with sadness, these are very important experiences for parents and families. For parents who have an unexpected death of a baby, they often revisit their experiences during pregnancy to create meaning afterwards. The mother of Paul, who died unexpectedly 5 days before his due date, expressed:

> I see Paul's life as the 9 months that he lived. He had his own kind of life. He lived his own life in another world that was very real, very his own. He had his own experiences.

He got to have all the adventures I had. He got to go swimming. He got to go to San Francisco. He got to taste funny food. He got to go to the cinema. He got to have all those experiences in his own way. He had his own life. We shared it in lots of ways and we didn't in other ways.

Spiritual care has much to offer parents as they search for meaning. The first step is to assess what is important to parents. Spiritual assessment can take many forms, but all should have the same aim of identifying the important strands that the chaplain can then help parents to hold. Identifying sources of strength from spiritual, religious or secular sources particular to each parent is important; however, it is also significant to be aware that previously used and relied-upon supports may not now work. Challenging questions require a depth of spiritual sensitivity and maturity on the part of the chaplain so that they are not avoided. This necessitates a level of discernment and judgement in any spiritual intervention(s) to help parents in their search for meaning. For the parents of Aoife, Michael and Paul the pastoral response to allow each family to weave the story of each baby into their particular family was important. This personal approach in a large maternity hospital honours the uniqueness of each baby and his or her family, and in so doing helps to celebrate the meaning of life of each baby.

Maintaining hope

Maintaining hope is a hallmark of human resilience in the face of adversity. Bereaved parents, even in the midst of devastating loss and grief, struggle with the confusing dynamic of trying to maintain hope, on the one hand, and yet feeling an utter hopelessness, on the other, as they come to terms with the harsh reality of death and a life of bereavement. When parents are given the news that their baby might die, there is a natural reticence to hear and accept this news. Parents will often experience an internal struggle hoping that the news is wrong and can feel unable to accept the reality presented to them. To accept such a reality can feel like giving up hope. The sense that something might be wrong can evoke a deep visceral response from parents akin to a fight-or-flight response. Baby Michael's mother who sensed that he had stopped moving described this as: 'I remember lying up on my bed hitting my tummy trying to get some response... I went to the GP and I literally burst in the door and collapsed to the floor... I was hysterical.'

Pastoral care for parents during this conflicting time of trying to maintain hope can be challenging. It is a bewildering experience for parents who can still feel the vibrant life of their baby moving and kicking and yet at the same time try to come to terms that their baby's life will come to an end. Baby

Joan's mother expressed this conflicted hope as: 'I knew that although she was vibrant and active and I so wanted to meet her, every day closer to Joan's birth was also a day closer to her death, and that was just heartbreaking.'

Responding pastorally to Joan's parents provided an opportunity for them to reframe their hope from one of an incorrect diagnosis to one where they found new hope where Joan was a part of their family and that death would not change that. This led Joan's parents to create many memories with her during pregnancy while she was still alive. These memories helped to record Joan's story. Pastorally there is much that can be drawn from the experience of palliative care chaplaincy in situations like this. Pastoral care, by recognizing and attending to the depth and reality of conflicted hope, can assist parents to recognize glimpses of hope even in the most devastating of experiences.

Importance of personhood

During pregnancy, parents develop a deep sense of the unique person of their growing baby. It is not uncommon for parents to describe characteristics and patterns of their unborn baby such as 'she's very active' or 'he kicks a lot'. These descriptors contribute towards forming the unique identity and affirm the importance of personhood of a baby. The significance of the personhood or uniqueness of a baby continues to be important after a baby has died. Although parents are devastated that their baby may not survive pregnancy or has already died through miscarriage or stillbirth, the value of the life and the uniqueness and personhood of their baby is of great consequence. This is expressed in many ways and continues to feature in how parents remember their baby into the future. Bereaved parents place importance on a stillborn baby being recognized and cared for as every other baby. The mother of baby Paul described the significance of the life of her son who died unexpectedly just before birth as:

> He played a big part in changing our lives in a year, not only in his own presence and the changes he would have brought – he also impacted other areas of our lives. He was a very powerful little person.

The personhood of the baby is one of the most important dimensions of meaningful spiritual care for those who support or care for bereaved parents and their families. How chaplains identify and respond to this is of immense importance. A therapeutic way to do this is for the chaplain to help parents and family members to tell the story of their baby. This narrative approach also has the benefit of identifying what are key reference points for co-construction of ritual or ceremony. Weaving these details into a personalized liturgy or ritual creates a poignant acknowledgement of the importance of the baby who has died as a person. The provision of opportunities for naming and blessing as appropriate to the wishes of parents helps them to honour the personhood of their baby. The use of a personalized memento of naming, such as a 'Naming Certificate', can be one of the few places where a baby's name is recorded in print. This is an important awareness pastorally, especially when babies who die following miscarriage may not receive any legal recognition or civil registration.

Protective care

All parents naturally wish to protect their baby from harm, as it is part of our evolutionary makeup to protect our young. For bereaved parents this sense of protective care is a very strong one. During pregnancy, parents (and mothers in particular) provide the ultimate protection for their baby *in utero*. This protective environment can, however, provide a challenging paradox for parents when they are powerless to change the outcome of a diagnosis of miscarriage, stillbirth or a life-limiting diagnosis for their baby. The experience of powerlessness and the inability to protect a baby from inevitable death is one of distress. Baby Rory's father described this existential struggle as one where he would have gladly given his own life in the place of his baby if that would have saved his baby's life.

The depth of protective care expressed by parents in the midst of perinatal loss is one of profound love. Above all, parents experience and express love for their baby in the same way as they do for any baby; a baby who dies is as loved as a baby who lives. When coupled with powerlessness to change the inevitable, the experience of love between parents and a baby is a disempowering and painful experience. This can come into sharp and painful focus at the time of birth and again at the time of burial or cremation when a final goodbye once again places parents into a place of powerlessness as they have to 'let go' and begin a new journey without their baby. The depth and range of emotions that parents can experience are varied. The desire to protect a baby can evoke what can be disturbing feelings which are important to bring to voice. Baby Thomas's mother described how she experienced strong protective feelings after his burial:

> I remember thinking, God I just wanted to take him out of the ground because I felt very cruel putting him into the ground. Even now you'd be thinking are there spiders or anything around the ground. I hope there's nothing touching him... I'd love to take him out and bring him home.

Another dimension of protective care is how parents often need to self-protect during perinatal bereavement. This need can arise from a desire to protect the memory of their baby or to protect themselves from ordinary social interactions when they might be placed in a situation of having to explain that something was wrong with their baby. Meeting other pregnant women or young babies can also be very difficult experiences, sometimes evoking feelings of jealousy and a painful reminder of loss.

The importance of sensitive pastoral care in this period cannot be overstated. In the midst of powerlessness and love, meeting and parting, parents and family members can experience a heart-numbing pain. This calls for an acknowledgement of the pain and a meaningful expression of love as parents and family say goodbye to their baby. Attention to detail and sensitivity to the individual needs of parents are important alongside pastoral flexibility and confidence, especially as most parents will not have experience of previous perinatal death and bereavement. This is unchartered territory where good pastoral care can provide the necessary compass points to aid navigation. The chaplain has an important opportunity here to empower parents to be parents to their deceased baby and help them regain some control when there is so much *beyond* their control.

Suffering

Perinatal loss brings both parents and healthcare professionals into close proximity with the profound depth of human suffering and existential pain. Bereaved parents wrestle with existential questions of 'why?' when faced with the tragedy of perinatal loss (Nuzum *et al.* 2017; Nuzum, Meaney and O'Donoghue 2017). Regardless of professed religious or spiritual belief, the suffering experienced following perinatal loss is a challenge to meaning and how we make sense of life. Suffering and belief arose as challenging realities for all parents interviewed. For those who professed religious faith, the death of their baby posed considerable challenges to their view of God. Bereaved parents experience the raw and searing edge of theodicy as they wrestle with deep and existential questions about their faith and belief – theodicy being expressed in terms of unfairness and injustice. The mother of baby Samuel, her firstborn child who was stillborn at 3 days after his due date, was a practising Christian and expressed, 'I wondered why this happened to me. I had no baby. Why me? It's beyond my capability of understanding, so I asked questions about God.'

Parents who have strong faith can find perinatal death very challenging on many levels – amongst them a conflict with their devotional practice, the presence of strong feelings of anger towards God and a sense of injustice or retribution. The father of baby Richard who was stillborn at 38 weeks of gestation was a committed and practising Christian. His son's death challenged his faith in a caring God: 'We always went to Mass…you're kind of saying "why?" You'd be wondering what you did wrong, what you did to anybody that drew this down on your doorstep.'

Many parents may experience their faith and spiritual practice as diminished following perinatal death, including for some a sense of abandonment by God when their prayers are not answered or when given a life-limiting diagnosis about their baby. They struggle with their faith when their deepest prayer was that their baby would be healed. On the other hand, some parents find their sense of faith strengthened.

The pastoral response in each of these situations is above all one of presence and accompaniment. It can be challenging to remain present to parents when their experience of faith and God is one of abandonment and desolation. Spiritual maturity calls a chaplain to attend to the enormity of spiritual pain, resisting the temptation to 'spiritualize' or fix the unfixable. The ability of the chaplain to engage in robust and searingly honest personal theological reflection is an important discipline for transformative care where there are no answers. Attentiveness to the chaplain's own spiritual journey and self-awareness, including reflection on suffering, theodicy, lament and wilderness, alongside ongoing pastoral supervision, will be reflected in the ongoing ability to attend to the spiritual depth of perinatal grief.

Relationships
Relationship between parents

As referred to above, pregnancy is a deeply relational experience. Regardless of the circumstances of conception, pregnancy loss impacts on relationships on a number of levels. Bereaved parents highlighted that the death of their baby impacted on the relationships between them, between themselves and their baby, and between themselves and healthcare professionals. This knowledge has an important pastoral dimension of which chaplains and other healthcare professionals need to be aware in the provision of care – a reminder that we are caring for people who are experiencing acute spiritual distress and crisis.

The impact of perinatal loss on the relationship between grieving parents following the death of a baby can be considerable (Gold 2010; Harper, O'Conor and O'Carroll 2011).

As well as the harsh reality of the death is the complexity of grieving styles and the individual experience of loss alongside the experience of the couple as a unit. Parents can find it hard to communicate the depth of their feelings to each other, which can in turn result in a discordant grieving process, isolation and reduced ability to support each other. Baby Rory's mother described the complexity of their grief:

We don't talk about it any more because it's too painful. It's very hard… I'd have a good day and Paul might be having a bad day, or it could be the other way around. If I am having a bad day I feel like I shouldn't make Paul feel that bad day…when I'm in pain I find it hard to comfort Paul. I can just feel the pain from him – it's like a double pain then.

Rory's father went on to say, 'It just breaks your heart because everything we have done together has been ruined, tainted.'

The depth of expression from Rory's parents demonstrates the enormity of spiritual pain experienced and its impact on the relationship between grieving parents.

Relationship between parents and their baby

The relationship between parents and their baby is one where parents can continue to feel protective towards their baby during the overall grieving process. During this period parents can experience an ongoing connection with their baby, and as they move through their grief process they can relocate their baby in the narrative of their family story. Mothers and fathers can experience this relationship differently during pregnancy, with fathers often experiencing that their relationship becomes stronger following birth. Unsurprisingly, mothers, on the other hand, often experience a strong relationship with their baby which can grow incrementally during gestation. The relationship of parent and baby is one that is of considerable spiritual significance as parents seek to express their love and loss. The acknowledgement of this love and loss is a key part of the co-construction of ceremony, ritual and memory-making. This has important implications for future grieving and helps to weave a rich tapestry of meaning and memory as parents and family return to their grief at various times into the future.

Most parents describe an ongoing and enduring relationship with their baby after he or she has died. This 'connectedness' can be a source of great comfort and can also help parents to relocate the memory of their baby in the ongoing and unfolding story of their family. The parents of baby James, who was stillborn at full term, described this sense of ongoing relationship:

I just go and talk to him and tell him what's happening with his sisters. Bríd is old enough now, so she talks to him, she knows that's her little brother. If we are driving past the graveyard, we say goodnight or good morning.

The place of burial is often a place where parents feel a particular closeness to their baby. The physical location of their grave can be a particular source of comfort and expression of grief and love for fathers. Fathers often value the privacy of grieving at a grave on their own. The father of baby Thomas expressed, 'I feel close to him in the graveyard. I prefer it when there's no one else there. I only feel it when I'm there on my own with him.'

The increasing use of cremation has provided alternative ways to create mementos with the ashes of a baby.

Relationship between parents and healthcare staff

The relationship between parents and healthcare staff is one that can be challenged following an adverse outcome such as the death of a baby. A previously trusting relationship can become strained as parents struggle with bad news. It cannot be overstated that every member of the healthcare team has a role in the support of grieving parents. Sadly, the outcome cannot be changed, but how parents experience care and compassion *can* be. Grieving parents can recall in precise detail the interaction they have with staff, and their experiences of supportive care can make an unbearable situation bearable. The mother of baby Rory who kept hoping against hope that Rory's diagnosis of a serious anomaly was wrong described her experience with her consultant: 'I could feel her kindness… I knew she really cared.'

Attention to detail, clear communication and a willingness to give of one's time are important to bereaved families and impact positively on the overall experience of care. Bad experiences of care can exacerbate an already distressing grieving process and impair recovery. This approach to spiritual care can best be summarized as person centred rather than institution centred. Pastorally, a chaplain, alongside other healthcare professionals, has an important role of recognizing signs of relationship strain and facilitating the sharing of personal pain and feeling, especially when couples are struggling to express such feelings to each other.

Conclusion

The experience of loss is a universal human phenomenon which for most of us is a natural part of life when we grieve the death of loved ones older than us. In this pattern of grieving we draw from a reservoir of memories to remember our loved ones. However, when faced with perinatal death, parents and families begin a journey where their loss and grief will accompany them for the rest of their lives. In this distinctive grief there is no reservoir of memories but rather grief takes on a palpable present as each new milestone is reached. This experience of grief calls for a sensitive and meaningful pastoral response. The lived experiences of bereaved parents in this chapter has given real-life vignettes to help us offer sensitive spiritual care at one of life's most vulnerable moments of acute grief and spiritual distress. To respond meaningfully is to attend to the spiritual depth of perinatal grief and existential pain, and doing so helps others find meaning in loss as well as build resilience and hope of recovery along with the capacity to live with loss.

References

Gold, K. (2010) 'Marriage and co-habitation outcomes after pregnancy loss'. *Paediatrics 5*, 1058–1059.

Harper, M., O'Conor, R. and O'Carroll, R. (2011) 'Increased mortality in parents bereaved in the first year of their child's life.' *BMJ Supportive and Palliative Care 1*, 3, 306–309. Accessed on 19/04/2018 at doi: 10.1136/bmjspcare-2011-000025.

Kelley, M. and Trinidad, S. (2012) 'Silent loss and the clinical encounter: Parents' and physicians' experiences of stillbirth – a qualitative analysis.' *BMC Pregnancy & Childbirth 12*, 1, 137–151. Accessed on 20/04/2018 at doi: 10.1186/1471-2393-12-137.

Kelly, E. (2007) *Marking Short Lives: Constructing and Sharing Rituals Following Pregnancy Loss.* Bern: Peter Lang.

Meaney, S., Corcoran, P., Spillane, N. and O'Donoghue, K. (2017) 'Experience of miscarriage: an interpretative phenomenological analysis.' *BMJ Open 7*, 3, e011382. Accessed on 20/04/2018 at doi: 10.1136/bmjopen-2016-011382.

Newitt, M. (2015) 'Chaplaincy support to bereaved parents – Part 1: Liturgy, ritual and pastoral presence.' *Health and Social Care Chaplaincy 2*, 2, 179–194.

Nuzum, D., Meaney, S. and O'Donoghue, K. (2017) 'The spiritual and theological challenges of stillbirth for bereaved parents.' *Journal of Religion and Health 56*, 3, 1081–1095. Accessed on 20/04/2018 at doi: 10.1007/s10943-017-0365-5.

Nuzum, D., Meaney, S. and O'Donoghue, K. (2018a) 'The impact of stillbirth on bereaved parents: a qualitative study.' *PLoS One 13*, e0191635. Accessed on 20/04/2018 at doi: 10.1371/journal.pone.0191635.

Nuzum, D., Meaney, S. and O'Donoghue, K. (2018b) 'The public awareness of stillbirth: an Irish population study.' *British Journal of Obstetrics and Gynaecology 125*, 2, 246–252.

Nuzum, D., Meaney, S., O'Donoghue, K. and Jackson, M. (2017) 'Stillbirth and suffering in Ireland: A theological reflection from healthcare chaplaincy.' *Practical Theology 10*, 2, 187–200.

Pierce, B. (2003) *Miscarriage and Stillbirth: The Changing Response.* Dublin: Veritas & SPCK.

Wretmark, A.A. (1993) *Perinatal Death as a Pastoral Problem.* Uppsala: Bibliotheca Theologiae Practicae.

Chapter 3

What Does Spiritual Need Feel Like?

Experience of Chaplaincy and Spiritual Care in Mental Health

Madeleine Parkes

Introduction

Some of my deepest spiritual needs have been met by an atheist psychiatrist; others have been met by a Christian chaplain; and others I am still working on meeting as I continue to live with chronic mental health conditions. These spiritual needs emerged when I was a young child and were made more serious by a diagnosis of chronic schizophrenia when I was 22 years old. Now, 30 years later, I am able to make some sense of my spirituality, how it affects my mental health problems and how spiritual care and chaplaincy has helped (and hindered) both my psychiatric recovery and spiritual recovery. In this chapter I discuss some of my experiences of having a severe psychiatric illness and some of the good and not-so-good treatment I have received from professionals in mental healthcare. I focus particularly on how my spiritual and religious needs have been expressed, assessed and met. It has been immensely difficult to relive some of the experiences I share here, and I have found it helpful to discuss them with a trusted friend and colleague who then wrote this chapter on my behalf. This is still my authentic voice, but with some of the distress and confusion removed in order that it makes sense to you as a reader.

Early years

I have always been a religious person right from my earliest memories; however, my understanding of what my religion actually means was flawed.

When I was 16 years old, I was confirmed into the Church of England. I then managed to make the whole experience into an achievement exercise, obsessively going over it: perhaps I wasn't really a Christian, not converted, had not done it 'properly'. I didn't realise at the time that I was missing the point that with faith even as small as a mustard seed, God loved me. The language of pressured Christianity bore down upon me with well-meaning students in the Christian Union obsessively asking me if I was 'saved'. I came to believe in a punitive, demanding God with a parental authoritarian voice. My parents' personalities, characterised by an overcritical emphasis on success, became mingled together with my early views of God. Oddly, we hardly ever went to church as a family – there was schoolwork to be done and goals to be achieved. The pressure in my household on myself and sibling was immense. I do believe that my parents wanted the best for me, and in their eyes, this came from academic achievement. My faith became something to 'achieve' and, as a result, I had many difficulties understanding what to believe. I had a misunderstanding that my relationship with God somehow had to be measured. This directly influenced the interpretation of the voices I heard later in my life.

I went to Oxford University to study medicine, despite music being my passion. My parents drove me to study medicine as they believed there were no jobs in music and medicine was a concrete career path. The lack of meaning and purpose in my life coincided with this decision. I entered Oxford with very little self-esteem after being socially isolated during my school years, and with very little confidence in my abilities as my parents had always done my schoolwork for me so that I might achieve. I worried that I was going to fail, be found out as a fraud and sent home in disgrace. However, I did not even consider that I might give up medicine. Failing to complete the course was something that I could not envisage.

Looking back on it, I started to become mentally unwell at this point. Strange things began happening to me. I thought I heard the voice of the Devil and started thinking I was possessed. Everything that was happening in my head was difficult to explain, and although I didn't explain it in terms of psychiatric illness, I can see that dimension to it now. Only in retrospect do I recognise that I was ill. I try not to dwell on these experiences or try to explain them in a cause-and-effect way as I'm not sure how helpful it is. I'm more concerned with how I cope on a daily basis with the symptoms that still persist.

I can only describe it as functioning like an empty eggshell. I was struggling with life, and a big part of this was my spirituality. My violin playing was of crucial importance – it was a spiritual outlet, although I wouldn't have described it as that at the time. I wanted to play, loved to play and got lost in playing. During my time training as a doctor I used to leave the ward, go to the hospital chapel and play the violin on my own. It was an escape. I wouldn't have survived without it.

The devils' voices I was hearing became more threatening and controlling. The day it first began I was in a church, which is perhaps why I understood the voices to be devils. After hearing the voices in a church, I felt petrified and then ashamed. I didn't know what to do. So, I did nothing. I heard these voices every now and again, but then they became more frequent and more persistent; louder. Then every day I would hear them. The first time I had an exorcism, it worked. The experiences went away, and I felt quite happy, which was an unusual emotion for me. I felt happy that someone – in this case the priest – really cared about me. I felt relieved and I came back into church. Unfortunately, after 3 weeks I heard another voice. I felt guilt immediately. What had I done to bring the voices back? I was too frightened to talk to anyone about it. I do wonder if things would have turned out better if I had been offered some support after my exorcism, some sort of prayer or support group (even though I'm not sure I would have been brave enough to attend due to my crippling shyness). By that point it was clear I had a range of religious, spiritual and psychiatric needs that desperately needed to be met.

After a few weeks I decided I had to do something as the voices were getting worse, so I told the same priest all over again. He suggested I needed another exorcism. Although I was given no theological explanation of the experience, I was also too frightened to think about it in any sensible way. After the second exorcism I left the church, ashamed to go back, as it hadn't worked. From that point on the damage was done. The exorcisms were quick fixes, with little support or explanation – quick fixes that would not have worked as I was so deep into psychiatric illness and spiritual distress. Ultimately, my deepest spiritual need at that point was the need for love and compassion, someone to explain that this wasn't my fault and that God did love me despite my experiences. This was never said.

I don't know how I got through the next 4 years. Most of it was in an alcohol haze. The voices continued to get more disruptive, with horrid and violent imagery. I was hearing several voices at that time, telling me that I was destroying the world. They were insistent that I would destroy the world if I didn't attempt suicide.

After injecting myself with potassium chloride, I was admitted to hospital where I spent the next year being selectively mute. My head was so full of confusion and distress after many years of suffering. I was worn out and didn't trust anyone. My faith was confusing, a source of guilt. My violin was in its case under my bed and I had very little human contact. I simply needed someone to trust, someone to show compassion and someone to help me understand my faith and perhaps redirect my theological understanding of what was happening to me. Unfortunately, nothing was offered – no spiritual or religious care, no referral to a priest, no chaplain. Nothing.

I was diagnosed with schizophrenia, filled full of drugs and given electroconvulsive therapy. I was very distressed that I had caused my parents such worry and problems. I don't think they had any warning that all this was going on until they were told that I was in hospital. They were of course devastated. Thus, my spiritual needs had become paramount. I had lost everything: my job, my identity as a doctor, anywhere to call home, my vocation and my friends – if I had ever had any. There was nothing to do in the hospital, and the boredom ate away at my soul. I could only see despair for the future. Worst of all, my religion was causing me much guilt, fear and deep distress. After quite a few years, I discharged myself, not really feeling much better.

Identifying spiritual needs

I had had enough of hospital, but there was nowhere to go and nothing to do. I rode on buses all day and drank tea on my own, the voices still there keeping me miserable. I had no church contact and agonised over Bible verses that I thought described the devils occupying space inside me. The first experience I had of spiritual care was from a community psychiatrist who was a convinced atheist and did not really even recognise the term 'spiritual'. Steven, the psychiatrist assigned to my care in the community, took my spiritual needs seriously. He saw that the violin was not just a hobby for me but was strongly linked to a sense of purpose in my life. It had been locked away in its case for many years, as I had become so disconnected from any sense of meaning in my life. During my many years in hospital the violin had been lying there under my bed, untouched. If only someone had bothered to ask about it, or encouraged me to hold it or play it, maybe I would have recovered quicker or my time in hospital would have been less miserable. But no one did, perhaps not understanding or not caring about that aspect of my life.

The first thing Steven did was change the medication I was on so that the side effect of the Parkinsonian-like tremor would be reduced. This was a practical but crucial first step towards my picking up the violin and being able to play again. He then encouraged me to play my violin even if only for a short time each day. Gradually, I began to take his advice. Even though I swung precariously from almost enjoying it to feeling absolutely hopeless after all the years of not playing, I stuck at it. It gave me something to do and some kind of purpose. Years went past when I was trying to find a life again, and I saw this particular psychiatrist quite regularly. Although I did not trust him with the details of my experiences, he still supported me and never gave up on me – and looking back on it, I don't know how he had the patience. It took over 5 years of building a trusting relationship with Steven before I began to talk about my religious needs – shame and fear hindered the conversation at every stage. But Steven showed me a tremendous amount of compassion and empathy.

I was scared that if someone found out what I was 'really' like, I would be rejected – I felt I already *had* been by the church I attended for the exorcisms. I didn't think anything could be done to help and I was in a very dark place. Steven slowly and cautiously asked gentle questions about my past, my beliefs and my self-harm. He was accepting of my understanding of what was happening to me – even though he was an atheist and I attributed my symptoms to the acts of devils. He stepped into my world of understanding and worked out my spiritual and religious needs from that standpoint. He saw that meeting my spiritual needs was a crucial dimension to my psychiatric recovery. He also knew where his interventions could be most effective, such as by encouraging my violin playing as a meaningful reason to live and facilitating this by adjusting my medication. He also knew his limitations and referred me to a specialist mental health chaplain who he thought might be able to meet my other spiritual needs that centred around my religious faith.

I was extremely hesitant to meet with Judy, the chaplain. I was worried that she would be able to sense the evil I believed was inside me and therefore be able to see what I was 'truly' like. It took a long time to build trust with Judy as I was intimidated at first by her authority as a priest and chaplain. For many of our initial meetings she just sat with me and held my hand for a few minutes. Sometimes she would pray out loud for me. At other times I knew she was praying but she was silent. Then when I did begin finally to talk with her, she too was very accepting of me – compassionate, caring and understanding. She used her expert discernment to distinguish what were symptoms of an illness and what were misconceptions of the religion I was trying to follow. She always tried to gently challenge these warped beliefs. Her authority meant that she had credibility in her teaching and wisdom. She helped me reread Bible verses, explored my early religious life and unpicked how my views of God influenced the perception of myself. Judy taught me that God is more powerful than devils. In addition, she suggested to me that devils, by their very nature, are going to lie; thus, I cannot and should not believe a word they say, and they should be ignored. Although I didn't believe this initially, now this means everything to me and my recovery. Crucially, Judy accepted that the voices I hear were understood as devils possessing me. Whether or not this is theologically correct didn't matter at the time and, in a sense, doesn't matter now – I don't find it helpful to think too deeply about this topic as I find myself going into dark places again. The point is that it didn't matter whether Judy held the same view of possession as me – or agreed that it was even possible – she accepted that this was my understanding of my experience and worked on how I could cope with it from this viewpoint. This was truly empathetic and extremely useful, because I couldn't simply change my mind about how I experienced or explained my voices.

We quite often had a cup of tea together, meeting up at a local café. This helped me to get out into fresh air and see the outside world. Together, we came up with strategies that worked to help me to manage my difficulties in more practical ways, such as teaching me distraction skills and how to challenge the voices I hear. I learned that I had to challenge some of the things I thought and believed. I also learned mindfulness techniques for coping with the extreme anxiety I sometimes suffer from. Judy helped me to discover who I am in God's eyes, not just who I 'should' be in the eyes of others. She helped me to find a church where I feel accepted and valued which I now attend regularly. As time has gone on, I have become more relaxed at church, and as I have done so, the devils or voices have become better. By 'better' I mean quieter, less persistent and easier to control.

Judy understood that I needed to have a purpose in my life, and this was to use the talents I have to give something back, talents I now believe are God given. I play my violin to elderly mental health patients on a weekly basis. Despite their advanced dementia, I see them react to music that is meaningful to them, which in turn gives me a sense of meaning. Playing my violin is akin to prayer to me; it is when I feel most connected with God. So, playing has become a large part of my life: I play at church and in multiple orchestras. Although sometimes this feels very stressful and induces a great deal of anxiety, I overcome this because of my love of music and my belief that it gives me a sense of purpose. Judy encouraged me to do voluntary work. She helped me cope with my feelings of inadequacy for the task and discover a new identity for myself, beyond that of a 'failed medical doctor'.

My experiences with chaplaincy and spiritual care

Both Steven and Judy showed me that you don't have to achieve anything to be loved – and this was a theological lesson. I felt Judy's love and compassion and appreciated how she took all 'conditions' off the relationship we had. This modelling met a deep spiritual, or simply human, need of mine which was to feel love and be shown some compassion. The fact that she understood and accepted my story and experiences helped to decrease my anxiety and was a huge relief. I did not feel judged in any way. I felt empowered by her holding hope for me and believing I could actually recover. I also felt safer in the knowledge that she, as a representative of the church, was assuring me of God's forgiveness. Through her theological training and pastoral care skills, Judy convinced me that the devils may *feel* in control of me, but they are not *of* me. She helped me to understand that my early life experiences were formative in both my religious beliefs and the foundations of my illness. I recognise now that there were features of depression, anxiety and psychosis that were compounded by a difficult religious faith and a pressured childhood. My idea of God was as an angry parent – an image that was persistent. I had to 'unlearn' this image, which is where Judy again was a great help. She re-taught me basic beliefs and doctrine and offered gentle challenge when my beliefs didn't fit established theological thought – again a testament to both her theological wisdom and pastoral competencies. It became clear to me that the religious faith I grew up with was immensely unhelpful, and some of my thinking contributed directly to my illness. My religious faith had to be unlearned, then relearned the right way, in order to become safe and useful. Religious issues, when solved, contributed in a satisfying way towards meeting broader spiritual needs such as meaning and purpose. All of this has transformed the way I feel about myself and my religion, not just while seeing Judy but also for my future life.

I also felt Judy's encouragement to use the talents given to me by God. This can be linked to Steven's earlier assessment that unlocking my spiritual needs would be a gateway to my recovery – but he realised that this could only happen if they could be identified and met. He realised that the key was hiding under my bed in the form of my violin – that picking up the violin again was the catalyst for my spiritual journey to evolve. What still surprises me about Steven is that he was a firm atheist who could put aside his own worldview and step into mine to talk about my spirituality. Perhaps he wouldn't call it that, but that's how I understand my violin playing.

Looking back now, I realise that there were many similarities in what Steven and Judy did for me. The major stumbling block they both encountered was my difficulty in confiding about my problems. This involved forming a trusting therapeutic relationship, a matter in which they were both extremely skilled. From both, I felt an acceptance at a *personal* level, not just as a service user or diagnosis. Both helped me to feel I could trust them by showing their care in practical ways as well as just talking in a consulting room. I felt that both were actually interested in me. From both, I felt compassion, care, understanding, empathy and unconditional acceptance, and both were very patient. Both understood my need for finding meaning, purpose, self-esteem and empowerment, and they did their best to help me achieve this, albeit in distinctly different ways. Steven's early realisation that addressing my spiritual needs would initiate my recovery didn't stop him from knowing his limitations in terms of providing more in-depth spiritual and religious care. He knew I needed more specialised help. Judy tackled the thorny problems of my warped religious beliefs in a more specific way in her role as a Christian chaplain. This has been essential in helping me to cope with ongoing difficulties and feel more at peace with myself and with God.

What have I learned that I could share?

After reflecting for a long time on my experience of chaplaincy and spiritual care, it has become clear that there are some simple but significant lessons from my story. No doubt these are reflected in the stories of many other service users who suffer from extremely difficult mental health issues. We know that mental health issues can affect one's identity, behaviour and the lens through which one sees the world. No matter the diagnosis, it is more often than not a very difficult and destructive illness to manage. If I had to highlight some crucial points from my own recovery journey, I would say that first we learn of the importance of the trusting therapeutic relationship. In my care this was a crucial first stage and was difficult to establish with my being a very distressed, isolated service user. For this you need great patience; it can take a long time and requires empathy, imagination and sincere compassion. Practical ways of demonstrating care can have special impact. I would suggest that this is good practice not just for chaplains but for any mental health professional who is committed to assessing someone's true spiritual state.

Second, some sense of positive spirituality is a common human need. We all need a sense of meaning and purpose however we individually discover it or define it. This tends to be eroded in people with mental health problems, especially if those problems are chronic or have really affected the person's sense of identity and worth. For some people this will be found in a specific religious belief, and for others it will be something more universal. A violin can even be a source of meaning and purpose, as it was for me. There is nothing religious about my instrument, but for me it was my saving grace. It is also important to highlight that spiritual needs do change. It's easy now, looking back, to track which spiritual need was more significant at a particular point in my illness and recovery, but at the time all I knew was that I felt an overwhelming sense of loneliness, guilt and fear. My spiritual needs ranged from simple ones, like needing to feel listened to and valued, to much more complex ones about my place in the world and relationship with

God. Many times I would experience multiple spiritual needs and wouldn't even recognise that they were a need because I felt unworthy of *having* needs.

Third, to those for whom a religion or spiritual belief is important, more specific specialised help with this may be crucial. A religion or spiritual belief can potentially be a hugely valuable source of meaning and purpose in life. However, for some – and I was in this category – religion is a source of great distress and confusion. For such people chaplaincy input may be transformative, particularly if the chaplain has both sound theological wisdom and a gentle, compassionate pastoral nature. For me it helped that the chaplain spoke from a place of authority – although some people react negatively when they encounter authority in religious people. I found that I could trust what the chaplain was saying precisely because of the expertise that comes with being appointed as a psychiatric chaplain. In my case it was important to speak to a chaplain who had good understanding of mental health and its interface with religion and spirituality. (A priest working in the local community who did not have this understanding unfortunately contributed to my distress and the deterioration in my illness.) In addition, the chaplain needs to be committed to the service user, both in terms of time and patience, as service users like myself have many years of trauma and distress to work through and we don't always know how to make sense of it. Clinical staff need to ask about this so that an appropriate referral to chaplaincy is made.

Finally, perhaps you might ask – well if spiritual care is not necessarily connected with religion, what is it? I think that many religions would probably agree on what it means. It involves treating others as you would like to be treated yourself if you were in that situation. To me, this means showing people sincere care, compassion and acceptance, and helping them to rediscover meaning out of despair. It is an approach that should be shown to all service users and can actually be practised by any member of the clinical team as a part of holistic care. I believe it is essential for facilitating recovery for all service users, whatever their faith or creed. I can only hope that my story goes somewhere towards illustrating this.

So how are things for me now?

For many years now, I have been a volunteer at my local mental health National Health Service trust. I derive a meaningful sense of satisfaction when I play my violin to entertain local elderly mental health service users, which is something I do every week. As time has gone on and my confidence has grown, I have designed and completed some research projects on the theme of spirituality and mental health recovery, which I am really enjoying.

I have even learned a lot about statistical analysis, which helps me find a sense of achievement. Although I am not able to manage the stress of paid work, I actually do feel a sense of fulfilment and satisfaction in life. I love my house and my cat and my various pieces of work. I go to church and find there a sense of acceptance, love and support. I do relapse every now and again. These relapses are characterised by a variety of strange and distressing thoughts and experiences. The most difficult and persistent signs of a relapse include believing that I have evil powers, caused by letting the devil in, and having the terrifying voice tell me that I will never be forgiven by God and am destined to go to Hell. Sadly, my relapses happen despite social support and a reasonably good mix of psychiatric medications. However, I am very grateful for the life I have now and can, with sincerity, say thanks be to God!

Part 2

Is Chaplaincy an Art or a Science?

'St Julian and the Leper'[1]
Though all ran from him, he did not
Run, but awaited
Him with his arms
Out, his ears stopped
To his bell, his alarmed
Crying. He lay down
With him there, sharing his sores'
Stench, the quarantine
Of his soul, contaminating
Himself with a kiss,
With the love
Our science has disinfected.

---

1   R.S. Thomas, *Selected Poems 1946–1968* (Bloodaxe Books, 1986; www.bloodaxebooks.com).

Chapter 4

Healthcare Chaplaincy as Professional Artistry

Mark Stobert

Introduction

The aim of my healthcare chaplaincy (HC) practice is for each pastoral encounter to be such that someone can experience and know love in the giving and receiving of it (Campbell 1986). However, I will make no determination as to who is the giver and who is the receiver in the encounter. A further aim is that in the encounter the search for meaning is replaced with the experience of it following Campbell and Moyers' (1988) observation that people are not searching for meaning but for experiences of meaning during life events, which have a resonance deep within, enabling them to feel in touch with the rapture of being. To fulfil those aims I have chosen to practise as a professionally artistic advancing reflective practitioner.

What is meant by 'professional artistry'?

Professional artistry (PA) was proposed by Schön (1983) as an alternative paradigm of practice to the technical rational mode of professional practice. Schön (1983, 1987) identified a crisis of knowledge in the professions. He was critical about the epistemology of professional practice and the dominant hierarchy of professional knowledge, describing it as technical rationality. Technical rationality often leads to a competency-based approach which tends to be mechanistic (Fish and Coles 1998), and assumes that practice is relatively simple, and interactions occur in which the practitioner gives and the patient receives. Technical rationality is based on skills that can be learnt, which are 'superficially reassuring in their ability to be seen and measured make professional accountability superficially easy' (Fish and Coles 1998, p.29). In PA only the principles can be predetermined and decisions are based on professional judgement, intuition and common sense. Artistic professional practice does not yield simple empirical evidence but requires professionals to reflect upon, articulate and refine and defend their practice. It is, therefore, difficult to measure, teach and research (Fish and Coles 1998, p.29). PA is concerned with both means and ends, and its activity is more akin to artistry where only the principles can be predetermined and activities cannot be pre-specified. HC can be understood as an example of a new (postmodern) profession wherein the expert and discrete knowledge related to the profession lies in the method of identifying need rather than in the act of providing a solution, in contrast to professions where expert knowledge imposes solutions upon perceived problems (Mowat and Swinton 2005, p.58).

PA enshrines *embodied reflection* (Kinsella 2010) revealed through intelligent action and tacit knowledge, where practitioners sometimes act spontaneously in ways that reveal a knowing that is not preceded by a prior intellectual operation (Schön 1983).

Reflective practice: a paradigm for healthcare chaplaincy

PA is founded on the use of reflective practice (RP) as a paradigm for action. It is a popular misconception that RP is simply an activity useful for supervision purposes; instead, it is better understood as a developing state of mind. It consists of four elements that are interwoven: reflection in action (RinA); reflection on action (RonA); critical reflection (CR); and reflexivity.

Reflection in action (RinA)

RinA is central to my chaplaincy practice and core of PA. Through RinA thought is turned back on action and back onto the knowing implicit in action (Schön 1983, p.50). In doing so I am conscious of action in the moment and of the knowledge that underpins it (Rolfe, Freshwater and Jasper 2001, p.128). The capacity to reflect in action enables me to be a reflective practitioner with the intent of producing change, yet with an openness to what that change might be. It is the foundation for the deep and attentive listening that pastoral care requires, being also a containing framework in which to interpret the empathetic affect that carers experience in those encounters. This leads to deeper understandings of patients, myself and practice. It is on-the-spot experimentation or action research in which a practitioner acts to see what happens, to produce an intended change with the purpose of move testing or hypothesis testing (Schön 1983).

RinA is event focused and immediate, and in dialogical relationship with RonA, which is also event orientated, but retrospective. Each are constant processes that I structure around a pastoral theological reflective cycle (Foskett and Lyall 1988), based on Kolb's (1984) cycle of experiential learning. Kolb's cycle encourages practitioners to reflect and make observations on their lived experience, to explore and construct abstract understandings and meanings of such, and then actively plan.

Reflection on action (RonA)

RonA involves three intertwined processes: noticing; reflection; and action (McLeod 1996). The intertwined nature of these processes means that analysis is rarely complete without RonA to provide deeper understanding and perspective transformation (Taylor *et al.* 2005). In the space provided by RonA, practitioners view their espoused theories, beliefs and contradictions with the aim of developing alternatives, intentionality and deliberative practice (McLeod 1996).

For me, RonA occurs on the go and through reflective supervision, individually and in groups in which, additionally, I experience the same relational safety that I provide for others. In the care of vulnerable and traumatised individuals, reflective supervision provides a place of holding (Heffron 2005; Shahmoon-Shanok *et al.* 2005). In such I am 'held' and enabled to hold others and their anxiety, when no solutions are apparent – a parallel process of relational engagement (Figure 4.1).

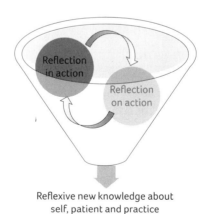

Reflexive new knowledge about
self, patient and practice

Figure 4.1 Reflective supervision: being 'held'

Critical reflection (CR)

My capacity to reflect in action is a function of the day-to-day dialogue between RinA and RonA. It is underpinned and grows through CR and reflexivity. CR is an in-depth review of events and pastoral exchanges and asks 'Why?' It brings feelings, thoughts, theory and other insights and perspectives to review and develop practice (Bolton 2014, p.7) as well as reframe problems (Schon 1987, p.31). It looks systematically and rigorously at my practice, enabling learning from actions and challenge to theory, making a difference to my practice (Rolfe, Freshwater and Jasper 2001, p.xi). Ethical, emancipatory or transformational claims can also be made for RP (Ferrell 1998; Glaze 2001; Heath and Freshwater 2000; Johns 1998, 2001; Quallington 2000; Todd and Freshwater 1999).

Reflexivity

Reflexivity deepens the reflective process by asking questions about my values and attitudes, theories used, prejudices and habitual actions and practices to understand my relationship to others (Bolton 2014, p.7). I find it sometimes exposing, embarrassing and grossly uncomfortable to stay with the uncertainty and challenge of other perceptions. This requires courage and willingness when I need to change deeply held ways of being (Bager-Charleson 2010, p.x). In my care of others, it is a professional, social and political responsibility. (Choosing to practise with a reflective paradigm requires me to act through my practice with or against the dominant forces that finance and politics dictate.)

CR and reflexivity require, and are enhanced by, the containment that the rigour of a systematic process brings. Bolton (2014) lists a series of espoused and implicit values and principles of RP (all the things a chaplain offers to those cared for) that also make the containment possible: trust; self-respect; responsibility; generosity; genuineness; positive regard; and empathy. These qualities are underpinned by certain uncertainty and the ability to sit with not knowing (Bion 1967) as well as a serious playfulness that leads to creativity and an unquestioning questioning to never let go of the possibility of otherness.

Reflective practice as paradigm and process

RP in my practice is a method of doing HC and a paradigm in which CR leads to the emergence of practical wisdom, an epistemology of practice and of new knowledge of self and others (Schön 1983; Taylor *et al.* 2005). This knowledge is produced in three domains (Habermas 1984):

- the *technical* domain of technical and scientific discipline and thought

- the *practical* domain, concerned with social interaction and the understanding of meaning

- the *emancipatory* domain, which is the knowledge of self and conduct of self in relation to social and institutional forces.

CR operates in these domains as technical, practical and emancipatory reflection (Taylor 2006) with descriptive, reflective and CR phases (Kim 1999).

Reflection on the descriptive phase constructs a personal and situational knowledge base which, when completed by the addition of a critical phase, enables the handling of complex situations without being entrenched in routinised practice (Kim 1999). The goals of CR, for me, are a perspective transformation of myself and freedom from imposed external social and psychological structures. Self-emancipation from routinised practice leads to an openness to new models of practice (Kim 1999) and generates new knowledge that challenges and changes professional practice in an ongoing fashion (Kim 1999).

As such, CR can lead to a number of outcomes:

- the shift of power to determine what counts as knowledge, from an elite to the workplace (Freshwater and Rolfe 2001; Freshwater, Taylor and Sherwood 2008)

- the generation of knowledge that becomes what practitioners know about practice (Smyth 1992)

- the creation of spiritual awareness to address the spiritual needs of the self and patients (Taylor *et al.* 2005)

- the development of emotional literacy and emotional intelligence (Freshwater 2004)

- a paradigm for the development of advancing practitioners (Jasper and Rolfe 2011).

My experience also resonates with Eby's (2000, p.53) model of reflective practice, which synthesises reflection, self-awareness and critical thinking, and identifies its philosophical roots in phenomenology and critical thinking. RP's home is in the intersection between the three and connects lived experience with a critical consciousness that resists oppression and leads to liberation. It also gives space for practical theology as a critical dialogue between experience and theological norms for the purposes of liberation (Pattison and Lynch 2005).

Contextual empirical evidence is, thus, generated through RP out of specific practice settings, in contrast to de-contextualised evidence produced by outside observers (Rolfe 2005a,b). It also makes research integral to RP, as on-the-spot experimentation and action research in RinA (Schön 1983), and as CR. As the continuous re-conceptualisation of what one is observing and doing, RP is a research paradigm in its own right (Fenichel 1992).

Whilst some identify the primary role of RP as being to learn through and from experience (Boud, Keogh and Walker 1985; Mezirow 1981), the primary role of RP in my practice is to develop my capacity for RinA. My understanding of RP is that of a paradigm within which I perform as a reflective practitioner and act as a researching professional. It is how I account for my practice to the institution, and the framework within which to critically evaluate the aim and performance of my HC practice of creating Safe Space for the Slow Questions (SSfSQs) for my institution and the inhabitants of that institution.

Professional artistry as chaplaincy practice: producing SSfSQs

I have described PA as the outcome of practice founded on RP as a paradigm for that practice. I have also set out a framework of RP as a basis for how a professionally artistic advancing reflective practitioner develops the capacity for RinA as the primary aim of practice for HC. I now want to describe how it works in my practice.

My practice as a reflective practitioner

SSfSQs is an embodied practice whereby the production of the 'space between' is created and offered by the nuanced and skilful use of self. The nature of this practice has been informed by psychotherapeutic understandings of therapeutic space, by socio-political theories of space and by practical theological understandings of the sacred and space.

The idea of SSfSQs was started when I heard a Dutch chaplain talk about how in her work with mental health patients she wanted them to feel safe so that they could ask slow questions (i.e. questions that could not be responded to with fast answers). This spark ignited a flame within me from which the poem below came, almost in an instant.

'The Slow, Slow Questions'
The slow, slow questions wait
In hiding.
They wait until they perceive that
Once exposed in the open they
Won't be dropped or damaged.
Even a 'space' (opened) between will suffice
Only after delicate testing

> Emerging from the shadows the slow, slow questions search for
> Somewhere to alight.
> A bird flying to a perch
> And sing its song.
>
> Does it matter that the song
> Is not replied to?
>
> The slow, slow questions
> Sing as sing they must.
>
> The reply? Ah! The slow, slow, slower answers
> Reach and embrace the questions,
> Not with words
> Not in song
> But as dance
> The dance of love.

It also captured the essence of my practice not just with patients but for the institution, which I had developed around the idea of creating seen and unseen sacred space illustrated in Figure 4.2.

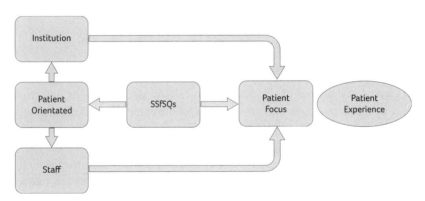

Figure 4.2 The production of Safe Space for the Slow Questions
as patient-focused and patient-orientated care

Seen and unseen sacred-space model of chaplaincy practice

The art of HC in my practice is to create SSfSQs for the institution that employs me and for the inhabitants of that institution. I have described my practice as nurturing sacred space, which can be a physical 'seen' place, an unseen intersubjective 'space between' people in relationship and an inner 'heart space' of an individual. The 'space between' is a function of the inner space of each person in relationship and a function of their fusion of horizons (Gadamer 1975). My working definition of the sacred is that which enables a person to 'open up' and facilitates a deepening relationship for persons to their psyche (soul), socially to others, cosmologically to the physical reality and metaphysically to the meanings that are constructed.

In my practice I aim to create and nurture seen and unseen sacred spaces through clinical pastoral expertise using reflective practice as a working paradigm, to empower staff to create it in their work and offer it directly to patients, visitors and staff.

Unseen sacred space has two elements. First, the interpersonal relational space or 'space between' engendered in every encounter between a chaplain and another. It is what Winnicott (1965) calls in counselling the facilitating environment for professional practice as carers. Soulful practice is the creation, holding and maintaining of this 'space between' in each encounter as carers. I identify some qualities of the 'space between':

- It is a meeting at the level of humanity and even of ourselves in the other.

- In the 'space between' pain and suffering can exist and find their place. Therefore, the 'space between' can contain and embrace the chaos of whatever crisis or difficulty might be happening for someone. It is fundamentally directed towards holding and containing, not orientated towards an outcome.

We suffer because
We suppose that there should
Be no fear or loneliness
No pain or doubt.
The chaos of these
Sufferings
Become creative when we
Understand them as wounds
That are part of being
Human.
If we can embrace
The chaos of pain
With compassion
We will give it space
Within us.
Then liberation starts
And there is a new creation.

– Mark Stobert

- Love is experienced and known in the giving and receiving of it.

- In the 'space between' meaning is experienced not because people are searching for meaning in life, but are searching for experiences of being alive – where their life experiences on the purely physical plane have resonances within their innermost being so that they feel alive in that moment.

- An additional quality to the space between is the capacity to 'not know' (Bion 1967), stemming from the quality of 'emptiness' (Moore 2002) that a practitioner needs to possess and bring to pastoral encounters. Holding and not knowing enhance SSfSQs.

- It is created, held and maintained by our own inner space, empathetic space or 'heart space'.

The second element of unseen sacred space is the inner boundaried 'heart space' which is generated through empathy by the practitioner. We need to be aware of our own empathy as a natural consequence of our capacity for compassion. This empathy needs inner space where it is safe to allow ourselves to be affected and moved by others. It can be helpful to imagine an inner space set aside and nurtured for the task of caring. Creating and maintaining boundaries to this 'heart space' makes this *empathetic space* safe for us to be affected by those for whom we care.

The boundaries are created in the intersection of the aspects of the self in practice (being, awareness and the more tangible in relation to doing), as illustrated in Figure 4.3.

Figure 4.3 The intersection of being, doing and awareness in practice

An overarching view of this intersection is shown in Figure 4.4.

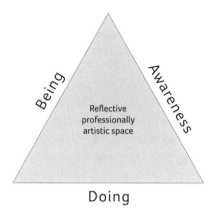

Figure 4.4 Reflective professionally artistic space created at the intersection

Within the unseen sacred space RinA and RonA can pursue a recursive dialogue.

The influence of CR

I will now illustrate how CR has drawn on contemporary understandings of the sacred, psychotherapeutic understandings, social theories of space and practical theology.

The sacred as an absolute reference point for life

Lynch (2007, p.138) defines the sacred as:

> An object defined by a quality of human thought, feeling and behaviour which is regarded as a grounding or ultimate source of power, identity, meaning and truth. This quality of human attention to the sacred object is constructed and mediated through social relations and cultural practices and resources. Religions are social and cultural systems which are orientated to sacred objects.

An object may take abstract form, such as a time and moment, but it becomes sacred because of the human thoughts, feelings and action that are motivated and directed towards it, and the images of them that are established internally (Greenberg and Mitchell 1983). This suggests that the sacred cannot exist other than in relationship. It also applies to things and places that sometimes become transitional objects. A bond established with a sacred object exerts strong influences on those same feelings, thoughts and motivations beyond the free agency of an individual – a kind of 'stickiness', which may be loving, empowering and compelling (Lynch 2007, p.139). Sacred objects may act positively to bind and hold things together, however provisional they may be. 'Stickiness' is not solely a function of the sacred object but also may be conditional on the needs and neediness of the individual.

In creating SSfSQs chaplains are often acting as transitional sacred objects that enable individuals to pass from one state to another, though their impact may be longer than the brief encounter through healthcare provision. The relationship between the 'stickiness' and the transitionality and provisionality of sacred objects may negate a sense of universality which only increases the importance of PA and RinA as an immediate practice for HC. In HC practice relationships are fostered such that objects retain their sacrality through recursive reproduction of specific practices yet ensuring that what is considered sacred does not remain fixed and static.

Therapeutic understandings

The frame and chaplaincy practice

The therapeutic frame in psychotherapeutic practice is a distinctive space that has an impact on clients, practitioners, practice and organisations (Bateman and Holmes 1995; Casement 1985; Gray 1994; Hoag 1992; Jordan and Marshall 2010; Langs 1979; Lemma 2003; McLoughlan 1995). Particular references are made to specific attributes of the frame such as abstinence (Freud 1968), containment (Bion 1967), the therapeutic frame and the artist's frame (Milner 1952), and holding (Winnicott 1968). Practical outworking of the frame allows for the development of the analytic relationship (Gray 1994). Even when organisational issues create limitations for its establishment, when established, the frame can provide benefit for the organisation as well as the patients (Hoag 1992).

Winnicott (1965, p.418) describes the secure frame as a place of therapeutic holding where the 'facilitating environment' consists of the physical surroundings and the helper, in whose person facilitation is achieved. It is a symbol of maternal holding whereby the frame holds the clinical setting and space so that the client can consciously encounter thoughts, experiences and feelings, and begin to tentatively resolve conflicts (Hoag 1992). Late in his career, D.W. Winnicott changed the emphasis of his analytical practice from interpretation to holding, the results of which proved transformational for his clients (Anderson 2014). The holding of the therapeutic frame is itself a therapeutic intervention (Lemma 2003).

Existential psychotherapeutic approaches

SSfSQs also draws from the phenomenological orientation of existential psychotherapy espoused by Laing (1967), May (1996) and Yalom (1980), amongst others, which attends to the 'ultimate concerns' (Tillich 1957, p.1) of individuals. These concerns are death, finitude, isolation and loneliness, and meaninglessness, and include guilt, loss, suffering and pain, which lead to anxiety to be defended against. This is the stuff of slow questions. Similarly, existential-phenomenologically informed therapy identifies that flights into denial, distraction and despair stem from the conflict that may exist with our ultimate concerns.

Conversational methods

The conversational method of psychotherapy (Hobson 1985) is premised on the possibility that one can know all one needs to know about another within the first 5 minutes of an encounter if we immerse ourselves in the totality of the relationship, initiated through conversation. This requires the holistic embodied stance that SSfSQs takes as described above.

SSfSQs is nurtured in different ways in different contexts. When alongside those experiencing pregnancy loss, it may be in the room in the hospital, at home or at the crematorium. In the hospital, on the corridor, it may be offered to someone who is needing support.

The social theory of space

In my CR on SSfSQs, I have explored social geographic theories of space and place. Spatial theory has transformed my way of seeing the professional healthcare world I inhabit.

Spatial theory offers a means to understand the knowledge and power issues that are at play in healthcare institutions and, therefore, how and where to place SSfSQs. Spatial theory has developed from social and humanistic geography and, by a reassessment of the role of space in social theory, from a structure-theoretical perspective on space to an action-theoretical sociology of space (Löw 2008), then to place:space theory (Thrift 2003) and finally to the interrelationship of space and place.

Dominant spaces and their production replicate power in society. Inevitably this means that in any space there will be a dialectic between demand and command. It follows that spaces cannot be the same twice, because social configurations are never the same. Even so, there are forces that seek to reproduce dominant meanings, and understandings (Tilley 1994), leading to the manipulation of boundaries and the exercise of power. Boundaries may serve to include or exclude and be related to the housing and development of ideologies and of constructed dominant spaces. Space and time come together, as spacio-temporal events, in place (Massey 2005) so that:

> a particular place not only brings together local and global influences, multiple cultures and identities, but it also contains historical influences which shape its present, as do its plans and potential for the future. (Buchanan 2009, p.63)

In that way, spaces are always now (Lefebvre 1991) but also synchronously contain the past. Massey (1993, p.155) refers to this as 'simultaneity' and that which makes social relations spatial, space being 'a moment in the intersection of configured and social relations'. This allows for the existence of multiple spaces in one place so that in any one place there exists a simultaneity of multiple spaces (Knott 2005; Massey 2005). These spaces are made up of dominant spaces and counter – and possibly utopic – spaces. Hospitals are places in which there exists the simultaneity of spaces that include the dominant spaces of finance, targets, medical and nursing paradigms and government policy, together with the counter spaces of compassion, humanity and spirituality. Counter spaces can exist within a dominant space. SSfSQs are counter spaces.

De Certeau (1984) bridges the homogeneous dominant spaces created through the strategies of classification, delineation and division that the 'strong' use as weapons by using the image of the 'nomad' as a way of encapsulating the way the 'weak' contest territorialisation by using furtive movements. For De Certeau power is about the creation of certainty, territory and boundaries, and the assertion of places. Hence, the nomad uses what De Certeau calls tactics to subvert the neat divisions and critique the spatialisation of domination. 'Tactics do not obey the laws of place, for they are not defined or identified by it' (De Certeau 1984, p.29). They are the ruses and tricks of the powerless using the space of the powerful in cunning ways to manipulate it. The 'nomad' is a postmodern citizen with new freedoms and movements for liberational practice (Cresswell 1997). It is an image that has resonance with the production of SSfSQs through the embodied practice of chaplains in healthcare institutions and offers new ways of chaplaincy creating and inhabiting healthcare spaces that are liberational. It's a way of seeing.

Professional artistry, reflective practice and practical theology

Using RP as a paradigm of practice, and, in particular, engaging in CR, has led to the development of my approach to practical theology (PT) from 'on the hoof' existential theology towards an emergent, immediate, postmodern, metaphoric, theological norm.

The shared purpose of PT and RP is to produce practical knowledge that is useful for people in the conduct of their lives and to enhance their holistic wellbeing in community. Whilst RP and PT are distinctive disciplines, there is considerable overlap, neither being a servant of the other. They exist in dialogue – theology being a normative discipline, contextual and dynamically reflective, in which the *theos* or god of the discipline can range from a personal subject that enters human lives and history, to god as the ultimate of the act of faith and the ultimate in the act of faith (Tillich 1957). Primacy is given to reflection upon lived contemporary experience, and an interdisciplinary approach as a preliminary to theological analysis (Pattison and Lynch 2005). Lynch (2005, p.94) defines theology as: 'The process of seeking normative answers to questions of truth/meaning, goodness, practice, evil, suffering, redemption, beauty in specific contexts.' As a chaplain I encounter these daily. Theology is concerned with what it means to live a good and self-fulfilling life, and the building of just and peaceful communities, in relation to the possibility of an absolute reference point to life (Lynch 2005). Lynch is inclusive of anyone who asks about the meaning and value of life; an interest in *theos* need not imply a commitment to a belief in a personal God but does require an openness that implies a commitment to the possibility of an absolute reference point for life. Theology involves developing an understanding of that absolute reference point and reflecting on the experience of life in relation to it. Nevertheless, as experience is always the starting point, sometimes it is important to keep God 'out of the way'.

Professional artistry and the NHS context of healthcare chaplaincy

The above framing of PA for chaplaincy practice must also consider the setting in which that practice takes place. Chaplains have been employed by the National Health Service (NHS), since its inception, to bring succour to the sick, dying and bereaved as well as those who care for them (Swift 2009). Models of chaplaincy practice and service have been proposed and adapted to meet the changing needs of the NHS (Folland 2006).

Much ink has been used to articulate the distinct role and place of chaplains in healthcare in the UK (Swift 2009), and discussion often centres around how chaplains might be best placed, in a multidisciplinary approach, to lead the provision of spiritual care (Billings 2015). Through a lament driven by marginalisation (Pattison 2015, p.23), a 'chaplocentricity' has emerged that appears to focus on finding a place for chaplaincy in healthcare, rather than the production of space.

Evidence-based chaplaincy: a defence against anxiety

The notion of evidence-based practice as the key to decision-making in healthcare has seen its growth in power and influence develop to the point where it is the dominant discourse and default mode of practice for most healthcare professions (Rolfe 2011). It is built on a symbiotic relationship between universities as the seat of theoretical ideas and suppliers of evidence and healthcare professions' need for that evidence to maintain a place in the hierarchy of the NHS. The financial crash and the subsequent reduction in public spending has pushed healthcare provision towards a model of transactional care away from a model of relational care. Transactional care is care that can be measured, given targets and costed, but often leads to de-personalisation and diminishment of relational care (Mulligan and Stears 2012). The economic policy of austerity has sharpened the need for chaplains to account for their practice as that which enhances the wellbeing of service users and gives value to taxpayers' money (Handzo *et al.* 2014; Kelly 2012).

There has been a dominant call for HC to progress towards the development of evidence-based chaplaincy practice and a research culture (Mowat 2008; Speck 2005). Outcomes-orientated chaplaincy is founded on a commitment to accountability that, Handzo *et al.* (2014) argue, answers questions of how chaplains show outcomes and demonstrate value to prove their case for being included and integrated into healthcare provision. I guess it depends on who is asking the questions as to whether the answers are sufficient. There are parallels to the way that the development of the ability to maintain therapeutic relationship has been supplanted by the teaching of communication skills. It suggests that if we do A, B and C, then X, Y and Z are likely to happen, and somehow it makes God and incarnation biddable and theology sterile.

There are similarities with psychological therapies and the advent of the NHS programme Improving Access to Psychological Therapies, which is dominated by the promotion of cognitive behavioural therapy as an evidence-based treatment for the support of patients with depression and anxiety. Lees (2016, p.4) sees this as the 'juggernaut of managed care' where professional practitioners are merely agents of the state, delivering regulated care to a government agenda that has an image of the ideal person. The evidence-based agenda advocated has the potential to limit the personal development of professionals (Lees 2016) and, through prescription and control, limit the enablement of patients (Morgan-Ayers 2016, p.35). The importance and centrality of the therapeutic relationship as the key to healing and in influencing long-term outcomes for psychotherapy has long been known. The centrality of the relational dimension of spiritual care over and above outcomes has also been acknowledged in chaplaincy (Carey 2015).

Nolan (2015) also identifies a managerialism agenda that is shaping spiritual care and distorting the focus of chaplaincy research towards outcome measures, to the detriment of research and a deeper understanding of process. He is critical of practices and interventions in which relationships become transactional and human attributes become commodities.

This trend in chaplaincy to follow the US and Australia in the pursuit of evidence-based and outcome-orientated approaches to practice sits at the 'doing' end of an epistemology of chaplaincy practice with little reference to the being and ontology of the practitioner.

Chaplains therefore need to consider that their practice is never apolitical – it is shaped in the context of political and economic forces – and that to choose a divergent way of practice is a political act. The professionally artistic reflective practitioner therefore must take responsibility for the political, social and cultural circumstances in which they live and work, and for their actions and values (Bolton 2014).

My professionally artistic HC practice has emerged and developed, within the context described above, through an embrace of RP as a paradigm of professional practice, with the capacity for reflection in action being the primary focus and the hallmark of an advancing reflective practitioner.

References

Anderson, J.W. (2014) 'How D.W. Winnicott conducted psychoanalysis.' *Psychoanalytical Psychology* 31, 3, 375–395.

Bager-Charleson, S. (2010) *Reflective Practice in Counselling and Psychotherapy.* London: Sage Publications.

Bateman, A. and Holmes, J. (1995) *Introduction to Psychoanalysis; Contemporary Theory and Practice.* London: Routledge.

Billings, A. (2015) 'The Place of Chaplaincy in Public Life.' In M. Cobb, C. Swift and A. Todd (eds) *Handbook of Chaplaincy Studies: Understanding Spiritual Care in Public Places.* Farnham: Ashgate Publishing.

Bion, W. (1967) *Second Thoughts.* London: Karnac.

Bolton, G. (2014) *Reflective Practice: Writing and Professional Development.* London: Sage Publications.

Boud, D., Keogh, R. and Walker, D. (1985) 'Promoting Reflection in Learning: A Model.' In D. Boud, R. Keogh and D. Walker (eds) *Reflection: Turning Experience into Learning.* London: Kogan Page.

Buchanan, C. (2009) 'Sense of place in the daily newspaper.' *Aether 4*, 62–84.

Campbell, A.V. (1986) *Rediscovering Pastoral Care* (2nd ed.). London: SCM. (Original work published 1981.)

Campbell, J. and Moyers, B. (1988) *The Power of Myth*. New York, NY: Doubleday.

Carey, L. (2015) 'Editorial. Healthcare chaplains responding to change: embracing outcomes of reaffirming relationships.' *Health and Social Care Chaplaincy 3*, 2, 85–92.

Casement, P. (1985) *On Learning from the Patient*. London: Routledge.

Cresswell, T. (1997) 'Imagining the Nomad: Mobility and the Post-Modern Primitive.' In G. Benko and U. Strohmayer (eds) *Space and Social Theory: Interpreting Modernity and Postmodernity*. Oxford: Blackwell.

De Certeau, M. (1984) *The Practice of Everyday Life*. Translated by S.F. Randall. Berkeley, CA: University of California Press.

Eby, M. (2000) 'Understanding Professional Development.' In A. Brechin, H. Brown and M.A. Eby (eds) *Critical Practice in Health and Social Care*. London: Sage Publications.

Fenichel, E. (1992) *Learning Through Supervision and Mentorship to Support the Development of Infants, Toddlers, and their Families*. Washington, DC: Zero to Three.

Ferrell, L. (1998) 'Doing the Right Thing: Customary vs Reflective Morality in Nursing Practice.' In C. Johns and D. Freshwater (eds) *Transforming Nursing Through Reflective Practice*. Oxford: Blackwell Science.

Fish, D. and Coles, C. (eds) (1998) *Developing Professional Judgement in Health Care: Learning Through the Critical Appreciation of Practice*. Oxford: Butterworth Heinemann.

Folland, M. (2006) *A Review of Some Theoretical Models of Healthcare Chaplaincy Service and Practice*. Sheffield: South Yorkshire Health Authority.

Foskett, J. and Lyall, D. (1988) *Helping the Helpers: Supervision and Pastoral Care*. London: SPCK.

Freshwater, D. (2004) 'Aesthetics and evidence-based practice in nursing: an oxymoron?' *International Journal of Human Caring 8*, 2, 8–12.

Freshwater, D. and Rolfe, G. (2001) 'Critical reflexivity: a politically and ethically engaged method for nursing.' *NT Research 6*, 1, 526–537.

Freshwater, D., Taylor, B. and Sherwood, G. (2008) *International Textbook of Reflective Practice in Nursing*. Oxford: Blackwell Publishing.

Freud, S. (1968) *The Future of an Illusion: The Standard Edition of the Complete Works of Sigmund Freud* (Vol. 21). Original work 1912. Translated by James Strachey. London: Hogarth Press.

Gadamer, H.-G. (1975) *Truth and Method*. London: Continuum.

Glaze, J. (2001) 'Reflection as a transforming process: student advanced nurse practitioner's experiences of developing reflective skills as part of an MSc programme.' *Journal of Advanced Nursing 35*, 5, 639–647.

Gray, A. (1994) *An Introduction to the Therapeutic Frame*. London: Routledge.

Greenberg, J.R. and Mitchell, S.A. (1983) *Object Relations in Psychoanalytic Theory*. Cambridge, MA: Harvard University Press.

Habermas, J. (1984) *The Theory of Communicative Action. Volume 1: Reason and the Rationalization of Society* (translated by Thomas McCarthy). Boston, MA: Beacon Press.

Handzo, G., Cobb, M., Holmes, C., Kelly, E. and Sinclair, S. (2014) 'Outcomes for professional healthcare chaplaincy: an international call to action.' *Journal of Healthcare Chaplaincy 20*, 2, 43–53.

Heath, H. and Freshwater, D. (2000) 'Clinical supervision as an emancipatory process: avoiding inappropriate intent.' *Journal of Advanced Nursing 32*, 5, 1298–1306.

Heffron, M.C. (2005) 'Reflective Supervision in Infant, Toddler and Preschool Work.' In K.M. Finello (ed.) *The Handbook of Training and Practice in Infant and Preschool Mental Health*. San Francisco, CA: Jossey-Bass.

Hoag, L. (1992) 'Psychotherapy in the general practice surgery: considerations of the frame.' *British Journal of Psychotherapy 8*, 4, 417–429.

Hobson, R.F. (1985) *Forms of Feeling: The Heart of Psychotherapy*. London: Routledge.

Jasper, M. and Rolfe, G. (2011) 'Critical Reflection and the Emergence of Professional Knowledge.' In G. Rolfe, M. Jasper and D. Freshwater (eds) *Critical Reflection in Action: Generating Knowledge for Care*. Basingstoke: Palgrave Macmillan.

Johns, C. (1998) 'Expanding the Gates of Perception.' In C. Johns and D. Freshwater (eds) *Transforming Nursing Through Reflective Practice*. Oxford: Blackwell.

Johns, C. (2001) 'Depending on the intent and emphasis of the supervisor, clinical supervision can be a different experience.' *Journal of Advanced Nursing 9*, 3, 139–145.

Jordan, M. and Marshall, H. (2010) 'Taking counselling and psychotherapy outside: destruction or enrichment of the therapeutic frame?' *European Journal of Psychotherapy and Counselling 12*, 4, 345–359.

Kelly, E. (2012) 'The development of healthcare chaplaincy.' *The Expository Times 123*, 10, 469–478.

Kim, H.S. (1999) 'Critical reflective inquiry for knowledge development in nursing practice.' *Journal of Advanced Nursing* 29, 5, 1205–1212.

Kinsella, A. (2010) 'The art of reflective practice in health and social care: reflections on the legacy of Donald Schön.' *Reflective Practice 11*, 4, 564–575.

Knott, K. (2005) *The Location of Religion: A Spatial Analysis*. Durham: Acumen.

Kolb, D.A. (1984) *Experiential Learning: Experience as the Source of Learning and Development*. Englewood Cliffs, NJ: Prentice-Hall.

Laing, R.D. (1967) *The Politics of Experience*. London: Routledge and Kegan Paul.

Langs, R. (1979) *The Therapeutic Environment*. London: Jason Aronson.

Lees, J. (2016) 'Introduction.' In J. Lees (ed.) *The Future of Psychological Therapy: From Managed Care to Transformational Practice*. London and New York, NY: Routledge.

Lefebvre, H. (1991) *The Production of Space*. Oxford: Blackwell.

Lemma, A. (2003) *Introduction to the Practice of Analytical Psychotherapy*. Chichester: Wiley.

Löw, M. (2008) 'The constitution of space: the structuration of spaces through the simultaneity of effects and perception.' *European Journal of Social Theory 1*, 11, 25–49.

Lynch, G. (2005) *Understanding Theology and Popular Culture*. Oxford: Blackwell.

Lynch, G. (ed.) (2007) *Between Sacred and Profane: Researching Religion and Popular Culture*. London: I.B. Tauris.

Massey, D. (1994) *Space, Place and Gender*. Cambridge: Polity Press.

Massey, D. (2005) *For Space*. London: Sage.

May, R. (1996) *Psychology and the Human Dimension*. New York, NY: Norton.

McLeod, M.L.P. (1996) *Practicing Nursing: Becoming Experienced*. New York, NY: Churchill Livingstone.

McLoughlan, B. (1995) *Developing Psychodynamic Counselling*. London: Sage.

Mezirow, J. (1981) 'A critical theory of adult learning and education.' *Adult Education 32*, 1, 3–24.

Milner, M. (1952) 'Aspects of symbolism and the not self.' *International Journal of Psychoanalysis 33*, 181–195.

Moore, T. (2002) *The Soul's Religion: Cultivating a Profoundly Spiritual Way of Life*. New York, NY: HarperCollins.

Morgan-Ayers, S. (2016) 'Regulation, Institutionalised Ethics and the Therapeutic Frame.' In J. Lees (ed.) *The Future of Psychological Therapy: From Managed Care to Transformational Practice*. London and New York, NY Routledge.

Mowatt H. (2008) *The Potential for Efficacy of Healthcare Chaplaincy and Spiritual Care Provision in the NHS (UK)*. Aberdeen: Mowat Research.

Mowat, H. and Swinton, J. (2005) *What Do Chaplains Do? The Role of the Chaplain in Meeting the Spiritual Needs of Patients*. Aberdeen: Mowat Research.

Mulligan, G. and Stears, M. (eds) (2012) *The Relational State: How Recognising the Importance of Human Relationships Could Revolutionise the Role of the State*. London: Institute of Public Policy Research.

Nolan, S. (2015) 'Healthcare chaplains responding to change: embracing outcomes of reaffirming relationships.' *Health and Social Care Chaplaincy 3*, 2, 93–109.

Pattison, S. (2015) 'Situating Chaplaincy in the United Kingdom: The Acceptable Face of Religion?' In M. Cobb, C. Swift and A. Todd (eds) *A Handbook of Chaplaincy Studies: Understanding Spiritual Care in Public Places*. Farnham: Ashgate Publishing.

Pattison, S. and Lynch, D. (2005) 'Pastoral and Practical Theology.' In D. Ford (ed.) *The Modern Theologians* (3rd ed.). Oxford: Blackwell.

Quallington, J. (2000) 'Ethical Reflection: A Role for Ethics in Nursing Practice.' In T. Ghaye, D. Gillespie and S. Lillyman (eds) *Empowerment Through Reflection*. Wiltshire: Quay Books.

Rolfe, G. (2005a) 'Evidence, Memory and Truth: Towards a Deconstructive Validation of Reflective Practice.' In C. Johns and D. Freshwater (eds) *Transforming Nursing Through Reflective Practice*. Oxford: Blackwell Science.

Rolfe, G. (2005b) 'The deconstructing angel: nursing reflection and evidence based practice.' *Nursing Inquiry 12*, 2, 78–86.

Rolfe, G. (2011) 'C. Wright Mills on intellectual craftsmanship.' *Nurse Education Today 31*, 2, 115–116.

Rolfe, G., Freshwater, D. and Jasper, M. (2001) *Critical Reflection for Nursing and the Helping Professions: A User's Guide*. Basingstoke: Palgrave Macmillan.

Schön, D. (1983) *The Reflective Practitioner: How Professionals Think in Action*. London: Temple Smith.

Schön, D. (1987) *Educating the Reflective Practitioner*. San Francisco, CA: Jossey-Bass.

Shahmoon-Shanok, R., Lapidus, C., Grant, M., Halperm, E. and Lamb-Parker, F. (2005) 'Apprenticeship, Transformational Enterprise and the Ripple Effect.' In K.M. Finello (ed.) *The Handbook of Training and Practice in Infant and Preschool Mental Health.* San Francisco, CA: Jossey-Bass.

Smyth, J. (1992) 'Teachers' work and the politics of reflection.' *American Educational Research Journal 29*, 267–300.

Speck, P. (2005) 'A standard for research in healthcare chaplaincy.' *Journal of Healthcare Chaplaincy 6*, 1, 26–40.

Swift, C. (2009) *Hospital Chaplaincy in the Twenty First Century: The Crisis of Spiritual Care on the NHS.* Farnham: Ashgate Publishing.

Taylor, B.J. (2006) *Reflective Practice: A Guide for Nurses and Midwives* (2nd ed.). Buckingham: Open University.

Taylor, B. Edwards, P., Holroyd, B., Unwin, A. and Rowley, J. (2005) 'Assertiveness in nursing practice: an action research and reflection project.' *Contemporary Nurse 20*, 2, 324–347.

Thrift, N. (2003) 'Space: The Fundamental Stuff of Geography.' In N. Clifford, S. Holloway, S. Rice and G. Valentine (eds) *Key Concepts in Geography.* London: Sage Publications.

Tilley, C. (1994) *A Phenomenology of Landscape: Places, Paths and Monuments.* Oxford: Berg.

Tillich, P. (1957) *The Dynamics of Faith.* New York, NY: Harper and Row.

Todd, G. and Freshwater, D. (1999) 'Reflective practice and guided discovery: clinical supervision.' *British Journal of Nursing 8*, 1383–1389.

Winnicott, D. (1965) *The Maturation Process and the Facilitating Environment.* New York, NY: International University Press.

Winnicott, D. (1968) *Psycho-analytic Explorations.* Cambridge, MA: Harvard University Press.

Yalom, I. (1980) *Existential Psychotherapy.* New York, NY: Basic Books.

Chapter 5

Different Trains

Liminality and the Chaplain

Kevin Franz

Introduction

One late October morning I was standing on a station platform between train journeys, scanning a departure board with unfamiliar destinations. I was on my way to an interview and, as it proved, the beginning of a decade working in mental healthcare in Glasgow. During the short journey two young families joined me. As I listened, with limited understanding, to their conversation I realised afresh how little I knew of this, Scotland's largest and most diverse city. I was aware of an anxiety which went beyond the interview itself. To paraphrase the poet Douglas Dunn (2003), I wondered if my accent would be at home here. I was conscious of being an outsider, a stranger in this place. Could I find my bearings?

It was a classic liminal moment. I was at a threshold – to cross would involve risk, adventure and fresh learning. The years which followed were rich in all of these things. I came to see that in spiritual care liminal spaces are ever-present, and being at ease in them is at the heart of the work. Moreover, what chaplains learn through the accompaniment they offer goes far beyond professional development. The experience of others and the sense they make of that living sheds light on the human project, what it means to be a human being fully alive. Our engagement invites us to venture into new ways of being ourselves. (I also came to appreciate how important train journeys are, opening up new landscapes and offering time to reflect on practice.)

In what follows I want to explore something of what those years taught me. First, I want to reflect on what I learned through encounters with those who inhabited liminal spaces and how they shaped my appreciation of its geography. In particular, I want to offer some thoughts on the hospitality of space. Second, and closely related, I want to reflect on how the chaplain makes personal sense out of the accompaniment of people in liminal spaces, the invitation offered and the risks taken. Finally, I want to suggest that the art and craft of chaplaincy, if it is to thrive, must embrace its own liminality. I had the rare opportunity to explore a little of what new patterns of health and social care chaplaincy might look like, to step over the threshold and look and learn. Before we undertake the journey, it may be helpful to have a more extended working definition of the liminal.

Liminality or living betwixt and between

Liminality's core meaning relates to being at a threshold, living in and through a time and place of transition. It has come to imply more generally a time of flux and change, the dissolving of older patterns and identities, the experience of ambiguity and disorientation. The theologian Richard Rohr (2016) describes it as '[the space] where we are betwixt and between the familiar and the completely unknown…[where] our old world [is] left behind, while we are not yet sure of the new existence'. For him it is a good, even sacred, space where genuine newness can begin. It is necessary for growth, for 'if we don't encounter liminal space in our lives we start idealizing normalcy. The threshold is God's waiting room. Here we are taught openness and patience…'

At times it is patience which liminality demands above all. In Jenny Erpenbeck's (2012) novel *The End of Days*, an old Jewish man in Galicia lies in bed in a dark cottage. People tell him he is close to death, but he notices that while for others dying seems to be a narrow antechamber which can be crossed in a single leap, it doesn't seem to be so for him. This business of dying is so huge he cannot find a way across. For him, as for so many I came to know in their search for mental wellbeing, the liminal can become a place of stasis, less a place of transition than of stranding.

In the broader human context liminal spaces, whatever their potential for growth, are not always entered freely or willingly. The geopolitics of our contemporary world as well as our private lives testify to this. Although at the outset the experience of the liminal I was invited to share was mainly an interior, spiritual landscape, I came to understand something of how social realities, such as poverty, loneliness and exile, are borne in the lives of individual people. I learned much from those I accompanied. It is their story which lies at the heart of what follows.

Learning from the patient

'When the student is ready the teacher will appear' is an ancient saying that tells us we, as chaplains, can learn much from our patients.

The key to all our practice as chaplains is the search to find ways of developing and exercising interpathy, that foundational skill and affect which John Swinton (2001) characterised as a genuine desire to immerse self in the unique worldview of the other and observing closely, as if theirs was the sole understanding of the world.

This is where our life in liminal spaces begins. We learn what the other may require of us, and as we seek to respond, we encounter in our turn our deepest personal and professional selves. It requires that we are open to learning.

There are many ways to learn the ways of a new city and a new role. William McIlvanney's writing offered me wonderful insights into living in Glasgow. His fictional detective Laidlaw spends his professional life among the city's marginal people and this is mirrored in his own life (McIlvanney 2013, p.213):

> [Laidlaw] was walking the edge of himself like a ledge… [She remembered him once saying to her] 'You know what I believe? There's no centre as such. The sum of the edges is the centre. You have to keep walking the edges.' But that was how you fell off. She sensed him teetering.

Most of my engagement with patients was that of individual accompaniment, often with those who were walking the edges or at risk of falling. In that intimate space the particularity of an individual life and its distinctive giftedness were most readily affirmed. I have written elsewhere of how in my search to develop a way of creative accompaniment I learned that the richest metaphors were those of hospitality and companionship (Franz 2013). Here I want to focus on the character of hospitality in liminal spaces and then more briefly consider how we ourselves are to 'be' in liminal spaces.

The experience of serious illness transports people to a liminal space. For most of us that journey is undertaken in the public intimacy of a hospital. They are quintessentially liminal spaces, at least for those receiving care. As physical contexts the transition they demonstrate from 'before' to 'now' is stark, marked by their physical design and distinctive language and culture. At best they offer safe spaces where the experiences of distress and disorientation are 'held', still embodying the older resonance of the word 'asylum'. They can be harbours for the repair of mind and body. They can also be places of transit with no prospect of return to what has been. It was this latter bleak experience of the liminal that Mark Skelton (2008) described. Reflecting on life with a diagnosis of terminal illness he wrote that, having done all the practical things to secure his family's future, he was forced to confront his changed 'place' in the world. He described his sense of himself as a pencil drawing, slowly being rubbed out.

From my perspective within mental healthcare the image of a life being erased captures the circumstances confronting many of those with whom I worked. It was particularly vivid for those living with, say, a diagnosis of early-onset dementia, but it was equally apposite for many confronting the broad range of mental illness. Many of the surface continuities of life were left behind; old routines and frames of reference remained but became hollowed out, shorn of their meaning. The liminality experienced was not hard to characterise but devastating to live with: loss of a settled sense of self, loss of a 'place in the world', loneliness, diminishing cognitive capacity or fearfulness of the person one is becoming. The future shrank and life choices shrivelled.

How is spiritual care to be expressed in such a time? Its most public manifestation may come through the hospitality of a physical space: designated sanctuaries; gardens; or sometimes our working spaces. In them we seek to create a receptive hospitality, open and in some sense 'other'. Such spaces can provide a sense of presence even when we ourselves are absent. In considering how to do this well I was introduced to the writing of French philosopher Gaston Bachelard (1969) and his unusual work *The Poetics of Space*. Bachelard helped me become more sensitive to the signals given by and within unoccupied spaces. Thus, when someone experiencing a psychotic episode described how the voices which pursued him were stilled while he sat in the sanctuary, and another of the inner freedom she experienced while looking at the artwork on the walls which protected her from self-harm, I wondered what strange chemistry was at work. I began to appreciate the difference between an empty or blank space and one which is, as it were, waiting for someone to occupy it. A liminal space can be a threshold to new ways of being, offering a moment of respite or perhaps a glimpse of what might be possible. As always, those who use such environments in our hospitals are our best guides to what makes them 'good spaces'.

A young man in one of our rehabilitation wards who came to the sanctuary most mornings asked me one day if I could provide some accessible reading material. Over time, we experimented and developed a daily bulletin of reflections, cartoons and short texts which were then left in a folder in the sanctuary. Many months after we had established this practice, I received a note from one of the medical staff. I learned it was part of her routine to spend time in the sanctuary at the end of the working day and to read what had been prepared. She had been struck the previous evening by a passage from the Old Testament, one of Jeremiah's laments. It seemed to her to capture the inner truth of mental distress, the spiral of negative thinking which plunges us into a seemingly irreversible journey in the dark. It reminded her, she wrote, of Beck's cognitive triad (Beck, Epstein and Harrison 1983) and she wondered if Jeremiah had been deeply depressed.

Over the next days, in the to and fro of an e-mail exchange, we explored how the language of psychology and formal religion intersected. We considered how religious lament not only names our distress but can move us beyond the loneliness of an inner, unarticulated experience through addressing it to something or someone outside of ourselves.

In my developing thinking about the hospitality of space, our conversation showed that moments spent in a safe and welcoming space could be transformative. Through the professional artistry of a clinician and the lived experience of a patient, I learned the capacity of an hospitable space to break the cycle of isolation, providing confidence to invite someone else into our place of sadness, a first step to arresting the apparently inexorable decline into depression. The hospitable space can itself be therapeutic.

There are times when the accompaniment we offer may not involve travelling the edges with a person but paradoxically staying still, opening a door and offering hospitality, providing a place for others to be themselves. I recall how someone who had come often, over many months, to sit in my office, sometimes in distress, sometimes in companionable silence, came to tell me of his imminent discharge. As we parted he looked around and said, 'I felt normal here.'

As hospitable spaces are a public expression of spiritual care, so alongside them we strive to cultivate a portable hospitality within the hospital environment, a hospitality of the heart to be offered wherever we are. I was humbled by the ability of chaplaincy colleagues in busy, animated general hospital wards to conjure moments of privacy and singleness of focus for those whose experience of liminality was being lived out in public.

For me, extending hospitality involved train journeys beyond the hospital, travelling to meet people in that imaginary land, 'the community', their time as inpatients over for at least a while. We would meet in their homes, or in public spaces such as coffee bars and art galleries. Visiting someone at home always offered a privileged glance into their private world. I learned that for them crossing the threshold, returning 'home' after a lengthy absence, was rarely simple. However skilfully prepared for by occupational therapy and community nursing staff, the 'coming home' often meant re-occupying a space where they had been deeply unhappy and at risk. The physical space had often changed little and was not yet ready to hold their changed personal realities.

Accompaniment in the first days after discharge required a different kind of engagement, shifting from providing hospitality to receiving it. It was helped by the physical journey the visit involved: the view from the train; the streets walked; the lift taken to the top of the tower block; noticing the smells and atmosphere of the building; the view from the window. It required recognising that the interpathic task had changed: the way the world looked from this place was different. This new phase was characterised by subtle shifts in the dynamic of the relationship. There was often an increased sense of mutuality, expressed in the reversed role of host and guest. There was also a new provisionality. This phase was a sign that a liminal time was drawing to a close. It asked of both partners that we recognise the threshold was behind us, the bridge to the new place crossed and that we must prepare for taking leave of one another.

Being ourselves in liminal spaces

What might be said of the chaplain's own liminality? It is a way of professional being which, to be effective, has to be rooted in our own search for authenticity. By its very nature the liminal is not permanent. Those we accompany move on. I recall working with someone carrying a weight of guilt and failure woven into a life dominated by addiction. Over time, the story was shared and we crafted together a simple ritual of regret and new beginnings. We thought carefully about what space would create the best environment and decided to meet in a summerhouse in the gardens of the hospital. There we sat, the doors open, looking across to a walled garden, and he chose the right time to speak the words he had written. Afterwards I asked if he had noticed anything. He, like me, had observed someone walking along one of the paths and, seeing the door into the walled garden ajar, had closed it. When I asked what response that provoked in him, he said he wanted to open the door again, to go through and see what lay beyond it, and to do so by himself if that was acceptable. It was the perfect embodiment of what we had been working towards. So, we went our separate ways. The liminal can be a place which opens up fresh and surprising perspectives.

What can make the liminal space perilous as well as creative is the change the accompaniment brings about in the accompanier. Willingness to share the view into a fractured or dystopic landscape is a precondition of good spiritual care. It is also a place of transition for the chaplain. What makes it a creative space for both partners is the search to tap into the other's wisdom, to be curious about how each understands their experience and meets the challenges to their wellbeing. Without such a meeting of minds and hearts the chaplain's wisdom will remain a latent resource and the patient's spiritual care will be impoverished. What the chaplain 'learns' is not simply how best to deploy what they already know, but how to be open to new ways of being human in the company of another as they make sense of things at the edge of meaning. At the end of each engagement, the chaplain must, like Hansel in the Grimm fairy tale, find the pebbles which lead home, back to a subtly changed reality.

The tale of Hansel and Gretel is a classic exploration of liminality. It touches on themes of transition, abandonment, exile, exploration and reconnection. The impossibility of return from the liminal to the pre-existing reality is captured in the image of the breadcrumbs. Hansel has left them to ensure his return, but the birds eat them and he finds there is no way back, only a way forwards, one which leads through loss and danger to newness.

The liminal and the marginal: learning in community

'Here is what we seek; a compassion that can stand in awe at what the poor have to carry rather than stand in judgement at how they carry it' (Burns 2017). Thus far we have considered liminality in the familiar context of individual patient care. We have drawn on the experience of persons living with chronic or acute ill health and reflected a little on what we can learn from them and other healthcare professionals. I have suggested that the liminal is the normative environment for the chaplain. There is now a broader context to be considered, one which asks radical questions of the inherited patterns of spiritual care. What if chaplaincy as a craft is being invited to embrace its own liminal moment? What if the exploration of what it means to be a health and social care chaplain involves the same boldness and stepping into the unknown we encourage in others?

One of the outcomes of the integration of health and social care, as it has been conceived and enacted recently in Scotland, is the reminder that people live lives in which a whole complex range of psychosocial factors frame the context in which their search for wellbeing takes place. Current innovations in care-system design and delivery simply mirror how individual lives are led. All chaplains know, as they listen to individual stories, the impact on people's wellbeing of where they live, the quality of their housing, of who their neighbours are or what access to public services is to hand. They know experientially that nothing can replace the effect of sharing what one arts project in tower blocks in the west of Glasgow called 'the view from my balcony'. In mental healthcare the shift to that broader canvas of health and social care has been perhaps easier to conceptualise, for the locus of the work has always been as much in 'the community' as in the hospital environment.

In finding its place in the new health and social care landscape in Scotland, chaplaincy has had the extraordinary opportunity to benefit from some innovative and creative thinking about public health. It arose from confronting some of Western Europe's most disturbing health statistics. Its prime mover was Sir Harry Burns, the Chief Medical Officer from 2005 to 2014, who, building on what he knew as a clinician in Glasgow, asked why in the previous three decades trends in life expectancy in Scotland's largest city, which till then had been broadly in line with other Western European conurbations, had failed to keep pace. Moreover, he asked which sectors of society were most likely to bear the brunt of this vulnerability and what that required of our understanding of healthcare.

Burns pointed to the rapid collapse of Scotland's industrial base as the consequence of Westminster government policy or inaction in the 1980s. He set out its effect on patterns of employment and the dislocation of traditional patterns of working and social life. It was this fundamental change, he argued, which lay at the root of Scotland's poor health profile. He argued that it presented a psychosocial crisis, one which required psychosocial remedies. The fundamental problem about Scotland's poor health is the health of the poor, he argued, but he vigorously resisted the dangerous conclusion that the poor should be blamed.

Burns' research and the debate it stimulated provided an analytical framework for what health and social care professionals knew from their practice. He was also unafraid to speak with passion about fundamental values. In similar vein, a report published by the Glasgow Centre for Population Health (Walsh *et al.* 2016) earthed the research in terms of its human cost.

If the key drivers of overall poor health are poverty and deprivation, the report states, there is an urgent need to narrow the widening gap in income, power and wealth, and as a consequence health inequality, within Scottish society. It is a call to action. It is in this context that chaplaincy in Scotland has been invited to find a place.

Scotstoun, in the west of Glasgow, provided a vivid example of a community marked by contrasting levels of prosperity and health. At its heart lay Kingsway Court, a complex of six high-rise flats – 'streets in the sky'. Built in the early 1960s the flats had housed families whose working lives had been spent in the nearby shipyards, factories and support industries. Scotstoun had struggled to recover from the impact of large-scale redundancies in the 1970s and 1980s following the closure of the yards. There was a concentration of 'hard-core' poverty, low incomes and unemployment. The area's health and wellbeing deficits were all too clear. The figures translated into what a local community action project (Kingsway Court 2011, p.11) described as

> [a] widespread and lengthy deprivation…debilitating to the wellbeing of many individuals… Residents range from those who are severely down-trodden and 'broken' with very little hope, to those who are down-trodden but determined, capable and aspirational.

There had been a further transformative element in Kingsway's social fabric: the arrival of a significant number of asylum seekers and refugees under the British Home Office's dispersal programme.

In the context of the scale of the health and social challenges facing the city, and in the context of the paradigm shifts for chaplaincy explored elsewhere in this book, what response was required of healthcare chaplaincy? What might a small action-research project in a community like Kingsway demonstrate?

With imaginative leadership from NHS Education for Scotland and underpinned by the professional support of skilled researchers, a project was established initially for 9 months and then extended to engage in a limited way with two other neighbourhoods, Drumchapel and Partick, for a further 18 months. All lay within the human communities Gartnavel Royal Hospital served. The time commitment agreed for the chaplain's involvement was modest, an average of half a day each week, but through the generosity of the host communities it provided a rich learning context. It afforded glimpses of what a genuinely integrated health and social care chaplaincy might look like and had an incalculable impact on my practice. It was an invitation to step across the threshold.

The theoretical framework underpinning such a project set out some of the adjustments the chaplain would have to make: the wisdom that the researcher enters a liminal state, separated from their own culture yet not incorporated into that of the host culture; learning how to be both participant and observer; and the challenge to develop self-reflexivity in the liminal state, one characterised as emotionally demanding and uncomfortable.

In concrete terms it required leaving behind a settled role and coming with 'a beginner's mind' to a community-run resource based in the flats. The project required skilled brokerage by others whom the community development staff and local management group trusted. There was no institutional solidity to fall back again, no role description to cling to, no history to appeal to. It required coming as a stranger and being met with curiosity, trust and a cautious welcome. It meant arriving empty-handed, open in the moment to whatever level of engagement my hosts chose.

I learned to set aside the default position of seeing one-to-one conversation as the norm and instead became intentional about spending time within groups trying to glimpse what belonging to them revealed about what made for community wellbeing. It meant negotiating in each encounter how to balance receptivity with curiosity. It required being content to deal with fragments which would be reflected on later with my research colleague.

Days were spent walking in the hills near the city with asylum seekers, listening to painful stories of exile; preparing lunch with a group of mainly older women who taught me much about hospitality; hearing stories from the local credit union about the impact of poverty; spending a festival day in the community garden as the full diversity of the community was celebrated.

It meant learning about the anger and distress in the local community a few years earlier when the Home Office 'dawn raids' on 'failed' asylum seekers had taken place, listening to the narratives of the active resistance that was mounted. It meant sharing the community's pride that the story had been made into a musical theatre production, *Glasgow Girls* (staged at Citizens' Theatre Glasgow in 2016).

I began to see that much non-intrusive mutual care and support was given in the gaps: while washing up or during a minibus journey. I saw how people afforded one another dignity and privacy, creating space for discrete support when someone was overwhelmed by sadness. I saw the importance of rituals and customs in the midst of the unpredictable everyday, how living is transfigured by ceremony in matters as simple as laying tables or playing bingo. I watched the way people managed their conflicts and arguments, heard how they experienced the healthcare system, how they managed life-diminishing chronic illness. I heard of the sense of loss of old community values which had seemed commonplace but were now at risk. I witnessed people's outrage at injustice and how they acted upon it and wondered about the impact on their wellbeing and peace of mind. I heard challenges to a healthcare system which used resilience as an excuse to avoid radical change. And then, at the end of the day, I would catch the train back to the hospital with the words 'what if?' in my mind.

In his groundbreaking article 'The patient's view', Roy Porter (1985) describes our profound ignorance of how ordinary people in the past actually regarded health and sickness. The challenge he set was to do 'history from below'. What if that was the invitation our project had uncovered for our own time? What if the resources of chaplaincy were to be re-oriented to respond to the needs and capacities of our poorest communities as they themselves identified them? What if our role was intentionally to uncover and to strengthen the human and spiritual assets in communities? What if the spiritual care we offered in those communities was to help build the resilience and confidence of local leaders in their task? What would it mean for chaplaincy formation and training to engage with a new paradigm? What would be lost? What would it take not only to step across the threshold but to make our professional home there?

Such an intentional shift to a fully integrated health and social care approach would have required a reconsideration of the human and financial resources available to chaplaincy. It would have demanded careful and honest conversation about what fresh skills, training and affects such a future would require of chaplains. It would have necessitated sitting light to established roles in the healthcare system, often hard won, and living with a degree of risk and provisionality. At that point the scale of those demands was too daunting and existing resources too modest. Yet in other contexts small initiatives were begun and some of these transitions undertaken. That, perhaps, is the character of the liminal. It invites us to venture, to experiment and test out what lies beyond the known. And as we have learned from the lives of those we have accompanied, timing is all.

Conclusion

We began with Richard Rohr's characterisation of the liminal as a waiting room. Perhaps, in conclusion, this implies too much passivity. Berdahl (1999), in her work on the communities which lay either side of the divide in Cold War Germany, suggests a more productive image. Borderlands (i.e. archetypal liminal spaces), she suggests, should not be thought of as marginal zones but simply places between established stable realities. Instead, they were active, creative spaces in which people worked to negotiate meaning and determine what was possible. Rather than being places to pass through, they were the natural home of the postmodern subject.

If this seems rather portentous for the modest role of the chaplain, it is worth recalling that life in the liminal space is serious but not solemn. We can develop a way of being and acting which is light on its feet, even playful. I have learned to value the reflection of the Catalan artist Joan Miró (Levy 2014, p.44): 'I want my work to emerge naturally, like the song of a bird or the music of Mozart, with no apparent effort, but thought out at length, and worked out from within.'

Miró's understanding of the creative processes which produced his painting came at a time when his work had become simpler, sparer. His words invite us to consider our creative life as chaplains, the mix of art and craft we develop and deploy in our work. Our accompaniment of others in liminal spaces may appear natural and effortless yet require that 'working out from within' of which Miró speaks. What makes that betwixt and between place we call the liminal a 'good' space is that we ourselves are welcomed and accompanied by the one who asks for our company and invites us over the threshold. In the liminal space the gifts are shared.

References

Bachelard, G. (1969) *The Poetics of Space*. Boston, MA: Beacon Press.

Beck, A.T., Epstein, N. and Harrison, R. (1983) 'Cognitions, attitudes and personality dimensions in depression.' *British Journal of Cognitive Psychotherapy 1*, 1, 1–16.

Berdahl, D. (1999) *Where the World Ended: Re-unification and Identity in the German Borderlands*. Berkeley, CA: University of California Press.

Burns, H. (2017) Notes from *Conversation with Sir Harry Burns*. Glasgow: Craighead Institute.

Dunn, D. (2003) 'Here and There.' In D. Dunn *New Selected Poems 1964–2000*. London: Faber and Faber.

Erpenbeck, J. (2012) *Aller Tage Abend*. Munchen: Albrecht Knaus Verlag.

Franz, K. (2013) 'In the land of unlikeness.' *Health and Social Care Chaplaincy 1*, 1, 75–83.

Kingsway Court Health and Wellbeing Centre (2011) *Summary Development Plan*. Glasgow: Kingsway Court Health and Wellbeing Centre.

Levy, D. (2014) *Modern and Contemporary Art*. Accessed on 31/03/2017 at https://issuu.com/artsolution/docs/davidlevy-low.

McIlvanney, W. (2013) *The Papers of Tony Veitch*. Edinburgh: Canongate. (Original work published 1983.)

Porter, R. (1985) 'The patient's view: doing medical history from below.' *Theory and Society 14*, 2, 175–198.

Rohr, R. (2016) *Richard Rohr's Daily Meditation: Transformation. Week 2 Liminal Space*. Accessed on 14/09/2016 at https://cac.org/liminal-space-2016-07-07.

Skelton, M. (2008) 'Our daughter will be an orphan.' *The Guardian*, 5 September 2008. Accessed on 06/09/2016 at www.theguardian.com/lifeandstyle/2008/sep/06/family.healthandwellbeing.

Swinton, J. (2001) *Spirituality and Mental Healthcare*. London: Jessica Kingsley Publishers.

Walsh, D., McCartney, G., Collins, C., Taulbut, M. and Batty, G.D. (2016) *History, Politics and Vulnerability: Explaining Excess Mortality*. Glasgow: Glasgow Centre for Population Health. Accessed on 01/12/2017 at www.gcph.co.uk/publications/635_history_politics_and_vulnerability_explaining_excess_mortality.

Chapter 6

The Role of Science in Enhancing Spiritual Care Practice

Daniel H Grossoehme

Introduction

A *spiritual autobiography*

The submission of a spiritual autobiography is required as part of the package of application materials to be submitted in order to become a board-certified chaplain through the Association of Professional Chaplains. Candidates are asked to relate those experiences where one's history directly affects one's clinical chaplaincy. Since there are experiences which not only inform my clinical chaplaincy but also how I think about the religion and science, I begin with an autobiographical account that includes how science is interwoven with how I practice chaplaincy, and how I understand myself in the context of a major academic pediatric medical center, which could also be considered a cathedral for science.

If asked as a child if I believed in God, the answer would have been 'Yes'. Our family went to church every Sunday. I squirmed through the sermons and appreciated the music. Faith didn't necessarily extend beyond that, though – until the day in tenth grade when I was taking senior biology and the teacher lectured on the Krebs Cycle of cellular respiration. It's a complex, cascading chain of chemical reactions that occurs countless times in each cell of our body. I recall very distinctly sitting in lecture and thinking, *What an incredible chemist God is!* And I was convinced that God was real and omnipotent for the first time.

At university, I took a degree in astrophysics, which is also the point when research entered my life, collecting data and modeling the atmosphere of a particular type of binary (Evans, Grossoehme and Moyer 1985; Grossoehme, Evans and Moyer 1983, 1984; Grossoehme *et al.* 1984). It was also the time when I found myself kneeling at the altar rail in an Episcopal parish next to a high-energy physics professor. His wasn't a profession I was to have, but his presence was a sign that the myth of the objective scientist as an atheistic egghead was just that, a myth, and that it was indeed possible for thoughtful religious belief and serious science to live together in a person's brain.

My university grades did not, however, support my intended path towards graduate work in astrophysics, and my focus turned elsewhere. I stopped looking up at the sky automatically when I went outside and thought I had closed the door on science. I was eventually ordained as an Episcopal priest and entered a residence in clinical pastoral education in a major academic medical center. I was standing in the chaplaincy office one morning when the mail arrived and brought with it a copy of the quarterly pastoral care journal. Someone noted that it contained an article by a chaplain educator we all knew. Our training supervisor said, 'Oh, he's from [name of center deleted] – they do research on chaplaincy up there.' One could hear the eye-rolling and disparagement in his voice. I immediately took two things away from this interaction: first, it was possible to do research and science in chaplaincy; and second, it was definitely regarded as inferior to clinical care, at best, and as a waste of time, at worst. The American model of training chaplains through clinical pastoral education emphasizes integrating disparate parts of one's personality into one's identity. And so the process of co-mingling of science and theology into my identity and vocation as a chaplain began.

I find myself frequently standing between two groups that are somewhat at odds with one another, and acting as an interpreter. On the one hand, I feel that part of my role as a chaplain is to help clinicians understand how and why their patients (and in pediatric hospital, why the patients' parents) are using faith to make healthcare decisions, and how faith influences their health behaviors. Even if you yourself do not have any religious or spiritual beliefs, many of your patients and families do – so wouldn't you be interested in knowing more? For example, my clinical assignment for the past 9 years has been with the cystic fibrosis team. Cystic fibrosis is a progressive, life-shortening disease in which mucus clogs the airways in the lungs and which must be loosened and coughed up through airway-clearance treatments several times a day. One young Christian parent told me that they didn't 'do' treatments or other things on the Sabbath. The Sabbath was a day for church and for family. With their permission, I was able to tell their story to the child's pulmonologist and facilitate a conversation between the pulmonologist and parents in which it became clear that the Sabbath being a day for family meant having the children running around playing outside – not the same as the prescribed airway-clearance therapy, but still an activity that meant the child was moving air and working to keep the airways open. The conversation also helped the pulmonologist experience the parents as loving and committed to their children and not rejecting medicine, though having a somewhat different set of priorities.

It is important that we as healthcare chaplains learn how to adjust our language as members of a minority to the dominant culture in which we find ourselves. This is not to say we must abandon our special language, but to say that it cannot be the only language we can speak. Clinical healthcare chaplaincy must be bilingual in the sense of having the ability to speak in ways that those in the dominant culture around us can understand. For healthcare chaplains, this means the language of the medical center, which means the language of science. Increasingly it also calls for chaplains to be conversant in the language of financial accountability and added value. The story from the Christian scriptures in which the Apostle Paul, speaking to the Greeks in Athens (Acts 17:22ff), is paradigmatic. Here is a religious figure able to communicate the content of his field of expertise without sacrificing his identity and to do so using imagery readily understood by those whose language and thought categories are quite different from his own. Why should clinicians care about spirituality if healthcare chaplains do not show an interest in the body and the ways it manifests disease and brokenness and healing? Developing and practicing these language skills may be an entrée into relationship for chaplaincy care of clinicians, or may lead to clinical collaboration based on relationship developed around a research conversation. For example, a chaplaincy colleague was interviewing physicians about their behavior (at least, that was what the chaplain thought was going to happen). The majority of these 'research interviews' became occasions in which the clinicians indirectly made use of the chaplain, seeking and accepting care in ways they had never done outside of the somewhat artificial setting of a research study. Clinician-researchers accustomed to measuring clinical values, such as blood counts or western blots, have expressed curiosity about how 'soft' topics like religion can be measured using 'real science'. These questions are sometimes expressed with a shake of the head and the comment 'You can't measure God, can you?'

Chaplaincy in a scientific world

Barbour (1990) has described four ways in which science and religion relate to one another. These paradigms are also useful for thinking of ways in which healthcare chaplains both respond to, and are influenced by, how they and others understand the relationship between religion and science. These are not evolutionary stages through which one should strive to move to arrive at the highest level. In the first of these four categories, scientific materialism and biblical literalism stand in conflict with one another. It may be that some of the origins of this conflict, at least from the religion side, stem from some of its sacred writings. The biblical book of creation tells a story in which the first humans ate of the fruit of the tree of knowledge of good and evil and were expelled from the primal garden (Genesis 2–3). Perhaps this story contributes to the fear some chaplains have about science and faith: to accept or undertake research would be as if they were reaching for the fruit of that tree, violating the command of God and usurping God's place in the universe. Another religious objection to science is scientific materialism's insistence on the primacy of the scientific method. This objective and deductive way of knowing may be seen completely contrary to the notion of 'meeting people where they are', which is a frequently quoted principle in chaplaincy education. Chaplaincy, by contrast, is understood by some to be a primarily objective and inductive endeavor. The chaplain starts with this particular patient in front of them, draws out their story and seeks to connect them in the end to the Absolute.

This deductive–inductive tension is beginning to blur. Discovery science and data mining are newer forms of science which are inductive. They do not deal with how the observer relates to a particular data point. They begin with data and look for patterns that lead to a hypothesis to be tested later. I have had interactions with adolescents who all have cystic fibrosis in many different ways over the past 9 years. At the same time, I have observed that there are patterns that suggest when it might be especially suitable for me to intervene. This is similar to the qualitative research method known as grounded theory (Charmaz 2014). This inductive approach moves from the particular story to an overarching theory that connects individual stories. That theory, 'grounded' in the words of particular individuals, can be tested subsequently to see how well it explains a phenomenon. It is a particularly accessible research methodology for chaplains to use (Swinton and Mowat 2006) and can lead to developing theories that influence chaplain behavior (Grossoehme *et al.* 2010).

The second paradigm holds that science and faith ask parallel questions, such as 'why' and 'how' things are as they are. This was my paradigm for many years as these two topics peaceably coexisted in my head. This could be what lies behind the statement I frequently encounter from both chaplains and physicians when talking about research: 'You can't measure God!' Of course, that is not what those of us doing research about spirituality and health are trying to do in the first place. What can be detected and measured are attitudes and behaviors. Knowing more about either could help answer questions of interest to chaplains, such as 'Who needs contact with a chaplain most today?' (Fitchett, Meyer and Burton 2000) or 'How do I help the treatment team understand why this person isn't doing their treatments at home?' (Grossoehme *et al.* 2015). A potential danger of viewing faith and science as parallel questions is that it could contribute to a chaplain's tendency to function as a 'lone ranger' who works in isolation from the healthcare team. This chaplain regularly sees patients, families and staff for care, but doesn't share salient information with the team nor work towards a plan of care that the team developed to benefit the patient. The third category has faith and science in a complementary relationship. The fourth category Barbour (1990) describes is one in which science and faith are integrated with one another. After years of attending or presiding at Episcopal Eucharistic worship, the priest's recitation of the Summary of the Law as part of the opening in the current, traditional language service ('Thou shalt love the Lord thy God with all thy heart, and with all thy soul and with all thy mind. This is the first and great commandment…') (*Book of Common Prayer* 1979, p.324) began to resonate in a new way for me. Using one's mind to love God was not only an option, but was part of the 'first and great commandment'. This was part of an internal shift of identity from a priest with an interest and some experience in science to a priest who *is* a scientist – or a scientist who is a priest. Research efforts are an affirmation that divine revelation continues. By engaging in research, the investigator implies that there is more to discover. In the case of chaplain researchers, or colleagues from other disciplines who study the role of faith and health, they imply that there is more that we can understand about who God is, and the ways in which God works in the lives of those for whom we care. Paying attention to God's presence and activity through listening to stories in qualitative research studies, discovering how religious beliefs or constructs are related to health outcomes in quantitative studies or reading these studies and reflecting on them are ways in which chaplains can experience and participate in God's ongoing revelation.

While the cognitive approach to God is perhaps not the major vein of ore that is mined, it *is* nevertheless a vein. Teilhard de Chardin wrote that science, and specifically research, is the highest form of adoration of God (de Chardin and Lindsay 1959). There are a number of clergy who were themselves scientists and there is the contemporary society of people doing science who are also ordained in their own faith traditions: the Society of Ordained Scientists.

Islam also has a tradition of valuing the pursuit of knowledge as part of faith. Islam has a long tradition of science, often conveniently forgotten by the West during times of violence. Although they are not written in the Qur'an, there are collections of words of the Prophet Mohammed which are known as *hadith*. Certain words directly address the relationship between science and faithfulness in Islam. These *hadith* include the idea that seeking of knowledge is obligatory for every Muslim (Al-Tirmidhi, Hadith 74). There are no limits on what kind of knowledge is to be sought, for evidence may be found anywhere, and it all points to the Almighty. For Muslims, the acquisition of knowledge is a means rather than an end in itself. Gaining knowledge must lead to disseminating the knowledge to the wider community. Another *hadith* (Al-Tirmidhi, Hadith 107) makes clear that knowledge is not only to be acquired, it must be imparted to the people. Gaining knowledge through research and study is only the first half of the process. Sharing that knowledge with others is important because knowledge of God belongs to the community and should not be hoarded as the private treasure of the researcher. Chaplain researchers should present their work publicly both for peer review as part of the scientific method, but also for the benefit of others. I suggested above that research is a means of experiencing revelation. It follows, then, that chaplains should also attend research presentations and read research journals as a means of gaining access to what has been revealed.

I want to suggest that research – conducting it or making use of it – does not take time away from chaplaincy, but that defining healthcare chaplaincy as only direct clinical care of the sick is too narrow. Chaplaincy has many faces, of which research is one. Elsewhere I have written about the learning experience I had when a research participant began to describe their experience to me as if it had been my bedside caring (Grossoehme 2011). Although some chaplains may distinguish between chaplaincy and research, it is equally the case that some of those for whom we care do not make such a distinction.

Chaplains as consumers of science

Healthcare chaplaincy, at least as it is currently practiced in the United States, is perhaps the last profession to have an evidence base for its practices. There has been a growing awareness that this must change. Canadian chaplain and educator Thomas St. James O'Connor (2002, p.253) defines evidence-based spiritual care as 'the use of scientific evidence on spirituality to inform the decisions and interventions in the spiritual care of persons'. This definition is helpful given the current state of chaplaincy research, because it allows chaplains to draw on the considerable and growing body of evidence on aspects of spirituality and health which have been published by psychologists, physicians, sociologists and others. The essential point is that whatever I do at the bedside should have a reason beyond my own experience that some people find whatever I'm doing beneficial. I should be research literate: aware of what literature relates to my clinical focus, reflect critically on its applicability to my practice and, when appropriate, be guided by it. For example, I'm aware of a considerable body of literature that shows a relationship between spiritual struggle and poorer health outcomes (Cotton *et al.* 2013; Fitchett *et al.* 2004; Grossoehme *et al.* 2013; King, Fitchett and Berry 2013; Thuné-Boyle *et al.* 2013). I also know that people experiencing spiritual struggle tend not to ask to speak with a chaplain nor be referred to me by other clinicians (Fitchett *et al.* 2000). In trying to determine the best use of my time in my clinical area today, I want to identify those persons with spiritual struggle and give them a relatively high priority (Grossoehme and Fitchett 2013; Grossoehme *et al.* 2016b). Chaplaincy practiced out of a research base shifts the field from one which placed a value on the non-directive, agenda-less, active listening style of Carl Rogers (Rogers 1951) towards one in which chaplains collaborate with patients, family members or staff to work towards an identified outcome (Peery 2012; VandeCreek and Lucas 2001). This shift is critical for chaplains to make in order to genuinely provide care at a deeper level than simple presence. To draw on a principle from another discipline of science (the second law of thermodynamics), left to themselves, systems tend to move towards increasing levels of disorder. In other words, someone's brokenness or 'dis-ease' will not improve without an active change. Sometimes the active change does not need to be dramatic. The Canadian psychologist Karl Tomm observed that the simple act of a therapist asking a question as part of their assessment process changed people's situations (Tomm 1987a,b, 1988). These changes might be noticed either during the therapeutic hour or in the client's reflection or discussion with others afterwards. This work strongly suggests that chaplaincy interactions are all, at least potentially, interventions. It is therefore incumbent on us to intervene well, by which I also mean well informed.

There is a justice issue involved here. Entering into relationship with someone as a chaplain means that we bring a level of power into that relationship beyond what the patient or family member's peer would bring to a relationship. This is most obvious in pediatrics, where adults have more power than children or adolescents, but is no less true in any other setting in which chaplains practice. Representing the sacred carries with it some of the power of the sacred. The right use of such power means always using it in the best interest of the other person; in the present discussion, that means offering interventions that are not only kind, but which we know are likely to benefit them. O'Connor and Meakes (1998) wrote that chaplains risk being ineffective, at best, and, at worst, injurious to the people they serve unless they draw on a base of evidence to support what they do. Chaplaincy needs to be informed by science. How one uses that at the bedside, clinic or office still leaves room for the 'art' of chaplaincy.

As Barbour's (1990) paradigm shows, there are different ways of conceiving the relationship between religion and science. Yet there are points of commonality which may make it easier for some chaplains to relate them to one another, and one of those is methodology, and specifically the use of descriptive language. Some spiritual concepts are difficult to put into words, for example a chaplain–patient conversation in which the patient is asking for a reason for their disease or suffering. Scientists also struggle to express their concepts in ways that are easily understood by not only their colleagues but by those from outside their discipline. Where a chaplain might draw on the use of metaphors or rituals to communicate a particular 'truth', scientists use numbers, symbols, equations and models to express the truth as they understand it.

No scientist believes that God obeyed Maxwell's equations, which articulate the laws by which light and all other forms of electromagnetic radiation behave, at the moment of creation as described in the biblical book of Genesis. Maxwell's equations are descriptive, rather than proscriptive. They describe the behavior of light as we now understand it. That nuance is important. To develop a mathematical model or a conceptual model of a phenomenon allows us to pose 'what if?' questions. Research about adolescents requesting chaplaincy care, and whether there are differences in the existential or faith-based content of those chaplaincy interactions (Chapman and Grossoehme 2002), can lead to questions such as: What if I deploy my chaplain resources differently? What if more requests come from adolescents with psychiatric admissions than from medical-surgical admissions? What if I rely on nurses to screen all patients for chaplaincy needs – will people with important needs be missed?

Quantitative research allows me to predict health outcomes based on observable characteristics and can influence my behavior as a chaplain. Spiritual struggle is related to poorer adherence to one's treatment regimen for cystic fibrosis (Grossoehme *et al.* 2015, 2016a) – the only means of slowing progression of this life-shortening disease. I cannot, as a chaplain, directly intervene to improve someone's rate of decline in pulmonary function. I can, however, screen for spiritual struggle (Fitchett and Risk 2009) and invite the patient or family member to discuss their struggles. Such a conversation could decrease their spiritual struggle, in which case it is reasonable to expect a downstream effect of slowing the rate at which their lung function declines. Without that knowledge and use of quantitative research to inform my clinical care, my chaplaincy would be more limited to one focused on merely active listening. To use research findings and the conceptual models of science is not to forsake the art of chaplaincy. How I engage a person after screening them for spiritual struggle and delve with them into their struggles is where the art of chaplaincy enters the picture.

Conclusion

This chapter is part of a section that questions whether chaplaincy is an art or a science. I prefer to have my cake and eat it too. Although I have drawn heavily on science, I have tried to argue that chaplaincy is both art and science, or perhaps more accurately, chaplaincy is an art informed and guided by science. The science we use and the science some of us undertake should always be in service to the artful relationships of clinical chaplaincy. To what extent could research be another color in your clinical palette or a new instrument in your orchestra? How might chaplaincy informed by research look and sound different from how you now practice it?

I never anticipated that a call to ordained ministry would lead me to where I am presently: as a practicing clinical chaplain who not only serves in a major academic medical center, but also is based within its academic structure. Although this brings with it the tension of explaining science and faith to both researchers and chaplains, it also brings with it the opportunity to do more than collaborate. Collaboration suggests people working out of a similar, if not identical, paradigm. What has evolved is more than that: it is engaging in a shared process with people who come from different paradigms and who each make unique contributions. I am continually challenged to find new ways to listen and communicate; to seek engagement with those who differ and resist the temptation to walk away in frustration because they don't understand what, to me, is obvious. What has evolved is, despite its tensions, one of the most exciting things I have done, allowing me to integrate mind and soul.

References

Barbour, I.G. (1990) *Religion in an Age of Science* (Vol. 1). London: SCM Press.

Book of Common Prayer (1979) Chicago, IL: Seabury Press.

Chapman, T.R. and Grossoehme, D.H. (2002) 'Adolescent patient and nurse referrals for pastoral care: a comparison of psychiatric vs. medical-surgical populations.' *Journal of Child and Adolescent Psychiatric Nursing 15*, 3, 118–123.

Charmaz, K. (2014) *Constructing Grounded Theory* (2nd ed.). Los Angeles, CA: Sage Publications.

Cotton, S., Pargament, K.I., Weekes, J.C., Grossoehme, D. *et al.* (2013) 'Spiritual struggles, health-related quality of life, and mental health outcomes in urban adolescents with asthma.' *Research in the Social Scientific Study of Religion 24*, 259–280.

de Chardin, P.T. and Lindsay, N. (1959) 'Building the earth.' *Cross Currents 9*, 4, 315–330.

Evans, E.E., Grossoehme, D.H. and Moyer, E.J. (1985) 'A photometric-study of AO Camelopardalis.' *Publications of the Astronomical Society of the Pacific 97*, 593, 648–652.

Fitchett, G. and Risk, J.L. (2009) 'Screening for spiritual struggle.' *Journal of Pastoral Care and Counseling 63*, 1–12.

Fitchett, G., Meyer, P.M. and Burton, L.A. (2000) 'Spiritual care in the hospital: Who requests it? Who needs it?' *Journal of Pastoral Care 54*, 2, 173–186.

Fitchett, G., Murphy, P.E., Kim, J., Gibbons, J.L., Cameron, J.R. and Davis, J.A. (2004) 'Religious struggle: prevalence, correlates and mental health risks in diabetic, congestive heart failure, and oncology patients.' *International Journal of Psychiatry in Medicine 34*, 2, 179–196. doi: 10.2190/UCJ9-DP4M-9C0X-835M.

Grossoehme, D.H. (2011) 'Research as a chaplaincy intervention.' *Journal of Health Care Chaplaincy 17*, 3–4, 97–99. doi: 10.1080/08854726.2011.616165.

Grossoehme, D.H. and Fitchett, G. (2013) 'Testing the validity of a protocol to screen for spiritual risk among parents of children with cystic fibrosis.' *Research in the Social Scientific Study of Religion 24*, 281–308.

Grossoehme, D.H., Evans, E.E. and Moyer, E.J. (1983) 'XY Leo and the star BD +18.' *Information Bulletin in Variable Stars*, 2335.

Grossoehme, D.H., Evans, E.E. and Moyer, E.J. (1984) 'Epochs of minimum light, displaced secondary eclipse of SW Lacertae.' *Publications of the Astronomical Society of the Pacific*, 648–652.

Grossoehme, D.H., Evans, E.E., Moyer, E.J. and Faulkner, D.R. (1984) 'New light elements and times of minimum light for AO Camelopardalis.' *Information Bulletin on Variable Stars*, 2497.

Grossoehme, D.H., Ragsdale, J., Wooldridge, J.L., Cotton, S. and Seid, M. (2010) 'We can handle this: parents' use of religion in the first year following their child's diagnosis with cystic fibrosis.' *Journal of Health Care Chaplaincy 16*, 3–4, 95–108. doi: 10.1080/08854726.2010.480833.

Grossoehme, D.H., Szczesniak, R.D., McPhail, G. and Seid, M. (2013) 'Is adolescents' religious coping with cystic fibrosis associated with the rate of decline in pulmonary function? A preliminary study.' *Journal of Health Care Chaplaincy 19*, 1, 33–42. doi: 10.1080/08854726.2013/767083.

Grossoehme, D.H., Szczesniak, R.D., Britton, L.L., Siracusa, C.M. *et al.* (2015) 'Adherence determinants in CF: cluster analysis of parental psychosocial and religious/spiritual factors.' *Annals of the American Thoracic Society 12*, 6, 838–846. doi: 10.1513/AnnalsATS.201408-379OC.

Grossoehme, D.H., Szczesniak, R.D., Mrug, S., Dimitriou, S.M., Marshall, A. and McPhail, G.L. (2016a) 'Adolescents' spirituality and cystic fibrosis airway clearance treatment adherence: examining mediators.' *Journal of Pediatric Psychology 41*, 9, 1022–1032.

Grossoehme, D.H., Teeters, A., Jelinke, S., Dimitriou, S.M. and Conard, L.E. (2016b) 'Screening for spiritual struggle in an adolescent transgender clinic: feasibility and acceptability.' *Journal of Health Care Chaplaincy 22*, 2, 54–66. doi: 10.1080/08854726.2015.1123004.

King, S.D.W., Fitchett, G. and Berry, D.L. (2013) 'Screening for religious/spiritual struggle in blood and marrow transplant patients.' *Supportive Care in Cancer 21*, 4, 993–1001. doi: 10.1007/s00520-012-1618-1.

O'Connor, T.S. and Meakes, E. (1998) 'Hope in the midst of challenge: evidence-based pastoral care.' *Journal of Pastoral Care 52*, 4, 259–267.

Peery, B. (2012) 'Outcome Oriented Chaplaincy: Intentional Caring.' In S.B. Roberts (ed.) *Professional Spiritual and Pastoral Care.* Woodstock, VT: SkyLight Paths.

Rogers, C.R. (1951) *Client-centered Counseling.* London: Constable. Society of Ordained Scientists. Accessed on 29/03/2017 at https://ordainedscientists.wordpress.com.

St. James O'Connor, T. (2002) 'Is evidence based spiritual care an oxymoron?' *Journal of Religion and Health 41*, 3, 253–262.

Swinton, J. and Mowat, H. (2006) *Practical Theology and Qualitative Research.* London: SCM Press.

Thuné-Boyle, I.C.V., Stygall, J., Keshtgar, M.R.S., Davidson, T.I. and Newman, S.P. (2013) 'Religious/spiritual coping resources and their relationship with adjustment in patients newly diagnosed with breast cancer in the UK.' *Psycho-Oncology 22*, 3, 646–658. doi: 10.1002/pon.3048.

Tomm, K. (1987a) 'Interventive interviewing: Part I. Strategizing as a fourth guideline for the therapist.' *Family Process 26*, 1, 3–13.

Tomm, K. (1987b) 'Interventive interviewing: Part II. Reflexive questioning as a means to enable self-healing.' *Family Process 26*, 2, 167–183.

Tomm, K. (1988) 'Interventive interviewing: Part III. Intending to ask lineal, circular, strategic, or reflexive questions?' *Family Process 27*, 1, 1–15.

VandeCreek, L. and Lucas, A.M. (eds) (2001) *The Discipline for Pastoral Care Giving: Foundations for Outcome Oriented Chaplaincy.* New York, NY: Haworth Press.

Chapter 7

Outcomes in Health and Social Care Chaplaincy

Core Business or Problematic Necessity?

George F Handzo and Steve Nolan

Introduction

Concluding this part, exploring to what extent chaplaincy is an art or science, is a transatlantic conversation about the role of, and recent higher priority given to, outcomes in contemporary specialist spiritual care.

As chaplains are increasingly required to show that they add value to the work of an organization or service as well as being value for money, the subject of outcomes has become increasingly important. This necessitates critical reflection as such a change in emphasis has far-reaching implications. In this engaging dialogue George F Handzo and Steve Nolan explore why outcomes-orientated chaplaincy may be of significance to chaplains, the people they work with and those who employ them. From this conversation emerge key considerations and concerns relating to the move towards outcome-orientated chaplaincy. These include:

- the requirement of the standardization of practice to effect replicable and predictable outcomes
- the place of relationship in chaplaincy research and practice
- the danger of the medicalization of chaplaincy
- reflections on the epistemological underpinnings of chaplaincy
- the pragmatic necessity of proving chaplains are of economic worth.

George F Handzo

'Outcomes' have had a chequered and often problematic history within the practice of health and social care chaplaincy. One could make the case that modern health and social care chaplaincy in fact emerged as a reaction to the 'outcomes' that were used in chaplaincy and still are in some places – the number of conversions, souls saved, worship attendance and Bibles given out. This time corresponded to the age when those in authority, including doctors and clergy, were considered to know the answer and lay people did what they were told. In response, we changed the model to one in which we at least claimed we have no outcomes. We aimed to shift the locus of power to the person being served and leave the agenda of the encounter completely in their hands. However, in fact, we never really had no outcomes. Chaplain Art Lucas, who designed and published a system of chaplaincy practice he called 'The Discipline' (Lucas 2001, p.20), often made the point with his students that when they say to themselves or others things like 'we hope that Mrs L…' or 'we pray that Mr D…', we are setting an outcome for our work. Thus, we had outcomes but refused to acknowledge them, which had the side effect of allowing chaplains to avoid accountability for their work.

Worse, in this system, there was no way to tell if chaplains ever did anything to help people. We did not even have a common definition of what 'help' is because we would not discuss outcomes. Another of Art Lucas's challenges to his students was 'How do you know?', which was usually in response to some assertion that the encounter had helped. What he was looking for in response was an observable behaviour or a direct verbal response from the person served. For example, the patient stopped crying, or the patient said they felt calmer. Without these kinds of responses, there was no way for chaplains to improve their practice, with improvement being defined as providing more patient-reported help.

In recent years, the health and social care context in the developed world has changed dramatically, making spiritual and chaplaincy care both more valued and central and, at the same time, more accountable and outcomes focused. The mantra is that the emphasis of care is shifting from volume to value (Porter 2010). Put simply, this is a shift from how many of something you do to what happens as a result of *what* you do. Put another way, this is a shift from 'how many?' (volume) to 'so what?' (value) and furthermore 'so what according to whom?' One of the major sticking points for chaplains and others in this new world is that it often appears that the 'whom' are institutional administrators and payers whose goals are driving down costs and driving up income to the detriment of patients, and this is not just a perception but a part of the reality. Healthcare is a business whether it is for profit, not-for-profit or government funded, and it must bring in more income than it spends in order to survive. However, it turns out that reducing costs and increasing patient satisfaction are not mutually exclusive goals. By example, reducing spiritual distress seems to be both what patients want and what reduces cost. However, as more and more chaplains are being hired and paid by health and social care providers and fewer and fewer by faith communities, focus does shift to satisfying spiritual need, which is what saves money. Focus shifts away from the traditional roles of chaplains to spread the faith and care for the faithful. Thus, while the goals of these two masters are not as divergent as many had assumed, they are not perfectly aligned. Chaplains have long been exempted from contributing to the business of the health and social care system. That day is fast coming to an end. The new reality is that if we continue to ignore the value-based reality of healthcare, we will increasingly be marginalized or eliminated and the integration of spiritual care in healthcare will suffer. Negotiating this dilemma while staying true to our calling is often not obvious or without compromise.

A second major influence is the rise of person-centred care that tends to include spiritual care as a fully integrated component of care. Palliative care is becoming increasingly universal in all phases and contexts of care with chaplains as full members of the team. However, this new integration usually assumes that chaplains will function as clinical professionals including providing spiritual assessments and care plans for those they serve and be fully integrated members of the team. It also means they will share spiritual care giving with those in other disciplines. Not all chaplains are at home with or trained for this role that is very much driven by the medical model of care. It is therefore focused on 'diagnosing' spiritual distress and 'treating' it. A difficulty for chaplains here is that the goal/outcome might displace the power of the relationship that has been the foundation of chaplaincy practice.

While there are certainly many dangers in the focus on outcomes, all of these dangers can be overcome. On the other hand, the result of not doing outcomes will include not being integrated into the client's care and having no idea whether we are doing anything worthwhile.

Steve Nolan

I agree that it is disingenuous, if not plain pretentious, for chaplains to claim disinterest in outcomes. We are caring, compassionate people, and we want to see the distress of those we work with relieved. We are also vulnerable individuals, and we need not only patients and families to recognise our effective work, we want commissioners and managers to acknowledge and value our activity as professionals, and to continue to commission us. We can add that, as people diversely committed to God (as we each understand God), we want the God we serve to be honoured. It seems to me that these motivating themes are all significant drivers for interest in chaplaincy outcomes: patient care; professional integration; and the integrity of our beliefs. But of these outcomes, the most pressing seems to be concern about the place of chaplaincy within a rapidly changing profession.

As you rightly describe, healthcare is a business. That truth is perhaps more obvious in the US context than in the UK, where our interface with the National Health Service (NHS) has shielded most of us from the price of health – although it is becoming increasingly difficult for us to ignore its costs. And I agree that the implications for chaplaincy are significant. What you call 'the new reality', the reality that chaplaincy faces marginalization or indeed elimination if as a profession it fails to adopt 'the new currency' (Handzo et al. 2014, p.43) of outcomes, is demanding that chaplains respond. What concerns me is not that chaplains need to become 'research literate' and 'evidence informed', but rather more accountable and collaborative. I have no issue with those requirements. What concerns me is the ways in which the spiritual care we offer will be reshaped by uncritically adopting the agenda of business – and it will be reshaped.

I notice that you acknowledge that 'there are certainly many dangers in the focus on outcomes', but I am troubled by the way you gloss over these dangers with the comment that 'all of these dangers can be overcome'. In my view, the dangers to the integrity of chaplaincy and spiritual care are more serious than you allow.

Striking in your description of healthcare as business is what you identify as a 'shift to satisfying spiritual need, which is what saves money'. Elsewhere, you and others have described how outcomes are 'enhanced if they can be achieved efficiently and predictably' (Handzo et al. 2014, p.44), adding that: 'Determining predictable outcomes typically involves standardization of practice, increased accountability of health care providers (HCP), and decreased decision-making ability on the part of clinicians in order to mitigate variance in practice' (Handzo et al. 2014, p.44).

It is the idea that chaplaincy and spiritual care could be 'standardized' that I find most difficult, especially when you go on to propose that chaplaincy should become a profession that has 'replicable and predictable outcomes' (Handzo et al. 2014, p.48, my emphasis). It seems to me that, while spiritual care may take many forms, and while it may be delivered through a variety of interventions, it is primarily offered in and through relationship, that is, real people caring for the spiritual needs of real people in all their various forms and with all their manifold eccentricities. I find it difficult to believe that you are suggesting that chaplains might have a standardized schedule of proven spiritual care interventions which, like pills from a drug trolley, they deliver as treatments to suitably diagnosed patients in anticipation of a predictable outcome. Such a possibility seems incongruous with any notion of spiritual care that could be considered person-centred.

For instance, we might take prayer as typical of a chaplain's spiritual care intervention (Handzo *et al.* 2008). We could imagine a skilled and experienced, theologically liberal, liturgically conservative Christian chaplain visiting two patients during the same round on a renal ward. One patient, an elderly Irish Roman Catholic, regards his religion as important and has for years been regular at confession and Sunday Mass, but has a somewhat formal relationship with his God. The other patient, a middle-aged, South African Pentecostal, is born-again and Spirit-filled, and has a vibrant walk with Jesus, whom she regards as her Brother. Both have requested that the chaplain visit for prayer. Given the degree of diversity separating these two patients, it is hard to imagine what kind of prayer could be considered a standardized intervention such as to affect a replicable and predictable outcome.

Or we could imagine that the same chaplain called in the middle of the night to baptize a dying baby and offer spiritual care to her family. On arrival, the chaplain would conduct what could be considered a standardized rite, but again it is hard to imagine what other standardized intervention would be appropriate for the child's traumatized mother who feels betrayed by her God, his or her angry father hurting for the pain of his wife, *and* his or her broken-hearted grandparents struggling to support their daughter and deal with their own overwhelming sadness. It is difficult to imagine *any* intervention that would not be dependent on the skills and experience of *this* chaplain, let alone one so standardized that *any other* chaplain could replicate it and be able confidently to predict an equally efficacious outcome.

I'm not arguing against the importance of outcomes. As a practising chaplain, I want a good outcome for all those for whom I care. I also understand the economic imperatives of the evolving healthcare environment. But I'm not convinced that the dangers of being outcomes oriented are as easily dismissed as you suggest. From my perspective, if we uncritically adopt an outcome-oriented approach that prioritizes value for money over improving patient care, and that, in the interests of predictability, aims to mitigate variance by standardizing practice, then the integrity of chaplaincy would be seriously compromised and the nature of the spiritual care we offer would be distorted to a parody. I wonder if you would address how you see that this particular danger can be overcome.

George

You raise some very cogent issues here that certainly deserve more in-depth consideration. The issue of standardization is, as you indicate, not so simple. I find it helpful to think about this in terms of the balance between the science of chaplaincy and the art. Many professions from medicine to the practice of art itself are some combination, it seems, of art and science. Most artists are trained and so, I would say, learn the science of their painting or piano playing. The technique allows their artistic being to express itself. But if they then apply the technique mechanistically and predictably, they will never be great artists.

I think we should see chaplaincy in much the same way. There is technique or science that can and should inform our practice. There are parts of what we do that should be standardized. Documentation, I think, is one example, and I happen to think that outcomes are another. I don't think it's acceptable to just come out wherever we come out. However, the art is where what you label as relationship comes in. For me the danger is being too far on either end of this art–science continuum. My perception at the moment is that chaplaincy has gone too far to the art end of the spectrum – thus the need to push outcomes and other forms of standardization. That said, you are right that going to the other extreme is not helpful either, but I don't see much danger of that any time soon.

The question I would love you to weigh in on (in part because I don't know the answer at all) is, how do we tell the right art–science balance for any particular situation like the ones you give or for any particular chaplain?

Steve

I'm afraid that your 'art–science continuum' doesn't work for me. Art and science are not polar opposites, and art should not be on a continuum with science. The opposite of art is reality, and the opposite of science is ignorance. So, I struggle with the idea of a 'science of chaplaincy'. Science is a method of enquiry that involves collecting data by observation or experiment in order to construct theory. We are a long way from anything that could be called a 'science of chaplaincy'. However, you link 'science' with 'technique', which is something different from science and which is, I think, a more appropriate term. Art has its techniques, and they are to do with the artist's craft. I'm much happier to talk about the '*craft* of chaplaincy'. It may seem that I'm being pedantic here, but describing chaplaincy as both an art and a science is to position it alongside medicine, which is genuinely a science, and which is frequently also described as an art.

So, I take your question to be concerned with the judgments that a chaplain must make in practising the craft of spiritual care across a wide range of situations. But I have to say that I find the question strange given that you see the development of replicable and predictable outcomes leads to 'decreased decision-making ability on the part of clinicians in order to mitigate variance in practice' (Handzo *et al.* 2014, p.44). I want to say that it is not possible to legislate for every eventuality, and that, to answer your question, the way we can tell the right way to respond in any particular situation is for any particular chaplain to exercise their professional judgment, which is informed by their knowledge and skills coupled with their experience, within the framework of their professional guidelines, supported by good supervision and ongoing reflective practice.

Describing chaplaincy as an art and a science lends it a certain status, and I can understand this has an obvious appeal. But the status is borrowed from the discourse of medicine and describing it this way roots chaplaincy all the more firmly within that discourse, *where frankly it does not belong.* The discourse of medicine is rightly driven by the imperative to diagnose and treat, and as chaplains we have no need to place ourselves under this imperative in order to know whether or not what we do is effective. We *know* what we do is effective, because people tell us it is. What we need to do is turn what we are told into data, for example by developing and using patient-reported outcome measures.

So, my concern remains. I worry that adopting the medical model of diagnosis and treatment, as you propose, would distort chaplaincy into a parody of itself, and I don't think you have said anything so far that addresses that concern and shows how chaplaincy can overcome that danger. To be explicit: while adopting an outcomes approach may offer the benefit of keeping chaplaincy integrated within healthcare, I am concerned whether the care that flows from an outcomes approach would be recognizable as spiritual care. Can you ease my mind on this concern?

George

I'm hearing some pretty strong feelings on your part with this art and science issue that I don't really understand at least in its depth and that may (or may not) go beyond what I have in mind. So, let me say some more about this. This is about integrating spiritual care and chaplaincy care into whole person, compassionate healthcare. To succeed in this mission and give patients and families the care they clearly say they want, I believe it is imperative that we integrate into the culture of medicine in which healthcare operates. Part of that integration is operating within the logic and language of that culture. I can't expect the medical culture to accommodate to my language and logic. This process is no different than what our missionary colleagues would subscribe to. At least in the US, the interplay between art and science and how each influence practice is integral to the medical culture and has been for many years (Peabody 2015). Yes, the definitions may not be what we would use, although I must say that I know some artists who would be upset with the implication that their art is not a representation of reality. Thus, if chaplaincy is going to be integrated into the medical culture, this is a dialogue that we need to be part of and a language form we need to use. To be clear, this is not about acceptance or status of chaplains or chaplaincy except in as much as we need standing to deliver good spiritual care. It is about creating a health system where patients are treated as whole persons and their spiritual beings are respected.

Now I would agree that if this process of integration resulted in chaplaincy becoming inauthentic or a parody of its proper self or selling its soul, then that would be too high a price to pay and we should find another way. However, I don't think that is the case. Take the following conversation for instance that has occurred numerous times between myself and chaplains I supervised. Question: 'Why did you pray with that patient?' Response: 'They seemed to have lost their connection to their God, which is important to them in coping with their illness, and I thought that prayer might help them re-establish that connection and support.' While this process could be named in various ways, to me 'diagnosis and treatment' is certainly one of them, and it is the one that communicates best in the medical culture when we want to explain what we do. So I would suggest that this language absolutely needs to be part of chaplain care in the healthcare culture – not because it reflects some basic way of spiritual being, but because it is the right tool to get the job done in this setting. The other side of this coin is that to call what we do a craft will not translate, at least in the US. I understand the comparison, but it simply won't get patients what they want in the culture in which we live.

So why is this issue so important to outcomes, which is our given topic? For outcomes to be replicable and improvable there needs to be a common language for talking about them, and the native language of healthcare is science. We in chaplaincy have long avoided using this language for various reasons that could be a whole chapter in itself. I agree we don't have a science of chaplaincy; that is exactly part of the problem. The lack of this science is a big reason your case book with George Fitchett is such an important contribution to the field (Fitchett and Nolan 2015). To have outcomes that can be understood and are therefore replicable, we need to use scientific language and standards of evidence. Should we abandon the ways of knowing – our craft, if you will – we have employed? No. But we should also use this other way of knowing that science represents both because it helps our profession discuss internally and because it communicates externally.

Steve

Perhaps your thinking on science is helpful in clarifying the difference between us, in which case we may find our perspectives are closer than we first thought – or we may find they are even further apart! It seems to me that you are using 'science' in two ways. On the one hand, you speak about 'science' as the scientific discourse of medical culture, which you say is 'a language form we need to use'. I agree, and here, our perspectives are very close. As chaplains, we do need to learn the language of our healthcare colleagues; this extends to the scientific language of research. And I think your analogy with missionary enculturation is helpful (as long as we don't push it too far!). In the same way that missionaries learn language and cultural values in order to communicate effectively and with integrity, so chaplains need to be bilingual and bicultural. I'd go further and say we need to be trilingual and tricultural: the language and culture of those who commission our services is equally (possibly more) important for us to master.

But, on the other hand, you also speak about 'science' as a 'way of knowing', and this, I think, is more problematic; this is where I think we are a long way apart. Adopting science as a way of knowing sounds like you are suggesting chaplaincy should adopt a scientific epistemology. I would be going too far if I accused you of adopting a positivist approach. My sense is that you are more pragmatist than positivist and that you are arguing from expediency, motivated by a desire to see chaplaincy and spiritual care fully integrated into clinical care. I understand the motivation, but here is my problem: scientific epistemology makes possible the belief that chaplaincy interventions could (should?) yield replicable and *predictable* outcomes, and this in turn ignites the ambition to have standardized schedules of spiritual care interventions, which I think are ultimately dehumanizing. I see this as an unnecessary distortion of spiritual care.

Let me emphasize that *I have no argument with the idea that chaplains can have outcomes*. I think definable outcomes are entirely consistent with good spiritual care and chaplaincy practice. But I am not comfortable with the epistemological dominance of 'scientific' knowledge – there are other valid ways of knowing; nor am I able to envision a spiritual care intervention that has replicable and *predictable* outcomes, and while I notice that you here speak of 'replicable and improvable' outcomes, the trajectory is still towards standardization. This is the parody of spiritual care that I fear.

So, to anticipate the obvious question…why do I fear standardization? It's because, in both my own practice and in observing that of others, I have witnessed what could be called 'the relationship effect'. I've written elsewhere about my meeting with Peter (Nolan 2015), and his reaction to the short time we spent together – little more than 20 minutes in which I offered attentive listening – which he recognized had had a positive effect on his sense of spiritual wellbeing. Some chaplains call this 'presence' ministry. This is not a term I like, but I have written about presence and described chaplains as a 'hopeful presence' (Nolan 2012). But not all chaplains like the designation.

Donovan (2012) is on record as wanting to outlaw the word, and he has a point. We sell ourselves short when we reduce our work to 'just being there'. What transforms 'just being there' into 'hopeful presence' is the way a chaplain – or anyone – is able to *attend to* the other person. Those who dismiss presence have failed to grasp its significance.

If I may speak personally: There was a period when I had to have treatment for an ongoing medical condition. On two occasions I visited the same hospital to have the same procedure. On both occasions the nurses who prepared me were very professional. The first nurse did her job well, but I was left feeling like one more object in her world. In contrast, the second nurse did her job equally well, but left me feeling uplifted and strengthened for the procedure. The first nurse processed me; the second nurse *attended* to me. Their interventions were the same and the outcomes should have been predictable – and medically they were – but I experienced a qualitative difference in the care they provided spiritually. This is why I have argued that research is needed to understand the spiritual care relationship (Nolan 2015), which is not to say that interventions and outcomes are unimportant, or that research into chaplaincy interventions is unnecessary, but the phenomenology of attending is little understood. Good-quality, practice-based research by chaplain researchers could help us to a clearer understanding about what we are doing when we do what we do.

George

You have nailed me on one point. I am absolutely a rabid pragmatist. Bravo on your diagnostic skills! This doesn't mean 'by any means necessary', but it does mean getting the job done as pretty much the highest goal. And I am a trained scientist, so I admit to being very comfortable with that language and way of knowing – or epistemology. It is a very useful way of understanding and thus engaging with a lot of what goes on in our world. But as much as it is very well suited for some of the situations in which we find ourselves, it is totally unsuited for others. For instance, the psalms would not communicate with the power and clarity they do if they were written as a scientific paper. Science simply does not have the language to communicate what the psalms communicate. So, I do think science is a very useful epistemology for understanding and growing spiritual care, but it is by far not the only one. Where you and I differ, I guess, is in which epistemology is most useful in what circumstances.

Your example of the nurse who 'attended' along with standard medical care is very instructive here. You suggest that the interventions and even outcomes were the same. I would argue that the interventions were markedly different, and there is a very good chance that the outcomes could be different even in medical terms if you include outcomes like pain level and even recovery times. I think the work of Shane Sinclair and his colleagues in Calgary is pivotal here (Sinclair *et al.* 2016). Turns out that patients know compassionate care when they see, hear and feel it, and they can tell you rather clearly what the components are. It turns out to look quite like what you called 'attending', and while I'm not sure one can claim to be able to train to these components, they are pretty clearly ones that training can maximize. So, is this about relationship? Absolutely! But I think it turns out that this attending is not as mystical as I hear you suggesting. That said, I acknowledge that when we do this, we run the danger of making this attending, this compassionate care, mechanical in such a way that I think would obviate its positive effects. As Ewan Kelly cautioned us at our *Caring for the Human Spirit* conference in the US a couple of years ago, in this rush to demonstrate knowledge and skill we do not want to lose the part of our training that he characterized as 'formation'.

Steve

I think the areas where we agree and where we differ are becoming clearer. We both agree that outcomes, whether conscious or not, are part of a chaplain's spiritual care. You made that point well with reference to Art Lucas. And we also agree that chaplains need to learn to speak the languages of our healthcare colleagues, those with whom we deliver care, and of our masters, those who commission our services and pay our salaries. Crucially though, we differ with respect to the extent to which we are prepared to buy-in to the medical model. For my part, I understand that it sets the context for healthcare, but as far as good spiritual care is concerned, I think it is inimical for the reasons I've advanced. It seems clear that the medical model itself needs rebalancing and, in my view, spiritual and social care offer insights that could aid that rebalancing.

George

I think the summary above is very well stated. I couldn't agree more with your last sentence, and the good news is that many other practitioners, patients and family caregivers agree as well. In our next go at something like this, I think we could fruitfully spend a chapter discussing what the medical model should look like in this rebalanced form. In the US, this proposed reality has often flown under the banner of 'compassionate care'. But what do we think it really should look like? What contribution does spiritual and social care have to make and, finally, how do we make it?

References

Donovan, D.W. (2012) 'Assessments.' In S.B. Roberts (ed.) *Professional Spiritual and Pastoral Care: A Practical Clergy and Chaplain's Handbook*. Woodstock, VT: SkyLight Paths.

Fitchett, G. and Nolan, S. (eds) (2015) *Spiritual Care in Practice: Case Studies in Healthcare Chaplaincy*. London: Jessica Kingsley Publishers.

Handzo, G.F., Flannelly, K.J., Kudler, T., Fogg, S.L. *et al.* (2008) 'What do chaplains really do? II. Interventions in the New York chaplaincy study.' *Journal of Health Care Chaplaincy 14*, 1, 39–56.

Handzo, G. F. Cobb, M., Holmes, C., Kelly, E. and Sinclair, S. (2014) 'Outcomes for professional health care chaplaincy: an international call to action.' *Journal of Health Care Chaplaincy 20*, 2, 43–53.

Lucas, A.M. (2001) 'Introduction to *The Discipline for Pastoral Care Giving*'. In L. VandeCreek and A.M. Lucas (eds) *The Discipline for Pastoral Care Giving: Foundations for Outcome Oriented Chaplaincy*. New York, NY: Routledge.

Nolan, S. (2012) *Spiritual Care at the End of Life: The Chaplain as a 'Hopeful Presence'*. London: Jessica Kingsley Publishers.

Nolan, S. (2015) 'Healthcare chaplains responding to change: embracing outcomes or reaffirming relationships?' *Health and Social Care Chaplaincy 3*, 2, 93–109.

Peabody, F.W. (2015) 'The care of the patient.' *Journal of the American Medical Association 313*, 18, 1868.

Porter, M.E. (2010) 'What is value in health care?' *New England Journal of Medicine 363*, 26, 2477–2481.

Sinclair, S., McClement, S., Raffin-Bouchal, S., Hack, T.F. *et al.* (2016) 'Compassion in health care: an empirical model.' *Journal of Pain and Symptom Management 51*, 2, 193–203.

Part 3

What Kind of Professionals Are Chaplains – Healthcare Professionals?

What does it mean to say chaplains are healthcare professionals? What has informed the development of chaplaincy as a healthcare profession? To what extent is such development wanted or needed? What kind of profession is chaplaincy? What kind of profession is it becoming? What kind of profession do chaplains want healthcare chaplaincy to be? And who decides? What further action is required to enable chaplaincy to become more fully integrated amongst more established healthcare professions? Where are the conversations exploring these issues happening – locally, nationally and globally? What kind of people do chaplains have to be?

Part 3 offers material which we hope stimulates reflection, discussion and debate about professionalism and chaplaincy.

Chapter 8

Charting the Journey Towards Healthcare Professionalisation in the UK

Derek Fraser

Introduction

At the time when the UK National Health Service (NHS) was established in 1948, it was an era when certain groups of people within society were particularly recognised and deemed to be 'professionals': doctors; lawyers; teachers; and priests/ministers. This long-established recognition and status continues even today. The same individuals are still acknowledged and given the authority to act as formal witnesses and to countersign or verify certain official documents such as passport applications and financial or other formal applications. As a reflection of the status and authority society still readily accepts and gives them, a number of these groups of professionals have developed the necessary infrastructures, accreditation and regulatory processes to help enhance their professional status and provide governance for the responsibility entrusted to them.

There is a careful attention to the development of professional chaplaincy in England in the early part of Swift's (2014) book *Hospital Chaplaincy in the Twenty-first Century*, where he traces that progression from the inception of the NHS in 1948 through to the 1990s, including the contributions of key figures like J. Gordon Cox, Norman Autton and Michael Wilson. His work suggests that, although the issue of professionalism of a chaplain was something assumed at an individual and personal level, there was no concerted drive to make chaplaincy a profession like other groups in the healthcare setting. One reason for this may well have been that chaplaincy at this time was still seen largely within a religious context. To have pursued a more systematic and overtly 'professional' systematic approach might have been criticised as being overly influenced by 'worldly things', of which members and authorities of different church groups have often been suspicious.

Market forces

From 1948 until the early 1990s chaplaincy was orientated largely towards responding to, and meeting the needs of, those from a particular religious background. However, in the 1990s, the establishment of hospital trusts in England allowed hospitals to act as independent units. This had a profound impact on chaplaincy. Trusts were forged within a very specific economic context, which asked questions about the purpose of things and queried value for money, accompanied by a move for greater accountability and efficiency – all key drivers in this 'new world' of healthcare.

Chaplaincy departments were not exempt from those challenges and many responded creatively to the opportunities arising: full-time posts were created so chaplains became directly employed by trusts, and numerous part-time posts were abolished. These part-time posts were often filled by local clergy, who were primarily concerned with their own local parish and had less investment in the hospital community as a whole and tended to operate within a religious framework ('visiting the flock' – either their own or others who claimed a religious allegiance).

Within the new frameworks and structures, chaplaincy posts were advertised and made subject to the same scrutiny as other posts in the hospital – with clearly defined job descriptions and person specifications. This new world of business planning and service strategies meant that chaplaincy was set to go in a new direction. NHS management started to treat chaplaincy like any other department in the hospital.

During this time in England, there was a particular influx of Free Church (non-Anglican and Roman Catholic) ministers into full-time chaplaincy posts. The changes afforded by the new management structures and values seemed to provide an opportunity and 'fit' where the particular pastoral gifts and experiences of clergy from these traditions could be recognised – and the dominance of posts held by clergy in the Church of England decreased.

At interview, these Free Church candidates often engaged very quickly with the new approach, showing an ability to articulate their position persuasively in terms of pastoral care, rather than limiting it to a traditional 'religious function'. It also coincided with an ideological change that saw chaplaincy beginning to move away from each person or patient of a particular Christian denomination being seen by someone of the same tradition, to a more generic and ecumenical approach. The question arising for hospital chaplaincy became: 'Does it matter who turns up at the bedside?' And, if so, 'Why?'

In Scotland this same shift towards a more ecumenical and generic model of chaplaincy had developed in the late 1990s and was the direct precursor to the ideological development about pastoral and spiritual care that predominates in the UK today. It was a subtle but significant shift of emphasis that enabled chaplaincy to develop further to meet the needs and complexities found in twenty-first century Britain.

By the early part of 2000, hospital chaplaincy continued to grow and change, with many hospitals having not just one 'main' chaplain, supplemented by members of local clergy giving their time freely, but the introduction of additional posts in key centres so that whole chaplaincy teams could begin to be developed.

There was great energy and dynamism to take this forwards and make the most of the opportunities of this 'brave new world' that had opened up. Professional associations, such as the College of Health Care Chaplains (CHCC), were keen to find a voice and speak up (and out) for chaplaincy. Along with its absorption into the Manufacturing, Science and Finance Union (MSF) in 1997 came additional political energy and determination. This union characteristically agitated for change and was keen to defend pay and conditions. It was with rigour and an increasingly forceful voice that it sought to defend chaplaincy.

It was because of union involvement and, in particular, Carol English's work, negotiating the terms and conditions for chaplaincy under the *Agenda for Change* (the national pay system for all NHS staff with the exception of doctors, dentists and most senior managers), that chaplaincy was recognised as a graduate profession (with posts classified as bands 5–7) within the NHS pay structure. Until this point, the level of training, competence, expertise and professionalism had largely been 'assumed' but not articulated formally and in detail. CHCC then became part of Unite (another large union), with one of the consequences being the splintering off of Scottish healthcare chaplains and the formation of the Scottish Association of Chaplains in Healthcare (SACH).

There were parallel changes taking place in the structures and shape of hospital chaplaincy in Scotland too. In the late 1990s the Church of Scotland relinquished its role in appointing chaplains to NHSScotland and chaplains became direct employees of the NHS. A key role of facilitator (Chris Levison) within NHS Education for Scotland (NES) took this development forwards creatively within the structure of the NHS and also ensured that there was the necessary underpinning thinking and ideological frameworks. This was a decisive moment for chaplaincy, not only in Scotland but also for chaplaincy in the rest of the UK. Acknowledgement needs to be given for the hugely creative initiatives that Chris and others have made, by virtue of their commitment, roles and willingness to collaborate with a wide network and range of chaplaincy colleagues across the NHS throughout the UK.

Reflection

It is interesting to note that the people, pressures and circumstances which have catalysed such profound and positive change in the recent history and development of chaplaincy have largely been external (and unexpected and/ or uninvited) ones.

The formation of trusts in England meant that chaplaincy departments were expected to behave in the same way as other departments in line with allied health professionals. The Leeds Hospitals were a case in point, where chaplaincy was managed within therapy services and the director of therapy services (a physiotherapist by training) set about ensuring chaplaincy conformed to the norms of the NHS. The chaplaincy department was required to use the standard time management tool 'KORNER' (Fraser 2013) and to develop business plans, policies and protocols.

The critical attention and growing interest in chaplaincy from NHS managers has been a key factor in chaplaincy's development as a profession. Audits began to be expected as good practice and research encouraged. One patient/staff survey (undertaken by chaplaincy in Leeds) was published under the title 'Is God good value?' (Fraser 1996). It was the beginning of new values and a new era.

On the broader canvas of chaplaincy, the move from a small grouping of CHCC (which had seen itself largely as a mutual support group or 'fellowship' meeting), into MSF, was another major shift. Union officers saw chaplaincy simply as 'one among many' others in the health professions and took that agenda forwards with the full collaboration of the chaplains involved. In negotiations on pay and terms and conditions, the professional status of the chaplain was fully assumed.

Within Scotland, as well as the move from the Church of Scotland facilitating chaplaincy provision to the direct employment of chaplains by the NHS, the creation of one national chaplaincy strategic post introduced a major sea change. Again, others from within the NHS drove the agenda forwards and simply expected chaplaincy to fit in and conform to their expectations, enabling major change based on the assumption that, as professionals, chaplains were naturally able to step up to the mark and embrace these new developments and challenges.

It is important to stress that it was this 'external' pressure on chaplaincy which was the catalyst for significantly beneficial changes and developments in its journey towards professionalisation. These were not only systemic, but instigated by many in NHS management roles, who recognised the value and potential in enabling chaplaincy to move forwards as part of good quality patient care. It is therefore important to record that chaplains themselves were not usually the 'drivers' of the professionalisation agenda, but rather acting in response.

Chaplaincy in England

During the 1990s chaplaincy in England was led in some measure by the Hospital Chaplaincy Council's (HCC) Chief Officer, Robert Clark. He had the vision, foresight and wisdom to develop the role of a national Chaplaincy Training and Development Officer, which sought to provide specialist training for hospital chaplains in developing the profession.

It was the Training and Development Officer of HCC who negotiated the first master's degree in healthcare chaplaincy beginning in Leeds at that time. It was located in the department of healthcare studies and provided an attempt to introduce postgraduate studies into chaplaincy. It was managed and overseen entirely by the theology faculty at Leeds University. The faculty academically and theoretically influenced the programme, with little input from serving chaplains, and, consequently, it was rather limited in its integration of theory and practice. But nevertheless, it produced a cohort of chaplains who began to think and reflect critically upon their setting, profession and practice.

In the 1990s and under the New Labour government, the NHS became keen to develop chaplaincy further, and part of that alliance translated into a need to make provision for more comprehensive guidance about inclusive or multi-faith provision. Guidance was issued in *NHS Executive Guidelines* (NHS England 1992) reaffirming chaplaincy but asking trusts to consider the needs of patients who came from non-Christian settings. For the first time in the issuing of NHS guidance around chaplaincy, other faiths were mentioned. The Christian 'stronghold' was being challenged and a more up-to-date service was envisaged; however, it was still predominantly focused on religious needs.

New guidance was eventually published by NHS England (2003a), the result of work done by HCC and the Multi-Faith Group for Healthcare Chaplaincy (MFGHC) – the latter having been established in 1998 as a result of a national chaplaincy conference in London.

At the same time, *Caring for the Spirit* (NHS England 2003b) was launched as a 10-year development plan for chaplaincy within the context of a developed management model. It sought to provide a focused dynamic for an employer-led professional development of chaplaincy. Sadly, however, these developments floundered and gradually expired – largely because of a lack of collaborative working and, thus, involvement of the wisdom and knowledge of practising chaplains. However, questions about the identity of chaplains and their purpose within spiritual care were brought into sharp focus.

Ideologically there was awareness and a growing fear on behalf of the 'old school' that a new model of chaplaincy was needed and wanted and was not going to go away. The prevailing paternalism of the Church of England was waning, and, with a change of personnel within the Church of England offices for chaplaincy, a mindset developed which saw the role of the chaplain confined to a 'religious expert' or 'functionary'. Such a perspective was at odds with the experience of many chaplains who had developed models of chaplaincy that were much broader in their reach and embraced a psychosocial–spiritual approach.

There was also a growing confidence among chaplains themselves and an assertiveness to define their identity and role within the healthcare setting. This change was overseen and enabled in England by the development of CHCC and its distinct agenda under Chris Swift's leadership. It was also reflected in Scotland and in the work of SACH. It became even more focused and formalised when the Chaplaincy Academic and Accreditation Board (CAAB) was established in 2003.

The CAAB Membership Board drew representatives from all the professional healthcare chaplaincy associations in the UK. Its remit was clearly defined as:

> an advisory board to the professional associations for Chaplaincy in the UK… It exists to develop the highest academic standards relating to the training and practice of healthcare chaplains and to promote the theory and knowledge of chaplaincy. (CAAB 2005, pp.1–2)

The board drew up recommendations relating to professional education and training for chaplains at all levels and operated a scheme for awarding points for continual professional development (CPD). This was a significant driving force in the next decade and enabled some very radical thinking. A clear direction of travel was established and a determination to drive forward the ideals underpinning the professional chaplaincy agenda.

A critical mass of motivated and like-minded chaplains was influenced across the UK. Those involved quickly discovered a common goal, language and vision for chaplaincy for the twenty-first century. There was an organic change in culture enhanced by the key players of CAAB relating robustly together within the board. A high value was placed on collaboration, networking and joint working for the benefit of the profession, including rigorous and open debate. CAAB and its successor, the UK Board of Healthcare Chaplaincy (UKBHC), had garnered itself from *within* the profession, and to lead the agenda in defining and shaping its future. Individual chaplains, with a clear ideology and confidence about professional chaplaincy in its own right, and underpinned by robust theological thinking, precipitated swift change.

In many ways, 2003 was an ideological 'watershed' for chaplaincy in England. From this point in time, the worlds of the various parties involved in chaplaincy split and went off in their own ways and directions: CAAB, along with its partners CHCC, SACH, the Association of Hospice and Palliative Care Chaplains (AHPCC) and the Northern Irish Healthcare Chaplains Association, continued to consolidate and develop the professional agenda, while MFGHC, HCC and other groups focused on faith authorisation and accreditation within their own and individual faith communities.

However, the pace of change and the direction of travel had begun and were increasingly led by the chaplains and bodies within the profession, with a whole series of new developments continuing to emerge in shaping the journey towards professionalisation. This led to a profound change in the landscape and understanding of chaplaincy throughout the UK.

An ideological watershed for chaplaincy
Education and training

An initial challenge for CAAB in 2003 was to define its terms of reference and its remit. The initial remit was clarified under seven headings:

1. to make recommendations on academic policy pertaining to the profession

2. to monitor the implementation of approved policy

3. to establish procedures and standards for the validation of new and existing courses

4. to provide a mechanism for monitoring standards of teaching and the content of new and approved courses

5. to make recommendations concerning appropriate professional education and training for chaplains at all levels, including minimum entry requirements

6. to make recommendations concerning minimum and relevant continuing professional development and education for chaplains at all levels

7. to further develop its role in consultation with HCC.

CAAB's membership was delineated such that it will comprise serving chaplains who:

- possess academic credentials of a minimum of master's level themselves

- are experienced practitioners in healthcare chaplaincy ('in that they have had many years of experience')

- have current experience of training students for chaplaincy

- have access to the academic world.

It established an external Academic Reference Panel whose purpose was to ensure the credibility and integrity of CAAB and to provide the necessary academic oversight, supervision and accountability for such a professional group. This was part of ensuring that robust quality-assurance processes were established.

The objectives of accreditation were clearly spelled out so that any academic chaplaincy-related courses developed were consistent with the defined body of knowledge for chaplaincy and standards appropriate to the levels of chaplaincy specified. Critical other criteria also needed to be met, such as clear aims and objectives identified for any training and education.

A key priority for CAAB was to define a distinct body of knowledge for chaplaincy. Eight aspects were elucidated, with fuller details developed in relation to each one:

1. knowledge of the current sociological context

2. knowledge of philosophical understandings of personhood

3. knowledge of moral thinking

4. knowledge of organisational/institutional dynamics

5. knowledge of pastoral care models

6. knowledge of human interrelationships

7. knowledge of current worldviews

8. knowledge of one's own faith tradition.

The group recognised that the agenda was large, and attention was particularly focused on the training necessary for chaplains working at different grades. CAAB continued to work in collaboration with colleagues across the UK and to develop some of the dimensions and infrastructures used in the nursing profession: including their clear requirement for CPD. To be on a par with other professions, chaplains needed to keep their learning and development up to date. CAAB provided clear guidance about requirements for this and an annual CPD summary form was produced, inviting registered individual chaplains to self-declare that they had undertaken learning in four spheres:

1. individual self-directed learning

2. individual professional activities

3. work-based learning

4. external formal educational activity.

The form also gave individual chaplains the opportunity to describe the impact of the learning on their practice. Annual completion and submission of CPD summaries became a requirement if chaplains wished to continue to be registered members of UKBHC (established in 2008 by CAAB). Collaboration enabled CAAB to produce a comprehensive CPD portfolio document, describing the need for CPD as well as providing resources to promote reflective and consistent practice. In 2011, CHCC then agreed to fund folders and print hard copies of this resource portfolio to send out to all associated chaplains.

Chaplaincy CPD and its importance as part of professional life in chaplaincy has been detailed elsewhere (Fraser 2013) and continues to be a vital dimension in driving forward the professional agenda. The whole issue of scrutiny of such summary reports is currently under review, with a growing realisation that each year approximately 10% of submissions need to be audited by senior practitioners to ensure quality control is duly exercised. UKBHC is piloting several ways of taking this forwards to ensure that chaplains continue to grow and develop as practitioners so that those entrusted to their care receive the very best of care. This is consistent with emerging practices in other professions such as nursing.

At the same time as CAAB came into being, the NHS was reviewing and developing its work around terms and conditions in *Agenda for Change* (Department of Health 2004a). New work to develop post-profiles across the whole of the NHS was also simultaneously being undertaken through the *Knowledge and Skills Framework* (KSF) (Department of Health 2004b) agenda. CAAB collaborated with the national KSF development group in developing KSF post-outlines for all chaplaincy posts. This had a major contribution in defining healthcare chaplaincy as a profession.

Until that time, the minimum qualifications required in appointing chaplains had never been specified – other than someone being a minister of religion in good standing with their church and with at least 3 years of pastoral experience. CAAB decided that in order to apply for an entry-grade post, candidates should be able to fulfil the academic entry requirements for postgraduate diploma level. In addition, they should be able to demonstrate expertise in pastoral care through a minimum of 3 years in a ministry role formally authorised through either ordination or being commissioned by a recognised faith community. The first year of an entry-grade post was seen as a foundation year with chaplains receiving ongoing training and education (particularly in reflective practice) and the completion of sufficient modules to equate to postgraduate certificate level. The requirement for reflective practice training was recognised as crucial to the practice and development of chaplaincy (echoed in the early work produced on CPD) and grew to be a defining feature of healthcare chaplaincy as it is today.

Code of conduct

For many years chaplaincy had a code of conduct promoted and published by CHCC (its professional association). But 2005 saw a significant updating and revision of that document through the involvement and input of CAAB, which was piloted and tested across all chaplaincies in the UK before being formally launched as *the* code of conduct for chaplaincy. Subsequently, it has gone through a number of iterations (the most recent version is UKBHC 2014). Its purpose was to set out the professional standards of conduct expected of healthcare chaplains towards those in their care. It has been accepted and adopted by all the different groups involved in and representing chaplaincy.

It has also been adapted as a 'best-practice guide' for volunteers, students and others linked with chaplaincy. Employers have embraced the code as a tool in facilitating the management of those involved in chaplaincy. The clear definition of expectations and standards within the code has been a major building block in the foundation of the profession more generally.

The code covers matters relating to:

1. general conduct of chaplains

2. relationships between chaplains and those in their care

3. working with colleagues

4. probity in professional practice

5. procedures for dealing with misconduct.

It is important to clarify at this point the purpose of the different key documents shaping chaplaincy. The *code* specifies the clear criteria for professional conduct, just as other healthcare professions do. For example, in the UK, the General Medical Council and Nursing and Midwifery Council. It is quite distinct from the *Standards for Healthcare Chaplaincy Services* (UKBHC 2009) which delineate the service standards necessary for chaplaincy. While the *Capabilities and Competences Framework* (UKBHC 2017) tabulated the level of competencies for individual chaplains at different levels of practice.

Chaplaincy standards

The *Standards for Healthcare Chaplaincy Services* (NHS Education for Scotland 2007) were developed in Scotland to support those seeking the implementation of policy around spiritual care. They built upon work already undertaken by AHPCC (2006, first published in 2003), *Standards for Hospice and Palliative Care Chaplaincy*. The standards were devised to enable the auditing of chaplaincy services, as well as ensuring equality across services and the development of an integrated approach to the delivery of NHS-funded services. They provide a description of chaplaincy services in terms that are familiar to NHS managers. Each of the seven identified standards contains a rationale, a statement and measurable descriptive criteria:

1. spiritual and religious care

2. access to chaplaincy services

3. partnership with faith communities and belief groups

4. staff support

5. education, training and research

6. resources

7. chaplaincy provision to a particular hospital or unit.

The standards have an accompanying audit tool which can be used to provide chaplaincy services with a baseline from which they can be understood, measured and prove their efficacy and value. They have been adopted and adapted as necessary across NHS services.

Capability and competence framework

The next logical step, following from the development of professional standards, was then to produce a capability and competence framework for chaplains to help (a) develop education and training, (b) the pastoral development of individual chaplains and (c) the development of teams. The framework was devised under four headings (each with subsections) as follows:

1. Knowledge and skills for professional practice

    1) Knowledge and skills for practice

    2) Practising ethically

    3) Communication skills

    4) Education and training

2. Spiritual and religious assessment and intervention

    1) Spiritual assessment and intervention

    2) Religious assessment and intervention

3. Institutional practice

    1) Team working

    2) Staff support

    3) Chaplain to the hospital or unit

4. Reflective practice

    1) Reflective practice

    2) Personal spiritual development.

This framework acknowledged that chaplaincy requires certain competencies but recognised that these also need to be attuned to capability. 'Competence' defines terms of knowledge, skills and attitude, whereas 'capability' describes the extent to which an individual can apply, adapt and synthesise new knowledge from experience (see also Chapter 21 on growing chaplains for new paradigms for a fuller exploration of the significance of competencies and capabilities in chaplaincy education and training). Thus, a capability framework was produced, with certain competencies contained within each one.

This work was spearheaded by NHS Education for Scotland (2009) but was supported by CAAB, AHPCC, CHCC and SACH. Those involved in its design aimed for a framework which would be relevant, applied and fit for purpose, and the framework was based on a progressive four-level model to reflect fitness in a gradual progression of a chaplain through the profession. Role definitions are as follows:

- *Trainee chaplain* is a person in training, working under supervision of a chaplain.

- *Chaplain* is an autonomous, qualified practitioner whose role is to seek and respond to the spiritual and religious needs of individuals, their carers and staff.

- *Senior chaplain* is a chaplain with additional responsibilities and experience, including the management of a chaplaincy team.

- *Specialist chaplain* is a chaplain with specialist knowledge and experience of a particular aspect of healthcare chaplaincy (e.g. acute, mental health, paediatrics, palliative care).

- *Lead chaplain* is a chaplain with management responsibility for spiritual and religious care policy and services across a health board area.

This clarification and demarcation of levels within chaplaincy became crucial in its development and self-understanding as a profession. When the work of designing the framework was initially undertaken in 2009, it was simply focused on chaplains working as autonomous and qualified practitioners with no resources allocated for further development of a local service.

Since 2009, UKBHC has further developed and enlarged the framework and scope of chaplaincy by giving relevant criteria and describing the different levels and duties of chaplains across a wider range, as outlined above (UKBHC 2017).

This newer framework also sets out the knowledge and skills chaplains should be evidencing to demonstrate professional practice. A vital part of the developing progress for the chaplain resides within their own personal development in particular reflective practice and personal spiritual and theological growth and development.

The 2009 version of the framework was an excellent tool to use in conversation with academic partners as they devised and initiated new courses for chaplaincy. By 2009, a number of them were already in place and have subsequently remodelled themselves around the new framework, whereas newer courses based their course structure on the new framework from the outset.

The masters programme in Cambridge with its innovative Pastoral Reflective Practice module, alongside the course at the South London and Maudsley Hospital, have both drawn on the paradigm of the clinical pastoral education model which has been so dominant in the US. It sought to develop a distinctive programme that enabled individuals to be trained and equipped in pastoral encounters within the context of an academic framework.

The work combined an academic theoretical approach alongside practice-based work, so that people could be trained in healthcare chaplaincy and practitioners could also be assessed as 'fit to practise' (or not). This was a major development in thinking for chaplaincy, because the universities involved required increasing evidence to justify the decisions made about whether people were fit to practise as chaplains. Whereas previously it was assumed that every clergy person was deemed fit to practise based on their training and formation as a minister of religion, professionals now had to ensure their programmes of study were robust enough to withstand scrutiny and challenge of both their pastoral and academic ability combined. In addition, experience has also shown that although clergy may have been 'academically' qualified, they were not necessarily pastorally skilled – although this had been difficult to prove before any professional standards and frameworks were in place. There was now an appetite to build robust systems to ensure that only those 'fit for purpose' would be appointed. The use of objective criteria meant that appointments to chaplaincy posts could no longer be based solely on prior knowledge and experience of a candidate or on 'personal hunch'. This began a major qualitative shift in appointments to chaplaincy posts.

Registration

As part of its remit, UKBHC moved towards the establishment of a voluntary register for healthcare chaplains. The register was devised as a means to demonstrate the accountability and professional credibility of its members to the public and to potential or actual employers: a mechanism to promote high standards of best practice and behaviour and a way to support and encourage professional regulation.

In 2012, the UK Government established the Professional Standards Authority (PSA) to oversee the work of the nine statutory bodies regulating health professionals in the UK. They also created standards for organisations holding voluntary registers for people in unregulated health and care occupations, to accredit those organisations that meet those standards. Even prior to the PSA's inception, UKBHC has worked hard to be accepted within the Accredited Voluntary Registers Scheme, which enables further developments in the PSA accreditation work.

The journey to professionalisation reached a major milestone in August 2017 when formal acceptance of UKBHC as holding an accredited register was recognised by the PSA. This is a clear and confident sign of the growing public recognition, credibility and status being given to professional healthcare chaplaincy, a profession which now has a proven commitment and the systems in place to provide the highest standards of personal behaviour, clinical competence and business practice.

Bringing these practitioners into a broad framework of assurance is good for patients, service users and the public, and is the best way to promote quality. The programme offers a new layer of protection for people receiving health services, and gives healthcare chaplains the opportunity to demonstrate their commitment to good practice.

The future of chaplaincy

Having reached one milestone, it is vital that the achievements to date continue to be built on and embedded into practice with a clear articulation of what chaplains provide. This will require a wide and vigorous engagement and debate with many chaplains and critical friends with a varied range of reflected experiences of engagement with, or working within, the health service. As well as developing a more rigorous evidence base, chaplaincy will require an increased focus on what makes its services unique within the healthcare setting. As the pastoral theologian within the institution, it is vital that such clarity of purpose be maintained. This is not to be dominated by an outcomes-based agenda but to take due cognisance of it while at the same time affirming the distinctive contribution of chaplaincy within the whole health economy. The internal drivers within the NHS, alongside the external pressures, will always create tensions that can be challenging or destructive. A key factor is the self-definition and understanding of the chaplains themselves as they delineate their unique contribution as part of the healthcare team. Now is a time for courage, confidence and clarity in what chaplaincy has to offer. The future of the story and evolution of chaplaincy will depend partly on the ability of practitioners to develop, refine and articulate their work as professional clinical practitioners as well as pastoral theologians. It is a contribution which will be vital in maintaining that necessary balance and rigour for the flourishing of the profession as a whole.

References

Association of Hospice and Palliative Care Chaplains (2006) *Standards for Hospice and Palliative Care Chaplaincy*. (Original work published 2003.) Accessed on 02/11/2018 at www.ahpcc.org.uk/wp-content/uploads/2014/07/standardsguidelines2006.pdf.

Chaplaincy Academic and Accreditation Board (2005) *Annual Summary Report*. Accessed on 23/10/2018 at www.ukbhc.org.uk/publications/reports.

Department of Health (2004a) *Agenda for Change: Final Agreement*. Leeds: Department of Health. Accessed on 28/12/2018 at https://webarchive.nationalarchives.gov.uk/20080728114822/http://www.dh.gov.uk/en/Publicationsandstatistics/Publications/PublicationsPolicyAndGuidance/DH_4095943.

Department of Health (2004b) *The NHS Knowledge and Skills Framework (NHS KSF) and the Development Review Process.* London: Department of Health Publications. Accessed on 02/11/2018 at www.libraryservices.nhs. uk/document_uploads/KSF/NHS_KSF_ Document.pdf.

Fraser, D. (1996) 'Is God good value?' *Health Service Journal*, 11 July, 28–29.

Fraser, D. (2013) 'CPD: an essential component of healthcare chaplaincy.' *Health and Social Care Chaplaincy 1*, 1, 22–34.

NHS Education for Scotland (2007) *Standards for Healthcare Chaplaincy Services.* Edinburgh: NHS Education for Scotland. Accessed on 09/12/2018 at www.nes.scot.nhs.uk/ media/290156/chaplaincy__standards_final_ version.pdf.

NHS Education for Scotland (2009) *Spiritual and Religious Care Capabilities and Competences for Healthcare Chaplains.* Edinburgh: NHS Education for Scotland. Accessed on 10/12/2018 at www.ukbhc.org.uk/sites/default/files/nes_ chaplaincy_capabilities_and_competences.pdf.

NHS England (1992) *NHS Executive Guidelines: Meeting Spiritual Needs.* London: Department of Health.

NHS England (2003a) *NHS Chaplaincy: Meeting the Religious and Spiritual Needs of Patients and Staff.* London: Department of Health.

NHS England (2003b) *Caring for the Spirit: NHS Chaplaincy Guidelines.* London: Department of Health.

Swift, C. (2014) *Hospital Chaplaincy in the Twenty-first Century.* Farnham: Ashgate. (Original work published 2009.) Accessed on 25/11/2018 at www.professionalstandards.org.uk/news-and-blog/latest-news/detail/2017/08/23/ independent-quality-mark-for-healthcare-chaplains.

UK Board of Healthcare Chaplaincy (2009) *Standards for Healthcare Chaplaincy Services.* Cambridge: UK Board of Healthcare Chaplaincy. Accessed on 02/11/2018 at www. ukbhc.org.uk/sites/default/files/standards_for_ healthcare_chaplaincy_services_2009.pdf.

UK Board of Healthcare Chaplaincy (2014) *Code of Conduct for Healthcare Chaplains.* Cambridge: UK Board of Healthcare Chaplaincy. Accessed on 02/11/2018 at www.ukbhc.org.uk/sites/ default/files/ukbhc_code_of_conduct_2010_ revised_2014.pdf.

UK Board of Healthcare Chaplaincy (2017) *Spiritual and Religious Care Capabilities and Competences for Healthcare Chaplains Bands (or Levels) 5, 6, 7 and 8.* Cambridge: UK Board of Healthcare Chaplaincy. Accessed on 02/11/2018 at www.ukbhc.org.uk/sites/default/files/ukbhc_ spiritual_and_religious_capabilities_and_ competences_bands_5_-_8_2017.pdf.

Chapter 9

Reflections on Research and Professionalization in Healthcare Chaplaincy in Europe

Anne Vandenhoeck

Introduction

Late August 2018. In Tartu, Estonia, Liidia Meel is preparing her doctoral defence. She has written a doctoral thesis on the topic of interdisciplinary team based pastoral care. Meel is a healthcare chaplain in a general hospital and has performed qualitative research on the integration of pastoral care in interdisciplinary teams (Meel 2015, 2016, 2017, 2018ab; Meel and Lehtsaar 2017). Elsbeth Littooij, a Dutch chaplain, also finished her doctoral research around the same time. Littooij's qualitative research involved exploring the change of meaning-making in patients living with a spinal cord injury or a stroke during their rehabilitation (Littooij *et al.* 2015, 2016a,b, 2018a,b). In Belgium, Eva Buelens received the good news of funding for her doctoral research. She is a chaplain in the University Hospitals in Leuven and will perform research using a variety of instruments, including the Scottish spiritual care Patient Related Outcome Measure (PROM) (Snowden and Telfer 2017). In Switzerland, Simon Peng Keller and Pascal Mösli, and others, are setting up a conference about charting in electronic patient records. These four examples are in no way the result of an exhaustive search; they came to mind when reflecting on the word 'professional' with regard to chaplains (each passing through my email box very recently). There is a gathering momentum regarding research in healthcare chaplaincy in Europe. Undoubtedly, this will impact on the way chaplains will look at themselves and, on the way, how they will be perceived by others.

Building momentum in research in healthcare chaplaincy in Europe

I start from the presupposition that the amount and the quality of research is a measure for a growing professional base for chaplaincy in healthcare. A professional base refers to chaplains knowing what they are doing, being able to communicate what they are doing and integrating results of research into practice, in order to be a research-informed profession. It goes without saying that there is more to chaplaincy than research and professionalism. But even spirituality, the necessary and fundamental roots of every chaplain, needs to be handled in a professional way in relation to patients, loved ones and staff. The spirituality of chaplains and their professionalism have to be paired up for life.

In describing building momentum in research in healthcare chaplaincy in Europe, I would like to touch upon some factors that have played an important role: the political and religious changes in Europe; the European Network for Health Care Chaplaincy (ENHCC); the changes in healthcare; and the foundation of the European Research Institute for Chaplains in Healthcare (ERICH).

The recent changes in healthcare, religion and society have had a huge influence on European chaplaincy. A lot has happened in the past four decades in Europe on a political level. One of the biggest changes has been brought by the fall of the Berlin Wall. New chaplaincy associations arose in countries such as the Czech Republic, Latvia and Estonia. They have been looking to the west and north of Europe for knowledge and training, which they have adapted to their own culture. They were, and are, very eager to move ahead with training and education and to participate in research. What is particularly interesting is the reciprocity in learning. Chaplains in western and northern Europe are learning from those in the east how they are dealing with the offset of mandatory secularist societies under Russian occupation. Sharing good practice and knowledge exchange has been one of the founding goals of the ENHCC. In the 1980s, a Swedish chaplain (Sten Lundgren) took the initiative to meet with ten fellow chaplains in Berlin in 1990, right after the fall of the Wall, in a (re)uniting Germany. They talked about critical ethical issues in healthcare and experienced how enriching it was to exchange knowledge and practice. They found paradoxically that their experiences were both very alike and different. Differences were found in cultural, historical, healthcare and religious backgrounds. Five consultations later, in 2000, the ENHCC was officially founded in Crete. The purpose of the ENHCC is described in the founding document as follows (ENHCC 2000):

...to *enable* its participants, who serve in the area of the multi-disciplinary field of healthcare: to *share and learn* from one another, to work for the *development* of professional guidelines required to minister to the existential and spiritual needs of patients, relatives and staff, drawing on personal, religious, cultural and community resources, to *promote* a high-quality standard of Health Care Chaplaincy in Europe.

From the beginning the emphasis was on raising the profile of the chaplain in order to deliver high-quality spiritual care. Biannually, the ENHCC holds a consultation for its members – representatives of professional associations, churches or faith communities. In 2018 also, other interested chaplains participated in the consultation. What have the gatherings shown in the past 20 years? They have shown the following:

- The manner in which one becomes a chaplain is dependent not only on educational opportunities, but also on the faith traditions of a country. There is no single route that leads to becoming a healthcare chaplain in Europe. The road map is quite diverse and rarely the same in more than one country. In quite a few countries, it suffices to have an education in a seminary and be ordained in order to become a chaplain. The necessary competencies and attitudes to be acquired when finishing a seminary education varies from country to country. After ordination one can be appointed as a chaplain in a healthcare institution or as a minister or priest in a community with a responsibility to visit patients in the local hospital or nursing home. Similarly, for non-Christian faith groups there is a general education approved by the faith group, followed by being appointed either to a local faith community and visiting healthcare institutions as part of their remit or being appointed part- or full-time to a healthcare institution. In most countries churches or faith groups organize continuing professional development for healthcare chaplains. For example, supervision, inter-vision (a gathering of professionals discussing cases among themselves according to an agreed structure and method), conferences and further formational programmes like clinical pastoral education (CPE). Not every European country has CPE and, if they have, the programmes are adapted accordingly to different cultures and traditions. In other countries there is mandatory additional training for chaplains over and above the general training they received in their own faith tradition. Such training includes specialized postgraduate university courses, additional regional training programmes and courses offered by other institutes for higher education or indeed CPE.

- There are different models of chaplaincy across Europe. One model is the 'denominational' approach. Patients receive a visit from a chaplain from their own denomination. Sometimes in countries where there are multiple Christian churches, Christian chaplains will visit everyone who is a Christian, no matter their tradition. Catholic or orthodox priests in such an approach tend to focus more on giving sacraments, and lay Christian chaplains more on counselling and supporting. Muslim chaplains in such a system will only visit Muslim patients. Every affiliation has its own chaplain, hired by the healthcare institution as a staff member or on a consultancy basis. The challenge of this approach is, who visits those who are not religious or do not identify with a faith community? The groups of people who define themselves as spiritual or non-believers are sometimes supported either by humanist or pagan chaplains or by Christian chaplains.

  Another model of chaplaincy is the 'generalist' approach. No matter your own spiritual background as a chaplain, you are responsible for all patients on the wards that are assigned to you. You visit everyone who is referred to you or you make cold calls, but if patients explicitly want to see a chaplain from their own faith community, referrals are made. It is quite remarkable that this model is both used in a one denominational system (for example, in countries where chaplains are coming out of one denomination that has an absolute domination) and also in very plural societies. For example, in Portugal the vast majority of chaplains are Catholic priests who visit everyone on their units, as well as in the Netherlands where, if you are appointed to a ward as a chaplain, you visit everyone who requires spiritual care, no matter their or your background. Both societies are very different: in Portugal Catholicism is the dominant religion, whereas the Netherlands has always been very pluralistic – yet they use the same model from a different perspective. The challenge with this model is not to become a total chameleon as a chaplain.

  In the Netherlands there are chaplains who are no longer tied to any specific spiritual tradition. Their undergraduate degree is not theology but, for example, philosophy. They then do a 1-year master's degree in healthcare chaplaincy. They belong to that group in society that no longer identifies with faith traditions but is searching for meaning in other ways. The question here is if they are equipped enough in a 'generalist' approach to offer spiritual care to people that do identify with faith traditions. A more fundamental question is: What is the impact on spiritual care practice if you do not belong to a story that is shared by others?

- There is a growing interest in research among European chaplaincies. In the 14 years that I have been involved with the ENHCC I have witnessed how chaplains are growing professionally and, therefore, are more interested in research. Chaplains have an increased awareness that they work in a professional environment. Such a working context requires an awareness of what they are doing with patients and their loved ones and a capability to communicate their contribution to the care of a patient or loved one. In short, the world chaplains inhabit is being increasingly driven by research that contributes to an evidence base for safe, effective and value-for-money quality care. On the other hand, chaplains are also becoming interested in research because of their love for their vocation and a commitment to practising and living out that vocation as well as they can. A remarkable counterpoint was the 2014 ENHCC consultation in Salzburg which focused on chaplaincy research. The consultation put forward the Salzburg statement (ENHCC 2014), which expressed the will of those present to invest more in research, especially that which was outcome oriented, in order to promote chaplaincy as a research-informed profession. The statement was an answer to the international call, developed by researchers from across the globe in the field of chaplaincy, to do more outcome-oriented research as chaplains (Handzo *et al.* 2014). At the same time, the participants recognized in the statement the importance for chaplains to be rooted in spirituality.

The changes in healthcare and religion have likewise been very significant for chaplaincy. Everywhere in Europe secularization, de-traditionalization and pluralization have left their traces, but in very different ways. The changes in the religious and faith landscape put the emphasis more on spiritual care than on pastoral care. Spiritual care connects with the spiritual dimension of every human being. Every human being is occupied with the search for meaning, the highest fulfilment in a human life according to Viktor Frankl (2000). Pastoral care as healing, sustaining, guiding and reconciling in the name of Christ, the Good Shepherd, became a specific form of spiritual care. The integration of spiritual care into healthcare has been enhanced through the vision of palliative care, which not only theoretically states that it is fundamentally based on whole-person care, including spiritual care, but actually seeks to put this into practice (Puchalski, Ferrell and O'Donnell 2016). However, healthcare is also governed by contemporary paradigms that influence chaplaincy. The economic paradigm has a huge impact. Vacant chaplaincy posts are re-graded or disappear in the never-ending search to save money. Non-medical professions are suffering under the rationalizing waves that keep rolling through healthcare systems, but chaplains are specifically vulnerable because they lack evidence, method and language to communicate what they contribute. Under these conditions, it is hard from the perspective of the predominant economic paradigm to see chaplaincy as efficient. Chaplains' need for research is fed by the need for spiritual care to keep being present in the healthcare system.

On the other hand, the paradigm of quality of care, and therefore person-centred care, another significant paradigm in contemporary healthcare, potentially promotes chaplaincy. Tools which measure the wellbeing of patients and include aspects of their spirituality are based on a whole-person concept and raise the profile of spiritual care (for example, questionnaires measuring quality of life and satisfaction of patients and their relatives in a palliative care setting) (Sewtz *et al.* 2018). Care paths can include spiritual care as well as protocols. The quality paradigm offers opportunities for chaplains to be more integrated and opens space for spiritual care.

Another influencing factor that has led to momentum in research is the existence of chaplaincy professional associations. When the ENHCC gathers, most participants are representing the professional associations, for example the association for chaplains in Latvia, the association for chaplains in the Netherlands or associations for chaplains in the UK. Some participants are representing churches or faith communities, for example the national chaplaincy association of the protestant chaplains and the national chaplaincy association of the catholic chaplains in healthcare in France. Either way, professional associations and national associations within faith groups have contributed in a significant way to the professionalization of chaplaincy. Sometimes faith groups are hesitant to embrace chaplaincy as a healthcare profession because they fear spirituality will become less important or the tie with the faith community will suffer from chaplaincy becoming more integrated into the healthcare system. We must not forget that there are still countries in Europe, for example Austria, Germany and Sweden, where most chaplains in healthcare institutions are recruited and paid for by their faith communities and not by the healthcare institutions themselves – although attempts are being made in some of those countries to let the healthcare institutions pick up the bill. In other countries, such as Greece and Cyprus, most healthcare chaplaincy is done by priests based in parishes who spend a proportion of their time in healthcare institutions. It is another fact that shows the diversity within the healthcare chaplaincy landscape in Europe.

In general, most professional associations are promoting research and placing it front and centre on their agenda. They aim for their members to be research literate and use traditional and new forms of communication in education (such as online lectures and live webinars) to bring their members up to date on the latest research findings. The whole consultation of the ENHCC in Debrecen, Hungary, in 2016 consisted of invited presentations about various aspects of research performed by chaplains. During the consultation, 94% of participants voted in favour of the creation of a European research institute that would enhance research done by chaplains to enhance specialist spiritual care practice. Professional associations and academics also play a key role in stimulating chaplaincy research. In general, chaplains have come late to contributing to the rapidly growing literature on spiritual care research compared with other healthcare professions, such as nurses, psychologists and psychiatrists, but momentum is gathering. The ENHCC consultation in Blankenberge, Belgium, in 2018 was the first to put out a call for papers whereby European chaplains could present their own research. Both of these recent consultations are an example of the recognition of the need for chaplaincy research whilst also showcasing the increase of recent initiatives from across Europe.

Raising the profile of the profession

Raising the profile of the profession needs to be done for one goal only: the best possible spiritual care provision for patients, loved ones and staff. The best possible spiritual care for patients, loved ones and staff is coached (in a generalist-specialist model), enhanced (in the whole of the institution) and delivered (relationally) by specialists. Chaplains are the only professionals in the spectrum of healthcare professions who are trained in the language of spiritual care, have explored in depth their own spirituality and personality in order to deliver nuanced spiritual care, have scientific knowledge regarding spiritual traditions and spiritual care, know how to perform rituals, such as prayers and sacraments, and have well-developed spiritual antennae.

Some professional associations have been very active on several fronts to raise the profile of chaplaincy. The Dutch association has been advocating on a national political level to include the costs for healthcare chaplaincy in health insurances. Recently a major breakthrough has been realized: the Dutch government has approved a budget of 25 million euros to enhance spiritual care in the context of home care (VGVZ 2018). The spiritual care will mostly be done by chaplains who work part-time in healthcare institutions and part-time on a freelance basis outside the healthcare institutions. Political lobbying is happening in many European countries, such as Belgium, regarding chaplaincy. Often such political influencing is incidental through existing relationships with politicians or because of contacts between churches and government. However, it needs to be systematic, well organized and thought through. From my experience with the Flemish professional association for chaplains in healthcare, in any political lobbying it is very important to do the following:

1. Let yourself be assisted by professional advisors. Talking to professional lobbyists and lobby firms is a must and will enhance your professional communication and networking.

2. Have an attractive 'curb' appeal, for example a clear message, an attractive logo, a digestible one-page information sheet and an attractive, informative website.

3. Talk to as many politicians of different parties as you can in an ongoing manner. Keep them informed of the progress you are making by, for example, inviting them to your conferences or holding an event with a debate on recognizing chaplaincy as a healthcare profession with representatives from every party (with a well-known professional moderator).

4. Get spiritual care included in strategic national or organizational policies, for example on care for chronically ill patients or patients with dementia, and to be integrated into care paths.

5. Make the narrative of chaplaincy a story which is valued by society, for example by offering written opinion pieces to major news outlets, appearing in documentaries or reality shows in healthcare institutions, giving interviews to popular magazines and by constantly advocating chaplaincy, including through social media; invest in short video clips showing what chaplaincy means in practice and involve patients or loved ones in talking about the outcomes of chaplaincy so as to be able to be utilized when the opportunity presents itself.

6. Advocate for chaplaincy with stakeholders: from patient groups to healthcare consortiums and insurance firms. It is worth getting as much sympathy and support as possible for the profession of chaplains.

7. Work continuously on an extensive online file on chaplaincy which can be shared again when the opportunity arises to showcase the professionalism of chaplaincy, for example job descriptions, results of recent research, competencies, code of ethics, mandatory education and training, and the impact on quality and patient outcomes. Give your stakeholders and politicians access to the online file so they can educate themselves on chaplaincy and, at the same time, remain updated on the achievements of your advocacy.

Concurrently, is it very important to intentionally keep raising the profile of chaplaincy in healthcare institutions themselves. Again, it is advisable to connect with as many people as possible to advocate for the ongoing integration and validation of spiritual care. The task at hand is big and an addition to an already overloaded agenda for chaplains. Therefore, chaplains need supporters and fellow thinkers in advocating for spiritual care – organizing a spiritual care group with other interested professionals or holding a 'spiritual care day' where special events are held in an institution or organization to profile chaplaincy and spiritual care. There are endless possibilities to creatively and collaboratively express the importance of spiritual care for patients, loved ones and staff which can involve many interested parties together with chaplains.

The daily contacts of chaplains with patients, loved ones and staff remain the most powerful advocacy for spiritual care. I remember a meeting in the Flemish parliament with a member of the Care Think-Tank, a group consisting of members of the parliament from different parties who come together to discuss issues in healthcare. After the meeting, where we shared information and research about spiritual care, he came to me and simply said, 'You don't need to convince me of the importance of spiritual care. I recently met with a chaplain when my brother-in-law was severely ill.' Nothing more was necessary, and he went on to organize a meeting with a government minister. (In Chapter 11, John Swinton writes about confidence and professional identity.) Chaplains do more, and mean more, than they realize and have every reason to be confident in engaging with other healthcare professionals and the healthcare system.

Spiritual care PROM and ERICH

Raising the profile of chaplaincy in the context of professionalism and healthcare ties chaplaincy to research. My students know I am slightly allergic to chaplains' reaction when asked by other professionals or by patients what they are doing and their sole answer is: 'I am here to listen.' Yes, of course chaplains are there to listen. Yes, active listening for a few hours a day is hard work. And yes, listening to patients' stories is fundamental and makes them feel accepted – and one needs training for listening. But we have passed the era of Carl Rogers as our only frame of reference. We are no longer in a therapeutic model for spiritual care where psychology is the main influencer for chaplaincy work in healthcare. The backpack of chaplains needs more (and has more!) than listening skills, and spiritual care is more than listening too. Why would a chief executive and her board attribute money out of a tight budget to a chaplain who is there to listen? Any discerning chief executive –

and yes, this is also a loss – who is not familiar with chaplaincy or does not practise a particular religion would recruit volunteers to listen to patients and write a farewell email to the chaplains. Just listening is too meagre an answer. We need to communicate more about the added value and impact of chaplaincy from the growing body of evidence of chaplaincy research. That is precisely what a research-informed profession is all about.

Scotland has played a prominent role in developing an instrument that promises to find a language to name the difference that is made by chaplains when visiting patients and their loved ones. The differences made can be called outcomes of spiritual care. To capture such impacts, it is not only necessary to ask chaplains but also patients. Thus, the spiritual care PROM was born. PROMs are measurements that are being used in other healthcare disciplines to measure the outcomes of treatments. (See Chapter 13 for further information about the development and validation of the Scottish spiritual care PROM.)

The fact that an outcome-oriented research instrument was being validated in Scotland combined with the need for a European research initiative led to applying for a grant to do PROMs research in different European countries and to the founding of ERICH in June 2017. ERICH is strongly tied to the ENHCC and the Academic Centre for Practical Theology at the KU Leuven, which hosts the research institute. Currently the spiritual care PROM is being used to do chaplaincy outcome-oriented research in Belgium, the UK, the Netherlands, Estonia and the Czech Republic as well as Australia. Ireland will join the European collaboration at a later stage. ERICH seeks to contribute to chaplaincy becoming a research-based profession in order to deliver the best possible care. Results from the spiritual care PROM research in Scotland and Australia show that the item 'Being able to talk about what is on my mind' proves to be the most valued aspect of the relationship between a chaplain and a patient (Lobb *et al.* 2018). Outcome-oriented results clearly give an insight into what patients value in spiritual care. Chaplains thus are able, based on this research, to express part of their unique contribution to healthcare by saying they are there to listen to what's on a patient's mind in the here and now.

Conclusion: moving forward

Both despair and hope are tied to the future of chaplaincy. On the one hand, we see chaplains' positions disappear in different parts of Europe as this chapter is read. Rationalizing in healthcare continues to threaten the future of specialist spiritual care in healthcare institutions. Chaplains will continue to have difficulties fully explaining what we do as professional spiritual care providers. That is not a bad thing, though, because we share this with all other healthcare professions. There is that unexplainable thing that helps transform care into compassionate care – in every profession – and it has to do with spirituality. On the other hand, there is perspective and, thus, hope. Every piece of research performed by chaplains on spiritual care helps develop a language that we need in order to be aware of what the best possible care is for patients, their loved ones and staff. At the same time, it will help us survive and thrive in contemporary healthcare. Consistent professional practice, supported by continuous professional education based on research information, will be beneficial for all. Chaplains will not be selling themselves out nor deceiving their vocation or calling. We will just have learned more about the spiritual needs and resources of patients and be able to better respond to them. This does not exclude offering patients, loved ones and staff relevant aspects from the great spiritual traditions that may enhance their spiritual wellbeing. Chaplaincy, of course, is more than an answer to formulated needs. Sometimes a chaplain is like a beggar who shows another beggar where the bread is to be found today.

References

European Network of Health Care Chaplaincy (2000) *Statement of Purpose*. Crete: ENHCC. Accessed on 19/10/2018 at www.enhcc.eu/about.htm.

European Network of Health Care Chaplaincy (2014) *Salzburg Statement*. Salzburg: ENHCC. Accessed on 19/12/2018 at www.enhcc.eu/2014_salzburg_statement.pdf.

Frankl, V. (2000) *Man's Search for Meaning*. Boston, MA: Beacon Press. (Original work published 1946.)

Handzo, G., Holmes, C., Sinclair, S., Cobb, M. and Kelly, E. (2014) 'Outcomes for professional health care chaplaincy: an international call to action. *Journal of Health Care Chaplaincy 20*, 2, 43–53.

Littooij, E., Widdershoven, G., Stolwijk-Swüste, J., Doodeman, S., Leget, C. and Dekker, J. (2015) 'Global meaning in people with spinal cord injury: content and changes.' *Journal of Spinal Cord Medicine 39*, 2, 197–205.

Littooij, E., Leget, C., Stolwijk-Swüste, J., Doodeman, S., Widdershoven, G. and Dekker, J. (2016a) 'The importance of "global meaning" for people rehabilitating from spinal cord injury.' *Spinal Cord 54*, 1047–1052.

Littooij, E., Dekker, J., Vloothuis, J., Leget, C. and Widdershoven, G. (2016b) 'Global meaning in people with stroke: content and changes.' *Health Psychology Open 3*, 1–9.

Littooij, E., Dekker, J., Vloothuis, J., Widdershoven, G. and Leget, C. (2018a) 'Global meaning and rehabilitation in people with stroke.' *Brain Impairment 4*, 1–10.

Littooij, E., Widdershoven, G., Leget, C. and Dekker, J. (2018b) 'Inner posture as aspect of global meaning in healthcare: a conceptual analysis.' *Medicine, Health Care and Philosophy*. Accessed on 19/10/2018 at https://doi.org/10.1007/s11019-018-9853-y.

Lobb, E., Snowden, A., Schmidt, S., Swing, A.M., Logan, P. and Macfarlane, C. (2018) '"What's on your mind?" The only necessary question in spiritual care.' *Journal for the Study of Spirituality 8*, 1, 19–33.

Meel, L. (2015) 'Implementing spiritual care at the end of life: Estonia.' *European Journal of Palliative Care 22*, 1, 36–37.

Meel, L. (2016) 'Socio-cultural aspects of the development of contemporary clinical pastoral care in Estonia: a systematic review.' *Health and Social Care Chaplaincy 4*, 1, 57–70.

Meel, L. (2017) 'Defining the context for best practices: institutional setting for clinical pastoral care in Estonia.' *Journal of Religion and Health 57*, 1, 328–332.

Meel, L. (2018a) 'Interdisciplinary team based pastoral care model for Estonian healthcare institutions.' *Dissertationes Theologiae Universitatis Tartuensis 35.* Tartu: University of Tartu Press.

Meel, L. (2018b) 'Interdisciplinary team based pastoral care model for Estonian healthcare institutions: the professionals' insight and the model adjustments.' *Occasional Papers on Religion in Eastern Europe 38,* 2, article 2. Accessed on 19/10/2018 at https://digitalcommons.georgefox.edu/ree/vol38/iss2/2.

Meel, L. and Lehtsaar, T. (2017) 'Interdisciplinary team based pastoral care: a potentially adaptable model for Estonian healthcare institutions.' *Occasional Papers on Religion in Eastern Europe 37,* 3, 2. Accessed on 19/10/2018 at https://digitalcommons.georgefox.edu/cgi/viewcontent.cgi?referer=&httpsredir=1&article=2019&context=ree.

Puchalski, C., Ferrell, B. and O'Donnell, E. (2016) 'Spiritual Issues in Palliative Care.' In S. Yennurajalingam and E. Bruera (eds) *Oxford American Handbook of Hospice and Palliative Medicine and Supportive Care.* New York, NY: Oxford University Press.

Sewtz, C., Muscheites, W., Kriesen, U., Grosse-Thiel, C. *et al.* (2018) 'Questionnaires measuring quality of life and satisfaction of patients and their relatives in a palliative care setting: German translation of FAMCARE-2 and the palliative care subscale of FACIT-Pal.' *Annals of Palliative Medicine 7,* 4, 420–426.

Snowden, A. and Telfer, I. (2017) 'Patient reported outcome measure of spiritual care as delivered by chaplains.' *Journal of Health Care Chaplaincy 23,* 4, 131–155.

VGVZ (2018) 'Press release. Doorbraak: financiering voor geestelijke verzorging thuis.' Accessed on 19/10/2018 at https://vgvz.nl/wp-content/uploads/2018/10/Persbericht_KamerbriefGVEerstelijndef.pdf.

Chapter 10

The Architecture of Chaplaincy and Spiritual Care

Contemporary Sustainable Building

Hans Evers

Introduction

The social context for spiritual care in the Netherlands has undergone change. Before 1960, religious and philosophical institutions had a major influence on how society and individuals understood themselves. The academic world then took over the function of being a source of self-understanding, with 'truths' and 'best practice' replacing 'dogmatic beliefs' and 'moral tomes'. Both before and after 1960, individuals 'derived' their self-understanding and associated moral direction from an external source. In today's world, internal sources prevail, with individual experience and perception forming the basis for self-understanding and making decisions on how to behave. Whereas in the northwestern hemisphere individuality was formerly subordinate to the collective, the collective is now the communicative context for individuals wishing to explore who they are. Individuals talk about themselves in dialogue with those around them. This exciting and probably irreversible change also calls for a change within spiritual care.

This chapter first describes this change in context and its implications for the work of chaplains. Their field – 'philosophy of life' – is broadly understood as the personal understanding of one's own life, of others, of existence and of God. This personal awareness finds expression in identity and morality, which are articulated to varying degrees. The changes in self-understanding have also led to a new approach to daily tasks. This new pastoral 'building' is exemplified through individual discussion and supervision of a treatment team. The keystone of this chapter is a plea for professional transparency that fosters the reliance needed for successful support.

Dominant life philosophy models in chaplaincy and spiritual care

Until after the Second World War, it was standard practice in the Netherlands to link your personal philosophy first and foremost to the group to which you belonged. Dutch society was organised into 'pillars', with fellow believers forming self-sufficient societies within the larger whole – for example, Roman Catholic, Protestant, Jewish and socialist groupings. Engagement with the public domain, including healthcare, schools and social services, was linked to a person's religious or political beliefs. Even day-to-day activities took place within these pillars. When individuals faced with sudden health problems or challenges in the workplace, for instance, didn't know what to do, they sought advice from moral leaders within their own pillar. Everyone was familiar with the same rules. From the upper to the lower social classes, from poorly to highly educated, young and old, modern and conservative – they all sat under the same pulpit. By complying, individuals were assured of support and the belief that they were doing the right thing. Of course, they paid a price for that certainty.

From 1960 onwards, the Netherlands changed profoundly. Institutions which had hitherto governed public life and the lives of individuals were stripped of this function very rapidly by science and technology, which replaced the church and politics as the dominant reference points for personal and collective philosophies. Faith became part of private life and many people no longer broadcast it in public. Society was viewed as an organic whole and its members as people who were ruled by reason. Identity was mainly discussed in terms of the empirically based human sciences. People talked about themselves using the same words that doctors, psychologists and sociologists used. And in bookshops, books on morality were replaced by those on self-help. The belief in manufacturability and striving for perfection were accepted without reservation. Guidelines and protocols were drawn up and best practice was identified for all domains. Professional conduct became subject to quality-control routines involving extensive registration, while new institutions emerged to monitor and encourage compliance and quality. 'Value-free empirical research' played a key role in this normative practice. On the margin of this development, which was dubbed as 'secularisation', practitioners of hermeneutic sciences and representatives of religious and political institutions lost their traditional authority and power.

Since the turn of the twenty-first century, it has clearly emerged that 'secularisation' did not transpire as expected. The theory of secularisation had assumed that academia would replace the church and that religious beliefs would be exchanged for scientific truths. The former has happened to a degree. There are far fewer local church communities and people no longer belong to churches on a mass scale. Churches play a modest role in public life. They have been replaced not only by academia, however. Large monetary and commercial institutions also play a big role. The second development has not occurred. Although people acknowledge scientific truths, it seems they live primarily by their beliefs (Donk *et al.* 2006). Motivaction, a Dutch research agency that conducts ongoing studies of behaviour, sheds light on these beliefs (Motivaction n.d.). Their studies look at coherence in the choices respondents make in all aspects of life, revealing a picture of the philosophical differentiation present in Dutch society. It is not church membership or scientific knowledge that are important variables for beliefs about personal identity and morality, but rather people's life and working status and the extent to which they support change (flexibility). Through factor analysis, groups can be distinguished that have their own lifestyle (mentality). People are shown to differ not in terms of their norms and values – as often suggested – but primarily in terms of how they prioritise these things. Each identity or mentality has its own moral focus. For example, there is a large group of women who stop work for a time when they have children. Family is the core value for which these women set all else aside. Others allow their motherhood to be shaped by the importance that is attached to their career: several weeks after giving birth, they take their children to a crèche. They see themselves as 'good mothers' because of their concern for their own development and the wellbeing of their family. Another group of mothers believes in the importance of health and healthy eating, and they raise their children on a diet containing lots of raw vegetables.

Clearly, all these mothers share a belief in the value of 'motherhood'; in each group, there beats a warm, moral heart. These differences are not confined to motherhood: they also relate to participation as citizens in society, to how people think about health and how neighbourhoods are organised. There is no domain without its own special flavour. In practice, groups also adopt very different standpoints on the principles laid down in protocols by science. Thus, living as long as possible and going to extremes is not a guiding principle for people who lead their lives in accordance with the motto 'you only live once'.

Models for spiritual care

The above philosophical approaches within public life differ markedly as a context for the work of a chaplain.

Before 1960, chaplains in the Netherlands provided advice to individuals, acted as moderators in departments and professional associations, sometimes sat on an institution's board or even held the post of care institution director. They were also responsible for the liturgy and for administering the sacraments so that patients in care institutions who would otherwise miss out could participate fully in church life. In other words, chaplains were *ambassadors of religious and philosophical institutions and authorised interpreters of doctrine and morality*. As 'carers of souls' they also looked after concrete, physical aspects of human life and society.

After 1960, chaplains were primarily approached as *care workers* concerned with culture and spirituality, in the same way that others were concerned with somatics, the psyche and social life. They were mainly there for patients who were active to varying degrees in a church or another association (category). They supported them in a medico-technocratic world, based on their own tradition and morality. Chaplains played a modest role within organisations as consultants when it came to dealing with deviant behaviour and thinking among patients. Chaplains seldom or never sat on boards by virtue of their position. As 'care workers' they had difficulty formulating care needs that could be directly linked to the reason for a patient's admission and treatment. The care need was often expressed in ethical terms, such as 'meeting the needs of the patient as a human being'. If justifying their involvement was problematical, they could appeal to the 'refuge function' or more generally to the fundamental right to practise religion. If attempts were made to generically position their role as care worker, the added value of spiritual care was primarily articulated from the perspective of empirical research. Psychology and sociology operationalised this added value with outcomes for welfare and wellbeing. New academic subdisciplines, such as pastoral psychology and pastoral psychotherapy, emerged.

The fact that Dutch people no longer tend to derive their identity and core moral beliefs from external institutions (such as church/religious texts and science/best practice), but make discoveries within themselves (in communication with one another and based on their own experience and perception), is bound to have consequences for chaplains. It obliges them to shift their role and position from 'ambassador/authorised interpreter of doctrine and morality' or 'care worker who provides coaching based on ideas about best practice' to a third role and position which can perhaps best be labelled 'facilitator'. As facilitators, chaplains place their own competencies in the hermeneutics of life at the disposal of people who, for themselves and together with others, are compelled to reformulate their assumptions about meaning and coherence. The ability to identify and name the way in which issues of meaning and coherence are raised is indispensable. Viewed in these terms, facilitation is always a rhetorical-critical approach used to encourage internal dialogue. The facilitator operates at all levels of an organisation.

Chaplains facilitate in cases where there are profound changes in an individual's personal orientation. Following a major change, many patients are faced with the task of reinventing themselves. The 'new person' who emerges after, say, a trauma or a life-threatening illness will seek appropriate treatment. This is sometimes a matter of urgency because a doctor may explicitly ask which path they wish to take. For many people, it can be a major challenge to know which choice will eventually offer peace, a home and a future. Which path will mean they won't feel uprooted and distressed? The search will often focus on the weighing up of facts and meanings. Careful planning can bring solace, even if the desired result cannot be enforced.

The chaplain then supports the individual when they communicate their beliefs to those close to them. There may be differences of understanding with immediate and extended family and friends, or between the patient and the medical practitioners and carers. The patient's personal beliefs may differ from the convictions inherent in protocols and guidelines, which can be a source of frustration for patients, supporters and medical practitioners. Although dedicated healthcare staff are often prepared to dress up best practice in a different guise, they are less willing to abandon the underlying principles. They are accustomed to responding to 'non-compliant behaviour' by providing more information, by training their own communication skills and by modifying the protocols. In this area of tension, chaplains can help to identify, label and discuss the differences with a view to obtaining consent. This leaves the patient and medical practitioner jointly in control and they can both rely on their own conscience regarding treatments for which they do not wish to be responsible (de Groot 2008).

Lastly, chaplains help society (and subsocieties) to cope with many – sometimes conflicting – beliefs. Without a dominant and unequivocal moral core, society is seeking a new coherence. The common concerns of life philosophies or the uniformity of science are no longer reference points for individuals or groups. A new frame of reference is required that will meet the needs of the moral heart of individuals and groups. Now that religious and scientific convictions are no longer absolute and it has become commonplace to legitimise different priorities, what now matters is the care with which individuals distinguish their own identity and make and communicate their ethical choices.

Combination

It is essential that work at the micro-, meso- and macro-levels be combined or interlinked. This helps to create a climate in which individual beliefs do not pose a threat to society's coherence, while society in turn offers individuals the space to work things out.

It is clear that the dominant models for life philosophies in public life have not succeeded one another seamlessly. There is a mismatch in timing, not only worldwide but regionally as well. Chaplains who, in the first instance, present themselves as facilitators can, if required, take on other roles or refer people to colleagues. Chaplains are always facilitators and also – on demand – ambassadors or care workers. This sequence also works for people who see themselves first and foremost as members of a group. They are approached in this sequence in accordance with their religious tradition. This sequence also makes sense because it obviates a situation in which someone is assigned a label they do not want on the basis of external characteristics.

Building

Chaplains who primarily present themselves as facilitators of inner beliefs are faced with the task of attuning their professional practice accordingly. This is a comprehensive operation. It involves how they present themselves within the organisation and to patients, as well as the method they use to be of service to patients, supporters, departments and their organisation. By way of example, we describe below (a) the systematic discussions that have been developed to facilitate patients (micro-level) and (b) how we work with departments to develop appropriate care in a specific case (meso-level).

The crux of this two-pronged approach is that a conviction is not seen as a conclusion following a rational consideration, but as an 'intuition' that people express as metaphors from a wide range of viewpoints. Chaplains facilitate the individual or group until, once the different viewpoints have been articulated, the essence is automatically summarised in an image. What was previously present as an intuition then becomes comprehensible and can be shared with others.

In both these exercises chaplains make themselves available as hermeneutic experts. They listen in such a way that their clients find the courage and patience to listen to themselves until they feel they are understood and can share their experience. I see the academic and professional training of chaplains as a lengthy, multifaceted exercise in listening, in which the subject and outcome are seen as an added personal bonus. The ability to listen with curiosity, selflessness and vigilance is a powerful skill.

Contemplative listening

From the outset, chaplains show in their contact with clients how they understand themselves. Chaplains who address a patient without asking whether it is convenient, without stating the reason for, and purpose of, their visit and without agreeing about the approach are basing their action on the self-evident nature of their office or position. To illustrate how this differs from the approach a chaplain should make, I will describe a situation that occurs in teaching hospitals on a daily basis and in many variations.

The situation involves a meeting with clients who, following a critical life event, feel that the change in their life has undermined their familiar self-understanding and who feel unable to simply pick up the thread once more. For example, after a serious trauma, a client may have to live with a permanent disability, as well as discover that business relationships and friendships were less close than he or she thought. If asked to reintegrate, they discover that they have lost not only a particular ability, but also something of themselves. The change makes it necessary for them to reinvent themselves. There are many changes that prompt a need of this kind: hearing that the child you are expecting will require a good deal of ongoing care; the discovery of a life-threatening condition or illness; or being deployed as a soldier to a war zone. Any critical life event can create such a need, although this does not mean that all such changes will prompt everyone to seek internal dialogue. Clients who do feel a need for reorientation can ask the chaplain for space and time in which to talk about their own core. So in the situation outlined thus far, the chaplain can act in line with the three life-philosophy models in the public domain and the associated role patterns.

The *ambassador/interpreter of doctrine and morality* informs or instructs the patient, whether solicited or unsolicited, about the community's view of the most important issue. For example, a critical life event can be called a trial that purifies the patient, preparing them for their ultimate destination. Besides this example, there are many other responses to the question of suffering (theodicy). In addition to this instructive role, chaplains can opt for a liturgical approach. As explicit representatives of the community, they can pray with the patient and the patient's supporters or administer the sacraments.

The *care worker* does not focus on morality, doctrine or the need for liturgy, but will want to contribute to the welfare and wellbeing of the patient and his or her supporters. The care worker will see the critical life event primarily as an occurrence that drastically alters the physical situation, places a burden on the psyche, makes it difficult to perform ordinary social roles and tasks, and creates doubt about participation in the culture. The care worker will seek to heal or prevent possible despair through a therapeutic approach. Chaplains can select from a wide range of sociocultural and psychological techniques and methods. As well as these tools from the field of human sciences, there are others such as general philosophical or ethics coaching, legal support and literary critical reflections.

Chaplains who present themselves as *facilitators of internal dialogue* focus on articulating inner convictions. Clients who do feel a need for reorientation can ask the chaplain as auditor for space and time in which to talk about their own core in a multidimensional exploration. This internal dialogue simply demands of an auditor that they listen and try to understand (Evers 2017). The auditor knows that the clients are the sole explorers and only experts when it comes to content. The auditor cannot directly observe that about which the clients are talking. The clients know that they are the only ones who will determine the topic, the approach and the frame of reference in the discussion (Stiles 1992). They know that the auditor will do everything possible to leave the content of the discussion undisturbed and will give them ample space to calibrate their picture of their life experience. The clients and auditor agree that the clients will not ask for information, advice or interpretation in the discussion.

If, after such listening, a client would like to use a different discussion technique with the auditor, such as a brief therapeutic discussion or an explanation of a passage from a holy book, this calls for a new, clear agreement. If the auditor changes the discussion technique without explanation and without the client's express consent, there is a danger that he or she will use deeply personal information in a didactic way or to exert influence on the client. This is ethically undesirable in view of the agreed contract with the client (de Groot and van Hoek 2017).

Deliberation of views on care

The chaplain facilitates internal dialogue not only for clients, but also for professionals. To illustrate the difference in approach by the chaplain, I will describe a situation that occurs daily in many variants within teaching hospitals. In healthcare, it frequently happens that a treatment is not only a 'solution' but is also part of the tragedy. We see this in struggles with meaning among patients and their supporters (challenged meaning, existential crisis, suffering from life or a temporary 'handicap' and in the process of attributing meaning), professional and/or personal discomfort among medical practitioners, observing that current guidelines and protocols are inadequate, and sometimes a need for common communication or consensus. In this situation, it is impossible to only do good, and the patient, their supporters and medical practitioners face the same dilemma. The unique reality of the case does not usually fit into the regulatory framework (protocols, guidelines, needs assessment) and institutions on offer (for example, care institutions, Health Care Inspectorate, insurance companies or jurisprudence). We also observe that the customary solution strategies do not suffice. In treatment practice, refuge is frequently sought in the four classical approaches: 'That's how we do things here!' (variant of *'Cuius regio eius religio'*, e.g. 'This is Scotland, not Nigeria'); 'That's what we think!' (variant of *'Pars maior pars sanior'*, e.g. these are the protocols of the professional group); 'That's my decision, you'll have to be content with that' (Judgement of Solomon on form or content); and 'He who pays the piper calls the tune.' These statements cause dissatisfaction among people who feel they are subject to a power argument and will not usually have an opportunity to tackle things differently next time. So in summary thus far, the chaplain can act in line with the three life-philosophy models in the public domain and the associated role patterns.

The *ambassador/interpreter of doctrine and morality* informs or instructs the people concerned, whether solicited or unsolicited, about the opinion of his or her organisation. Inasmuch as these people are members of the same organisation, the chaplain asks, tacitly or explicitly, in their intervention that norms and values of the institution be respected. Non-compliant behaviour can have consequences for a person's bond with the organisation and may even be regarded as culpable guilt or sin. It is not difficult to think of past examples of this kind of professional practice. In contemporary reality too, this behaviour is commonplace. For example, chaplains who set themselves up as custodians of human norms and values are 'guardians of virtue' in the same way that their counterparts were a century ago. The same applies to chaplains who see themselves as having primary responsibility for setting up an ethics committee or arranging specific times for an ethical assessment.

Chaplains in the role of *care workers* do not focus on morality and doctrine but rather seek to contribute to the welfare and wellbeing of patients and their supporters. They prefer to act as co-practitioners. They represent the 'spiritual dimension' in the discussion about good care. Their contribution is seen as part of psychosocial or holistic care. Their colleagues in the care discussion are psychologists and social workers, who represent empirical science. Chaplains also invoke their religious belief or philosophical background. Care is based on a direct link, either assumed or demonstrated, between religious practices and healing and rehabilitation. There are also chaplains who, during treatment decisions or a palliative process, appoint themselves as spokespeople regarding 'what benefits most people in a situation like this' (e.g. by referring to research or WHO guidelines).

Chaplains who act as *facilitators in the joint discussion about appropriate care* focus on formulating a shared belief. Their expertise lies primarily in guiding the discussion of a case in which the participants do not primarily proceed from their disciplinary differences but from their shared humanitarian concern. They possess the cognitive and communication competencies to transcend the situation together in a safe and dignified discussion. The discussion results in a prioritised set of advice that makes the shared belief explicit. The medical practitioner can use it to enter into discussion with the patient and their supporters. Experience has taught us that this intervention by the chaplain does not usually lead to spectacular changes in medical policy or in responsibilities. The shared shift in emphasis from curative to palliative policy is the exception here; nor is the deliberation a paranormal panacea in medically hopeless cases. The main outcomes are that the team works more effectively, more efficiently and more agreeably. The following aspects can be identified:

- It is about optimising understanding and consensus in the communication between medical practitioners. It helps to ensure that the multidisciplinary policy is implemented consistently.

- It helps with the development of tailored communication to patients and those around them.

- It smoothens and accelerates decision-making processes in cases where a stalemate has been reached through indecision resulting from a lack of shared beliefs.

- It is also a practical reflection on guidelines and protocols.

- It reinforces treatment quality and the department's quality policy.

Introduction keystone: transparency fosters reliance

For care organisations, the loss of a dominant, self-evident moral focus means the loss of control over content. What constitutes appropriate care is governed in part by the patient's self-understanding and moral orientation. Chaplains help the client and organisation to decide on the desired treatment outcomes. They can only fulfil this role if they have the confidence of all those involved. Today's chaplains are asked to provide tangible proof of their added value in engaging with meaning. The trust that the organisation places in its chaplains also gives them credit with patients. If the picture is clear, this creates and guarantees a place for chaplaincy. Professionalism is clearly embodied in four practices that presuppose one another: regular formulation of a mission statement, drawing up protocols, registration of client contacts and peer review.

Drawing up and adopting a mission statement

A mission statement describes, briefly but comprehensively, what employers, colleagues and clients of chaplains can expect. Because of the importance of a specific added value, the professional profile needs to be well defined. The job description, the desired outcomes, the methods used and the quality policy show how chaplains connect with clients and the care system to which they are affiliated. This description may explain how chaplains relate to the religious and philosophical transformation and to the spirituality of clients. The desired outcomes and methods used can illustrate whether and how the approach relates to a patient's admission and supports their treatment. The description can also define who may have recourse to spiritual care and what admission and treatment reasons indicate a change, such that the client should be informed about the option of spiritual care. A chaplain's specialisation must be reflected in a clearly formulated focus, the competency they have acquired and maintained, and the practicability of the activity's aims. Following stakeholder approval, a mission statement containing these elements constitutes a clear agreement with the institution and society. The mission statement is therefore one of the documents in which a care institution gives concrete form to appropriate, value-oriented care.

Drawing up protocols

The transparent functioning of chaplains within the clinic and organisation is served by protocols that can be viewed by all clients and staff. Protocols describe day-to-day activities briefly and in a way that can be verified. Thus, a protocol should describe how and when the client encounters the chaplain. A second protocol can describe how the client and chaplain reach agreement on the need for, as well as the form and content of, that contact. A third protocol can outline the method the chaplain uses in that contact, while a fourth describes documentation. These descriptions show the minimum due diligence requirements that the professional sets. Against a background of the transformed role and the resulting strong demand for professionalism, protocols must provide an answer to the following questions:

- How does the activity accord with the consensus within the institution about good care and priorities?

- How does the activity accord with the care needs of the patient and those around him or her?

- What makes the activity a suitable offering?

- What makes the activity a systematic and methodical activity that can be expected of a professional?

- How are the practices and presumed skills safeguarded (quality manual, reviews, accreditation)?

Documentation of encounters with clients

Maintaining a client record is axiomatic within care. The quality, diligence and privacy that are so important here are generally laid down extensively in legislation. For chaplains, too, it is important that their contributions to care be well documented. Maintaining client records, particularly within the hospital's overall electronic information system, means that professionalism and transparency can be clearly demonstrated. There are at least five functions that make this explicit: proactive investigations; documentation that supports processes; supporting collaboration; facilitating management; and quality-boosting and scientific research.

Chaplains who can access the hospital's electronic information system are able to select patients in a timely fashion who are eligible for notification about spiritual care options. Process-support documentation means noting relevant information about contact with patients. This documentation helps chaplains in their efforts to ensure continuity, as well as assisting team members in the event of a transfer. In addition to information that is only available to chaplains and their team, parts of the record can also be offered to other medical practitioners. The record allows chaplains to continually formulate and reflect on outcomes, with or without the client. Registration in the hospital's electronic information system also enables chaplains to chart the results of their efforts in quantitative terms. It yields information on the number of patients who are seen, their response and the number of contacts that result. Lastly, documentation can be helpful when conducting quality-enhancing and scientific research. For example, the effect of changes to a protocol can be monitored. Documentation also makes it easy to gather material for case studies or to evaluate the use of special discussion techniques.

Peer review

Peer review is an ideal instrument for teams to continue working on professional development and specialisation. The transition from life philosophy in the public domain and the private sphere obliges chaplains to make a profound transition in terms of their position and role. This calls for considerable creativity and critical reflection, as well as solidarity regarding the loss of what is familiar and becoming accustomed to something new. There are also big differences among chaplains when it comes to clinging to the past or looking forward to new experiences. Everything can come up for discussion within a safe peer-review climate based on enlightened self-interest. This includes how they present themselves, the methods they use, how things are recorded, and publicity within the hospital. Peer-review sessions can generate a new understanding of the mission statement, protocols, documentation and peer review itself.

Conclusion

If professional practice is transparent, it fosters the trust that chaplains need to do their work. After the changes in the way individuals and society deal with life philosophies, this practice – now more than ever – involves what comforts people and gives them the courage to *be*. In this way, chaplains not only support their clients but also help those around them and society to deal with the call that each life makes on our humanity. Accepting the new situation, in which individuals explore life itself in dialogue with those around them, is a sound basis for sustainable chaplaincy and spiritual care.

References

de Groot, J. (2008) 'Morele counseling voor de patiënt als pendant voor moreel beraad.' *Tijdschrift voor Gezondheidszorg en Ethiek 18*, 4, 107–111.

de Groot, J. and van Hoek, M. (2017) 'Contemplative listening in moral issues: moral counseling redefined in principles and methods.' *Journal of Pastoral Care and Counseling 71*, 2, 106–113.

Donk, W.B.H.J. v.d., Jonkers, A.P., Kronjee, G.J. and Plum, R.J.J. (2006) 'Geloven in het publiek domein: verkenningen van een dubbele transformatie.' *Wetenschappelijke Raad voor het Regeringsbeleid-Verkenningen* 13.

Evers, H. (2017) 'Contemplative listening: A rhetorical-critical approach to facilitate internal dialogue.' *Journal of Pastoral Care and Counseling 71*, 2, 114–121.

Motivaction (n.d.) Accessed on 07/11/2018 at www.motivaction.nl.

Stiles, W.B. (1992) *Describing Talk: A Taxonomy of Verbal Response Modes*. Newbury Park, CA: Sage.

Chapter 11

Professional Identity and Confidence[1]

John Swinton

Introduction

Chaplaincy sits at the spiritual heart of the National Health Service (NHS) in the UK. Chaplains inhabit that space within healthcare that is described as the realm of 'the spiritual'; a realm where the importance of such things as meaning, purpose, value, dignity, love and the Divine are intentionally brought to the fore within the lives of people living with illness and staff who strive to offer care that is truly holistic. In a system that can easily lose sight of the importance of spirituality, the continuing presence of chaplains enables the NHS to retain a sense of soulfulness that is vital for the provision of care that is truly person centred. For patients, the value of chaplaincy is often quite apparent (Raffay, Wood and Todd 2016; Snowden and Telfer 2017). Illness is a meaningful *experiencing* that transcends the biological and impacts upon a person's relationships, mortality, sense of purpose and reason for being in the world. Chaplains and the language of spirituality find their primary focus in drawing out this dimension of healthcare and offering creative spiritual strategies to meet people's expressed spiritual needs. There is a growing evidence base that indicates that the presence of chaplains is not only desirable for patients and for staff but also can have measurable health benefits (Lichter 2013; Timmins *et al.* 2018). However, chaplaincy is in transition. It is moving, both in reality and perception, from being a discipline that is closely associated with the church to one that has a primary affiliation with healthcare providers. This complex transition raises several very important questions that need to be addressed, such as:

---

1   This chapter is an updated version of the following article: Swinton, J. (2003) 'A question of identity: What does it mean for chaplains to become healthcare professionals?' *Scottish Journal for Healthcare Chaplaincy* 6, 2, 2–7.

- What exactly does it mean for chaplains to be healthcare professionals?

- What are the sources of identity that make chaplains chaplains?

- What exactly does chaplaincy do that other disciplines don't already do?

- What evidence base should they draw upon in order to prove their authenticity, worth and value?

Such questions are not 'by the way' questions. Chaplaincy has opponents who suggest that the money spent on chaplaincy would be better spent elsewhere (Hamburgh 2017). In a post-Brexit, post-religious Britain, which may end up seeing the world and its priorities quite differently from our current assumptions, being proactively clear on issues of identity, distinctiveness and professional practice is a pressing necessity for the long-term stability and security of chaplaincy as a healthcare discipline.

In this chapter I reflect on some of these questions with a particular focus on chaplaincy in Scotland, although the general arguments also will apply elsewhere. I raise some important issues with a view to contributing to the ongoing conversation around the nature of chaplaincy and its role within healthcare institutions. I do so not in any sense to criticize the discipline of chaplaincy or to question the professionalism of healthcare chaplains. As will become clear, it is my view that chaplaincy offers a vital healing conduit which is crucial for the sustaining of a genuinely person-centred healthcare system. It offers a powerful prophetic challenge to healthcare systems to hold onto aspects of caring that can become occluded by an unbalanced focus on technological solutions that forget about *people*. By asking challenging questions and laying out potential options and possibilities, I hope to add to the continuing development of healthcare chaplaincy in the UK and beyond. What I offer herein is not intended in any sense as a theory of professionalization or a theory of chaplaincy. Rather, this chapter should be read as a series of critical observations and questions intended to raise important issues with a view to helping to ensure the place of chaplaincy as a healthcare profession within contemporary healthcare provision. The point of the chapter is to encourage constructive conversation, rather than to win any argument, as it is only through such dialogue that creative change can emerge.

What does it mean to be a professional?

It is clear that many healthcare chaplains feel that developing the primary identity of 'healthcare professional' is the best way to describe their discipline and locate it within healthcare systems. Previously chaplains would, for the most part, be ordained ministers with a direct connection to the church, but nowadays the entry point into chaplaincy is not ordination but rather education (Paterson and Clegg 2013). Chaplaincy is conceived as an independent discipline which continues to respect the Christian church and other religious communities but is not formally bound to any given religious community with regard to training, accreditation or oversight. Chaplains are healthcare professionals.

There is no problem with this shift. Disciplines develop and shift in their shape and form. That is inevitably the case. If chaplains are to continue to be taken seriously, it is vital that they be viewed by other professionals as engaging in forms of practice which are relevant, efficient, well informed and credible according to the standards of credibility that are placed on any healthcare profession. In order to achieve this, they must be seen to be acting in a manner that is professional in the broad sense of the term; however, we do need to be clear on what we mean when we describe chaplains as professionals.

Professionalism or professionalization?

It will be helpful to draw a distinction between *professionalism* and *professionalization*.

Professionalism

It is clear that professionalism is very important for chaplains. Alison Elliot (personal correspondence) suggests that the beginning point of professionalism is the existence of a system and structure which ensures that chaplains have the resources to do a professional job. Elliot suggests that in order to do a professional job (in the broader sense), chaplains require the following:

- *integrity*, which can be maintained by the provision of some sort of code of conduct such as that which is largely outlined in the various chaplaincy guidelines that are currently available

- *autonomy*, that is, the ability to work unsupervised in a way which makes a distinct contribution to the practice of healthcare

- *back-up*, for example being able to keep up with colleagues in things such as utilizing information technology and social media, giving PowerPoint presentations, general efficiency and so forth

- *support*, that is, from other chaplains, the church, professional bodies, people who know what chaplains are going through and so forth

- *respect* (an additional dimension we are adding to Elliot's list), both for oneself and for the dignity, autonomy and personhood of others.

At this level, becoming a professional is vital for any chaplain and a central dimension of good practice. This would seem to be a wise and worthy goal for chaplaincy and one which has been achieved in various ways. Chaplains should act in a professional manner.

Professionalization

If becoming a healthcare professional means the 'professionalization' of chaplaincy, that is, developing chaplaincy in line with other healthcare professions, such as nursing or medicine, then other questions have to be raised and answered. Professionalization relates to the social process wherein an occupation moves towards formally ensuring that its practices are of the highest integrity and competence. Precisely what constitutes a profession is contested (Bondi *et al.* 2011). For current purposes we will explore some generic (i.e. not belonging specifically to any one theory) features that can help us to reflect clearly on what it might mean for chaplains to be healthcare professionals in this more focused sense of the term. We can describe the five primary components necessary for a discipline to have professional status as:

1. a body of knowledge which supports and underpins practice

2. a code of professional ethics

3. an occupational organization controlling the profession

4. substantial intellectual and practical training

5. provision of a specialized skill or service.

A body of knowledge which supports and underpins their practice

The Cambridge dictionary defines a professional as 'a person who has the type of job that needs a high level of education and training, e.g. health professionals. This education provides the professional with the necessary body of literature that underpins and sustains its practices' (Cambridge Dictionary 2019). At first glance one might think that chaplains clearly meet this criterion as full-time chaplains are educated to the level of university education and sometimes to postgraduate level; however, there is a tension.

Historically, chaplains have been ordained Christian ministers who have specific training within the field of biblical studies and Christian theology, in order to attain their status as ordained ministers of word and sacrament. This provides a certain set of skills and particular understandings of religion and spirituality which may or may not be useful in the current climate, which focuses on a much more generic understanding of spirituality and sees religion as optional. It could be argued that the body of literature which has traditionally underpinned chaplaincy is now too narrow for the needs of current healthcare chaplains (Barclay 2003). Chaplains desire to be seen in more generic terms as spiritual carers who are able to cater for the spiritual needs of *all* people of all faiths (and none). Becoming a spiritual carer in this sense is not in itself problematic insofar as chaplains within a secular healthcare context are quite correctly called to care for *all* of the people they encounter and not simply those with an expressed religious commitment. This position finds some support in the broader scientific literature that indicates that all human beings have spiritual needs if spirituality is defined in broad terms which include, but are not necessarily defined by, religion (Hay 2006). Some chaplains satisfy these needs through religious structures, but many express them in varied ways which do not include religion, transcendence or a concept of a deity. If this is so, becoming a spiritual carer in this generic sense is an important dimension of the chaplain's role: spiritual needs need to be catered for and chaplains are a group of people charged with the responsibility of caring for this dimension of human beings.

However, in moving away from the body of literature that provided identity and theoretical/theological guidance – theology and biblical studies – chaplains risk having no unique body of literature to underpin their practices and help define their identity. In distancing themselves from the Christian tradition as its primary body of professional knowledge, it becomes unclear what body of knowledge underpins the practice of chaplaincy. Is it psychology, counselling or psychotherapy, or is there in fact a big enough body of information to create a formal discipline of 'chaplaincy studies'? Depending on how we answer that question, we could be faced with the following potentially awkward question: In terms of the ability to carry out spiritual care and the knowledge base that is necessary to do this well, what is the difference between a spiritually oriented counsellor, or a trained listener with an interest in spirituality, and a professional chaplain?

The problem is that the uniqueness of the previous underlying body of literature has been superseded by literature that is shared with other healthcare professionals, thus making it difficult to see what the specific theoretical basis of chaplaincy actually is. This makes chaplains vulnerable. It would be quite difficult to argue that you could get rid of, for example, doctors and nurses, and substitute them with another profession. That would be so both in terms of theory and practice. Evidencing chaplaincy on the basis of its unique body of validating literature is more difficult. It is certainly the case that there is a growing body of literature that indicates the positive effects of chaplaincy and its importance for patient care. However, the research that is done tends to focus on what chaplains *do* rather than what they *are* and why they are what they are. So, for example, chaplains are present and listen, empathize, counsel and interact with other professionals to help increase knowledge and practice within the area of spiritual care. This is all highly beneficial for patients and staff, and that can be evidenced. However, none of these skills are unique to chaplains. Even the area of spirituality is contentious. There are multiple definitions of what spirituality is, coming from various healthcare disciplines and perspectives, some of which differ sometimes radically (Swinton and Pattison 2010). So, it may not be enough simply to state that spirituality is what defines chaplaincy and marks it out from other disciplines. If we do not think these challenges through, even the evidence base may not be as helpful as we may think it is. It could be argued that the research is certainly done on chaplains, but what chaplains are doing is not necessarily unique to chaplaincy. If that is the case, it would be fairly straightforward for chaplaincy's detractors to argue that it is not chaplaincy per se that is important in improving care within any given situation, but rather human presence and the shared need to be heard, encouraged, valued and assisted in dealing with questions of mortality and the meaning of life.

The second, third and fourth components

Let me take the next three components – a code of professional ethics, an occupational organization controlling the profession, and substantial intellectual and practical training – together. These three dimensions of the professional role appear to be relatively uncontroversial, at least in principle. Chaplaincy is a discipline which is deeply implicated in issues of value and meaning. Its daily encounters with people on an intimate and deeply trusted level, combined with the primary task of caring for the person's spirituality, a dimension of experience which is inherently caught up in systems of meaning and belief, means that ethics and moral principle provide some of the implicit 'grammar' of chaplaincy. Chaplaincy codes of ethics enable the development of ethical standards and assumptions that provide important guidance for chaplains as they wrestle within the complex ethical environment of the healthcare system. Such codes of ethics are vital not only to enable chaplains to practise ethically, but also to ensure that patients be protected from potential abuse or malpractice. Similarly, having unified professional bodies which oversee the profession is a vital dimension in terms of setting boundaries, establishing professional qualifications and training, dealing with disciplinary issues, setting standards and so forth. All of these elements are in place in different ways and in different contexts.

Even here some critical thinking may be required, however. Take, for example, the issue of training and dedicated chaplaincy qualifications. At the moment in Scotland the gateway into chaplaincy is via a postgraduate certificate which currently comes from the University of Glasgow. At the time of writing this chapter a new tender has gone out for chaplaincy education, so it may be a good time to ask a few potentially important questions. All of the healthcare professions – medicine, nursing, social work, occupational therapy and so forth – have specific courses with particular qualifications, which it is necessary to acquire before a person can practise within any given area. For chaplains to become healthcare professionals in the way that the other healthcare disciplines understand this term, a similar dedicated training qualification has been developed. If it is to hold credibility, the chaplaincy qualification must be at a similar level to that of other healthcare professions.

Significantly, however, the qualification is only for people *coming into* the profession of chaplaincy. Chaplains currently in post, some of whom have been trained and formed in ministry and some who have not been, do not have to do the qualification. There are fewer ordained people applying for chaplaincy jobs in Scotland and some increased interest in chaplaincy by people from other healthcare disciplines. So, the nature of chaplaincy is shifting in terms of practice (from religion to spirituality) and also in terms of spiritual affiliation (from ordained person to spiritually mature person without any formal religious affiliation). This is inevitable as chaplaincy shifts its identity from a religion-centred to a healthcare discipline. Chaplaincy remains in transition, and aspects of its professional status are emerging rather than fixed.

Nevertheless, the fact that there is a two-tier system of education is problematic in terms of professional identity. If we are to argue that chaplaincy is a healthcare profession and that it has a specific body of literature on which to base its practices and a set of unique practices that make them irreplaceable, then the current mixed economy of education and practice is a hindrance. The challenge is how best to manage the inevitable and not necessarily negative mixed economy of chaplaincy practice and education whilst at the same time striving to support the claim that chaplains are best perceived as healthcare professionals. The piecemeal nature of formation and education (Paterson and Clegg 2013), alongside the variations in practice and approach, makes the identity and uniqueness of chaplaincy somewhat fragile in ways that other healthcare professions may not be.

Provision of a specialized skill or service

Healthcare professionals are called upon to provide a specialized skill or service. We have discussed this above and I have highlighted some of the tensions around precisely what chaplaincy brings to the table and how best it might be articulated in the language of professionalism. Here I simply want to acknowledge the vital place of chaplaincy within healthcare in enabling a complex system to remain humane and person centred, and also to reprise the need for clarity as to the originality of the contribution that chaplains make in terms of skills and service provision. It is an old argument but always worth bearing in mind: *If it is the case that everyone can and should be delivering spiritual care, then what does that mean for chaplaincy?* Some certainly want to consider chaplains as spiritual experts and facilitators of spirituality in other disciplines and areas; however, bearing in mind how diffuse and unclear the concept of spirituality is, chaplains need to make sure that the precise nature of their expertise is apparent for all to see.

My intuition is that the uniqueness of chaplaincy lies in the formation of the chaplain (see Chapter 20). Traditionally this spiritual formation has been done via ecclesial formation. That is changing. The question is not so much what do chaplains *do*, a question that suggests that the importance of being a good chaplain lies primarily in what someone does; rather, the key question may be: *What kind of people do we have to be to be chaplains, and how can we form people in ways that help us to become people who do not just engage in spiritual care but are truly spiritual carers?* Perhaps the uniqueness of chaplaincy lies not so much in the tasks that chaplains perform, but rather in the type of people they are and their ability to see the spiritual in places and situations where other professionals cannot.

Evidence and intuition: buckets and waterfalls

All of this takes us into the issue of evidence-based chaplaincy and precisely what kind of evidence base might be required and appropriate. As I have suggested, proving that chaplaincy 'works' can be tricky. Previously in this book's Introduction we highlighted the tensions between empiricism and interpretivism as it relates to chaplaincy. When it comes to the type of evidence that best suits the needs of chaplaincy, we are faced with a similar issue. Let me try to illustrate the difficulties in assessing and understanding the meaning of spiritual care within a healthcare context that can have a radically different way of looking at the world. I will borrow an analogy used by Mark Cobb at a meeting on spiritual care in Edinburgh many years ago: Imagine yourself walking through a deep, dense wood. You are surrounded by beautiful, luscious foliage; the constantly changing aromas of the rich shrubbery makes your head swirl. Suddenly you reach a clearing. Right in the centre of the clearing is a beautiful stream headed up by a magnificent waterfall. You stand and watch in awe at the mystery and wonder of the waterfall. Multiple rainbows dance across the glistening surface of the water. The sound of the water, the taste of the spray, the sight of the magnificence and power of the waterfall touches you in inexpressible places and brings you into contact with a dimension of experience which you cannot quite articulate, but which you feel deeply and meaningfully. Eventually, your gaze of wonder begins to change as your curious side clicks into action: 'What is this thing called a waterfall?' 'What is it made of?' 'Why does it have such an effect on me?' So, you pick up a bucket and scoop up some of the water from the falls. You look into the bucket, but something has changed. The water is of course technically the same substance in each setting: H2O. It remains a vital constituent in your life; you need it to live, and without it you would perish. Yet, something has been lost in the movement from waterfall to bucket. In your attempts to break it down, analyse and explain what it really is, the mystery and awe of the waterfall has been left behind. Which is more real – the mystery of the crashing waterfall or the still waters of the bucket?

This vivid analogy reveals an important dimension which sits at the heart of the current debate over the role of the chaplain within a professional, evidence-based, scientifically driven healthcare system. On the one hand, chaplains are called to be spiritual healers and carers. They are called to mediate and care for a person's spirituality: that dimension of humanness which is in many senses unquantifiable, mysterious, individual and unique. On the other hand, they are called to justify their existence within a healthcare context which places great emphasis on that which is quantifiable, generalizable and universally applicable. The distinction between the waterfall and the still waters of the bucket symbolizes the difficulties that chaplains face when they begin to consider their identity and role within healthcare systems. In terms of professional development and the chaplain's long-term role within the healthcare system, this tension requires sensitive reflection for the uniqueness of chaplaincy to be fully recognized as well as effectively and meaningfully worked out.

The uniqueness of chaplaincy: square pegs in round holes

In significant ways which may be to the advantage of the healthcare professional, chaplaincy does not fit within the standard model. Chaplaincy is a unique discipline with a unique role within the healthcare system and it would be wise to establish itself on its own terms. Chaplaincy is a prophetic discipline which challenges many things within the healthcare system and forces it to begin the process of lateral thinking. One of its challenges may be to begin to redefine the meaning of 'health professional' and expand the boundaries of precisely what evidence base should underpin the practice of chaplaincy and how that evidence base can help enhance chaplains' professional identity and clarify their healing role. In a system which is often tempted to be death denying, chaplaincy calls us to notice that death and illness may have meaning beyond the understandable, but ultimately unrealistic, desire to avoid both. Chaplains are called to enable the system to redefine health and healing in ways which will enable it to realize that illness has meaning beyond the technical language of pathology, and that healing and health relate as much to the restoration of that meaning as they do to the elimination of suffering and pain. However, this is a goal which, in reality, will never be achieved. *Chaplaincy is the critical voice that makes holism possible.*

Bilingual chaplaincy: from symptoms to stories

Chaplains thus need to become bilingual (Hunsinger 1995). They need to learn the language of the empirical, but also hold on to, and teach people, the language of spirituality. At a minimum, spirituality has to do with issues of meaning, purpose, hope, love and for some people God. This is not the natural language of healthcare institutions. It is, however, the natural language of those who are suffering and the natural language of those who have been spiritually formed. One of the key things that chaplaincy brings to the table of healthcare delivery is engagement with a form of language that is often missing from professional practices but is central to human experience. In a context which demands empirical evidence based on the methodologies of science and the philosophy of empiricism, chaplaincy is called to reclaim the significance of the 'hidden' dimensions of the healing process as they are revealed in such things as narrative and human intuition. Much of what chaplains do relates to listening to and telling stories. Stories reveal a form of knowledge that is not only grasped with the mind but also with the heart. Stories demand interpretation, intuition and imagination – all gifts which are fundamental to chaplaincy when chaplains are practising well. In their day-to-day encounters with human pain, suffering and joy, chaplains struggle to understand the human spirit and to translate that into understandable forms of spiritual practice (Macritchie 2001), which can enhance the healing process within healthcare systems. They are called to reclaim the significance of intuition and empathetic imagination as legitimate dimensions of professional practice; intuition which reaches into the depths of the experience of suffering people not to *explain* their illness, but to try passionately to *understand* the meaning of what people are going through and to draw on the spiritual traditions to enable forms of deep healing which include, but are not defined by, particular religions. Such a practice of intuitive, narrative-based chaplaincy, when it is embodied and worked out, may offer a beginning point for the establishment of an identity of chaplaincy that retains its integrity without losing its relevance (Greenhalgh 1999). But chaplains need to be sure and confident of who they are and how they fit in before they can effectively challenge *anything*.

Conclusion: catalytic chaplaincy

Chaplaincy acts as a catalyst which has the potential to transform the way in which we deliver healthcare. A catalyst changes things not so much by what it *does* as by what it *is*. A catalyst changes things only by being itself. If a catalyst becomes something other than itself, it cannot function and there can be no change. That is why the questions surrounding the professional identity of chaplains that I have highlighted in this chapter are of such importance. Chaplains can only transform healthcare practices if they are certain of who they are and are confident enough to act accordingly. If chaplains are unsure about who and what they are, or unclear about the uniqueness and specific value that they bring to healthcare practices, nothing will change, and they may well find themselves swallowed up by lesser versions of themselves.

The suggestion that chaplains are catalysts for transformative healthcare practices is crucial. I hope that as people pick up on, reject and develop the questions and suggestions that I have made in this chapter, we can begin a dialogue that will take seriously an issue which has vital implications for chaplaincy now and in the future. The stakes are too high for us not to take the time now to reflect on, and for, the future.

Acknowledgements

Dr Alison Elliot is the associate director of the Centre for Theology and Public Issues at the University of Edinburgh. Professor Mark Cobb is clinical director of Therapeutics and Palliative Care at the Sheffield University Teaching Hospitals NHS Trust.

References

Barclay, E. (2003) 'Shaping Chaplaincy.' *Chaplaincy for Tomorrow Conference*, March 2003. Edinburgh: Church of Scotland, National Mission.

Bondi, L., Carr, D., Clark, C. and Clegg, C. (eds) (2011) *Towards Professional Wisdom*. London: Routledge.

Cambridge Dictionary. Accessed on 02/01/2019 at http://dictionary.cambridge.org.

Greenhalgh, T. (1999) 'Narrative based medicine in an evidence-based world.' *British Medical Journal 318*, 323–325.

Hamburgh, R. (2017) 'Are hospital chaplains a waste of NHS money?' *The Guardian*, 4 April 2017. Accessed on 05/07/2019 at www.theguardian.com/healthcare-network/2017/apr/04/hospital-chaplains-nhs-waste-taxpayers-money.

Hay, D. (2006) *Something There: The Biology of the Human Spirit*. London: Darton, Longman and Todd.

Hunsinger, D. van D. (1995) *Theology and Pastoral Counseling: A New Interdisciplinary Approach*. Grand Rapids: Eerdmans.

Lichter, D.A. (2013) 'Studies show spiritual care linked to better health outcomes.' *Health Progress 94*, 2, 62–66.

Macritchie, I. (2001) 'The chaplain as translator.' *Journal of Religion and Health 40*, 1, 205–211.

Paterson, M. and Clegg, C. (2013) *Education, Training & Formation for Healthcare Chaplains: Report of an NHS Review*. Edinburgh: NHS Education for Scotland.

Raffay, J., Wood, E. and Todd, A. (2016) 'Service user views of spiritual and pastoral care (chaplaincy) in NHS mental health services: a co-produced constructivist grounded theory investigation.' *BMC Psychiatry 16*, 20.

Snowden, A. and Telfer, I. (2017) 'Patient reported outcome measure of spiritual care as delivered by chaplains.' *Journal of Health Care Chaplaincy 23*, 4, 131–155.

Timmins, F., Caldeira, S., Murphy, M., Pujol, N. *et al.* (2018) 'The role of the healthcare chaplain: a literature review.' *Journal of Health Care Chaplaincy 243*, 87–106.

Part 4

Researching Chaplaincy
What Kind of Evidence Base Do Chaplains Actually Need?

'I would argue that the paradigm for professional chaplaincy for the first part of the twenty-first century is marked by efforts to be outcome oriented and evidence based.' So writes George Fitchett in Chapter 12.

A key component in enabling chaplaincy to become increasingly recognised as a profession within healthcare is the increased interest in, and performance of, research by chaplains. Also of importance is the developing understanding of the significance of such activity by chaplains. Such expanding activity and awareness are, we feel, slowly fostering pride in, and ownership of, research by the chaplaincy community. This is part of its gradual growing confidence as a healthcare profession. However, healthily, any such major developments within a professional discipline are subject to question and discussion. As highlighted in the Introduction, the debate about chaplaincy as an evidence-based profession is a key thread which weaves itself throughout this book. Other contributors, such as Steve Nolan, George F Handzo, Mark Stobert and Julian Raffay, explore questions about what sort of evidence base is required, who decides this and to what degree evidence-based practice is person centred.

Further exploration of why growing a relevant evidence base and research literacy is of significance to chaplaincy, as well as to those to whom chaplains relate within healthcare systems and beyond, is the focus of this section. Just as importantly, how chaplaincy research can be advanced, in what direction and by whom is discussed.

Part 4 also includes the story of the collaborative development of work aimed to bring together research, research education and an outcomes-orientated approach to chaplaincy. Emerging out of strategic political and pragmatic expediency, its iterative development has enabled much shared learning.

Chapter 12

Advancing Research in Healthcare Chaplaincy

Why, How, Who?

George Fitchett

Introduction

Leaders in healthcare chaplaincy and interested colleagues have recognized the importance of research for the profession since the later part of the twentieth century (Gleason 2004; McSherry 1987; VandeCreek 1988; VandeCreek and Lucas 1993). Despite this encouragement, during this period efforts to conduct research about chaplaincy were limited and sporadic (Berg 1994; O'Connor and Meakes 1998; VandeCreek, Ayres and Bassham 1995). At the same time, colleagues in other professions, such as nursing, medicine and psychology, became increasingly involved in research about religion and health (Larson, Sawyers and McCullough 1997; Pargament 1997). This led Larry VandeCreek (1998), a leader in chaplaincy research in the US, to express concern that chaplaincy was being left out and was in danger of becoming 'an absent profession'. In contrast to VandeCreek's prediction, the twenty-first century has seen an increase in research by and about healthcare chaplaincy. In fact, by 2008 there had been a sufficient quantity of research that a major review was published (Mowat 2008), and other reviews have followed (Fitchett 2017; Jankowski, Handzo and Flannelly 2011; Kalish 2012; Pesut *et al.* 2016; Proserpio, Piccinelli and Clerici 2011; Spiritual Care Victoria 2015).

In his analysis of changing paradigms in professional chaplaincy, Gleason (1998) describes how chaplaincy in the middle of the twentieth century was shaped by the Rogerian model of client-centred counselling. According to Gleason, by the beginning of the twenty-first century this paradigm was being replaced by a paradigm of pastoral care as a response to individual need. With the perspective offered by the years since Gleason's article, I would argue that the paradigm for professional chaplaincy for the first part of the twenty-first century is marked by efforts to be outcome oriented and evidence based. Art Lucas (2001) provided one of the first arguments for chaplains to develop care plans that would facilitate specific outcomes for their patients. Peery (2012) has offered a further description of this outcome-oriented approach to chaplaincy. A Statement by the European Network of Health Care Chaplaincy (ENHCC 2014) called for the promotion of 'research as an integral part of chaplaincy activity'. They further noted, 'This research must measure "outcomes" rather than "processes"' (ENHCC 2014). An international team of chaplaincy leaders emphasized the importance of outcomes by warning, 'If we do not develop, implement, and document these outcomes, there is a real danger that the profession may become redundant' (Handzo *et al.* 2014, p.47).

The inclusion of a standard about research (Standard 12) in the Standards of Practice of the US Association of Professional Chaplains (APC 2015) reflects the profession's recognition of the importance of research for its future. The Standard states, 'The chaplain practices evidence-based care including on-going evaluation of new practices, and when appropriate, contributes to or conducts research' (APC 2015). A similar commitment to evidence-based spiritual care can be seen in chaplaincy in the UK's National Health Service (Folland 2006; Speck 2005).

Several studies indicate there is broad support among chaplains for this paradigm shift. A study of 773 US healthcare chaplains working in the military, in Veterans Affairs (VA) hospitals and in civilian settings found that chaplains from all three contexts strongly endorsed an evidence-based approach to chaplaincy (Fitchett *et al.* 2014). Another survey of over 2000 chaplains from 23 countries suggests that these attitudes are not limited to chaplains in the US (Snowden *et al.* 2016). Over 80% of the respondents thought research was definitely important and nearly 70% thought chaplains should definitely be research literate.

In this chapter I share my views about the importance of research for the profession of healthcare chaplaincy. I also describe goals for future research and approaches to achieving them, including the different roles which chaplains and their research partners should play.

Why is chaplaincy research important?

There are two reasons why chaplains should embrace a research-informed or evidence-based approach to our work (Handzo *et al.* 2014). The first is that research provides a way to evaluate and improve the quality of our care. It helps us answer the question 'How do we know the care we are providing is the best care that can be offered?' In the first article to use the term 'evidence-based pastoral care', Canadian chaplains and researchers Tom O'Connor and Elizabeth Meakes (O'Connor and Meakes 1998, p.367) made the case for evidence-based chaplaincy in saying, 'Evidence from research needs to inform our pastoral care. To remove the evidence from pastoral care can create a ministry that is ineffective or possibly even harmful.' Some chaplains and those in other professions developing evidence-based approaches to their practice are uncomfortable with the idea of evidence-based practice because they believe that it requires a simple-minded application of standardized interventions. This is a misconception. Standard definitions of evidence-based practice, such as that of the American Psychological Association, note that it consists of three things: 'The integration of the best available research with clinical expertise in the context of patient characteristics, culture, and preferences' (APA Presidential Task Force on Evidence-Based Practice 2006, p.273).

The second reason for adopting a research-informed approach to practice is that it helps us communicate what we do and the benefits associated with our care. This is reflected in the 2014 ENHCC statement 'Sharing research findings will also inform healthcare providers and faith communities of the role and importance of chaplaincy and thus promote chaplaincy services'. Chaplains and the services they provide are not widely understood by the public, by the healthcare colleagues with whom we work or by the managers who make decisions about healthcare resources. Research is an important way to communicate about spiritual needs among the patients we serve, about the care we provide to address those needs and about the outcomes associated with that care. Using research to communicate about these things is especially important when we are addressing healthcare colleagues and decision-makers.

It is also noteworthy that this emphasis on research reflects, at least in part, the increasingly evidence-based contexts in which healthcare chaplains work. From the 1920s – when the profession of chaplaincy first started to emerge – to the present, healthcare organizations have become more complex, bureaucratic and resource constrained (Starr 1982). Inpatient stays are shorter, more care is provided on an outpatient basis and acuity is greater. In these contexts, healthcare colleagues across disciplines have struggled to identify empirically based standards of care. These organizational realities are shaping our commitment to research and the increasing pressure we feel to ground our practice in an evidence base (Cadge 2018).

How do we advance chaplaincy research?

While research about chaplaincy is growing, and there is enough that review articles are becoming important, the work is still in its early stages and it is useful to think about directions for our future research efforts. Several authors have published articles about the next steps for chaplaincy research (Damen, Delaney and Fitchett 2018; Nolan 2015; Weaver, Flannelly and Liu 2008). Suggestions for the next steps are also found in several of the reviews of chaplaincy research (Jankowski *et al.* 2011; Mowat 2008). In addition, in the palliative care context, reports on the state of the science of spirituality and palliative care research have been published (Balboni *et al.* 2017; Steinhauser *et al.* 2017), as have the results of an international survey of palliative care practitioners about priorities for research about spiritual care in palliative care (Selman *et al.* 2014).

It is understandable that when we consider the next steps in chaplaincy research, we imagine they should be like the randomized clinical trials (RCTs) we read about for medical interventions. In fact, two RCTs of chaplaincy care have been reported. In one study 50 patients with chronic obstructive pulmonary disease (COPD) were randomized to a daily chaplain visit or to usual care, which in this hospital was *no* chaplain visit (Iler, Obenshain and Camac 2001). Compared with those who did not receive chaplain visits, patients who did receive visits had a greater decrease in anxiety, shorter length of stay and higher ratings of satisfaction. In the second study 170 patients who received coronary artery bypass graft (CABG) surgery were randomized to receive chaplain visits or not (Bay *et al.* 2008). Outcomes were assessed 1 month and 6 months post-surgery. There were no differences between the two groups for changes in depression or anxiety. At 6-month follow-up, the patients who received chaplain visits had higher scores on positive religious coping and lower scores on negative religious coping.

As interesting as these two studies are, I think they skipped important steps that are necessary for developing and testing interventions (Czajkowski *et al.* 2015). Here I want to suggest a programme of research that can inform the development of spiritual care interventions designed to improve outcomes for patients and their families. The steps I describe are derived from recommendations for developing research about spiritual care in paediatrics by Feudtner and colleagues (2003). The first step is to understand the religious and spiritual (R/S) needs and resources of patients and families, to describe the ways they use R/S to cope with illness, injury and finitude. Just as effective spiritual care is built upon a sound spiritual assessment, research about spiritual care should be built upon knowledge about patients' and families' R/S needs, resources and coping. Qualitative research using interviews with a small number of patients with similar conditions can play an important role here. Examples of this work include studies of patients with advanced cancer or heart failure (Grant *et al.* 2004; Murray *et al.* 2004), a study of African-American patients with diabetes (Polzer and Miles 2007) and a study of adolescents and young adults receiving haemopoietic stem cell transplantation (Ragsdale *et al.* 2014). This is also a place where surveys can be used to learn about the R/S resources, needs and coping of people in specific clinical situations. Many such studies have been conducted including studies of adult and adolescent patients receiving psychiatric care (Fitchett, Burton and Sivan 1997; Grossoehme, Cotton and Leonard 2007). Other examples include investigations about cancer patients (Alcorn *et al.* 2010), older adults in long-term care (Daaleman *et al.* 2008) and parents of children who died in the ICU (Meert, Thurston and Briller 2005). This is also a place where case studies can be very informative (Fitchett 2011; Fitchett and Nolan 2015).

While a body of research has examined the R/S resources, needs and coping of people facing specific clinical situations, there is room for additional work at this basic level. For example, there are many conditions that have not been examined, and there is a need for studies of key subgroups of people with those conditions: young and old, men and women, racial/ethnic subgroups, those with low and high distress and people who are religious as well as those who are spiritual but not religious. In addition, few studies have followed patients, or their families, over time to describe the trajectory of R/S coping with illness. Examining these trajectories may disclose points of vulnerability where chaplains' spiritual care may be especially important. We also need critical reviews of the existing research about patients' R/S resources, needs and coping to bring into focus what has been well established based on high-quality research and where additional research is needed.

The next step is to synthesize this descriptive research into theories about the role of R/S in coping with illness. Figure 12.1 shows a model my colleagues and I developed to describe the role of R/S in coping with serious illness (Murphy, Fitchett and Canada 2008). The model is based on the stress and coping model of Lazarus and Folkman (1984) and Pargament's (1997) work on religious coping. The model emphasizes four important elements in using R/S to cope with serious illness: the process of appraisal; the personal and environmental resources that people bring to coping; the R/S coping activities (e.g. prayer) that are employed and their focus (problem solving, emotion focused); and the outcomes of R/S coping.

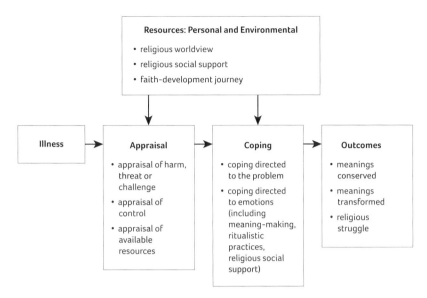

Figure 12.1 A model of religious coping with serious illness
(From Murphy, Fitchett and Canada 2008, p.195)

Another example of model building is the work of chaplain and researcher Daniel H Grossoehme and colleagues who used interviews with parents of children with cystic fibrosis to develop a model of the role of religion in the parents' coping with this difficult situation (Grossoehme *et al.* 2010). A different model is described by chaplain Steven Spidell (2014) who, using the work of George Bonanno and others, suggests a model for spiritual care focused on resilience.

After a model or theory has been developed, the next step is to develop and test interventions based on that model. This part of the research process has several critical components. One component is to specify the outcome that is the target of the intervention. As noted earlier, an outcome-oriented approach to chaplaincy care is relatively new. Chaplaincy training has not helped us learn to identify outcomes that are benefited by our care. A team of Scottish chaplains and researchers has offered a helpful list of outcomes associated with chaplains' care (Figure 12.2; Snowden *et al.* 2013).

Some chaplaincy research may focus on outcomes aligned with the mission of the institutions in which we work, for example patient satisfaction scores, which in the US are now a consideration in reimbursement. This points to the importance of replicating and extending the finding that chaplain visits are associated with higher satisfaction scores (Marin *et al.* 2015). As mentioned earlier, Iler and colleagues (2001) examined the impact of chaplain care on the anxiety of patients being treated for COPD. Anxiety is a common and distressing symptom for these patients, so the finding of a positive impact of chaplain care on their anxiety is important.

Figure 12.2 Outcomes associated with chaplain care
(From Snowden *et al.* 2013, p.4)

There is growing evidence of the painful and harmful effects of R/S struggle (e.g. feeling abandoned or punished by God). These harmful effects include poorer quality of life, greater depression, greater functional limitations and possibly increased risk of death (Fitchett *et al.* 2004; Pargament *et al.* 2001, 2004; Sherman *et al.* 2009). This evidence supports the choice of negative religious coping, as an important outcome for the RCT with the CABG patients, by Bay and colleagues (2008). A recent study found that helping patients and families with decisions about goals of care was a common activity for chaplains working in palliative care (Jeuland *et al.* 2017). Identifying the extent to which chaplains help patients and families make these difficult decisions in light of their beliefs and values is another important outcome to consider for chaplaincy research.

Related to decisions about intervention outcomes are decisions about the participants who are the target of the intervention. As the resilience research shows, many people cope well with potentially traumatic events. Interventions that include a large number of such people are unlikely to show an effect. The overall low levels of anxiety and depression in the participants in the CABG study (Bay *et al.* 2008) may be one of the reasons those investigators found no effects of the chaplains' visits on patients' anxiety and depression. Repeating that study but focusing it on patients with moderate or high levels of anxiety, depression or R/S struggle might produce very different results.

The next component of research about chaplain interventions is developing and testing the intervention. Because chaplains' training focuses so narrowly on providing empathic interpersonal support, on being present, we have limited vocabulary for our interventions. This is reflected in the report by Iler and colleagues (2001) of what they did with the COPD patients they visited. (They report that they made daily visits to them.) Beyond that, we do not know much about what occurred in those visits. Observing this, I have argued for the need for case studies that would include detailed descriptions of chaplains' interventions (Fitchett 2011). Nearly 30 case studies have since been published and additional cases are being prepared for publication (Cooper 2011; Fitchett and Nolan 2015, 2017, 2018; King 2012; Risk 2013). These cases can provide one source of information to describe chaplains' interventions. In addition, a comprehensive, evidence-based description of chaplain activities has been published and offers another resource for identifying chaplain interventions (Massey *et al.* 2015).

Chaplain and researcher Katherine Piderman has developed *Hear My Voice*, a spiritual life review intervention designed to promote spiritual wellbeing and quality of life for patients facing serious progressive illness such as brain cancer. The intervention and reports of pilot studies based on it have been published in a series of papers (Piderman *et al.* 2015, 2017a,b). Testing interventions begins, as Piderman and colleagues have done, with small single-group pilot studies, the aim of which is to determine the feasibility and acceptability of the intervention. The small samples in pilot studies generally preclude finding a statistically significant effect of the intervention on the main study outcomes; however, they provide an initial estimate of the effect of the intervention that will be needed if the results from the pilot study are positive and there is evidence that a larger trial of the efficacy of the intervention is warranted.

To review the steps of the research process I have outlined here, I want to point to the work of palliative care researcher Karen Steinhauser and her colleagues. To understand the needs of patients and families with advanced illness, they began with focus groups in which they asked them for their views of a good death (Steinhauser *et al.* 2000b, 2001). Information from the focus groups was used to build surveys in which large samples of patients with advanced illness and families who had recently lost a loved one were asked about their views of a good death (Steinhauser *et al.* 2000a). This and other work led to developing outcome measures to assess patient and family quality of life at the end of life (Steinhauser *et al.* 2002, 2004). Next the team developed interventions to improve quality of life at the end of life for both patients and families, and they tested the feasibility and acceptability of these interventions in small pilot studies (Steinhauser *et al.* 2016). The Caregiver Outlook intervention was delivered by a chaplain. The pilot studies of both interventions showed they were feasible and acceptable, so the next step for this team will be larger studies of their effectiveness.

We can see from this example that developing a programme of research leading to an intervention is a long and complicated process. Chaplains are just beginning to develop the commitment to evidence-based practice and the training in research that are necessary to carry out such sustained research. As we develop evidence-based interventions, we need to remember that work is also necessary to disseminate them. These efforts must focus both on the training of new chaplains and the professional development of practising chaplains. There are other important areas for chaplaincy research in addition to developing evidence-based interventions. Here I will describe research about what chaplains do, especially research about spiritual assessment, spiritual screening and the documentation of chaplaincy care. I will also consider the implications of this research for identifying the competencies and education of professional chaplains.

In the US, for most health professions there are standard procedures and procedure codes that allow for billing. These codes are also essential for research about the delivery and utilization of services across practitioners, institutions and healthcare systems. No similar uniformly accepted descriptions exist for the services provided by healthcare chaplaincy. There have been a few reports of efforts to describe what chaplains do (Gibbons, Retsas and Pinikahaha 1999; Kinnard and McSherry 1998). Colleagues in Australia have developed descriptions of chaplain activities that are consistent with the World Health Organization's International Classification of Diseases (ICD) format (Carey and Cohen 2015). The *Chaplain Taxonomy* (Massey *et al.* 2015) represents the most comprehensive effort to describe what chaplains do. The development of the taxonomy included a literature review, retrospective chart review, focus groups, self-observation, experience sampling, concept mapping and reliability testing. The current published version includes 100 activities representing intended effects, methods and interventions. Further research to revise and improve the taxonomy has been conducted (Nash *et al.* 2018) and is encouraged.

Spiritual assessment is one of the most important activities performed by professional chaplains. Unfortunately, there is almost no research to support the current published models for spiritual assessment (Fitchett 2012). In addition, there is some evidence that many chaplains are unfamiliar with these models and prefer to employ a locally developed one (O'Connor *et al.* 2005). Developing evidence-based models for spiritual assessment is one of the most pressing areas for spiritual care research. An important exception to the limitations in this area is the work of a Swiss team that developed the Spiritual Distress Assessment Tool (SDAT) for use with geriatric rehabilitation patients. Their work began with a review of existing tools for describing spiritual needs (Monod *et al.* 2011) and conceptualizing five central spiritual needs of geriatric rehabilitation patients (Monod *et al.* 2010b). Chaplains using the SDAT conduct an interview with a patient and then score the intensity of unmet spiritual need for each of the five areas (Monod *et al.* 2010a). The team has conducted tests of the validity and reliability of these scores and reported acceptable results (Monod *et al.* 2012). Their work represents an important milestone in the development of an evidence-based, condition-specific, quantifiable model of spiritual assessment that deserves replication.

Determining who is experiencing R/S need and should be referred to a professional chaplain is another pressing area for spiritual care research. Valid and reliable methods to screen for potential R/S need can help guide referrals by professional colleagues and help chaplains prioritize deployment of their limited resources. There are a number of protocols for spiritual screening but limited research about their validity and reliability (Mako, Galek and Poppito 2006; Steinhauser *et al.* 2006). The RUSH protocol is a popular approach to spiritual screening (Fitchett and Risk 2009), but recent research suggests problems with it, including less than desirable sensitivity, that is, the inability to correctly identify those who are experiencing R/S struggle (Fitchett, Murphy and King 2017). King and colleagues (2017) recently examined the reliability of six approaches to screening for R/S distress. They found that using two items together ('Do you struggle with the loss of meaning and joy in your life?' and 'Do you currently have what you would describe as religious or spiritual struggles?') yielded acceptable net sensitivity of 82%, although net specificity (the ability to correctly detect those who are not experiencing R/S struggle) remained problematic at 50%. This work demonstrates that rigorous research about R/S screening tools is possible and provides a foundation for continuing research in this area.

The spread of electronic medical records (EMR) in healthcare and the invitations to chaplaincy departments to design templates to record their work has given rise to conversations among chaplains about the purposes that should be served by their documentation. Chaplain documentation in the EMR allows multiple members of a chaplaincy department to provide coordinated care to a given patient and/or family. It provides evidence (documentation) about whether chaplain care has been offered or provided, including whether specific services (e.g. sacraments) have been provided or specific conversations or tasks have been completed (e.g. discussion about treatment preferences, completion of Power of Attorney forms). Healthcare colleagues may rely on the chaplains' documentation of these activities, but little is known about whether they consult chaplain chart notes and what information they find helpful. Some research has relied on evidence of chaplain care in the EMR to examine utilization of chaplains (Choi, Curlin and Cox 2015) and the effect of chaplain care on patient and family satisfaction (Marin *et al.* 2015; Wall *et al.* 2007). Two studies have examined the narrative notes written in the EMR by chaplains working in the ICUs of academic medical centres (Johnson *et al.* 2016; Lee, Curlin and Choi 2016). Research about chaplain documentation is just beginning and is an important area for future work.

All of the areas for research that I have described – developing evidence-based interventions, using a standardized taxonomy to describe chaplain activities, and developing and using evidence-based spiritual assessments – have implications for the competencies expected of professional chaplains and for chaplaincy education. Identifying the competencies expected of professional chaplains and determining whether chaplaincy training programmes are helping people develop these competencies are also areas where the research is very limited. Cooper and colleagues (2010) have published one of the few reports of research about identifying competencies for chaplains, in this case competencies for chaplains working in palliative care. Using a modified Developing a Curriculum process, this team identified 14 major areas of responsibility and 81 major tasks for chaplains working in hospice and palliative care. My colleagues and I (Fitchett *et al.* 2015) conducted a survey in which we examined utilization of certification competencies in the chaplaincy training curricula of 26 clinical pastoral education (CPE) programmes in the US. We found that the curricula of 38% of these programmes had substantive engagement with the certification competencies, 38% only introduced students to the competencies and 23% of the programmes had no engagement with them.

Several studies have reported on the use of patient simulation in chaplain education (Kraus and Div 2008). For example, Tartaglia and Dodd-McCue (2010) reported on the use of a standardized patient interview at the beginning and end of training for students in their first unit of CPE. Students responded positively to being able to view and discuss the videotaped interviews. The faculty appreciated the opportunity for direct observation of student functioning and the interview evaluation form, which allowed rating of the students' interview behaviours. Identifying competencies for professional chaplains and identifying what training practices are most effective in helping students achieve those competencies are important areas for future research.

Who is needed to advance chaplaincy research?

Who needs to be involved in the substantial work to advance chaplaincy research that I have described? The first point to emphasize in answering this question is that not every chaplain needs to be a chaplain *and* researcher; however, it is important for every chaplain to be research literate so that they can critically review emerging research and integrate it into their professional practice as appropriate. Beyond this there may be a group of chaplains who wish to develop more advanced research literacy that will enable them to direct or participate in departmental quality-improvement projects or to collaborate in research being led by others. Furthering chaplaincy research will also require chaplains with advanced research education, which will equip them to design and lead more sophisticated research efforts. These three levels of chaplain involvement in research are similar to those described in the APC Research Standard (2015) and the levels of involvement in the UK Standard (Speck 2005).

A group of chaplains with advanced research education are essential, but not sufficient, for advancing chaplaincy research. This work will also require departments, institutions and healthcare systems that see the value of chaplaincy research, and are willing to commit the resources, to support this work. Finding sponsors with an interest in underwriting centres that can develop and sustain programmes of chaplaincy-related research is an important way for institutions and healthcare systems to support chaplaincy research. Advancing chaplaincy research will also require collaborators. Even modest quality-improvement projects or investigations often require a research team whose members bring the diverse expertise needed to successfully plan and carry out the project. For more complex projects with a larger scope, research collaborators are essential. This is especially the case for developing projects that can be successful in rigorous and highly competitive grant-review processes such as those of the National Institutes for Health in the US.

Conclusion

Research about chaplaincy is developing quickly with contributors from around the world (Fitchett, White and Lyndes 2018). However, as I have shown in this chapter, research in our field is at an early stage, and much time and effort will be required to develop an evidence-based approach to our work. There are interesting and important opportunities to contribute to chaplaincy research at different levels: small, medium and large. Chaplains with a modest level of research literacy can partner with interested colleagues to replicate a small survey or other project in their local setting, to conduct a quality-improvement project (e.g. Gomez-Castillo *et al.* 2015) or to contribute to the growing body of chaplain case studies. Other chaplains may find the partners and resources to carry out a survey-based project (e.g. Jeuland *et al.* 2017) or a series of qualitative interviews that shed light on how patients with a specific condition use R/S to cope with their illness (e.g. Ragsdale *et al.* 2014). Finally, some chaplains will have the opportunity to partner with sophisticated major research efforts and address substantial questions about spiritual care and its impact (e.g. Johnson *et al.* 2014; Monod *et al.* 2012). The number of chaplains and collaborators who are interested in advancing this research is growing, and it is an exciting time to be involved in chaplaincy research. As we engage in this work it is important to remember that the main reason for our efforts is to advance the quality of our spiritual care for patients and families. In addition, research plays an important role in communicating what we do, and its value, to our healthcare colleagues and managers who must make decisions about healthcare resources.

Acknowledgements

I am grateful for Wendy Cadge's comments on a previous version of this chapter and for Annelieke Damen's assistance in the preparation of the manuscript.

References

Alcorn, S.R., Balboni, M.J., Prigerson, H.G., Reynolds, A. *et al.* (2010) '"If God wanted me yesterday, I wouldn't be here today": religious and spiritual themes in patients' experiences of advanced cancer.' *Journal of Palliative Medicine* 13, 5, 581–588.

APA Presidential Task Force on Evidence-Based Practice (2006) 'Evidence-based practice in psychology.' *American Psychologist* 61, 4, 271–285.

Association of Professional Chaplains (APC) (2015) *Standards of Practice for Professional Chaplains.* Accessed on 29/03/2017 at www.professionalchaplains.org/content. asp?pl=198&contentid=198.

Balboni, T.A., Fitchett, G., Handzo, G.F., Johnson, K.S. *et al.* (2017) 'State of the science of spirituality and palliative care research. Part II: Screening, assessment, and interventions.' *Journal of Pain and Symptom Management* 54, 3, 441–453.

Bay, P.S., Beckman, D., Trippi, J., Gunderman, R. *et al.* (2008) 'The effect of pastoral care services on anxiety, depression, hope, religious coping, and religious problem-solving styles: a randomized controlled study.' *Journal of Religion and Health* 47, 1, 57–69.

Berg, G.E. (1994) 'The use of the computer as a tool for assessment and research in pastoral care.' *Journal of Health Care Chaplaincy* 6, 1, 11–25.

Cadge, W. (2018) 'Healthcare chaplaincy as a companion profession: historical developments.' *Journal of Health Care Chaplaincy,* 13 August, 1–16. [Epub ahead of print.] doi: 10.1080/08854726.2018.1463617.

Carey, L.B. and Cohen, J. (2015) 'The utility of the WHO ICD-10-AM pastoral intervention codings within religious, pastoral and spiritual care research.' *Journal of Religion and Health* 54, 5, 1772–1787.

Choi, P.J., Curlin, F.A. and Cox, C.E. (2015) '"The patient is dying, please call the chaplain": the activities of chaplains in one medical center's intensive care units.' *Journal of Pain and Symptom Management 50*, 4, 501–506.

Cooper, D., Aherns, M. and Pereira, J. (2010) 'The competencies required by professional hospice palliative care spiritual care providers.' *Journal of Palliative Medicine 13*, 7, 869–875.

Cooper, R.S. (2011) 'Case study of a chaplain's spiritual care for a patient with advanced metastatic breast cancer.' *Journal of Health Care Chaplaincy 17*, 1, 19–37.

Czajkowski, S.M., Powell, L.H., Adler, N., Naar-King, S. *et al.* (2015) 'From ideas to efficacy: the ORBIT model for developing behavioral treatments for chronic diseases.' *Health Psychology 34*, 10, 971–982.

Daaleman, T.P., Williams, C.S., Hamilton, V.L. and Zimmerman, S. (2008) 'Spiritual care at the end of life in long-term care.' *Medical Care 46*, 1, 85–91.

Damen, A., Delaney, A. and Fitchett, G. (2018) 'Research priorities for healthcare chaplaincy: views of U.S. chaplains.' *Journal of Health Care Chaplaincy 24*, 2, 57–66.

European Network of Health Care Chaplaincy (2014) *The European Network of Health Care Chaplaincy Statement: Healthcare Chaplaincy in the Midst of Transition.* Accessed on 21/03/2017 at http://enhcc.eu/2014_salzburg_statement.pdf.

Feudtner, C., Haney, J. and Dimmers, M.A. (2003) 'Spiritual care needs of hospitalized children and their families: a national survey of pastoral care providers' perceptions.' *Pediatrics 111*, 1, 67–72.

Fitchett, G. (2011) 'Making our case(s).' *Journal of Health Care Chaplaincy 17*, 1–18.

Fitchett, G. (2012) 'Next Steps for Spiritual Assessment in Health Care.' In M. Cobb, C. Puchalski and B. Rumbold (eds) *Oxford Textbook of Spirituality in Healthcare.* Oxford: Oxford University Press.

Fitchett, G. (2017) 'Recent progress in chaplaincy-related research.' *Journal of Pastoral Care and Counseling 71*, 3, 163–175.

Fitchett, G. and Nolan, S. (eds) (2015) *Spiritual Care in Practice: Case Studies in Healthcare Chaplaincy.* London: Jessica Kingsley Publishers.

Fitchett, G. and Nolan, S. (2017) 'Chaplain case study research.' *Health and Social Care Chaplaincy 5*, 2, 167–173.

Fitchett, G. and Nolan, S. (eds) (2018) *Case Studies in Spiritual Care: Healthcare Chaplaincy Assessments, Interventions and Outcomes.* London: Jessica Kingsley Publishers.

Fitchett, G. and Risk, J. (2009) 'Screening for spiritual struggle.' *Journal of Pastoral Care and Counseling 63*, 1–2, 4.1–12.

Fitchett, G., Burton, L.A. and Sivan, A.B. (1997) 'The religious needs and resources of psychiatric in-patients.' *Journal of Nervous and Mental Disease 185*, 5, 320–326.

Fitchett, G., Murphy, P.E., Kim, J., Gibbons, J.L. *et al.* (2004) 'Religious struggle: prevalence, correlates and mental health risks in diabetic, congestive heart failure, and oncology patients.' *International Journal of Psychiatry in Medicine 34*, 20, 179–196.

Fitchett, G., Nieuwsma, J.A., Bates, M.J., Rhodes, J.E. *et al.* (2014) 'Evidence-based chaplaincy care: attitudes and practices in diverse healthcare chaplain samples.' *Journal of Health Care Chaplaincy 20*, 4, 144–160.

Fitchett, G., Tartaglia, A., Massey, K., Jackson-Jordon, B. *et al.* (2015) 'Education for professional chaplains: Should certification competencies shape curriculum?' *Journal of Health Care Chaplaincy 21*, 4, 151–164.

Fitchett, G., Murphy, P. and King, S.D.W. (2017) 'Examining the validity of the Rush protocol to screen for religious/spiritual struggle.' *Journal of Health Care Chaplaincy 23*, 3, 98–112.

Fitchett, G., White, K.B. and Lyndes, K. (eds) (2018) *Evidence-Based Healthcare Chaplaincy: A Research Reader.* London: Jessica Kingsley Publishers.

Folland, M. (2006) 'Opportunity and conflict: evidence-based practice and the modernization of healthcare chaplaincy.' *Contact 149*, 12–20.

Gibbons, G., Retsas, A. and Pinikahaha, J. (1999) 'Describing what chaplains do in hospitals.' *Journal of Pastoral Care 53*, 2, 201–207.

Gleason, J.J. (1998) 'An emerging paradigm in professional chaplaincy.' *Chaplaincy Today 14*, 9–14.

Gleason, J.J. (2004) 'Pastoral research: past, present, and future.' *Journal of Pastoral Care and Counseling 58*, 4, 295–306.

Gomez-Castillo, B.J., Hirsch, R., Groninger, H., Baker, K. *et al.* (2015) 'Increasing the number of outpatients receiving spiritual assessment: a pain and palliative care service quality improvement project.' *Journal of Pain and Symptom Management 50*, 5, 724–729.

Grant, E., Murray, S.A., Kendall, M., Boyd, K. *et al.* (2004) 'Spiritual issues and needs: perspectives from patients with advanced cancer and nonmalignant disease. A qualitative study.' *Palliative and Supportive Care 2*, 4, 371–378.

Grossoehme, D.H., Cotton, S. and Leonard, A. (2007) 'Spiritual and religious experiences of adolescent psychiatric inpatients versus healthy peers.' *Journal of Pastoral Care and Counseling 61*, 3, 197–204.

Grossoehme, D.H., Ragsdale, J., Wooldridge, J.L., Cotton, S. *et al.* (2010) 'We can handle this: parents' use of religion in the first year following their child's diagnosis with cystic fibrosis.' *Journal of Health Care Chaplaincy 16*, 3–4, 95–108.

Handzo, G.F., Cobb, M., Holmes, C., Kelly, E. *et al.* (2014) 'Outcomes for professional health care chaplaincy: an international call to action.' *Journal of Health Care Chaplaincy 20*, 2, 43–53.

Iler, W.L., Obenshain, D. and Camac, M. (2001) 'The impact of daily visits from chaplains on patients with chronic obstructive pulmonary disease (COPD): a pilot study.' *Chaplaincy Today 17*, 1, 5–11.

Jankowski, K.R., Handzo, G.F. and Flannelly, K.J. (2011) 'Testing the efficacy of chaplaincy care.' *Journal of Health Care Chaplaincy 17*, 3–4, 100–125.

Jeuland, J., Fitchett, G., Schulman-Green, D. and Kapo, J. (2017) 'Chaplains working in palliative care: who they are and what they do.' *Journal of Palliative Medicine 20*, 5, 502–508.

Johnson, J.R., Engelberg, R.A., Nielsen, E.L., Kross, E.K. *et al.* (2014) 'The association of spiritual care providers' activities with family members' satisfaction with care after a death in the ICU.' *Critical Care Medicine 42*, 9, 1991–2000.

Johnson, R., Wirpsa, M.J., Boyken, L., Sakumoto, M. *et al.* (2016) 'Communicating chaplains' care: narrative documentation in a neuroscience-spine intensive care unit.' *Journal of Health Care Chaplaincy 22*, 4, 133–150.

Kalish, N. (2012) 'Evidence-based spiritual care: a literature review.' *Current Opinion in Supportive and Palliative Care 6*, 3, 242–246.

King, S.D. (2012) 'Facing fears and counting blessings: a case study of a chaplain's faithful companioning a cancer patient.' *Journal of Health Care Chaplaincy 18*, 1–22.

King, S.D., Fitchett, G., Murphy, P.E., Pargament, K.I., Harrison, D.A. and Loggers, E.T. (2017) 'Determining best methods to screen for religious/spiritual distress.' *Supportive Care in Cancer 25*, 2, 471–479.

Kinnard, W. and McSherry, E. (1998) 'The development and use of codes for chaplain interventions (procedures and products) in the Veterans Affairs Healthcare System.' *Chaplaincy Today 14*, 14–22.

Kraus, J.K. and Div, M. (2008) 'From reel time to real time: patient simulation for chaplain interns.' *Journal of Pastoral Care and Counseling 62*, 4, 331–336.

Larson, D.B., Sawyers, J.P. and McCullough, M.E. (1997) *Scientific Research on Spirituality and Health: A Consensus Report.* Rockville, MD: National Institute for Healthcare Research.

Lazarus, R.S. and Folkman, S. (1984) *Stress, Appraisal and Coping.* New York, NY: Springer.

Lee, B.M., Curlin, F.A. and Choi, P.J. (2016) 'Documenting presence: a descriptive study of chaplain notes in the intensive care unit.' *Palliative and Supportive Care 20*, 1–7, 190–196.

Lucas, A.M. (2001) 'Introduction to the Discipline for Pastoral Care Giving.' In L. VandeCreek and A.M. Lucas (eds) *The Discipline for Pastoral Care Giving.* Binghamton, NY: The Haworth Pastoral Press.

Mako, C., Galek, M. and Poppito, S.R. (2006) 'Spiritual pain among patients with advanced cancer in palliative care.' *Journal of Palliative Medicine 9*, 5, 1106–1113.

Marin, D.B., Sharma, V., Sosunov, E., Egorova, N. *et al.* (2015) 'Relationship between chaplain visits and patient satisfaction.' *Journal of Health Care Chaplaincy 21*, 1, 14–24.

Massey, K., Barnes, M.J., Villines, D., Goldstein, J.D. *et al.* (2015) 'What do I do? Developing a taxonomy of chaplaincy activities and interventions for spiritual care in intensive care unit palliative care.' *BMC Palliative Care 14*, 10. Accessed on 13/11/2018 at www.advocatehealth.com/chaplaincy-research.

McSherry, E. (1987) 'The need and appropriateness of measurement and research in chaplaincy: its criticalness for patient care and chaplain department survival post-1987.' *Journal of Health Care Chaplaincy 1*, 1, 3–41.

Meert, K.L., Thurston, C.S. and Briller, S.H. (2005) 'The spiritual needs of parents at the time of their child's death in the pediatric intensive care unit and during bereavement: a qualitative study.' *Pediatric Critical Care Medicine 6*, 4, 420–427.

Monod, S., Rochat, E., Büla, C., Jobin, G. *et al.* (2010a) 'The spiritual distress assessment tool: an instrument to assess spiritual distress in hospitalised elderly persons.' *BMC Geriatrics 13*, 10, 88.

Monod, S., Rochat, E., Büla, C. and Spencer, B. (2010b) 'The spiritual needs model: spirituality assessment in the geriatric hospital setting.' *Journal of Religion, Spirituality and Aging 22*, 271–282.

Monod, S., Brennan, M., Rochat, E., Martin, E. *et al.* (2011) 'Instruments measuring spirituality in clinical research: a systematic review.' *Journal of General Internal Medicine 26*, 11, 1345–1357.

Monod, S., Martin, E., Spencer, B. and Rochat, E. (2012) 'Validation of the spiritual distress assessment tool in older hospitalized patients.' *BMC Geriatrics 29*, 12–13.

Mowat, H. (2008) *The Potential for Efficacy of Healthcare Chaplaincy and Spiritual Care Provision in the NHS (UK): A Scoping Review of Recent Research.* Aberdeen, Scotland: Mowat Research Ltd.

Murphy, P.E., Fitchett, G. and Canada, A.L. (2008) 'Adult Spirituality for Persons with Chronic Illness.' In V.B. Carson and H.G. Koenig (eds) *Spiritual Dimensions of Nursing Practice* (revised edition). West Conshohocken, PA: Templeton Foundation Press.

Murray, S.A., Kendall, M., Boyd, K. and Worth, A. (2004) 'Exploring the spiritual needs of people dying of lung cancer or heart failure: a prospective qualitative interview study of patients and their carers.' *Palliative Medicine 18*, 1, 39–45.

Nash, P., Roberts, E., Nash, S., Darby, K. and Parwaz, A.A. (2018) 'Adapting the Advocate Health Care Taxonomy of chaplaincy for a pediatric hospital context: a pilot study.' *Journal of Health Care Chaplaincy*, 27 July, 1–15. [Epub ahead of print.] Accessed on 16/11/2018 at doi.org/10.1080/08854726.2018.1473911.

Nolan, S. (2015) 'Making Spiritual Care Visible: The Developing Agenda and Methodologies for Research in Spiritual Care.' In J. Pye, P. Sedgwick and A. Todd (eds) *Critical Care: Developing Spiritual Care in Healthcare Contexts.* London: Jessica Kingsley Publishers.

O'Connor, T.S. and Meakes, E. (1998) 'Hope in the midst of challenge: evidence-based pastoral care.' *Journal of Pastoral Care 52*, 359–367.

O'Connor, T.S., Meakes, E., O'Neill, K., Penner, C. *et al.* (2005) 'Not well known, used little and needed: Canadian chaplains' experiences of published spiritual assessment tools.' *Journal of Pastoral Care and Counseling 59*, 1–2, 97–107.

Pargament, K.I. (1997) *The Psychology of Religion and Coping: Theory, Research, Practice.* New York, NY: The Guilford Press.

Pargament, K.I., Koenig, H.G., Tarakeshwar, N. and Hahn, J. (2001) 'Religious struggle as a predictor of mortality among medically ill elderly patients: a 2-year longitudinal study.' *Archives of Internal Medicine 161*, 15, 1881–1885.

Pargament, K.I., Koenig, H.G., Tarakeshwar, N. and Hahn, J. (2004) 'Religious coping methods as predictors of psychological, physical and spiritual outcomes among medically ill elderly patients: a two-year longitudinal study.' *Journal of Health Psychology 9*, 6, 713–730.

Peery, B. (2012) 'Outcome Oriented Chaplaincy: Intentional Caring.' In S. Roberts (ed.) *Professional Spiritual and Pastoral Care: A Practical Clergy and Chaplain's Handbook.* Woodstock, VY: SkyLight Paths Publishing.

Pesut, B., Sinclair, S., Fitchett, G., Greig, M. *et al.* (2016) 'Health care chaplaincy: a scoping review of the evidence 2009–2014.' *Journal of Health Care Chaplaincy 22*, 2, 67–84.

Piderman, K.M., Breitkopf, C.R., Jenkins, S.M., Lovejoy, L.A. *et al.* (2015) 'The feasibility and educational value of Hear My Voice, a chaplain-led spiritual life review process for patients with brain cancers and progressive neurologic conditions.' *Journal of Cancer Education 30*, 2, 209–212.

Piderman, K.M., Breitkopf, C.R., Jenkins, S.M., Lapid, M.I. *et al.* (2017a) 'The impact of a spiritual legacy intervention in patients with brain cancers and other neurologic illnesses and their support persons.' *Psycho-oncology 26*, 3, 346–353.

Piderman, K.M., Egginton, J.S., Ingram, C., Dose, A.M. *et al.* (2017b) 'I'm still me: inspiration and instruction from individuals with brain cancer.' *Journal of Health Care Chaplaincy 23*, 1, 15–33.

Polzer, R.L. and Miles, M.S. (2007) 'Spirituality in African Americans with diabetes: self-management through a relationship with God.' *Qualitative Health Research 17*, 176–188.

Proserpio, T., Piccinelli, C. and Clerici, C.A. (2011) 'Pastoral care in hospitals: a literature review.' *Tumori Journal 97*, 5, 666–671.

Ragsdale, J.R., Hegner, M.A., Mueller, M. and Davies, S. (2014) 'Identifying religious and/or spiritual perspectives of adolescents and young adults receiving blood and marrow transplants: a prospective qualitative study.' *Biology of Blood and Marrow Transplantation 20*, 1238–1257.

Risk, J.L. (2013) 'Building a new life: a chaplain's theory based case study of chronic illness.' *Journal of Health Care Chaplaincy 19*, 3, 81–98.

Selman, L., Young, T., Vermandere, M., Stirling, I. *et al.* (2014) 'Research priorities in spiritual care: an international survey of palliative care researchers and clinicians.' *Journal of Pain and Symptom Management 48*, 4, 518–531.

Sherman, A.C., Plante, T.G., Simonton, S., Latif, U. *et al.* (2009) 'Prospective study of religious coping among patients undergoing autologous stem cell transplantation.' *Journal of Behavioral Medicine 32*, 1, 118–128.

Snowden, A., Telfer, I., Kelly, E., Bunniss, S. *et al.* (2013) 'The construction of the Lothian PROM.' *The Scottish Journal of Healthcare Chaplaincy* 16, 3–16.

Snowden, A., Fitchett, G., Grossoehme, D.H., Handzo, G. *et al.* (2016) 'International study of chaplains' attitudes about research.' *Journal of Health Care Chaplaincy* 21, 1–10.

Speck, P. (2005) 'A standard for research in healthcare chaplaincy.' *Journal of Health Care Chaplaincy* 6, 1, 26–40.

Spidell, S. (2014) 'Resilience and professional chaplaincy: a paradigm shift in focus.' *Journal of Health Care Chaplaincy* 20, 1, 16–24.

Spiritual Care Victoria (2015) *Review of Literature June 2015.* Accessed on 16/10/2016 at www. spiritualhealthvictoria.org.au/research.

Starr, P. (1982) *The Social Transformation of American Medicine.* New York, NY: Basic Books.

Steinhauser, K.E., Christakis, N.A., Clipp, E.C., McNeilly, M. *et al.* (2000a) 'Factors considered important at the end of life by patients, family, physicians and other care providers.' *Journal of the American Medical Association* 284, 19, 2476–2482.

Steinhauser, K.E., Clipp, E.C., McNeilly, M., Christakis, N.A. *et al.* (2000b) 'In search of a good death: observations of patients, families, and providers.' *Annals of Internal Medicine* 132, 10, 825–832.

Steinhauser, K.E., Christakis, N.A., Clipp, E.C., McNeilly, M. *et al.* (2001) 'Preparing for the end of life: preferences of patients, families, physicians, and other care providers.' *Journal of Pain and Symptom Management* 22, 3, 727–737.

Steinhauser, K.E., Bosworth, H.B., Clipp, E.C., McNeilly, M. *et al.* (2002) 'Initial assessment of a new instrument to measure quality of life at the end of life.' *Journal of Palliative Medicine* 5, 6, 829–841.

Steinhauser, K.E., Clipp, E.C., Bosworth, H.B., McNeilly, M. *et al.* (2004) 'Measuring quality of life at the end of life: validation of the QUAL-E.' *Palliative and Support Care* 2, 1, 3–14.

Steinhauser, K.E., Voils, C.I., Clipp, E.C., Bosworth, H.B. *et al.* (2006) '"Are you at peace?": one item to probe spiritual concerns at the end of life.' *Archives of Internal Medicine* 166, 1, 101–105.

Steinhauser, K.E., Olsen, A., Johnson, K.S., Sanders, L.L. *et al.* (2016) 'The feasibility and acceptability of a chaplain-led intervention for caregivers of seriously ill patients: a caregiver outlook pilot study.' *Palliative and Support Care* 14, 5, 456–467.

Steinhauser, K.E., Fitchett, G., Handzo, G.F., Johnson, K.S. *et al.* (2017) 'State of the science of spirituality and palliative care research. Part I: Definitions, measurement, and outcomes. *Journal of Pain and Symptom Management* 54, 3, 428–440.

Tartaglia, A. and Dodd-McCue, D. (2010) 'Enhancing objectivity in pastoral education: use of standardized patients in video simulation.' *Journal of Pastoral Care and Counseling* 64, 2, 2.1–10.

VandeCreek, L. (1988) *A Research Primer for Pastoral Care and Counseling.* Decatur, GA: Journal of Pastoral Care Publications.

VandeCreek, L. (1998) 'Professional chaplaincy: An absent profession?' *Journal of Pastoral Care* 53, 4, 417–432.

VandeCreek, L. and Lucas, A. (1993) 'Defining the value of pastoral care services: research strategies related to the patient's coping process.' *The Caregiver Journal* 10, 2, 13–27.

VandeCreek, L., Ayres, S. and Bassham, M. (1995) 'Using INSPIRIT to conduct spiritual assessments.' *Journal of Pastoral Care* 49, 1, 83–89.

Wall, R.J., Engelberg, R.A., Gries, C.J., Glavan, B. *et al.* (2007) 'Spiritual care of families in the intensive care unit.' *Critical Care Medicine* 35, 4, 1084–1090.

Weaver, A.J., Flannelly, K.J. and Liu, C. (2008) 'Chaplaincy research: its value, its quality, and its future.' *Journal of Health Care Chaplaincy* 14, 1, 3–19.

Chapter 13

The Story of the Scottish Patient Reported Outcome Measure

An Example of Innovation, Collaboration and Education in Chaplaincy Research

Austyn Snowden and Iain Telfer

Introduction

This chapter introduces the Scottish Patient Reported Outcome Measure (PROM),[1] an original five-item measure constructed specifically to measure the outcomes of chaplain interventions. It provides an overview of the creation and initial testing of the Scottish PROM. It focuses on its conceptual underpinnings because those are what support all subsequent claims to validity. It also includes a discussion of the value of undertaking practical research from the perspective of a practising healthcare chaplain. We discuss some common misgivings about the project and address them by showing the Scottish PROM to be fit for purpose: it measures the outcomes of spiritual care as delivered by chaplains. Furthermore, we examine the PROM's implications for workforce planners and chaplains, and conclude with a short summary of ongoing research, where the Scottish PROM is, or is about to be, included in studies globally.

Construction of the Scottish PROM

Chaplaincy leaders worldwide recognize that the outcomes of chaplaincy interventions need to be measured in order to provide a stronger evidence base (see also Chapters 7, 9 and 12; Healthcare Chaplaincy Network 2016). In

---

1   The Scottish PROM is copyrighted but free to use with written permission from NHS Education for Scotland (NES).

Scotland, NHS Education for Scotland (NES) commissioned the construction of a spiritual care PROM to generate this evidence.

A PROM is a measure of health, as defined by the patient, in relation to treatment they have received (Wolpert 2014). PROMs are used in health settings around the world to inform planners and clinicians alike about the effectiveness of interventions. The best PROMs are short, easy to understand and important to the group under study (Meadows 2010). They need to be psychometrically valid and reliable, and should ideally measure a unidimensional construct (Fries, Rose and Krishnan 2011). In other words, a PROM should measure what it is supposed to measure, and *only* what it is supposed to measure. To create a PROM from scratch takes years and requires a series of iterative steps (Streiner and Norman 2008). In summary these steps are:

1. theoretical underpinning

2. item development

3. face and content validity

4. reliability

5. dimensionality

6. construct validity.

The most important step in this whole process is the first one: theoretical underpinning; from that, the others follow. The purpose of the Scottish PROM is to measure patient outcomes of chaplaincy interventions. Providing a robust theoretical underpinning of the PROM required a systematic examination, not just of what chaplains do but also the *impact* of what they do.

For this, we turned to the literature. The literature search strategy is detailed in the full report of the first phase of PROM development (Snowden *et al.* 2012). In summary, we systematically reviewed and synthesized the literature. This was an iterative process requiring many cycles of theory building, testing and reviewing, with the aim of elucidating all common chaplain activities and outcomes. The process continued until no new themes emerged. At this point the themes were reviewed for consistency and generalizability. We concluded that despite chaplains undertaking a broad range of activities, there were nevertheless generalizable aspects. Chaplains enabled hope, comfort and understanding to be found, for example. There was wide agreement on these and other key themes in the literature (Figure 13.1).

Figure 13.1 Themes associated with chaplaincy

The key phase in turning these themes into outcome statements was to understand where they fit within the process of chaplaincy. Note how some of them are clearly outcomes, whereas others better describe activities that occur during a meeting with the chaplain. Being 'listened to' is something that happens during an encounter, for example. 'Peace' is an outcome. It was at this point that we realized that we should try to measure both activities and outcomes in order to understand the relationship between the quality of the chaplain encounter and the outcome of it. For example, being authentically listened to is likely to generate a deeper sense of peace than only being cursorily listened to (Agledahl *et al.* 2011).

So, although we were only tasked with developing an outcome measure, we decided during this phase of development to extend our remit because this seemed important. If we could analyse the relationship between how the encounter felt for a patient and the subsequent outcomes of that encounter, then a deeper understanding would emerge of how positive outcomes arise. Furthermore, thinking of chaplaincy as a process is entirely coherent with Mowat and Swinton's (2007) conceptualization of chaplaincy. Identifying and responding to spiritual need is what chaplains do. Some of the themes in Figure 13.1 describe the activity of identifying and responding to need, and should therefore also be measured as:

> an active process of finding people who need spiritual care, identifying the nature of the need and responding to the need through theological reflection and the sharing of spiritual practices. (Mowat and Swinton 2007, p.8)

Consequently, the themes illustrated in Figure 13.1 were categorized into those that represented 'outcomes' of chaplain encounters and those that represented activity during encounters. Figure 13.2 shows the result of this exercise. The themes on the left could all follow the statement 'During intervention(s) with the chaplain I felt [listened to, understood and so forth]', whereas the themes on the right represent outcomes; for example: 'As a consequence of [having my faith and beliefs valued, being understood] I felt [hope, comfort, peace and so forth].'

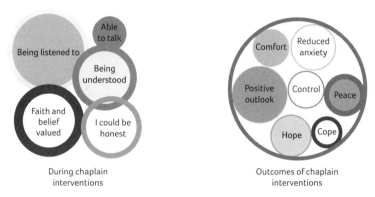

Figure 13.2 Themes divided into whether they describe activity during the chaplain encounter or outcomes of the encounter

Once we had our themes situated within a process of chaplaincy, the next task was to turn the themes into questionnaire items. Over the next 18 months survey items were drafted and redrafted in an iterative series of focus groups and chaplain conferences (Snowden and Telfer 2012). As an example of the kind of changes made, during this time it was felt that being honest with oneself was more important as an outcome for patients rather than an aspect of the chaplaincy intervention, so honesty became an outcome. The first version of the questionnaire was called the Lothian PROM, as NHS Lothian was the geographical health board where initial testing occurred.

The PROM was then tested for face validity (i.e. Does the questionnaire appear to measure what it is meant to measure?) and content validity (i.e. Are the various items of the questionnaire essential for ensuring what is being measured, in this case the intervention of a chaplain?). The pilot study included inpatient acute, paediatric and mental health units (Snowden *et al.* 2012). Results were extremely encouraging as the questionnaire made sense to all who completed it.

Chaplains wrote 'referral records' detailing their view of the patient's needs as part of the recruitment procedure. This meant we had a record from the chaplain against which we could compare the patient response. Free text responses showed us that the chaplains had a very clear understanding of their patients. We had expected this because listening and understanding is core to chaplaincy. What we had not expected was the degree of concordance. Quite often the chaplains and the patients would use identical language to describe a particular problem or encounter (Snowden *et al.* 2013b). This finding merits further study. The degree of coherence between patient and clinician language is likely to be important evidence that the patient was listened to and understood (Snowden and Marland 2012) In using identical language, we hypothesize that chaplains may be unique in this regard. For example, Gray, Wykes and Gournay (2002) found that when nurses and patients discussed important aspects of medicine management, such as side effects, and the relationship between prescriber and patient, each prioritized very different elements, suggesting incoherence and greater potential for misunderstanding between patient and clinician.

We also found in the Lothian PROM study that, regardless of faith or belief, patients obtained equivalent benefit from chaplaincy intervention. We have been keen to probe that relationship further, as it is still often viewed as a source of contention.

Further minor changes were made to the PROM as a consequence of feedback from the pilot study. The current version of the questionnaire, the Scottish PROM (see Figure 13.3), has remained consistent since then. It asks people for their age, gender and whether they self-describe as religious, spiritual, both or neither, as well as four questions about people's experience during their meeting(s) with the chaplain. The PROM items are next: five questions which ask people to describe their state of spiritual health in the previous 2 weeks. Finally, there is a free text box where people can expand on any related issue, important to them.

Age		How would you describe yourself?	
Male	O	Religious	O
Female	O	Spiritual	O
Other	O	Both	O
		Neither	O

During my meeting(s) with the listener I felt…

	None of the time	Rarely	Some of the time	Often	All of the time
I was listened to	O	O	O	O	O
I was able to talk about what was on my mind	O	O	O	O	O
My situation was understood	O	O	O	O	O
My faith/beliefs were valued	O	O	O	O	O

In the last two weeks I have felt:

	None of the time	Rarely	Some of the time	Often	All of the time
I could be honest with myself about how I was really feeling	O	O	O	O	O
Anxious	O	O	O	O	O
I had a positive outlook on my situation	O	O	O	O	O
In control of my life	O	O	O	O	O
A sense of peace	O	O	O	O	O

Thank you. If you want to add any other relevant information, please do so in this text box/overleaf:

Figure 13.3 The Scottish PROM

Other studies using the PROM

The Scottish PROM has subsequently been used in a number of studies and service evaluations globally. It was last used in Scotland to analyse the impact of Community Chaplaincy Listening (CCL), a service offered by chaplains in general practice settings (see Chapter 17). Patients who are referred to

CCL services by family doctors or general practitioners (GPs) have a range of spiritual needs and emotional issues relating to transition and loss.

Results have again been very positive, with the Scottish PROM showing consistency of measurement over time (reliability) and that it is measuring what it was designed to measure (validity) (Snowden and Telfer 2017). GP feedback on the value of chaplaincy was also extremely positive. Patients whom they referred showed improved mood, with less attendance at surgery. In some instances, GPs felt less need to prescribe, thought patients' ability to cope was improved and felt less pressured themselves.

A SELECTION OF FEEDBACK FROM GPS WHO REFERRED PATIENTS TO CCL

- Comment 1: 'Less attendance, less prescribing, somebody with time and willingness to listen. Also notable is to reduce the emotional pressure on me. We may deal with 30 or even up to 60 patients in a day. When one or more has existential or emotional problems and needs [to be] listened to, while the waiting room is full and there could be medically urgent things waiting, it is an additional emotional stress on me over and above the usual effects of doing counselling. We have no de-briefing or supervision – just rush on to the next patient who is angry about waiting so long.'

- Comment 2: 'Patient feels supported; improvement in symptoms; less reliance on [GP] practice; more confidence for patients to deal with and gain control of their symptoms and lives in general.'

- Comment 3: 'Greater wellbeing, more motivation; less reliance on doctors and taking more active role in their own health rather than the prescribed traditional passive role of "fix me."'

- Comment 4: 'Reduction in stress, anxiety; improved mood, calmer perspective on life.'

- Comment 5: 'Reduced prescribing, less attendance at surgery, very positive impact on patients' coping ability.'

- Comment 6: '…non-medical model is very helpful.'

- Comment 7: '…coping better by themselves; especially helpful for people with existential issues.'

- Comment 8: '…less use [of] antidepressants, benefit from time and sharing issues.'

The results in the box above are not a direct outcome of using the PROM but an example of the type of secondary evidence that can be obtained by using the PROM as a primary measure.

In order to pursue the potentially important economic benefits alluded to by the GPs in the box above, the Scottish protocol now includes more systematic and prospective feedback from them. GPs will record levels of attendance, prescription usage, mood and any other metrics they feel are relevant and feasible. For the first time, the study also includes a before-and-after health-related quality-of-life score (EQ5D-3L) which will enable a cost-effective analysis of chaplaincy in primary care. (Further ongoing PROM research is given at the end of this chapter.)

The difference between listening and enabling people to talk

Recall that the Scottish PROM (Figure 13.3) was designed to understand the relationship between the quality of the patient encounter and subsequent outcomes. This was done statistically by examining correlations between the responses to the 'during my meeting with the chaplain' items and the outcome items ('in the last two weeks I have felt…'). A noticeable finding from the original Lothian PROM study was the striking relationship between the item 'I was able to talk about what was on my mind' and all the outcome items (Snowden *et al.* 2013a). There was a strong, significant positive correlation in every case. In other words, 'I was able to talk about what was on my mind' was associated with the person feeling able to be honest, less anxious, having a positive outlook, in control and feeling a sense of peace. None of the other items showed this relationship. 'I was able to talk about what was on my mind' was a better indicator of subsequent positive outcome than any of the other three statements:

- 'I was listened to.'
- 'My situation was understood.'
- 'My faith/beliefs were valued.'

However, this finding was based on only a total of 37 responses, and so the generalizability of the finding was questionable. It was therefore very interesting when the finding was replicated in a much larger Scottish PROM study with over 100 participants (Snowden and Telfer 2017). Then, the same pattern was noted in a sample of over 500 PROMs completed by Australian participants (Elizabeth Lobb, personal communication). Three independent studies obtained the same result, and so it is reasonable to assume that this was a consistent finding. 'I was able to talk about what was on my mind' is more important and qualitatively distinct from being listened to, understood or valued; all are important, but there is something extra special about people being able to talk about what is on their mind.

Future studies could be designed to test the prediction that being able to talk about what is currently important would lessen anxiety and give a sense of control and peace. If this study could establish that being able to talk about what is currently important leads to improved outcomes, this would be a step closer to valuing the skills of chaplains in facilitating the conditions for allowing people to talk *as an end in itself*. Space prevents a deeper discussion of the distinction, but to summarize, talking is generally seen as a means to an end, a method of ascertaining the outcome. Following an argument developed by Mowat and colleagues (2013), where authentic listening is viewed as a desirable endpoint, or *outcome*, this line of thought will be investigated further in future PROM studies, where being 'able to talk about what was on my mind' will be systematically examined in depth.

Reducing the irreducible

Throughout the development of the PROM there have always been sceptics. One of the biggest conceptual issues that had to be addressed was the claim that the PROM was actually a PREM – a patient-reported *experience* measure. This argument obviously turns on the conceptual distinction between experience and outcome, somewhat similar to the distinction drawn in the last section. The debate was eventually resolved with reference to PROMIS (Pilkonis *et al.* 2011), the largest repository of PROMs in the US, which supported the contention that the PROM items pertain to outcomes. (For a philosophical distinction and a detailed examination of the conceptual difference, see the summary report of the Lothian PROM: Snowden *et al.* 2012.)

Another challenge to the PROM came from American colleagues who questioned whether the PROM might be measuring *mental* wellbeing rather than spiritual wellbeing.[2] Our belief is that it measures spiritual wellbeing because it is conceptually grounded in the spirituality literature and faithfully reflects the secular culture of twenty-first-century Scotland (Alison *et al.* 2014). On the suggestion of American colleagues, it was decided to incorporate a definition of spirituality into the PROM questionnaire,

---

2   The conversation with American colleagues was part of a tabled discussion during a Skype meeting of the Joint Research Council of the Association of Professional Chaplains.

namely 'Spirituality has to do with what gives meaning, purpose and a sense of wellbeing to life. For some people, this may include belief in a Superior Being, though this is not the case for everyone.'

Where is God?

If the criticism is actually about the absence of God in the Scottish PROM, then this is a different matter. Recall that the purpose of the project was to devise a measure that captured the outcomes of spiritual care as delivered by chaplains in Scotland. The assumption we made at the outset about spiritual care was that chaplains deliver it: spiritual caring is what they do (Mowat and Swinton 2007). The items in the Scottish PROM therefore represent outcomes of spiritual care as delivered by chaplains. The reason the Scottish PROM does not contain any overt statement of a religious nature is because such a statement would be meaningless to half the Scottish population (Alison *et al.* 2014) and therefore run the risk of people of no faith disengaging. Patients in Scotland can express concern when the suggestion of referral to chaplaincy is raised. For example, in one study many non-religious bereaved parents expressed anxiety about being proselytized or patronized (Kelly 2007). Nurses and other referrers may then assure people that meeting a chaplain does not have to include discussion about religion. Subsequently, to ask them about their relationship with God would be disingenuous.

We kept the item about faith and belief in the items about the meeting with the chaplain. We also considered adding 'voluntary' questions, that is, questions to be answered only if religious, but decided instead that a short, fully inclusive measure that would be meaningful to everyone who had seen a chaplain would be more coherent with our brief. We have considerable evidence that people seeing a chaplain in Scotland benefit equivalently, regardless of whether they describe themselves as religious, spiritual, both or neither (Snowden *et al.* 2012). This is not to dismiss the importance of religion, ritual or any form of faith to anybody. However, we were tasked with constructing a generalizable measure that captures *everyone*'s experience. Excluding overtly religious statements from the outcomes was the only way to capture the impact of chaplaincy in a systematic manner.

This decision clearly impacts on the utility of the PROM in other cultures. The Scottish PROM is a necessary and sufficient measure of outcomes of spiritual care as delivered by chaplains in Scotland. In more overtly religious countries, the Scottish PROM still fulfils the necessary criteria, but perhaps is not sufficient. We are working with colleagues globally to develop solutions. Perhaps different countries should consider the Scottish PROM as a 'minimum data set' and supplement it with culturally specific questions where relevant. The key take-home message is that the items themselves cannot be changed in any way, because any subsequent findings would be invalid and, thus, impossible to explain and situate in the literature. In other words, there may be room for additional items as long as the original (see Figure 13.3) remains intact. (More research is needed.)

A final hurdle is that not all chaplains think that an outcome measure of their work is either possible or desirable. Reducing an essentially irreducible transformational and transcendent process to five Likert-scale items (see Figure 13.3) is too big a leap for some chaplains. We are very sympathetic to this position, and when confronted with it, we respond by clarifying what we understand the purpose of the PROM to be. It is simply a method of obtaining robust generalizable data for those who need this type of information. It is not meant to represent all chaplaincy research. For some chaplains it is a 'way in' to research. To give an example of this, Iain Telfer, a practising healthcare chaplain and co-author of the PROM, now discusses his relationship with the PROM and how it helped him get to grips with the wider chaplaincy research agenda.

PROMs and personal and professional development

From my perspective, engagement with the Scottish PROM research project has been both challenging and immensely stimulating. It has meant a commitment, first, to becoming actively involved in helping establish chaplaincy as a research-based profession. Second, it has reinforced the importance of listening to the patient voice, recognizing that being made aware of spiritual care outcomes, 'from the patient's point of view', is entirely necessary if integrity in chaplaincy is to be reaffirmed. Third, developing new confidence in what we do as chaplains has been one of the most rewarding benefits of participating in this groundbreaking research.

I came into healthcare chaplaincy from a background of education, training, formation and practice in parish ministry in Scotland, a context where there was little in the way of supervision or encouragement to engage in research. It was initially daunting to be faced with the expectation that chaplaincy might require a deliberate intention to engage in reflective practice. Such engagement took the form, at the very least, of learning the skill of searching for and reading critically what others are writing about spiritual care.

Perhaps, most obviously, it is the context within which this care takes place that marks it out as different, namely the secular nature of the National Health

Service in Scotland. Certainly, since the end of the Second World War, in the UK we have witnessed a steady social disengagement from institutionalized religion. Consequently, people are no longer sure what to make of a suggested referral to a chaplaincy service. Explained in terms of 'additional support' that might allow them to think about the impact of a health problem or difficulty (with no mention of religion), they will often agree, commenting afterwards, that being listened to and enabled to talk about what was on their mind, with someone who is non-medical, has been beneficial.

The authority of institutionalized religion may have been found wanting; yet, many people feel somewhat at sea, unsure of how to re-establish their bearings in life, perhaps even yearning after something to replace the so-called certainties of the past.

It is into this world that the chaplain steps when called to offer spiritual care, sometimes unsure of what it is she or he has to offer; and the patient or client may be equally unsure of what form or shape the help they seek might take. Perhaps unsurprisingly, this has led practitioners in Scotland, and elsewhere, to re-examine the language of spiritual care.

So, the conversation begins – not only a conversation between practitioner and patient, but also an important dialogue within the profession itself; asking such fundamental questions as 'What do we mean by spiritual care?' and 'What shape might that take?', 'How do we assess a person's spiritual need?' and 'How might we begin to tackle that concern with them?' Also, 'How might we gauge the effectiveness or otherwise of the support chaplains offer?' and 'How best might we gather "robust evidence" that spiritual care is central to holistic compassionate care?'

Being 'research-informed' (Fitchett 2002) entails becoming aware of aspects of this conversation. It leads to an examination of what is at the heart of chaplaincy; the irreducible minimum, we might say. It means a commitment to reflective practice, which means being humble enough to learn from colleagues and from one's own mistakes, enhancing skills, refining practice and improving outcomes. It means some chaplains becoming actively engaged in research projects to produce the much sought-after evidence we need to secure the future of spiritual care within budgeting priorities (Snowden *et al.* 2017).

Core elements of the *Healthcare Quality Strategy for NHSScotland* (Scottish Government 2010) include listening to people's views and gathering information about their lived experience to improve care. Out of this grew the conviction that one of the essential drivers to securing the future of spiritual care within the healthcare setting in Scotland must be research into what people themselves see as the value of such care. In other words, seeking the patient voice in assessing the significance of what chaplains do became a priority. This led directly to the development of the Scottish spiritual care PROM.

This journey into research has revealed how colleagues globally are wrestling with similar questions around meaningful encounters with people facing challenging existential questions as a result of acute injury or illness – how, as chaplains, we cope when our vulnerability is exposed; when the faith we thought should sustain us does not; when life is turned upside down; when our dreams and our sense of security are shattered; when nothing makes sense any more. These are all important matters that touch our lives, as well as the lives of those we hope to support. Our own personal reflection and sense of vulnerability equip us, as much as anything, to be an attentive presence for others in their time of need.

There are no shortcuts to becoming gainfully self-aware; nor does the satisfaction that we do a good job come without the hard work of taking the journey inward, which R.S. Thomas's (1996) poem 'Groping' describes. This job we have chosen to do (or, that has chosen *us*) demands integrity of life and practice. More than that, engaging with research positively assists the vital, ongoing cycle of personal and professional development. We owe nothing less to those we encounter, who choose to allow us to accompany them for a while, in the mutual discovery, spirit to spirit, of what makes us truly human.

Further research

Our original remit was to provide *evidence*. This continues to be our challenge. For example, we need to examine the function of the Scottish PROM in a wider range of settings and populations. More data are needed to ascertain population norms and meaningful thresholds across a range of clinical settings. For example, what score constitutes spiritual wellbeing? What score constitutes distress? Could this be used as a referral measure? Colleagues in Australia, the US and mainland Europe are using the PROM in different contexts and will help with this process shortly.

The clinical utility of the Scottish PROM in practice is what is likely to be of more interest to most chaplains. Recall that the PROM allows for comparison between chaplain and patient understanding, thereby offering a way to explore the coherence between chaplain and patient at that point. The PROM's usefulness in helping facilitate personal and team reflection is clear, but further work is required to help chaplains communicate their worth to others, not least workforce planners.

Ongoing phases of our research include:

- testing the utility of the Scottish PROM as a before-and-after measure of chaplain intervention in CCL; this study will also test convergent validity with EQ5D-3L and explore the cost-effectiveness of chaplain interventions

- translation and validation of the PROM in Belgium, the Netherlands and other European countries; replica studies will then be conducted across Europe under the auspices of the European Research Institute for Chaplains in Healthcare

- an observational pre–post cohort study in several UK hospice day services, including children's services

- a PhD project examining the utility of the PROM in a Belgian context

- a large multi-centre randomized study using the PROM in Australia.

Conclusion

The Scottish PROM is a reliable, valid measure of the outcomes of chaplain interventions in Scotland. It is the first measure designed specifically to capture the impact of chaplain interventions. As such, it has focused international attention on this important area of research. This agenda is new to many chaplains, so this chapter went back to the beginning to tell the story of how the PROM was developed, what it was developed from and how it has been refined along the way. We hope that we have demonstrated the importance, for the professional healthcare chaplain, of engaging with spiritual care research. As the contexts within which chaplains operate change, chaplains need research more now than ever to demonstrate their worth and articulate their value. Finally, we hope that by showing the process from the beginning and discussing common misgivings, readers will have gained a balanced understanding of the pros and cons of using the PROM to measure outcomes of spiritual care (chaplaincy) interventions. The PROM was never meant to be a panacea, and chaplaincy research clearly requires different methods and tools to address all its different questions. Having said this, we believe the Scottish PROM does what it was designed to do: it measures the outcomes of spiritual care as delivered by chaplains. All colleagues needing to do this now have a valid and reliable tool to do so.

References

Agledahl, K.M., Gulbrandsen, P., Førde, R. and Wifstad, Å. (2011) 'Courteous but not curious: how doctors' politeness masks their existential neglect. A qualitative study of video-recorded patient consultations.' *Journal of Medical Ethics* 37, 11, 650–654. Accessed on 29/09/2018 at doi.org/10.1136/jme.2010.041988.

Alison, A., Siddiqui, M., Snowden, A. and Fleming, M. (2014) *Faith and Belief Scotland*. Edinburgh. Accessed on 29/09/2018 at http://faithandbelief.div.ed.ac.uk/wp-content/uploads/2014/07/Faith-and-Belief-Scotland-FINAL-VERSION-OF-REPORT.pdf.

Fitchett, G. (2002) 'Health care chaplaincy as a research-informed profession: how we get there.' *Journal of Health Care Chaplaincy* 12, 1–2, 67–72.

Fries, J., Rose, M. and Krishnan, E. (2011) 'The PROMIS of better outcome assessment: responsiveness, floor and ceiling effects, and Internet administration.' *The Journal of Rheumatology* 38, 8, 1759–1764. Accessed on 29/09/2018 at www.ncbi.nlm.nih.gov/pubmed/21807798.

Gray, R., Wykes, T. and Gournay, K. (2002) 'From compliance to concordance: a review of the literature on interventions to enhance compliance with antipsychotic medication.' *Journal of Psychiatric and Mental Health Nursing* 9, 3, 277–284.

Healthcare Chaplaincy Network (2016) *What Is Quality Spiritual Care in Healthcare and How Can We Measure it?* Accessed on 29/09/2018 at www.healthcarechaplaincy.org/docs/research/quality_indicators_document_2_17_16.pdf.

Kelly, E. (2007) *Marking Short Lives: Constructing and Sharing Ritual Following Pregnancy Loss.* Oxford: Peter Lang.

Meadows, K.A. (2010) 'Patient-reported outcome measures: an overview.' *British Journal of Community Nursing* 16, 3, 146–151.

Mowat, H. and Swinton, J. (2007) *What do Chaplains do?* Aberdeen: Mowat Research.

Mowat, H., Bunniss, S., Snowden, A. and Wright, L. (2013) 'Listening as health care.' *The Scottish Journal of Healthcare Chaplaincy* 16, 39–46.

Pilkonis, P.A., Choi, S., Reise, S.P. and Stover, A.M. (2011) 'Item banks for measuring emotional distress from the patient reported outcomes measurement information system (PROMIS): depression, anxiety and anger.' *Assessment 18*, 3, 263–283.

Scottish Government (2010) *The Healthcare Quality Strategy for NHSScotland*. Edinburgh: Scottish Government. Accessed on 29/09/2018 at www.gov.scot/Publications/2010/05/10102307/0.

Snowden, A. and Marland, G.R. (2012) 'No decision about me without me: concordance operationalised.' *Journal of Clinical Nursing* 22, 1353–1360. Accessed on 29/09/2018 at doi.org/10.1111/j.1365-2702.2012.04337.x.

Snowden, A. and Telfer, I. (2012) 'A Patient Reported Outcome Measure for Spiritual Care.' In *Spiritual Care and Health: Improving Outcome and Enhancing Wellbeing*. Clydebank, Scotland. Accessed on 29/09/2018 at www.nes.scot.nhs.uk/education-and-training/by-discipline/spiritual-care/about-spiritual-care/presentations-from-conferences/spiritual-care-and-health-improving-outcome-and-enhancing-wellbeing,international-conference,-march-2012.aspx.

Snowden, A. and Telfer, I. (2017) 'A patient reported outcome measure of spiritual care as delivered by chaplains.' *Journal of Health Care Chaplaincy* 23, 4, 131–155. Accessed on 29/09/2018 at doi.org/10.1080/08854726.2017.1279935.

Snowden, A., Telfer, I., Kelly, E., Mowat, H. *et al.* (2012) *Healthcare Chaplaincy: The Lothian Chaplaincy Patient Reported Outcome Measure (PROM)*. Gourock. Accessed on 29/09/2018 at www.snowdenresearch.co.uk.

Snowden, A., Telfer, I., Kelly, E., Bunniss, S. *et al.* (2013a) '"I was able to talk about what was on my mind." The operationalisation of person centred care.' *The Scottish Journal of Healthcare Chaplaincy* 16, 14–24.

Snowden, A., Telfer, I., Kelly, E., Bunniss, S. *et al.* (2013b) 'Spiritual care as person centred care: a thematic analysis of chaplain interventions.' *The Scottish Journal of Healthcare Chaplaincy* 16, 25–35.

Snowden, A., Fitchett, G., Grossoehme, D., Handzo, G. *et al.* (2017) 'International study of chaplains' attitudes about research.' *Journal of Health Care Chaplaincy* 23, 1, 34–43.

Streiner, D. and Norman, G.R. (2008) *Health Measurement Scales: A Practical Guide to their Development and Use* (4th ed.). New York, NY: Oxford University Press.

Thomas, R.S. (1996) *Selected Poems*. London: J.M. Dent.

Wolpert, M. (2014) 'Uses and abuses of patient reported outcome measures (PROMs): potential iatrogenic impact of PROMs implementation and how it can be mitigated.' *Administration and Policy in Mental Health 41*, 2, 141–145. Accessed on 29/09/2018 at http://Doi.org/10.1007/s10488-013-0509-1.

Part 5

Creative Engagements

In the latter half of this book arguments are made, and creative examples offered, describing a chaplain's role at different levels of healthcare activity, which includes, yet is more than, working with individuals. This section is the first of two which explore the influence chaplains potentially have working with people and teams as well as on organisations and systems in relation to promoting spiritual wellbeing. These sections begin to point the way for new models of chaplaincy, such as working as a spiritual enabler or leader of transformation within challenging and rapidly changing contexts.

Part 5 concerns chaplains creatively engaging with institutions and care teams. A junior doctor (Sharp 2017, p.361) recently wrote in an opinion piece in the *British Medical Journal* entitled 'Has NHS workforce morale hit rock bottom?': 'None of my colleagues have lost their love of their profession but the reality of working in the modern NHS is taking its toll.' How can chaplains creatively and collaboratively influence healthcare culture and enhance staff experience? How do chaplains engage in ways that have integrity, have impact on individual and collective wellbeing and are at the same time deeply spiritual? How can chaplains creatively support, and learn from, others in their provision of person-centred, including spiritual, care?

Reference

Sharp, T. (2017) 'Has NHS workforce morale hit
    rock bottom?' *British Medical Journal 356*, 361.

Chapter 14

The Chaplain and Organizational Spirituality of Church-Sponsored Healthcare Institutions

Neil Pembroke and Raymond Reddicliffe

Introduction

Commonly cited definitions of organizational spirituality (OS) (Ashmos and Duchon 2000; Graber, Johnson and Hornberger 2001; Howard 2002; Jurkiewicz and Giacalone 2004) refer to features such as meaning and purpose, positive feelings (e.g. joy, wholeness, fun), self-actualization (developing personal potential) and an experience of community. Identifying these core elements in spirituality in the workplace is helpful to a degree, but it does not take us very far in our quest to construct a model of corporate spirituality. What is described in most of these definitions is an *individual* employee's quest for enjoyment at work, meaning, personal fulfilment and the experience of fellowship. The approach taken by Jurkiewicz and Giacalone (2004) is an exception. In their definition they situate self-transcendence, the experience of community and a positive emotional state in the context of organizational culture and the values that shape it. The culture of an organization is certainly built up by, and expressed in, individual values and actions, but it also transcends the personal. Culture is, by definition, a shared or corporate phenomenon.

When it comes to OS in a healthcare context, there are extra factors that need to be considered. While a great deal has been written on the topic of spiritual care by clinicians, there is relatively little literature available on corporate spirituality. There is also the fact that there are differences between a healthcare organization and other organized entities. The most prominent is that something is required beyond the care of staff – namely, the care of patients and their families. Finally, the fact that many healthcare organizations are not-for-profit must be taken into account. It is, therefore, not possible to simply transpose the central principles and practices from OS onto a healthcare setting.

This chapter focuses on certain key values and practices that spiritualize the culture of a healthcare organization. We have chosen to focus on a particular context – that of the church-sponsored facility. Though the core principles and theological reflection have a general application, the empirical research is set exclusively in church-run hospitals.

In an earlier work, Pembroke (2012) presented a model of OS in a healthcare context consisting of six elements: availability; compassion; inclusion; empathy; confirmation; and social justice. In this chapter we build on, develop and extend Pembroke's work. We include an element – compassion – that is fundamental in a caring environment and add two other very important elements – identification with an ethos and trust. When staff members identify with the vision of the organization and experience working relationships characterized by trust, they have a strong sense of belonging. They feel personally connected to their place of work and to the people in it; it feels like home to them. In summary, our discussion is around the nature of a spiritualized organizational culture characterized by a shared commitment to building a climate of compassion, trust and sense of belonging, and the role that chaplains have to play in this task.

Our discussion of OS in a healthcare context begins with setting up a conversation between organizational theory and covenant theology. This is followed by a report on empirical work carried out by Reddicliffe (2013) that includes illustrations of the model at work and reflections on the role of the chaplain in spiritualizing a healthcare organization.

Theology of a spiritualized organization: covenantal perspectives

In this section we set up a dialogue between covenantal theology, on the one hand, and a model of OS centred on compassion and belonging, on the other. The attempt to correlate covenantal and organizational perspectives is fraught because of the almost infinite distinction between God and humankind. Though God is massively unlike human beings, clearly there are also significant points of similarity (we are created *imago Dei*).

Compassion in the covenant and in a healthcare facility

Bergant (1996) observes that in the cluster of Hebrew words for compassion found in the Old Testament, *rhm* is the most prominent. It has the primary meaning of 'cherishing', 'soothing' or 'a gentle attitude of mind'. Bergant concludes that this Hebrew word group indicates a bond like that between a mother and the child of her womb. The New Testament writer Paul uses the Greek word *spláncna* for compassion. It is 'a very forceful term to signify an expression of the total personality at the deepest level' (Köster 1985, p.1068).

Observing the visceral connotation in the biblical words, we can say that compassion is about 'feeling it in your guts'. A compassionate person is deeply receptive to the pain of others.

Compassion is clearly a significant human response, but can we really speak of the compassion of God? For all but the very recent history of Christian thought, the doctrine of the impassibility of God has reigned supreme. The thinking associated with this position runs like this: God is the 'unmoved Mover', and since to feel something means being influenced or 'moved' by something outside the self, God is not passionate.

Theologians today often make a distinction between the God of the philosophers and the God of the Bible. The God we encounter in the scriptures is a passionate one. We find clear evidence of this in God's response to the persistent rebellious streak in Israel: the heart of God is grieved. God chose Israel to be God's own and lavished blessings upon the people. But time and time again they wandered from the straight path that YHWH had set before them. Israel is God's own and God is faithful in the divine love for her. When God is faced with infidelity, God is overcome with grief (see, for example, Hosea 11:7, 8c).

In Jeremiah 31:20 we find this beautiful expression of divine compassion: 'Is Ephraim my dear son? Is he the child I delight in? As often as I speak against him, I still remember him. Therefore, I am deeply moved for him; I will surely have mercy on him, says the Lord.'

The expression 'I am deeply moved' is a translation of *me'ay hamui*, which literally means 'my inner parts trembled' (Hoass 1997, p.152). 'Inner parts' parallels the womb in the Bible. With this in mind, Phyllis Trible translates this expression as: 'Therefore, my womb trembles for him' (Trible 1976, p.276, cited in Hoass 1997, pp.152–153). God is the source of all compassion in the world. The wondrous mercy of God infuses God's creatures and moves them at the deepest level.

Compassion is an expression of the deepest part of an individual; it is at the centre of a spiritualized healthcare facility. Healthcare providers and chaplains are constantly faced with human suffering and sorrow. A spiritual approach to their work requires them to allow themselves to feel this pain. Offering a compassionate response day in and day out is clearly very demanding. The temptation is to put up a barrier, to shield oneself from the suffering. Healthcare professionals and pastoral caregivers are understandably afraid that it will all become too much. Indeed, compassion fatigue is a very real issue today (Hegney *et al.* 2014; Hooper *et al.* 2010; Yoder 2010). However, it is possible to allow oneself to feel compassion without it becoming an impossible burden and completely draining one's emotional energy (Pembroke 2016). We all know that this is easier said than done. Each person will have her or his own strategy in this regard; some of these will be better than others. There is a useful literature available on managing compassion fatigue (Joinson 1992; LaRowe 2005; McHolm 2006; Pembroke 2016).

Being at home: organizational and covenantal dimensions

A number of social scientists and organizational theorists have observed that institutions are actually mini-societies, and that it is therefore appropriate to refer to corporate or organizational culture (Hofstede, Hofstede and Minkov 2010; Kotter and Heskett 1992; Morgan 1986; Nicotera, Clinkscales and Walker 2003). Of course, there are often competing desires in relation to the shape of the organizational culture. For a person to feel that she belongs in her organization, she needs to be able to identify with the prevailing culture. If a staff member finds herself on the wrong side of an ideological divide, she will likely feel frustrated, angry and depressed. Rather than enjoying the feeling of being at home in her work, she will experience the pain of alienation.

Identification with an ethos also plays a central role in building trust. While trust in working relationships has different shapes (Reynolds 1997; Shapiro, Sheppard and Cheraskin 1992), identification-based trust is commonly acknowledged to be the highest form (Guohong and Harms 2010; Ole Borgen 2001; Reynolds 1997; Shapiro *et al.* 1992). It is the kind of trust that is established when the agents internalize each other's preferences.

There are significant connections between these observations on belonging and trust in an organization and covenantal theology. 'I will be your God and you will be my people' is fundamentally a declaration of belonging. For the Hebrew, his or her personhood was established through the covenant. As Brueggemann (1979, p.120) puts it: '[T]he act of claiming is the act of giving life and identity to that person. Before being called and belonging to, the person was not. In the Bible, "person" means to belong with and belong to and belong for.'

YHWH's loving glance, YHWH's calling word, was responsible for Israel's existence. YHWH loved the people of Israel into existence. Before God called out to them, they were no people. They had no existence, no life and no sense of belonging. To belong meant to exist as the property of the Egyptian overlords. But YHWH's love brought redemption and constituted them as a people: '[I]t was because the Lord loved you and kept the oath he swore to the forefathers that he brought you out with a mighty hand and redeemed you from the land of slavery, from the power of the Pharaoh king of Egypt' (Deuteronomy 7:8).

Trust was a significant factor in the covenantal relationship that began with this saving act. YHWH moved from relying on the 'machinery of external enforcement' associated with the Mosaic covenant (Mendenhall and Herion 1992, p.1192) to a new covenant (Jeremiah 31:33) involving a total internalization of YHWH's will. In this way, a much firmer foundation for trust in the covenantal relationship was established.

It is interesting to compare this with observations by organizational theorists. Reynolds (1997, pp.7–9) refers to three types of relationship in an organization. First, there are power relationships. The power of management is established through the mechanisms and procedures it has at its disposal to discipline staff members. This approach meets with some success, but a relationship shaped by constant monitoring and deterrence is oppressive. The second form of relationship was set up in many organizations in reaction to the oppressive nature of power relationships. Management sought to give workers a great deal of freedom and thus to 'empower' them. Such an approach is naïve and built on hope. Management simply hopes that workers will respect and appreciate the latitude and trust accorded them and will respond appropriately. The third type of relationship is established through identification. Workers and management commit to a common set of values and beliefs. In this scenario, workers do not need to be subjected to constant monitoring and the threat of punishment. Rather, they are inspired and energized in their work. The movement in the covenantal relationship to internalization of the divine vision through law written on the heart is reflected in the best wisdom of organizational theory today. When the partners in a project own a common vision, a high level of trust ensues.

We have presented an overview of core elements in a spiritualized healthcare organization through a correlation between organizational theory and covenantal theology. Our final tasks are to illustrate the model at work and to discuss the contribution that a chaplain may make to spiritualizing her or his organizational culture.

Illustrations and examples of compassion, belonging and trust

We noted earlier that organizational spirituality is not so much to do with whether particular rhetoric is employed, but rather with the presence of notable characteristics in the cultural life of an organization or institution. For example, compassion essentially involves receptivity to the pain of others, that is, a person's inner readiness to be open, welcoming or hospitable is a key indicator of someone having and expressing compassion. The degree to which receptivity becomes a cultural value within an organization could be said to provide a reliable indicator of its spirituality. Similarly, where a strong sense of belonging is experienced by people comprising an organization and gestures or other symbolic behaviours are in evidence, these too may be regarded as signs of spirituality. Third, we have asserted that optimal expressions of trust are typically associated with high levels of interdependence, and this characteristic can also be regarded as a marker of organizational spirituality.

Below are instances of how spiritually resonant core values are being expressed in and through chaplaincy services in healthcare organizations in Southeast Queensland (Reddicliffe 2013).

Lily is a young woman who from infancy has coped with intellectual, emotional and physical disability. Soon after her move to semi-independent living arrangements she needed hospitalization for surgery and was anxious at the prospect. In response, arrangements were made for Lily to visit and meet hospital staff, including chaplain Cheryl. On admission, during preparation for surgery and post-operatively there was further pastoral care and support for Lily and her family.

A second example of compassionate care involved patient Mary. In conversation with chaplain Elise, Mary indicated that a close relative planned to visit later that day and was celebrating a significant birthday. Elise selected an appropriate birthday card and acquired a bouquet of flowers. Mary wrote a greeting on the card to accompany the flowers for presentation. Mary was 'blown away' by this spontaneous caring gesture – as was her relative!

While compassionate care is important, empathic understanding is an indispensable prerequisite. Martin (a chaplain/manager of a hospital pastoral care department) made the observation: 'My wellbeing is caught up with the wellbeing of others. When sitting beside a patient, I try to feel some of their pain, and to understand what their journey is like for them.'

When chaplains and other professional staff work closely together in a hospital context, they share a commitment to core corporate values such as compassion, respect, justice, working together and leading through learning

(Reddicliffe 2013). Over time, close and strong relationships tend to develop and frequently people share a deep sense of belonging to the organization in which they serve. Martin also described the relationship between his department and hospital management as 'healthy and positive', noting that sometimes it is necessary to raise concerns or act prophetically. His perception is that interdepartmental relationships are covenantal in nature, describing them as analogous to a mature marriage relationship founded on genuine mutual respect.

Another key element in any enduring and meaningful personal or organizational relationship, as indicated earlier, is the trust associated with efficacy and spirituality in organizational life. The example was given of how one hospital erected four huge banners on its premises to highlight the excellent quality of care provided. One banner featured the contribution of the hospital's chaplain/manager depicting the level of trust that existed and the esteem in which the chaplaincy team was held.

The role of chaplains in a spiritualized healthcare organization

In respect to a spiritualized or humanized healthcare organization that is church related, chaplains are among those often strategically placed to assist internalization of the organization's vision. They may achieve this by grounding the core values of the organization in their work commitments and helping relationships, and also through advocating for, and helping facilitate, a spiritualized culture in the corporate life of the organization.

From recent pastoral experiences, observations and reflections of chaplain/managers and others in a church-related healthcare organization (Reddicliffe 2013), along with other sources, it is suggested that there are signs of an emerging vision with implications for healthcare chaplains. Three key elements in this vision are:

- working from a theology of care reflecting an open and welcoming stance (the guest/host dynamic)

- an emphasis on spiritual care over traditional expressions of pastoral care

- encouraging wider participation in the delivery of spiritual care through involvement of clinicians from other healthcare disciplines.

Conclusion

We conclude this chapter with brief reference to future challenges for healthcare chaplains working towards internalization of this vision.

Guest or host?

Informed engagement with theological ideas needs to play a vital role in helping chaplains think through organizational spirituality issues. For example, what are the implications of the notions of 'guest theology' and 'host theology' (Slater 2012, p.317; Steddon 2010, pp.11–12) with their distinctive orientations and *modus operandi* for promoting the mission of God in the world? Guest theology is characterized as 'other oriented', while host theology may be described as adopting a 'presiding posture'.

However, we contend that a different style of host theology is also valid. In discussing the element of compassion, reference was made to receptivity. There is a strong inference here to a welcoming host inviting another to enter and to feel quite at home. We noted earlier how chaplain Cheryl exemplified the idea of being 'other oriented' by attending to Lily's needs and those of her family. She provided a ministry of compassionate care as a welcoming and hospitable host. There are clear biblical and theological precedents for understanding an invitational message from a presiding host in an alternative yet positive way (e.g. John 21; Mark 10:45).

Spirituality and pastoral care

Chaplains are also contributing to the spiritualizing of their healthcare organizations by applying recent empirical research in healthcare environments and grappling with the implications of the changing focus from pastoral to spiritual care.

Chaplain/manager John commented on efforts by chaplaincy staff to apply research undertaken by organizations such as the Templeton Foundation in the US. The implications of positive associations found between hope, prayer and healing are alluded to in the following observation (Reddicliffe 2013, Interview 3):

> …there is evidence mounting that people usually heal faster if they pray regularly, or are part of a church, mosque or synagogue. We approach this from a clinical point of view rather than a chaplaincy perspective. We look at how we as a Pastoral Care Department can fit into that approach.

While there is empirical evidence for a positive relationship between the practice of spirituality and better health outcomes (e.g. Jankowski, Handzo and Flannelly 2011; Koenig, McCullough and Larsen 2001), the evidence is far from unequivocal. For example, Benson and colleagues (2006) did not find support for the hypothesis that intercessory prayer has positive effects in recovery of cardiac surgical patients. Other research highlights the potential for a broader application of spiritual and pastoral resources in clinical healthcare settings. In an Australian study, over two-thirds of participating chaplains reportedly believed it was part of their pastoral role to assist patients and family members make decisions about healthcare treatment (Carey and Cohen 2008). However, this study also questioned whether there is empirical evidence that chaplains are doing enough to assist healthcare institutions to move beyond 'tokenism'. If future chaplaincy ministries are to be economically viable, active engagement with clinical healthcare settings must become the principal context for chaplaincy-related research and for undertaking spiritual/pastoral care interventions and their evaluation.

Alongside the more traditional focus on the provision of pastoral care from a predominantly Christian perspective, there is growing recognition of major shifts in the ways that the relationship between religion and spirituality are understood and described (Walton 2012; World Health Organization 2002). Viewed from what seems a much broader perspective, Swinton (2001) describes a migration of spirituality from the religious to the secular domain. Consequently, there has been 'a constructive transition from religion as an encompassing concept to spirituality as an encompassing context' (Swinton 2001, p.11). Features of this shift are reflected in chaplain/manager John's comments (Reddicliffe 2013, Interview 3):

> You have these two views of how religion and spirituality relate… My experience is that we have this huge need for people to connect with spirituality in the community, but who do not want a bar of the church. They don't trust or understand it.

Spiritual care across clinical healthcare disciplines

The trend towards understanding spiritual care as unfettered by interdisciplinary boundaries is consistent with Swinton's (2001) conceptual framework of spirituality, has strategic intent and is understood to have broad applicability. Consequently, spiritual care is no longer regarded as the exclusive domain of chaplains or other religious professionals, but rather has relevance for all members of an interdisciplinary healthcare team.

A 'praying-hands programme' implemented in a church-related hospital aims to deconstruct the notion that only chaplains and other religious professionals ought to pray with patients and visitors. The voluntary programme encourages the extension of the ministry of prayer by particular staff members in their respective clinical contexts. As chaplain/manager John explains (Reddicliffe 2013, Interview 3):

> If we believe in the priesthood of all believers, we should also believe in the chaplaincy of all believers. The idea was that within the bounds of discipline, to be able to spread this ministry out and involve others…in the ministry of prayer.

While coordinating and facilitating healthcare chaplaincy services within the organization is a necessary component in the work of chaplain/managers, it is the promotion of the healthcare organization's vision and commitment to developing a culture characterized by resonant values that are regarded as absolutely vital and essential elements in their work.

Challenges of internalizing a shared vision

At the very least, clear signals are needed from the corporate owners and managers regarding the vital importance of internalizing the vision of a spiritualized culture. Posing the issue another way, we may enquire: Is there congruence between the vision being enunciated by key managers and leaders of the organization with what is observed in the cultural expressions of the organization? In particular, is spirituality understood to encompass more than the provision of pastoral and/or spiritual care for patients, visitors and staff?

We turn now to consider how chaplain/managers and other chaplaincy staff of church-related healthcare organizations help create ownership and internalize a common vision. Feedback from chaplain/managers and directors of mission suggest they function as the principal brokers of spiritual and pastoral care in their respective healthcare organizations. They are usually well informed about the main issues for chaplains working 'at the coalface' through the reporting and supervisory mechanisms already in place. In addition, invariably these middle-management leaders are familiar with the governance structures of their organization. They can readily appreciate the perspectives of organizational leaders on policy development and implementation in respect to shaping future directions for the chaplaincy services provided.

Internalizing a common vision

Chaplains may contribute to the spiritualizing of their organization by helping ground its core values. This task can be achieved by engaging in personal conversations with other staff and volunteers and participating in events that celebrate the facility's achievements. They can also participate in meetings or group activities that provide opportunity for reflection and/or discussion of the organization's vision and values. In one facility, regular interdepartmental consultations take place that raise awareness of 'above the line' and 'below the line' behaviours (Reddicliffe 2013, Interview 2). In this context, the observation was made that an important aspect of the work of the chaplain is 'to help create an environment in which the good, the bad, and the ugly, can be shared'. This comment points to the importance of working towards the humanizing of the culture and the internalization of a common vision that may represent the essence of its spirituality.

It would be inappropriate to generalize about the future directions of healthcare chaplaincy and, in particular, about how chaplains can contribute to the spiritualizing of their organizations, from the small sample of case descriptions presented. Nevertheless, emerging trends identified are considered of value as indicators of how chaplain/managers, directors of mission, chaplains and other staff are currently contributing to the spiritualizing of their respective church-related healthcare organizations. It is hoped that ministry planners and chaplaincy practitioners in other contexts will be encouraged as they reflect upon and address their own unique challenges in developing best-practice spiritual and pastoral care within and beyond their own organizational environments.

The particular context is critical; however, we conclude with this general comment: Our reflections suggest that chaplains – especially those in a leadership position – have a vital role to play in shaping a culture in their healthcare facility that is characterized by compassion, a sense of belonging and trust. When it comes to creating an environment of deep trust and belonging, internalization of a shared vision is crucially important. This is confirmed by current organizational theory, covenantal theology and the reports we have received from practitioners.

Acknowledgements

The authors thank the following Uniting Healthcare Chaplaincy interviewees: Reverend Heather den Houting, Reverend Helen Dick, Reverend Murray Fysh, Ms Colleen Geyer and Pastor Theo Masselos.

References

Ashmos, D.R. and Duchon, D. (2000) 'Spirituality at work: a conceptualization and a measure.' *Journal of Management Inquiry 9*, 2, 134–145.

Benson, H., Dusek, J., Sherwook J., Lam, P. *et al.* (2006) 'Study of the therapeutic effects of intercessory prayer (STEP) in cardiac bypass patients: a multi-center randomized trial of uncertainty and certainty of receiving intercessory prayer.' *American Heart Journal 151*, 4, 934–942.

Bergant, D. (1996) 'Compassion.' In C. Stuhlmueller (ed.) *The Collegeville Pastoral Dictionary of Biblical Theology*. Collegeville, MN: The Liturgical Press.

Brueggemann, W. (1979) 'Covenanting as human vocation.' *Interpretation 33*, 115–129.

Carey, L.B. and Cohen, J. (2008) 'Religion, spirituality and health care treatment decisions: the role of chaplains in the Australian clinical context.' *Journal of Health Care Chaplaincy 15*, 25–39.

Graber, D.R., Johnson, J.A. and Hornberger, K.D. (2001) 'Spirituality and healthcare organizations.' *Journal of Health Management 46*, 1, 39–50.

Guohong, H. and Harms, P.D. (2010) 'Team identification, trust and conflict: a mediation model.' *International Journal of Conflict Management 21*, 1, 20–43.

Hegney, D.G., Craigie, M., Hemsworth, D., Osseiran-Moisson, R. *et al.* (2014) 'Compassion satisfaction, compassion fatigue, anxiety, depression and stress in registered nurses in Australia: Study 1 results.' *Journal of Nursing Management 22*, 506–518.

Hoaas, G. (1997) 'Passion and compassion of God in the Old Testament.' *Scandinavian Journal of the Old Testament 11*, 1, 138–159.

Hofstede, G., Hofstede, G.J. and Minkov, M. (2010) *Cultures and Organizations: Software for the Mind*. New York, NY: McGraw-Hill. (Original work published 1991.)

Hooper, C., Craig, J., Janvrin, D.R., Wetsel, M.A. *et al.* (2010) 'Compassion satisfaction, burnout, and compassion fatigue among emergency nurses compared with nurses in other select inpatient specialties.' *Journal of Emergency Nursing 36*, 420–427.

Howard, S.A. (2002) 'A spiritual perspective on learning in the workplace.' *Journal of Managerial Psychology 17*, 3, 230–242.

Jankowski, K., Handzo, G.F. and Flannelly, K.J. (2011) 'Testing the efficacy of chaplaincy care.' *Journal of Health Care Chaplaincy 17*, 100–125.

Joinson, C. (1992) 'Coping with compassion fatigue.' *Nursing 92*, 22, 116–121.

Jurkiewicz, C.L. and Giacalone, R.A. (2004) 'A values framework for measuring the impact of workplace spirituality on organizational performance.' *Journal of Business Ethics 49*, 129–142.

Koenig, H., McCullough, M. and Larsen, D. (2001) *Handbook of Religion and Health*. Oxford: Oxford University Press.

Köster, H. (1985) '*Splánchnon*.' In G. Kittel and G. Friedrich (eds) *Theological Dictionary of the New Testament*. Translated by G. Bromiley. Grand Rapids, MI: Eerdmans.

Kotter, J. and Heskett, J. (1992) *Corporate Culture and Performance*. New York, NY: The Free Press.

LaRowe, K. (2005) *Transforming Compassion Fatigue into Flow*. Boston, MA: Acanthus.

McHolm, F. (2006) 'Rx for compassion.' *Journal of Christian Nursing 23*, 4, 12–19.

Mendenhall, G. and Herion, G. (1992) 'Covenant.' In D. Freedman (ed.) *The Anchor Bible Dictionary* (Vol. 1). New York, NY: Doubleday.

Morgan, G. (1986) *Images of Organization*. Beverly Hills, CA: Sage Publications.

Nicotera, M., Clinkscales, M.J. and Walker, F.R. (2003) *Understanding Organizations Through Culture and Structure*. Mahwah, NJ: Lawrence Erlbaum.

Ole Borgen, S. (2001) 'Identification as a trust-generating mechanism in cooperatives.' *Annals of Public and Cooperative Economics 72*, 209–228.

Pembroke, N. (2012) 'Healthcare Organizations: Corporate Spirituality.' In M. Cobb, B. Rumbold and C. Puchalski (eds) *Oxford Textbook of Spirituality and Healthcare*. Oxford: Oxford University Press.

Pembroke, N. (2016) 'Contributions from Christian ethics and Buddhist philosophy to the management of compassion fatigue in nurses.' *Nursing and Health Sciences 18*, 1, 120–124.

Reddicliffe, R. (2013) 'Health Care Chaplaincy Interviews: Edited Transcripts of Five One-on-One Semi-Structured Interviews with Chaplain/Managers of Pastoral Care Departments of Church-Owned Hospitals, and with Directors of Mission from UnitingCare, Queensland.' Unpublished interview series, Queensland.

Reynolds, L. (1997) *Creating the High Trust, High Performance Organization*. London: Nicholas Brealey Publications.

Shapiro, D., Sheppard, B. and Cheraskin, L. (1992) 'Business on a handshake.' *Negotiation Journal* 8, 4, 365–377.

Slater, V. (2012) 'Living Church in the world: chaplaincy and the mission of the Church.' *Practical Theology* 5, 3, 307–320.

Steddon, P. (2010) *Street Church: Fresh Expressions...and Beyond?* Oxford: Self-published.

Swinton, J. (2001) *Spirituality and Mental Health Care: Rediscovering a 'Forgotten' Dimension.* London: Jessica Kingsley Publishers.

Trible, P. (1976) 'The gift of the poem: a rhetorical study of Jeremiah 31:15–22.' *Andover Newton Quarterly 17,* 271–286.

Walton, M.N. (2012) 'Assessing the construction of spirituality: conceptualising spirituality in health care settings.' *Journal of Pastoral Care and Counseling 66,* 3, 1–16.

World Health Organization (2002) 'WHO-PI: Pastoral Intervention Codings.' *International Classification of Diseases* (10th revision). Geneva: World Health Organization.

Yoder, E.A. (2010) 'Compassion fatigue in nurses.' *Applied Nursing Research 23,* 191–197.

Chapter 15

Chaplaincy and Its Potential Contribution to Cultural Transformation

Kenneth J Donaldson and Ewan Kelly

Introduction

The authors met through participating in a transformational leadership programme sponsored by the Scottish government. As their relationship developed, they discovered a common interest in, and commitment to, the person-centred care and wellbeing of all who inhabit healthcare contexts. In this chapter Ewan offers some background to a resource, Values Based Reflective Practice (VBRP), developed within Scottish chaplaincy to help staff reflect on their practice. Ken then describes how VBRP has influenced his practice as a doctor and medical leader, as well as some of the wider impact of this resource on healthcare culture in Scotland.

This chapter seeks to introduce an innovative approach to inter-professional transformative learning, VBRP, which was created and tested within the Scottish chaplaincy community and then rolled out within NHSScotland from 2011 onwards. The initial aim of the initiative was to foster staff engagement as part of the Scottish government's person-centred agenda (Scottish Government 2010) through regular small-group facilitated, group-reflective practice. The Scottish government advocates that an engaged and well staff community 'have been shown to improve the patient experience and outcomes' (p.43); however, with time, not only did VBRP have an impact on individuals' practice (at a micro-level of healthcare activity) as a model of reflective practice, it also began to influence attitudes, behaviours and the promotion of staff support within teams, departments and in localities (meso-level) as well as at organizational and national (meta) levels. This was primarily through VBRP tools being increasingly used reflexively in practice by clinicians, teachers, managers and leaders. It is thus argued in this chapter that healthcare chaplaincy has influenced cultural transformation towards a more person-centred approach within Scottish healthcare at different levels of activity. Chaplains have been involved in the development of VBRP, the strategic planning of its rollout, facilitation of group reflective practice and education of other healthcare professionals about VBRP tools as well as how to facilitate VBRP reflective groups. Such influence is illustrated particularly through Ken's engagement with, and use of, VBRP as a renal physician and as a medical leader.

What is work or organizational culture?

In short, culture in a place of work 'is the way we do things around here' (Boston 1995, p.19). What informs such culture is complex, yet cultural theorists commonly have 'understandings of culture being underpinned by notions of shared values, beliefs and meanings' (Patterson *et al.* 2011, p.24). A significant exploration of cultural theory is beyond the scope of this chapter; however, in the context of describing how chaplains, through the embedding of VBRP and its tools, may have influenced Scottish healthcare culture, it is helpful to briefly outline how, in relation to cultural theory, this may have occurred.

Culture exists on three levels (based on Schein and Schein 2016):

1. observable phenomena

2. values and beliefs

3. underpinning mindsets and attitudes.

Observable phenomena or artefacts are aspects of culture which are most easily objectively noticed. They include, for example, behavioural norms and routines, the language people use, the way decisions are made as well as how information is communicated. Values and beliefs are the foundation of the phenomena which are experiences within a culture, influencing individual and corporate behaviour. Artefacts represent the lived experience of those engaging with an organization, whereas values represent people's aspirations. Patterson *et al.* (2011, p.25) significantly note that 'it is important to distinguish between espoused values and values in use'. This is where often stress is found for staff – the lived experience of the clash (in difference) between the espoused values of an organization or healthcare system, organizational values as they are enacted and experienced. Furthermore, to enable meaningful work requires staff to be able to live out their values in a work environment which not only enables such but also in which organizational values in practice resonate with theirs (Lips-Wiersma and Morris 2011).

Underpinning mindsets and attitudes are the ingrained assumptions of individuals and groups which are largely unconscious and rarely made explicit (unlike values which are often expressed). They influence beliefs and values in a mainly unquestioned and taken-for-granted manner. Therefore, to invoke cultural transformation there is a need to change not only individual behaviours and other observable phenomena but also underlying individual mindsets and basic assumptions. Thus, reflection 'upon their [staff] thinking and their spirits is essential. When people become conscious, their ability to change increases dramatically' (Hacker 2015, p.14).

What is VBRP?

VBRP evolved from a method of facilitated group theological reflective practice developed and utilized by healthcare chaplains across Scotland. It was found that chaplaincy teams who regularly met together to reflect theologically in the present on past practice to inform future work, over a period of 18 months, felt that such shared learning:

- deepened their individual spiritual care practice

- enhanced relationships amongst their team

- promoted vocational fulfilment. (Kelly 2013)

Other healthcare professionals began to show an interest in the potential for regular facilitated reflective practice and the realization was made that such a method could be 'translated into a vocabulary and conceptual framework where vocation, values, attitudes and behaviours can be explored by practitioners from a range of healthcare disciplines' (Paterson and Kelly 2013, p.60). At its core such a translation involved the replacement of asking the presenting practitioner 'What of God might be glimpsed in this situation?' with 'What values are being lived out or not?' It was envisaged that VBRP could also 'help staff reflect on the relationship between their personal stories, including their values, beliefs, experiences and sense of vocational fulfilment, and the shared story of their workplace. The interface of the two influencing behaviours, attitudes, decision-making and wellbeing' (Kelly 2012, p.472).

Essentially, VBRP involves the creation of a safe, non-judgemental space held by a trained facilitator in which a small group of practitioners reflect together on a piece of practice of a colleague to inform their future practice. It is not about judging, fixing or telling one another what to do, but rather exploring and deepening awareness. This is promoted in group reflection using a tool known as the 'three levels of seeing'.

The 'three levels of seeing' are taken from the Greek translation of the resurrection story in John 20. (A full description can be found in Leach and Paterson 2015.) In brief, the first level of seeing (*blepo*) is that which is noticed or observed whilst a piece of practice is presented. The second level (*theoreo*) is interested in that which arouses curiosity or makes a practitioner wonder and want to chew something over more. The third level (*horao*) relates to those 'a-ha' moments – when the penny drops and a realization occurs (Paterson and Kelly 2013).

Any contributions made to help a practitioner reflect on their practice must begin with 'I notice' or 'I wonder', and only the person whose practice is being shared can 'realize' – express a moment of potentially deep learning for themselves prompted by group reflection.

The focus on values and meaning during group reflection are aided by utilizing aspects of the 'NAVVY' tool to aid learning:

- **N** – whose needs are being met or overlooked in my or our practice?

- **A** – what abilities, assets and/or capabilities are at work or are missing in my or our practice?

- **V** – whose voices are being heard or silenced, included or excluded from my or our practice?

- **V** – what and who is being valued, undervalued or overvalued in my or our practice?

- **Y** – what does this situation reveal about you, me and us as practitioners and as a team or organization?

Such an approach affords the opportunity for 'double loop' learning where the impact of reflection is not just on strategies for practice but on a practitioner's values (Sandage and Jensen 2013). In addition, as can be seen from Ken's experience of VBRP (below), deeper unconscious assumptions are also potentially touched and recalled to stimulate transformation.

As outlined in the Introduction, chaplains trained in VBRP initially facilitated inter-professional reflective practice groups. Using a cascade model to roll out VBRP, chaplains then began to train practitioners from a variety of disciplines throughout NHSScotland to facilitate VBRP reflective groups. In time, VBRP tools, or aspects of them, became increasingly used reflexively by practitioners, managers and leaders to reflect in practice.

Influencing culture at a micro-level
Ken's introduction to VBRP

In 2011, a friend of mine (Ken's) died in hospital. The way he and his family were treated left me sad and bewildered. I witnessed firsthand the impact of the lack of empathy and compassion experienced by his family and on their subsequent bereavement. Through sharing their story in a variety of healthcare educational contexts with a focus on person-centred care, I realized this was not a one off; other healthcare professionals had had similar experiences as they sought to support sick or dying loved ones in their personal lives. Why? What was behind this apparent lack of care and what could we do to prevent this happening?

Stimulated by discussion with some colleagues, we developed the concept of using such patient experiences in a constructive manner with multidisciplinary teams within NHS Dumfries and Galloway (the geographical health board in which I work, in southwest Scotland). It was suggested VBRP may be a method to help teams reflect together on patient stories to inform future practice. I had never heard of VBRP – the use of noticing and wondering about experience as opposed to making assumptions, quick judgements or fixes and the power of an individual's own realizations or deep learning to enhance sustained behaviour change. What about the NAVVY tool? I must confess I was a little sceptical. In particular, the language of 'I notice' and 'I wonder' felt clunky and contrived, and I struggled to see how this would enable transformational learning. However, I was persuaded to integrate the method into our locality's multidisciplinary continuing professional development sessions which we had named *Enhanced Patient Experience* events.

It was important that a facilitated VBRP session be modelled before event participants could begin to give it a try. Therefore, we needed a practitioner willing to share a story, a piece of their practice which had stayed with them, to enable facilitated reflection involving five or six others to help that healthcare worker reflect on that incident to inform future practice. An ideal case emerged from my own practice. As a consultant nephrologist I am often involved in decisions around whether to dialyse acutely ill individuals. In this instance I had decided to dialyse an elderly lady, who died the next day. At the time I recognized that dialysing her had been a mistake but had not discussed her case in any detail with anyone else. After talking it through with the rest of the team, I agreed to share it as part of a VBRP session at our learning event.

I therefore found myself sitting in a semi-circle with the facilitator, a chaplain and six others who were involved in modelling VBRP in a lecture theatre in front of an audience of 50 or so of my peers telling them the story of 'Mary' as the focus of a VBRP session.

Mary's story

I had known Mary for several years and had reviewed her in clinic a month or so before her final admission. She was elderly, virtually housebound and had multiple medical problems, including progressive kidney failure. We had discussed the consequences of her failing kidneys and the options available to her – hospital-based haemodialysis, peritoneal dialysis at home or full supportive care which involves managing with medicines and other support but not progressing to dialysis. She had chosen the latter as she felt dialysis would be too much for her, a decision with which I agreed. On the day of her final admission, however, she became acutely breathless over a matter of hours and, by the time she arrived in hospital, was critically ill. She knew her lungs were full of fluid because her kidneys had finally failed. Emergency dialysis was an option of which she was aware and was now requesting. Significantly, shortly before Mary's final admission to hospital, I had been made head of the renal unit in the hospital.

One of my more junior colleagues, Jane, saw Mary in our admissions unit and discussed the possibility of dialysis with Mary and her family. Jane, by her own admission, struggles with end-of-life discussions and, after seeing Mary, she came to talk through the situation with me. Mary wanted dialysis. Jane agreed, but the family were not so keen. I explained to Jane that I trusted her judgement and that she should proceed to insert a dialysis line into Mary. This involves numbing an area of the patient's neck with local anaesthetic, and inserting a needle, then a wire and finally a long plastic tube into the jugular vein. This 'line' is then used to dialyse the patient. Although a relatively routine procedure for a kidney doctor, this is an uncomfortable and sometimes painful process for the patient.

About 30 minutes after my discussion with Jane, I went to our 'line' room to see how things were going. I found a very breathless patient who was clearly distressed, a red-faced and sweaty Jane struggling to get the line in and our senior charge nurse looking extremely anxious. I made a quick decision and took over the procedure and, after another 10 minutes or so, managed to insert the line. Mary was given some morphine to ease her distress and had dialysis. The next morning, I went straight to our high-dependency unit to review Mary. I was told that she had had a fairly settled night and was having some breakfast. I stuck my head into the room where she was and found her slumped in her bed. She was barely breathing, and I called over a nurse. We sat with Mary for the next 2 minutes as she died.

VBRP and the impact on Ken's practice

I finished the story and the inter-professional group involved in performing VBRP then started using the 'three levels of seeing' and NAVVY tools, enabled by a facilitator, to help me reflect on this piece of practice.

What they noticed and wondered about was not quite what I was expecting. Someone noticed that I had become a little emotional when I had mentioned Jane's name. Somebody else wondered to what extent I felt a sense of responsibility and ownership for the renal unit and the decisions made by the unit's staff. My discomfort when discussing the dialysis decision was noticed, as was some remorse about the degree of family involvement. But they offered no opinions or judgements, or shared comparative stories; they just noticed and wondered. I was left to consider their comments and reflect on them and, ultimately, come to my own realizations. When these realizations came, they were powerful and emotional, and I found myself close to tears.

Through engagement in VBRP with others, I had come to the realization that I had deliberately stepped back from making decisions about Mary as I had recently taken on the role of lead of the renal unit and felt I needed to give others some freedom. I knew Jane would struggle with the decision but did not want to overrule her. I knew that dialysis was the wrong thing to do as I walked into the room and saw Mary. When asked to consider *Whose needs were being met?* by one of the group, it became clear to me: Jane's needs were met, my needs were met (at least in terms of my understanding of my new role as head of the renal unit), perhaps the nursing team's needs were met – but Mary's needs were *not* met. Her *voice* may have been heard – she had said she wanted dialysis – but she was extremely unwell and clutching at straws. I had heard my inner *voice* too but had not acted on it at the time. Experience had told me that dialysis was not in her best interests and the family knew that too. Ultimately it did her no good; it only put her through a distressing procedure 12 hours before she died.

After the VBRP session, I felt drained emotionally and physically. The audience members were clearly moved too, and several came up to me and thanked me for being so open and honest. They recognized the power of what had just happened. I also realized the power of a senior physician prepared to do what I had just done – being open and vulnerable in front of peers. I hoped that this would influence others to do likewise, albeit in small groups and not in front of a large audience. On reflection, I realized the power of VBRP to provide a safe space to explore my practice and the values informing my practice, and to do so in a non-judgemental way. More than that, I had realized some deep truths about myself and some attitudes and behaviours that I would need to address to improve my clinical practice.

There is no doubt that what happened to me following that VBRP session was a slow but profound change in how I considered the needs of patients and their families, as well as my own needs. This caused me to further reflect on what had befallen my friend and his family. Had any staff members involved in his care had the opportunity to reflect and learn from their involvement? I suspect not. What this had offered me was a chance to reconnect with my values – compassion, empathy and respect for others – values which may have been buried by the pressures of work, the responsibility of the renal unit and caring for other staff members. It helped me reconnect with what vocationally matters to me.

Following my 'realization' that VBRP was an approach to reflection on practice that could dig deep and release those inner emotions that are so often buried in healthcare workers as well as help enable them to reconnect with vocational values, I started to explore how I could spread the word and influence my colleagues locally and further afield. However, even as I started to look ahead, I noticed how VBRP was affecting my clinical behaviours in real time. I had reflected *on* practice by telling Mary's story, but now I was increasingly reflecting *in* practice. I found myself entering a ward and being faced with difficult clinical decisions and, quite literally at times, 'taking' a step back, intentionally noticing and wondering and asking staff around me 'Whose needs are being met?' and 'What about the voices of the patient and relatives?' I quickly noticed that this change in my approach led to different outcomes – outcomes which were much more inclusive of the patient's opinions and feelings and which often involved far more lengthy and detailed discussions with families at an earlier stage in the patient's journey.

Influencing culture at a meso-level

I (Ken) now describe two examples where VBRP has been used to influence organizational culture change in a locality.

Example 1: a merging of organizations in a locality

In 2015, the Scottish government directed local councils and health boards to establish 'integrated joint boards' (IJBs) to help facilitate the overall integration of health, social and independent care. In the geographical area where I work, the IJB comprised an equal number of elected members from the local council and non-executive health board members along with professional leads and other representatives. As medical director for NHS Dumfries and Galloway, I am part of the IJB. It became apparent quite early in the IJB's 'forming' that there was a clear clash of cultures between the health and social (council-run) care bodies, which up until then had worked entirely strategically and organizationally independently.

This chapter described earlier some of the theory underlying cultural development, and it is interesting to examine the IJB through this lens. Council members were keen to discuss governance and process in depth, and often their language around these discussions could be direct and to the point. Health board members, whilst recognizing the importance of the governance structure, had a more pragmatic approach – a wish to 'get things done' – and it was obvious that both these visible behaviours, or artefacts, were causing friction. I can look back now and realize that the values and beliefs underlying these behaviours were subtly different. Whilst there was a common feeling of 'trying to do the best for the local population', this was being expressed in different ways, which were being directed by basic underlying assumptions about 'how things get done' within each system.

The chair of the IJB wished to address this and employed several methods, one of which was to engage in a session of VBRP. The majority of the IJB met and spent an afternoon in a facilitated session in which everyone had the opportunity to express the values that informed their work. All were then encouraged to notice and wonder about how these values expressed themselves in their work, and the realizations that emerged were explored further using the NAVVY tool. The afternoon started, as these workshops often do, with a general feeling of disquiet and perhaps 'what have I got myself into?' but, by the end, conversation was flowing and the overall feeling was that it had been worthwhile.

Several months later, we had another workshop to explore where we were regarding the overall functioning of the IJB. What was noticed by everyone, and explored in the last hour of the session, was the general feeling of a 'difference' to the group. It was wondered out loud, 'Have we created our own IJB culture that is neither council nor health board but instead unique?' There was much laughter, shared stories and a general warmth that had been absent before. This has persisted throughout subsequent IJB meetings, and they are more productive as a result. It would be a little presumptive to suggest that this is all down to one session of VBRP as other workshops had taken place. However, there is a noticeable change in the language used around the board table and a kinder approach that is less accusatory, gentler and more curious. Instead of bickering over who has told what representative body a certain fact, there is a focus on the end user – 'Are their needs being met?', and if not, why not and how can we respond?

Example 2: influencing junior doctors' attitudes and behaviours

In 2017, I delivered an educational session to a selection of junior doctors on the topic of *Realistic Medicine* (Calderwood 2016). This describes a shift away from traditional practice to one that is more inclusive of patients and their families and has shared decision-making, a focus on value in healthcare, less variation and waste, and innovation in collaboration with public partners. I used a story of an elderly patient who was admitted to hospital for several weeks and underwent numerous tests and procedures when, in fact, he was actively dying. His wishes were not to have aggressive treatment, but rather to die peacefully at home. Sadly, his wife was not engaged with meaningfully by staff until late in this process, and by this time the patient was too muddled to articulate things clearly. After telling this story, I introduced VBRP as a method of reflecting on practice and learning from stories like this. When I mentioned the 'three levels of seeing', a doctor in the front row laughed. I noticed his response out loud and wondered what was so funny. He said that it sounded ridiculous. I believe a lot of medics feel this way initially; he was just being open about his cynicism. Once we chatted this through with the group, I was able to move them to a different place. This approach is different – it does not focus on finding solutions or fixing problems but on exploring the values and motivations for care. It may feel odd at first, but it has power.

I believe that it is extremely important to engage young doctors in training with tools such as VBRP at as early a stage as possible. I have observed and experienced newly qualified doctors quickly becoming entrenched in established cultures and accepting 'that is the way things are done around here'. If we are to prevent this happening so readily and challenge some of their basic underlying assumptions, in particular those around *Realistic Medicine* (Calderwood 2016), then we need doctors who feel safe noticing and wondering about their experience and comfortable to engage in a session of VBRP to explore some of the difficult situations that they encounter on a daily basis.

Junior doctors move around a great deal, so it is difficult to measure how much of an impact a session like the one I delivered above will have had. I did receive some formal feedback a week or so later with a number of positive comments such as: 'Overall the most useful lecture I have had this year'; 'Thank you for this, I will attempt to "notice and wonder" more often'; 'Recognizing whose needs are met and how to reflect effectively is very important'; and unsurprisingly, 'The consultants need to hear this too!'

So, there is work to be done with other groups of healthcare staff, but my experience with the junior doctors was positive and I believe this is a good place to start. Cultural transformation does not happen overnight, but by small steps and by hope. By engaging the senior doctors of tomorrow, we can start that change.

Influencing culture at a meta-level
Examples across NHSScotland

VBRP is not just about behavioural change or seeing things differently. In the current environment of the NHS – financial strain, recruitment shortages, constant change – VBRP also has a role in staff support. It is a tool which can be used to promote staff wellbeing. Following from the success of local *Enhanced Patient Experience* events, I (Ken) have spoken at several interdisciplinary *National Patient Safety* conferences in Scotland raising the national profile of VBRP; however, the focus remained on learning as opposed to support. It was not until I was invited to a national British Medical Association meeting on staff support that I felt able to explore this important aspect of the tool. This was a chance to speak to a body of doctors and explain how taking an opportunity to notice and wonder at what was happening in the moment between them, and those they were relating to, could lead to building resilience at work. Simply by sharing stories in a safe environment, they found they were able to reconnect with vocational values and what mattered most to them, both clinically and in their leadership roles. This ultimately led to an increased self-awareness and attentiveness to those around them. In short, they became kinder to themselves and others.

VBRP is becoming increasingly recognized throughout the Scottish healthcare system as a valuable tool to aid learning, change behaviour and enhance staff wellbeing. A recent chief executive officer's report from NHS Grampian (Wright 2018, p.2), in northeast Scotland, includes the following:

> In NHS Grampian there appears to be an appetite for VBRP. 42 sessions have been delivered this year (January till April), with some 178 participants, mostly drawn from ward-based teams… VBRP is particularly helpful when demands on time and activity are high, in that by stepping back for 20–30 minutes, reviewing what is seen and making a re-assessment, teams are in a better place to respond to their perceived needs.

In central Scotland, NHS Forth Valley's (2016–2017) annual report into *Feedback, Comments, Concerns, Compliments and Complaints* records that there are 12 facilitated VBRP groups regularly taking place across the organization which enables, as appropriate, identifying key lessons from complaints.

In NHS Lanarkshire (south of Glasgow), VBRP is being rolled out widely. A pilot has been developed to use the tool to help staff reflect on and learn from adverse incidents. Paul Graham (2017), head of Spiritual Care and Wellbeing at NHS Lanarkshire, significantly says this about participating in VBRP:

> we hear that we're not the only one to feel or think this way; we grow in respect and admiration for our colleagues who press on through the doubt, fear, or hurt to deliver the best possible care; and we see colleagues be affirmed by their peers. We witness people being restored and replenished, ready to go back into the arena and give themselves generously for others.

Nationally VBRP is being recommended as an approach to aid the debriefing for staff following end-of-life events by NHS Education for Scotland (2019) on their *Support Around Death* website.

Conclusion
Ken's perspective

With increasing use of tools like VBRP in healthcare, it is possible that we shift the underlying culture from one of investigate and treat to a more balanced one of quality and value. Sir Muir Gray describes 'value-based healthcare' (Gray and Abbasi 2007) which, it is important to note, is different from values-based practice. The NHS has a finite resource, and we need to ensure that ever-dwindling finances are directed appropriately and deliver treatments which provide the best value to our patients. This is an extremely complex and ethically challenging area, but it is with the use of tools like VBRP that we can open our eyes to the experiences of the people we treat and engage in more meaningful conversation to ensure we deliver the best value. This depends upon shared decision-making (involving patients, their families and healthcare professionals) which, in turn, depends upon healthcare professionals having the skills to reflect both on and in practice; to notice in the moment, wonder why and subsequently *realize*. Asking 'Whose needs are being met?', 'Whose voice is being heard?', 'What does this say about you?' – these questions are so powerful in the moment that they can change the direction of a consultation and help enable outcomes which are of value. They encourage an emotional connection which promotes engagement at a human level with our patients and their loved ones. They can also influence decision-making at a higher level, encouraging co-design of services with citizens and development of policy that can deliver value.

VBRP is not the only tool which can aid in this way, but it is one that I have used in many different scenarios and the one I continue to return to because of its striking effect and influence. I have noticed a change in myself and I no longer wonder why – I have realized!

Ewan's perspective

Ken has offered his own personal reflections and observations on the impact VBRP, both as a model of reflective practice and as a reflective approach which offers tools to aid reflexivity in practice, has had on his own work as a clinician and leader. His reflections resonate with significant findings of a national evaluation of VBRP (Bunniss 2014, p.11) which reveals key impacts observed by VBRP facilitators. These impacts include:

1. increased self-awareness and therefore an enhanced ability to reflect on practice at the point of care and be responsive to patient and staff needs in the moment

2. increased personal wellbeing, satisfaction and resilience as a result of remembering, recovering or reclaiming the motivation and desire to become NHS healthcare staff.

In enabling individuals to (re)engage with their inner and spiritual selves, to revisit and question 'given' cultural norms and assumptions, and practise from a sense of vocational purpose as well as with increased self-awareness and discernment, VBRP promotes transformational learning and deepened vocational fulfilment for individuals. Moreover, as Ken's examples show, in relation to cultural theory, VBRP also affords the potential for contributing to cultural transformation at meso- and meta-levels of healthcare activity.

References

Boston, C. (1995) 'Cultural transformation.' *Journal of Nursing Administration 25*, 1, 19–20.

Bunniss, S. (2014) *Values Based Reflective Practice Evaluation Report.* Glasgow: Firecloud Research. (Unpublished report.)

Calderwood, C. (2016) *Realistic Medicine: Chief Medical Officer's Annual Report 2014–15.* Edinburgh: The Scottish Government. Accessed on 27/12/2018 at www.gov.scot/Resource/0049/00492520.pdf.

Graham, P. (2017) 'We are listening to staff.' *Care Opinion.* Accessed on 27/12/2018 at www.careopinion.org.uk/blogposts/659/we-are-listening-to-staff.

Gray, J.M. and Abbasi, K. (2007) 'How to get better value healthcare.' *Journal of the Royal Society of Medicine 100*, 10, 480.

Hacker, S. (2015) 'Leading cultural transformation.' *The Journal for Quality and Participation 37*, 4, 13–16.

Kelly, E. (2012) 'The development of healthcare chaplaincy.' *The Expository Times 123*, 10, 469–478.

Kelly, E. (2013) 'Translating theological reflective practice into values-based reflection: a report from Scotland.' *Reflective Practice 33*, 245–256.

Leach, J. and Paterson, M. (2015) *Pastoral Supervision: A Handbook.* London: SCM. (Original work published 2010.)

Lips-Wiersma, M. and Morris, L. (2011) *The Map of Meaning: A Guide to Sustaining Our Humanity in the World of Work.* Sheffield: Greenleaf Publishing.

NHS Education for Scotland (2019) *Support Around Death*. Accessed on 21/12/2018 at www.sad.scot.nhs.uk.

NHS Forth Valley (2017) *Annual Report: Feedback, Comments, Concerns, Compliments and Complaints*. Larbert: NHS Forth Valley. Accessed on 21/12/2018 at https://nhsforthvalley.com/wp-content/uploads/2014/01/Feedback-Comments-Concerns-and-Complaints-Annual-Report-2016-2017.pdf.

Paterson, M. and Kelly, E. (2013) 'Values based reflective practice: a method developed in Scotland for spiritual care practitioners.' *Practical Theology* 6, 1, 52–68.

Paterson, M., Nolan, M., Rick, J., Brown, J. *et al.* (2011) *From Metrics to Meaning: Culture Change and Quality of Acute Hospital Care for Older People*. London: National Institute for Health Research Service Delivery and Organization Programme.

Sandage, S. and Jensen, M. (2013) 'Relational spiritual formation.' *Reflective Practice: Formation and Supervision in Ministry 33*, 95-108.

Schein, E. and Schein, P. (2016) *Organizational Culture and Leadership* (5th edition). San Francisco, CA: Jossey-Bass.

Scottish Government (2010) *The Healthcare Quality Strategy for NHSScotland*. Edinburgh: The Scottish Government. Accessed on 08/08/2018 at www.gov.scot/Publications/2010/05/10102307/5.

Wright, M. (2018) *Chief Executive's Report: April*. Aberdeen: NHS Grampian. Accessed on 21/12/2018 at www.nhsgrampian.org/files/item4for050418chiefexecutivereport.pdf.

Chapter 16

Spiritual Care and a New Art of Dying

Carlo Leget

Introduction

The place of chaplaincy at the end of life seems a natural one given the World Health Organization (2018) definition of palliative care which lists the spiritual dimension as one of the four dimensions in our care for dying patients and their families. For a good integration of chaplains in the healthcare team, however, it is essential that they be able to represent the spiritual dimension in such a way that it opens up a space in which patients, proxies and caregivers can learn from each other in a joint search for (existential) meaning. A new art of dying can be a helpful tool here, offering all parties involved a simple and non-judgmental framework which transcends the particularities of specific (non)religious traditions. In this chapter we sketch the possibilities of such a new art of dying, based on the experiences with this tool in the Netherlands in recent years.

Origin and outline of the new art of dying

Developing spiritual care at the end of life in a country as secularized as the Netherlands is a challenge in many respects (Van de Geer and Leget 2012). For centuries the Netherlands has been a country in which, globally speaking, half of the population belonged to the Roman Catholic Church and half of the population to a number of Dutch reformed churches in the Calvinist tradition. According to the most recent study in 2015, however, only 14% of the Dutch people still believe in a personal God, 28% of the population indicate belief in some higher power, 34% of the Dutch consider themselves agnostic and 24% of the population call themselves atheists (Bernts and Berghuijs 2016). Finding a common language for addressing the spiritual dimension in palliative care is difficult, for the debate already starts with the question of what to call this dimension: spiritual, existential or related to meaning? Other challenges are related to the image problem of chaplains in a secularized society (beginning with what name to give them that is acceptable to everyone) and the tendency to reduce the spiritual dimension to psychosocial issues.

The development of spiritual care as an interdisciplinary responsibility, in which chaplains have a special position because of their expertise, has proved to be an important and helpful step towards (re)integrating spiritual care into palliative care (Puchalski *et al.* 2009). One of the initiatives which has been successful in the Netherlands in this respect was the development of a model for communication and reflection on spiritual issues that puts the interaction of patients, proxies and caregivers at the centre of spiritual care. It is known as the *ars moriendi* model or diamond (because of its diamond shape form) and is used in many contexts.

The origin of the model lies in a project of participatory observation on two palliative care wards in Dutch nursing homes in the years 1998–1999. One of the most important observations made was the importance of the openness and inner freedom of the person listening to the spiritual concerns of another person. Depending on this openness and the atmosphere of humaneness and acceptance accompanying it, a conversation would be more or less open and in-depth. In one of the nursing homes the metaphor of space was used a lot. This metaphor is not immediately associated with a particular spiritual tradition but rather with an emotional and cognitive attitude of non-judgmental openness and inner freedom coined as 'inner space'. Inner space is not the same as inner peace. It may also be present whilst one experiences different conflicting emotions simultaneously. Important, however, is the experience that one is not entirely immersed in one or more of these emotions or inner voices: having inner space, one has the ability to experience and observe one's emotions simultaneously.

Searching for a way to embed the metaphor of inner space in the practice of conversation and accompaniment, a connection was made with an ancient tradition in which there is also an awareness that spirituality is about dealing with a plurality of inner voices. In the history of Western Europe, from ancient Greek and Roman culture until the nineteenth century, the confrontation with one's own mortality has given rise to a literary genre known as *ars moriendi* or art of dying (Laager 1996). One specific version of this genre has become known as the late medieval *ars moriendi* which was handed down in the form of block books (Bayard 1999; Girard-Augry 1986). In these medieval booklets patients were confronted with five challenges related to the loss of faith, hope, charity, patience and humility. The dying phase is depicted as a spiritual struggle in which the devils at one side of the bed represented the thoughts and feelings related to doubt, desperation, avarice, impatience and complacency. The angels and saints at the other side of the bed were there to inspire the moribund with faith, hope, charity, patience and humility.

Although the medieval model was restricted to the spiritual dimension of dying, and a good death was entirely framed in terms of staying connected with the Christian tradition, the five issues at stake seem to be universal issues. The idea of inner polyphony seems to be an important point of departure for spiritual care. Reframing the medieval *ars moriendi*, one could say that five existential issues are addressed: autonomy; suffering; human relations; guilt; and hope (Leget 2007, 2017). In the new *ars moriendi* these five issues are presented as basic anthropological tensions between two opposite poles that help create space to reflect on one's position or discover more than one inner voice (inner polyphony) with respect to an issue. Reflecting on how to deal with suffering, for example, one is drawn between the pole of doing (dominant in Western culture) and undergoing. At the centre of the new *ars moriendi* is the non-judgmental attitude of inner space, which is needed to find out how to face suffering without being dictated by one pole or the other. The goal of the model is not to transform the dialectical relation of the two poles into a new synthesis, but to live and die as freely as possible in between the tensions that are part of being human.

Framework for reflection: patients and families

Much of what has been written about spiritual care is written from the perspective of, and for, the professional caregiver (Cobb, Dowrick and Lloyd-Williams 2012). The central question is how to give spiritual care to patients. The *ars moriendi* model, however, takes a different point of departure. Like its medieval predecessor, *ars moriendi*, the art of dying, is seen primarily as the art of the one who is dying; or to put it more precisely, the art of dying is seen as a practice of those involved in which the patient is at the centre. As the model itself witnesses, 'no man is an island', and all human beings are related through identity building and life-sustaining networks. The inner space of patients and proxies are influenced by each other. The same is true for the inner space of formal and informal caregivers who are part of this shared practice.

Based on this idea, in one of the general hospitals in Arnhem, in the Netherlands, since 2011 the *ars moriendi* model has been introduced to patients during one of the longer intake conversations with nurse specialists. A graphic representation of the model is offered to the patient as a possible tool for organizing one's thoughts. Patients take home the leaflet with the tool and a short explanation, and they are invited to come back to it in a next conversation, when they feel it is important for them to do so. The message of the nurse is: 'We think this is an important dimension to take care of in the situation you are in now, so see if you think this is helpful. We do not want to impose anything on you, just empower you and your proxies to organize the deeper questions that may come up at the end of life.'

In the model five questions are central:

- Who am I and what do I really want?

- How do I deal with suffering?

- How do I say goodbye?

- How do I look back on my life?

- What can I hope for?

Reflecting on these questions, patients are encouraged to focus on their inner space. What are the difficult issues they are facing? Where would they like to be supported by conversations, rituals or other spiritual practices? Who do they think are the right persons for them to do this?

The *ars moriendi* tool is offered as a way to encourage reflection and conversation about their inner life. It does not lead to an evaluation in terms of right and wrong (as its medieval predecessor did) but helps to gain sight of where one's inner space might be under pressure. This is done with the help of the tension between the two poles. The question 'Who am I and what do I really want?' confronts us with the tensions between being connected with oneself and being connected with others. Both are constitutive to our identity and are related to our autonomy. Sometimes these tensions may result in conflicts of loyalties. The model helps to reflect on the limits of our human freedom as related to our identity. In the same way the other four central questions confront us with polarities that are constitutive of our human condition: the tension between doing and undergoing (How do I deal with suffering?); between holding on and letting go (How do I say goodbye?); between remembering and forgetting (How do I look back on my life?); and between knowing and believing (What can I hope for?).

Because these five questions and tensions are framed as generic anthropological tensions, there is sufficient openness to use them also for people who want to reflect on these issues from a religious perspective (Leget 2017). The starting point, however, is non-religious – not only because a religious perspective is only helpful for a minority of the general population, but also because spiritual needs may comprise situational needs and moral and biographical needs, next to religious needs (Kellehear 2000).

Patients who work with the model report that it is helpful in organizing their thoughts and feelings (Voskuilen 2012). What they often find difficult is to find the right words to speak about these issues. The model helps them here, partly because of its graphic representation(Figure 16.1). Although not every patient has the wish to engage deeply with spiritual issues, until now none of them have reported that something is missing in the tool as it is presented.

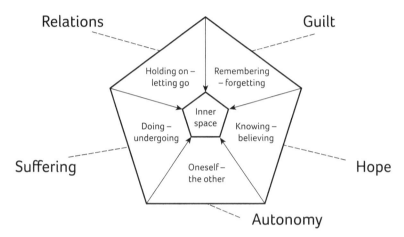

Figure 16.1 The ars moriendi model

Education: all healthcare professionals

In a country where 58% of the general population is either atheist or agnostic, it is no surprise that many caregivers have little to no background in dealing with existential, spiritual or religious issues. Therefore, a great deal of the success of integrating spiritual care in healthcare depends on (re)introducing attention to this dimension in clinical care. That brings us to the issue of education, where the *ars moriendi* model can be helpful in two major ways.

First, according to Part 2 of a European Association of Palliative Care (EAPC) white paper on education for palliative care generalists, to the core competency of providing spiritual care belongs the ability 'to demonstrate the reflective capacity to consider the importance of spiritual and existential dimensions in their own lives' (Gamondi, Larkin and Payne 2013, p.141). What is presented here as a first and basic competency presupposes a number of steps that are not so self-evident to a lot of healthcare professionals. First, many people will have to be ready to engage with the dimensions of spiritual and existential care, letting go of prejudices, allergies, bad experiences or other hindrances. Second, they will have to be ready and able to do some introspection and self-reflection on these issues. Third, they will have to find the language to express their position as regards these dimensions. Starting with the introduction of inner space as an experience all of us are familiar with in daily life, dealing with humour, stress, irritation, joy and sadness, the primordial step of fostering an attitude of openness can be made in a gentle way. Having people experience how inner space has an impact on what we perceive and feel is a first step of becoming aware of the non-rational aspects of human communication that are basic to spiritual care. This is the case for both professionals and patients and their families. Reflecting on the role of inner space and relating it to one's own experiences may thus be helpful in entering the field of spiritual care.

Second, one of the major obstacles of introducing spiritual care is the image of spirituality as something vague, religious or esoteric. Here the *ars moriendi* model can be helpful because it offers a framework that helps in organizing communication and reflection in formal and general anthropological categories that everyone understands at first sight. The graphic depiction of the model presents spirituality as an area that can be mapped out. What seemed to be vague and elusive thus becomes concrete and well defined.

A next step in education may be to enter those fields by small group discussions in which the caregivers reflect on the five themes from the *ars moriendi* model as they are present in their own lives. One might ask, for example, about the loyalties that are part of their own identity (autonomy); whether they are rather inclined to do or undergo, and how this works out with patients who are different (suffering); how they would like to say goodbye to their loved ones (relations); how one would like to be remembered and what one would choose to be written on one's headstone (guilt); and whether one believes in life after death (hope).

My experience in using exercises like these during training sessions is that healthcare professionals find it both interesting and important to do. They realize how little they know about how their colleagues think about these things. In daily care there is hardly time and opportunity to reflect on the impact of what they experience on their own life and values. Educational opportunities like these are a welcome moment of reflection that helps them to reconnect with the meaning of their work. It can also open their eyes to the existential dimensions of the concerns their patients have.

Apart from using the model as a tool to reflect on one's own inner life, it can be used to develop a critical perspective on contemporary culture (Leget 2016). Looking at the five tensions in the *ars moriendi* model, one could say that contemporary culture is more focused on me than others (autonomy); more on doing than undergoing (suffering); more on holding on than letting go (relations); more on forgetting than remembering (guilt); and more on knowing than believing (hope). In this respect the model can help to create inner space by identifying which cultural tendencies have an impact on the way we appreciate the situation we are in and the choices we have. By sketching a broader landscape, more options can be developed and more inner freedom can be realized.

Spiritual history taking: healthcare professionals with an education in spiritual care

In the Netherlands, physicians who want to specialize in palliative care at a generalist level can take part in a 20-day training with a group of 40 colleagues. One of the elements of the training is a 1.5-hour introduction to spiritual care and the *ars moriendi* model. After this introduction the physicians are given a take-home assignment. They are asked to analyse one of their patients with the help of the *ars moriendi* tool. This can be done through a conversation with the patient or as a mental exercise, looking back on one of the patients of whom they have taken care. The goal of the assignment is to experience how it is to work with the model and what it does for their professional practice. They are asked to report about their experiences by showing how they worked with the model and what they discovered about the patient and their practice.

In the many years that I have given these courses, the physicians almost unanimously report that the model helps them to get a grip on an area that they always had found difficult to manage. The structure of the model helps them to get insight into the issues that are relevant for patients and the model helps to discuss things with patients. Most physicians report that their relationship with the patients has deepened, and for many of them this has led to further conversations with patients and their families. As far as the physicians are concerned, the model is complete and does not lack any themes (Leget, van Daelen and Swart 2013).

Although the model was considered complete, the physicians felt the most comfortable discussing the questions about autonomy (relation with myself versus relation with others), suffering (doing versus undergoing) and saying goodbye (holding on versus letting go). Their own explanation for this is that these themes are closest to their work as doctors. The question about looking back on life (remembering versus forgetting) was seen as more difficult because the physicians felt this was more a private thing related to guilt and remorse. The question about hope (knowing versus believing) was the most difficult one, because they felt they were not experts in this field, and they were afraid to make mistakes by saying the wrong thing.

Although physicians reported that the model was helpful, and it opened their eyes to the dimension of spiritual care in a concrete way, they also found that it was time-consuming. Many found it hard to integrate in their daily care, and some also found that they would need more training to feel confident to work with the model. Others reported that the more the model was used, the more it became an internalized checklist to alert them to themes about which they would normally not think. A positive outcome, finally, was that they had a better view on what a chaplain actually does, and some had even referred patients to a chaplain after they had used the model.

Spiritual assessment: chaplains

Although the basics of the *ars moriendi* model can be taught within 1.5 hours, the possibilities of working with the model in a more sophisticated way make it especially apt to work with for chaplains. From 2007, eleven 4-day masterclasses on spiritual care in palliative care have been organized in the Netherlands. Originally meant for healthcare chaplains, through the years the masterclasses have developed into interdisciplinary masterclasses during which both chaplains and other healthcare professionals are taught to work with the *ars moriendi* model. Next to an introduction to the background of the model, different ways of fostering inner space, and the many ways in which the models can be used, most of the time is spent on an in-depth case discussion.

After having read a complex case aloud, a joint exploration is made of how our own inner space is affected by hearing the case. Collecting the great variety of emotional responses to the case helps in seeing how the different participants bring their own frame of reference to the table. In a very effective way it can be shown: (a) how great a variety of first reactions – ranging from compassion and love to anger and pain – one single case can elicit; (b) to what extent our own biography may be helpful to have deep or superficial access to the problems that are central to the case; and (c) how much most people are inclined to act and solve problems rather than to observe their own inner world and analyse the complexity at hand.

Subsequently, the case is discussed in a group that has a maximum of 12 persons, allowing them to have a discussion of 15–20 minutes on every theme. By discussing the five central questions in their complexity, the participants learn that there can be a polyphony of voices, emotions and positions in each one of the five fields. Someone may want to hold on and let go of their family at the same time, and the central question then is to what extent these wishes are accompanied with anger, fear, guilt or inner space.

As well as learning to see the complexity in each separate field, the participants also discover how the different fields are interrelated. The five fields are all different routes of access to the same inner space of this person. Looking at the case through the lens of one of these fields will show new aspects of the same case – like the same light being fractured in different colours through different facets of a diamond. Often, the different aspects are interrelated. In the case discussed, for example, a dying woman continues to cling to life because of motives that are related to social, psychological and religious issues that are found in four of the five fields.

There is a second way in which chaplains use the model, which is related to the way they write down notes about conversations they have with patients, and the wish to make a critical observation of their own functioning. In an experiment that we did with a number of chaplains in the Amsterdam region, we asked them to use the *ars moriendi* model to write down what they had discussed with a patient. In this way they were forced to analyse their conversations, and most of them discovered that they had particular themes and fields that they frequently explored and others that would be avoided or marginalized. Reflecting on these things it was found that many times there were hesitations to talk about specific subjects that were seen as private or that were avoided because of the fear of imposing one's own ideas and beliefs.

Communication: patient files and transfer

As the *ars moriendi* model is a simple tool that helps to organize issues and uses ordinary language, it is helpful for making notes in patient files and situations of transfer. The first clinical context where this has been developed was the palliative ward of the academic hospital in Leuven, Belgium (Leget *et al.* 2008).

Looking for ways to integrate spiritual care in their clinical palliative care practice, a multidisciplinary group of healthcare professionals started by reading papers and books on the subject that would be helpful to: (a) the development of an instrument for spiritual care; (b) the clarification of terminology; and (c) the development of one's own spiritual attitude.

As they felt that the *ars moriendi* model seemed to meet all of these goals, they began an experiment using the model in patient files. All patients received a spiritual file in which the five fields of the *ars moriendi* model were present. Instead of reporting spiritual issues and utterances among the information about physical and psychosocial matters, caregivers wrote down what they heard from patients in one of the five fields. When there was doubt, inexperienced caregivers would be helped by more experienced colleagues. The files would be discussed and interpreted in the multidisciplinary team.

As a result of this, people working on the palliative care ward reported a number of improvements as regards the implementation of spiritual care in everyday care. First, they reported an improvement in the recognition of spiritual issues. Second, they discovered that gradually a shared terminology was developing. Using the same instrument, and cooperating more intensely, people increased their vocabulary and a common language for spiritual issues was developed. Third, they developed their own instrument of interdisciplinary cooperation, which was used by *all* team members (not only by the few who had been advocating spiritual care from the outset). And lastly, they reported an improvement in the transfer of spiritual issues.

Apart from using the diamond framework for writing down fragments of spiritual issues, the team also made an addition to the model. When a sentence or utterance was written down, or a spiritual conversation in the night was reported, the caregiver would also add the intervention that had taken place: (a) observing and detecting; (b) accompanying; (c) informing and advising; and (d) coordinating and discussing. In this way it would be clear to what extent and in which way spiritual care was offered in the hospital.

Conclusion

The *ars moriendi* model has been developed in order to facilitate reflection and conversation on spiritual issues between patients, proxies and healthcare professionals. For the palliative care context, one could add volunteers here. By using the model in education and patient files, it is introduced into the day-to-day clinical practice of all healthcare workers. It becomes part of their way of looking at patients and families. It can also be offered to patients in order to give them back some autonomy in a field into which it is also hard for many patients to find their way. As chaplaincy is seen as the discipline which is most explicitly connected with expertise in spiritual care, the *ars moriendi* model helps chaplaincy to be better integrated in multi- and interdisciplinary care. Because the *ars moriendi* model contains five basic anthropological categories, it is easily transposed into other social and healthcare contexts.

References

Bayard, F. (1999) *L'art du Bien Mourir au XVe Siècle*. Paris: Presses de l'Université Paris-Sorbonne.

Bernts, A. and Berghuijs, J. (2016) *God in Nederland 2006–2015*. Utrecht: Ten Have.

Cobb, M., Dowrick, C. and Lloyd-Williams, M. (2012) 'What can we learn about the spiritual needs of palliative care patients from the research literature?' *Journal of Pain and Symptom Management 43*, 6, 1105–1119.

Gamondi, C., Larkin, P. and Payne, S. (2013) 'Core competencies in palliative care: an EAPC white paper on palliative care education. Part

2.' *European Journal of Palliative Care 20*, 3, 140–145.

Girard-Augry, P. (1986) *Ars Moriendi (1492) ou L'art de Bien Mourir.* Paris: Dervy.

Kellehear, A. (2000) 'Spirituality and palliative care: a model of needs.' *Palliative Medicine 14*, 2, 149–155.

Laager, J. (1996) *Ars Moriendi. Die Kunst Gut zu Leben und Gut zu Sterben. Texte von Cicero bis Luther.* Zurich: Manesse Verlag.

Leget, C. (2007) 'Retrieving the *ars moriendi* tradition.' *Medicine, Health Care and Philosophy 10*, 3, 313–319.

Leget, C. (2016) 'A new art of dying as a cultural challenge.' *Studies in Christian Ethics 29*, 3, 279–285.

Leget, C. (2017) *Art of Living, Art of Dying: Spiritual Care for a Good Death.* London: Jessica Kingsley Publishers.

Leget, C., Rubbens, L., Lissnijder, L. and Menten, J. (2008) 'Naar een spirituele "checklist" in een palliatieve zorgeenheid.' *Nederlands Tijdschrift voor Palliatieve Zorg 8*, 3, 93–101.

Leget, C., van Daelen, M. and Swart, S. (2013) 'Spirituele zorg in de kaderopleiding Palliatieve

Zorg.' *Tijdschrift voor Ouderengeneeskunde 3*, 146–149.

Puchalski, C., Ferrell, B., Virami, R., Otis-Green, S. et al. (2009) 'Improving the quality of spiritual care as a dimension of palliative care: the report of the Consensus Conference.' *Journal of Palliative Medicine 12*, 10, 885–904.

Van de Geer, J. and Leget, C. (2012) 'How spirituality is integrated system-wide in the Netherlands Palliative Care National Programme.' *Progress in Palliative Care 20*, 98–105.

Voskuilen, J. (2012) *Levensvragen van patiënten en het Ars moriendi model. Een kwalitatief onderzoek naar de betekenis die palliatieve patiënten geven aan de thema's van het Ars moriendi model.* Thesis, Hogeschool Arnhem Nijmegen, Master of Advanced Nursing.

World Health Organization (2018) *Integrating Palliative Care and Symptom Relief into Primary Care: A WHO Guide for Planners, Implementers and Managers.* Geneva: World Health Organization. Accessed on 01/07/2019 at https://apps.who.int/iris/bitstream/ha ndle/10665/274559/9789241514477-eng. pdf?ua=1.

Part 6

Caring Well, Caring Spiritually

To care well is as much a moral as an evidence-based issue. Who decides what is best for people spiritually as well as physically, psychologically and socially? Traditionally, professionals have been regarded as the 'experts' to whom persons go for advice, treatment or support when they are unwell or 'dis-eased'. Such a culture has promoted codependency.

Part 6 aims to help readers reflect on how chaplains might work counterculturally to empower and co-produce individual and communal health and wellbeing. Instead of working primarily with individuals when in deficit within institutions, chaplains can help promote resilience and spiritual wellbeing by enabling (re)connection with the assets of persons and people in community settings. In Part 6, examples of this from different parts of the UK reveal how chaplains and faith communities are tackling these issues in thoughtful and thought-provoking ways; pointing towards the co-creation of environments where people and professionals are willing to be vulnerable (Batalden 2018) and bound together in meaningful relationships where each other's assets of knowledge, skills, experience and communities are respected and utilized; co-producing spaces in which people together are cared for, or rather mutually supported, well and spiritually.

Reference

Batalden, P. (2018) 'Patient co-production is the key to quality care.' *British Medical Journal 362*, 266–267.

Chapter 17

Community Chaplaincy Listening

*From Interventions During Ill Health to
Enabling Wellbeing and Resilience*

Timothy P Bennison

Introduction

Community Chaplaincy Listening (CCL) is a form of 'spiritual' listening which engages with and responds to the things of the human spirit, that is, with that part of a person which is 'essential' to his or her being and wellbeing, and which:

- animates life

- gives purpose and meaning

- nurtures and sustains.

It is based on the principle that when people are given the space and safety to tell their story and be heard, their perspective can change and greater understanding can be gained. As an active listening service offered within acute care institutions, in primary and social care contexts, CCL helps people to begin to make sense of the issues facing them and find a way forward. In so doing, it identifies and draws upon personal and community assets and fosters increased wellbeing for the individual, as well as strengthens community resilience.

This chapter provides an overview of the CCL service in NHSScotland. After a brief account of the development of the service, it describes its setting within the broader context of changes in the way healthcare is both conceived and delivered in Scotland. This is followed by a description of the way the service works and an examination of its underlying principles. The 'assets-based' nature of CCL is explored and distinctions are drawn between CCL and counselling approaches. The question of what makes CCL 'spiritual' and expressive of spiritual care is then considered. Finally, the experiences of two patients who recently used the CCL service are cited as examples of how the service can work in practice.

How Community Chaplaincy Listening began

CCL grew out of the work of spiritual care departments in several health boards across Scotland as they sought to develop innovative ways of delivering person-centred spiritual care following both the restructuring and re-imagining of spiritual care services in NHSScotland over the previous 10 years or so, and the Scottish government's new emphasis on the community as the locus of care (Scottish Executive Health Department 2002; Scottish Government 2009ab, 2010, 2011, 2016). In particular, a number of spiritual care departments, notably those in Highland, Tayside and the Western Isles, had set up listening services in the primary care sector, based in general practitioner (GP) or family doctor premises. In 2011, NHS Education for Scotland (NES) commissioned an action research project designed both to support the development of such services and to evaluate their activity (Mowat and Bunniss 2011). This project embraced five health boards in total and, from its work, CCL emerged. From these beginnings, and following another round of action research, CCL has now become a chaplaincy national programme of work. Support was offered by the Scottish government, which provided funding for its development over the first 3 years. This was awarded on the condition that the service expand to over 40 sites during that period and develop a sustainable service-delivery model. CCL is now being delivered in 11 of the 14 geographical health board areas in Scotland with over 65 sites currently in operation. The use of trained volunteers in many sites has ensured that the service remains sustainable in the long term. More recently, some health boards are ensuring sustainability by negotiating funding for aspects of the service (e.g. volunteer expenses and supervision) either directly from the GP practices which use the service or from the local health and social care partnerships which manage community health and social care programmes.

Nationally, CCL is overseen by the programme director for spiritual care and chaplaincy in Scotland, based at NES, in conjunction with a CCL development group chaired by the national lead for CCL. As CCL has grown across Scotland, this group has focused, amongst other things, on the development of a robust governance structure including protocols for recruitment, training and registration as a listener. A 4-day 'formational' training programme has been developed and all CCL listeners are required to have successfully completed it.

Context

Within the last decade a significant paradigm shift has taken place in the way that healthcare is understood and delivered within NHSScotland. Amongst other things, this has involved movement from:

- treating ill health reactively to promoting wellbeing proactively

- a 'deficits-based' (trying to fix that which is broken) to an 'assets-based' approach to care focusing on positive sources of strength and building resilience at both individual and community level

- a focus on acute care in institutional settings to primary and community care in community settings. (NES: awaiting publication)

NHSScotland's *2020 Vision* (Scottish Government 2011, p.2), for example, articulates something of this changed approach, aspiring to enable everyone 'to live longer healthier lives at home, or in a homely setting'. This, it says, entails 'a healthcare system where we have integrated health and social care, [and] a focus on prevention, anticipation and supported self-management' (p.2). This echoes the direction of travel outlined in *The Healthcare Quality Strategy for NHSScotland* (Scottish Government 2010), with its stress on prevention and early intervention in the primary care sector. Similarly, NHSScotland's *Shifting the Balance of Care* initiative (Scottish Government 2009a, p.1) speaks, amongst other things, of 'shifting our view of individuals as passive recipients of care towards full partners in improving their health and managing their conditions'. More recently, the Scottish Government's (2016, pp. 4–5) *Health and Social Care Delivery Plan* again emphasises the need for a fundamental move away from a 'fix-and-treat' approach to an approach based on 'anticipation, prevention and self-management'. Alongside all of this, the initiation of integration of health and social care in Scotland in 2014 has led to a presumption that spiritual care services across the country will be refocused and re-prioritised to ensure that the community and primary care sector is properly catered for. Therefore, new approaches to healthcare with their stress, amongst other things, on building resilience and fostering assets will be reflected in practice.

The new *National Delivery Plan for Health and Social Care Chaplaincy and Spiritual Care Across Health and Social Care in Scotland* (Scottish Government: awaiting publication) details some of the implications of these changes for spiritual care. The following two changes are of most significance for CCL:

- the balance of activity expanding from almost exclusively one-to-one contact in institutions towards also facilitating group processes in primary care and community settings

- helping people not just to make sense of their circumstances and illness, but to be able to recognise and utilise their personal and communal assets to proactively develop their own wellbeing.

As we shall see, with its community-focused, assets-based, resilience-building approach, CCL fits well into this rapidly changing context.

Understanding CCL
How does it work?

Across Scotland, CCL is offered in a variety of settings within the local community, but most commonly, from GP practices. The service can be delivered either by chaplains or by volunteers recruited by local spiritual care departments. Typically, patients are referred to the service by their GP or other healthcare professionals, though self-referral is also possible at some sites. Referrals are usually prompted by the sense that a person is struggling with some life transition or finding it hard to make sense of a difficult experience or life event. The service is intended to be a short-term intervention with patients attending no more than three or four sessions with their listener for each episode of care. Patients present with a range of problems including bereavement and loss, relationship and work-related issues as well as struggles with loss and transition in relation to long-term conditions. Other issues include the experience of ongoing or historic abuse, anxiety, depression and various expressions of what we might call 'existential angst' (e.g. struggling to find meaning and purpose and, in several cases, strong mortality salience and death anxiety). Typically, patients come with a complex interweaving of narratives involving any combination of social, emotional, physical, psychological and spiritual dimensions – consistent with Saunders' (1993) concept of 'total pain'.

Listening sessions last for 50 minutes and, in line with the person-centred nature of the service, provide a space which the patient can use as he or she wishes. The patient decides what to talk about and the depth to which he or she wants to go. The listener's job is to listen, to hear the patient's story, to encourage and enable the patient in its telling and to help the patient reflect and gain perspective on his or her experience. He or she is not there to diagnose, offer advice or 'fix' things – simply to listen – and to enable the patient to draw upon his or her own resources as appropriate. Key to the success of an episode of care in CCL is the relationship that is established between listener and patient. It is the listener's task to try to foster an open, accepting, empathic and congruent relationship with the patient in which he or she feels safe and able to talk about, and reflect on, what are often deep and long-standing hurts, as well as profoundly painful and disorientating experiences.

Of significance here for the listener is that he or she comes with no theories or techniques to be applied to the patient. The only therapeutic tool the listener has at his or her disposal is his or her own reflexive self and the relationship that can be developed. Listeners have no toolkit from which they can prescribe a solution: they can offer only themselves with their strengths and vulnerabilities. This 'intentional use of self' is fundamental to CCL (as it is to spiritual care in other contexts too) and enables the care offered to be truly person-centred. As the listener offers his or her self in all his or her vulnerability, the patient is freed to be genuinely his or her self too and, in the safety of the therapeutic relationship, to (re)connect with that which sustains and nurtures them – their sources of strength or 'assets'.

As with all services offered within the NHS, it is important that CCL be supported by a strong evidence base and that its effectiveness be thoroughly evaluated. Building on the initial action research in the pilot phase, a Patient Reported Outcome Measure (PROM) has been developed to measure the impact of CCL on patients using the service (see Chapter 13).

An assets-based approach

Crucially, the main assumption underlying the CCL approach is that patients already have the resources they need to help them cope with their issues and find a way forwards. These resources, or 'assets', might be found within the patient (as perhaps an inner strength, values, memories or a particular ability or skill), around the patient (in their relationships and in their community) and, in some cases, 'beyond' the patient (e.g. through a sense of spiritual or transcendent connection). Whilst we might not go so far as to describe these sources of strength as what is known in the Rogerian person-centred counselling world as the 'actualising tendency', the principle is similar. The task of the listener, like the person-centred therapist, is not to advise or 'fix' or prescribe. It is rather to enable the patient to engage with the resources they already know, and have perhaps drawn upon previously, and through that engagement to build strength and resilience, thereby resourcing patients to be better able to manage their situation. This identification and fostering of assets underlie the whole enterprise of spiritual care and, as we have seen, the ability to draw upon and develop community and personal assets is fundamental to NHSScotland's vision and strategy.

This is an important principle, and it is easy to see how focusing on assets can help to foster in individuals and communities greater wellbeing, resilience and independence – a shift from passivity and powerlessness towards control and self-management. However, in the CCL context, the listener has to take care that the process of identifying and drawing upon assets does not descend into a careless 'count your blessings' exercise in which the patient is inadvertently, or deliberately, encouraged to reorient their perspective around the positive things identified and to resist the impact of the negative. The language of naming and drawing upon assets, in fact, points to something far deeper than simply a process of counterbalancing the negative with the positive; rather, it alludes to those strands in a patient's story, experience and wider environment which have in the past, and retain the potential in the future, to sustain, nurture, motivate and inspire. Far from being a list of blessings, our 'assets' are those deep-seated connections, relationships, strengths and values which give our lives meaning and purpose. They are the things in our lives which motivate and inspire us, get us out of bed in the morning and keep us going. The list of what these things might be is endless – a relationship, a value or ideal, some kind of spiritual practice or religious faith, or a combination of different things. Needless to say, in the midst of the frequently difficult and painful life situations and circumstances that many who attend CCL sessions find themselves in, it is easy to lose connection with those very assets necessary for survival, just at the time they are most needed. Indeed, sometimes, for some patients, it feels as though their only asset is the CCL *listener*.

This, in itself, is an important point. The notion of an assets-based approach applies just as readily to the service itself as it does to the patient who benefits from the service. In a very real sense, CCL utilises community assets in its delivery – drawing, as it does, on resources already present within the local area and people. These resources include, for example, space in the local community centre or GP surgery where CCL can be delivered and the structured network of connections that often emanate from these resources into the far reaches of the surrounding area. Importantly, CCL also offers the opportunity to local people to volunteer as listeners. Furthermore, these volunteers are resourced by NHS chaplains, who do not just deliver CCL but also use their assets to recruit, train, supervise, manage and support the local volunteer CCL listeners. In some places, listeners have also developed useful relationships with other local community assets, such as the Citizens' Advice Service, counselling services and social prescribers who, through their local knowledge, are able to connect patients with appropriate community groups, projects or resources. This has led to a fruitful cross-fertilisation of assets resulting in, amongst other things, useful referrals between different supportive organisations, thus enabling patients to make better use of the various community assets available, as is appropriate for them.

How does CCL differ from counselling?

The CCL Handbook (NES: awaiting publication) makes an emphatic distinction between CCL and counselling:

> CCL Listeners do **not** offer counselling or cognitive behavioural therapy or any kind of psychological intervention. Rather they walk alongside the person telling the story, ask the right questions and offer support and encouragement. The role of the CCL Listener is not to fix the problem or issue being described, but to create a safe space for the speaker to verbalise whatever gets in the way of their wellbeing and resilience.

This distinction, however, is perhaps a little more complicated than it first seems. Indeed, it could be argued that there are many similarities between CCL and at least some models of counselling. The term 'counselling' used in its broadest sense, to refer generally to all talking therapies, would seem to be equally applicable to CCL as to any other therapeutic approach based on talking and listening. However, there are many different models of counselling. Some are more directive and solution focused, and others are thoroughly person-centred and non-directive, relying only on the creation of a safe space and a reliable therapeutic relationship. The former are clearly distinct from CCL, which is purely a listening service and does not try to 'fix' people. However, the more person-centred approaches share, to a degree, some common ground with CCL – not least in their eschewing of therapeutic methods and techniques and their reliance on relationship and the intentional use of self.

Furthermore, there is a degree of overlap with the more established models of counselling at the level of the underlying principles on which they draw. Significantly, for example, the commitment within CCL practice to facilitate the patient's engagement with their own resources or assets mirrors to some extent the assumption lying behind the person-centred approach: that the patient has within his or her self the resources needed to cope with his or her situation. Hence, the role of the counsellor is to enable the patient to identify and draw upon those resources.

Despite this common ground, however, CCL remains distinct from models of counselling in that it does not draw upon the kind of strongly defined theoretical understandings of person and process that they do. Ultimately, whatever differences and similarities we might observe between counselling and CCL, a fundamental distinction between the two lies in the notion of 'intentionality'. In all models of counselling, to a greater or lesser extent, the intention is to help people to understand themselves and their behaviour, and to make changes. People who engage in counselling, both therapist and client, bring with them this intentionality. People involved in

CCL do not bring with them that same intentionality. CCL does not seek such a deep understanding of self, but stays, rather, with the patient's narrative, providing simply a safe space in which he or she can gain insight and perspective, and identify and draw upon appropriate assets. Furthermore, within CCL there is freedom, where appropriate, for the listener to share information or to signpost to local groups, services or places that might help the patient connect or reconnect with those assets and to gain a stronger sense of meaning, purpose, hope or joy.

What makes CCL 'spiritual' and how is it expressive of spiritual care?

CCL is spiritual because it engages with the human spirit. Together, listener and patient seek to uncover and explore that which lies at the centre of the patient's being, sustaining life and stimulating a sense of purpose and deep meaning. In addition, since the listener relies specifically on his or her intentional use of self, rather than some method or technique, it might be said that the listener responds also from his or her own deep spiritual centre or 'core'. Therefore, listener and patient meet and communicate at the level of the (human) spirit – a meeting of spirits which can, even in itself, foster growth and wellbeing.

This level of engagement is, of course, common to spiritual care in many different contexts. Our experience of, and engagement with, life in all its complex facets requires us to be constantly bringing together different stories, narratives and strands of experience. Our lives are set in many and varied interwoven cultural contexts which can connect or bump into each other all at once. Examples of such contexts include our family of origin, local community, workplace and educational experience as well as our national, spiritual and religious backgrounds. All of these different strands have the capacity to sustain and nurture, or to drain and diminish, at different times. At the centre of our being is a process which manages all these different strands and facilitates a creative interplay between them within which a sense of an integrated whole – meaning, purpose, direction, connectedness – can be realised.

All spiritual care, to a greater or lesser extent, engages with this process and seeks to enable those for whom the balance of those strands, stories and perceptions has been distorted, through illness, loss or other life event, to find a way of reassembling the different pieces to make sense of things again and to reconnect with that which sustains, nurtures and strengthens. CCL does this in a very intentional way by offering to patients the security of a safe, non-judgemental relationship in which they can rehearse their stories, make connections, identify and draw upon assets, and, hopefully, find a way of piecing things together.

More than merely fitting in with the broader picture of spiritual care provision in Scotland, CCL arguably lies at the vanguard of the way forwards for healthcare chaplaincy.

The process of change in Scotland in both the conception and practice of spiritual care since about 2009 has seen a decline in the place of the more 'religious' aspects of spiritual care. In the past, the healthcare chaplain was most often seen as the 'minister (or rabbi, or other faith leader) in the hospital'. That perception has been slowly reframed, and the healthcare chaplain is now increasingly recognised as a healthcare professional alongside others, with an important role to play in a holistic approach to patient care. In both community and acute contexts, spiritual care interventions are slowly beginning to be seen as complementary to the contributions of other professionals, and integral to the overall care plan. Nevertheless, frequently there are high levels of ambiguity both in the way staff perceive chaplains and in the way chaplains perceive themselves. In particular, the question of what is the unique or distinctive contribution chaplains make to patient care inevitably brings forth varied and ambivalent responses. In Scotland, spiritual care is gradually moving from the more traditional emphases on religion or theology (although this is still an important aspect of spiritual care work) to a thoroughly person-centred response to the fears, anxieties, hopes and passions of the individual patient – enabling and encouraging life-giving connections and supporting the process of meaning-making (which for some patients may mean prayer and ritual, for example). CCL, with its emphasis on compassionate witness and accompaniment, its fostering of personal and community assets and its response to unique individual need and circumstance, exemplifies this new approach to spiritual care.

CCL in practice

As noted above, patients present themselves at CCL sessions with a wide variety of issues and often with complicated combinations of issues in which the different narrative strands have woven together to create a complexity in which pain is experienced physically, socially, psychologically, emotionally and spiritually. Alongside this range of presenting issues, patients are encouraged to use the service in different ways as best suits them. For some patients a one-off session is sufficient, whereas for others an intense period of three or four weekly meetings is appropriate; and yet for other patients, several sessions or short episodes of care over the year are most useful for them as they deal with ongoing situations. Again, there are differences in how patients actually make use of the sessions they attend. For some patients it is simply a place to 'let off steam' and get things off their chest (and to be heard and affirmed in the process); others gain a degree of insight and new understandings are reached. On the other hand, for some people it is a place where they can receive ongoing support and encouragement as they deal with ongoing or recurring situations; and for a few, it provides an opportunity to work, very intentionally and insightfully, through a particular issue or situation.

Case studies

As a way of illustrating something of these differences in approach to the service and usage of CCL, I briefly outline the distinctive experiences of two patients.[1]

Working with Alison: fostering resilience in complexity

Alison has attended the CCL service at her local GP surgery on four separate occasions. On each occasion we have met around five times over a period of 2–3 months. Though each new episode of care has been sparked by a problem or crisis in Alison's life, much of our work together has focused on a cluster of complex and interrelated issues that underlie Alison's life and experience.

Since 2004 or so, she has faced several life-threatening episodes of illness and now suffers from a chronic condition which is gradually deteriorating. Treatment for this has left Alison with pain and numbness in parts of her body, reduced mobility, lack of energy and frequent fatigue. This has resulted in a gradual loss of self-confidence and bouts of anxiety.

In addition, Alison recently spent some time in prison. This was, for her, a terrifying and traumatic experience. Whilst there, she suffered severe bullying and experienced violence and sexual abuse from other inmates. This has added significantly to her levels of anxiety, and she lives in fear of further attacks or reprisals.

Alison also struggles to deal with a difficult family dynamic. One of her children is frequently in trouble with the police and is often verbally abusive. Alison experiences her partner as controlling and manipulative, and she has difficult relationships with several other members of her extended family. Compounding all this is Alison's own need for support and affirmation and, in particular, approval from her mother which is rarely forthcoming. All of

---

1   Whilst reflecting genuine experiences of CCL, these case studies are composite and illustrative.

this has an impact on Alison's spirit. She feels weary and that she has lost her zest for life. She feels unmotivated, depleted and powerless. She feels that her life has lost its purpose. She sees little hope for the future and struggles to find any sense of peace or wellbeing in the present.

Contrary to her own sense of herself, my experience of Alison is that her spirit is much stronger than she thinks. Despite her many emotional and physical struggles, Alison somehow finds the strength to keep going. She pushes herself physically to do as much as she can and, though it sometimes feels futile, she continues to 'put herself out there' emotionally with her mother and other difficult family members, in the hope that things will get better. Alison acknowledges this. She says she is a 'fighter' and that she believes she is strong enough never to completely lose hope or be overwhelmed by her situation. Much of my work with Alison has involved reflecting on this spiritual energy and on the ways in which it has strengthened her to deal successfully with past struggles. This has helped Alison feel affirmed, to find more confidence in herself and feel better able to find strength to face her current situation.

Alison and I have explored both the things that drain her and those which help her restore her sense of strength and energy, and have reflected on how she might keep an appropriate balance between the two. For example, dealing with difficult family members and the frustration and anxiety they bring is particularly de-energising – especially when she is already weakened by physical pain or fatigue. Quiet time alone, walking in the countryside and tending her garden are all energising and give Alison the chance to recoup her strength. Another part of Alison's experience has been a sense of powerlessness. In our work together, we have spent significant time thinking about how Alison might take a bit more control over the things that energise or drain her in order to maintain a better balance and to get the time and space she needs to rebuild her energy. She has good control over the practicalities of her physical condition and medication, but things are relationally challenging. Here, Alison is always drawn to the possibility of getting attention, support and affirmation from her mother – but in seeking this, she makes herself vulnerable to the de-energising, confidence-stifling elements of that relationship.

Amidst such frustrations, Alison has a positive and sustaining relationship with a life-long close friend who supports her in many of the practical ways. In addition, Alison feels that this friend understands her emotionally and is unconditionally on her side. This is a very particular source of strength and wellbeing for Alison.

There is little chance that Alison's circumstances will change drastically and, though more formal counselling may help her to understand some of the underlying issues and patterns of behaviour within herself that contribute to her anxiety and frustration, she remains uninterested in pursuing this. For Alison, CCL is a community asset which provides her, as and when she needs it, with the space, non-judgemental support and affirmation to reconnect with her assets and to gain strength when she is feeling drained and diminished in her situation. Alison says that simply being heard and accepted as she is in a CCL session leaves her feeling stronger, more energised and better able to cope with her life.

Alison's experience of life is complex. However, in the course of our CCL sessions, Alison and I have become aware of, and explored, several energising and strengthening resources to which she has access and reflected on how she might best connect with these assets and use them to promote her wellbeing in her particular circumstances.

Working with Olivia: enabling meaningful change

Olivia's story is somewhat simpler to recount than Alison's story. This is partly because, in total, I met her on only five occasions over two separate episodes of care, and partly because of the very focused and intentional way in which she used CCL.

Olivia is in her fifties. Her husband left about 15 years previously, leaving her with two young children to bring up alone. In the years following her husband's departure, Olivia had a number of brief relationships, none of which worked out, as well as a longer relationship which she ended when she became afraid that her partner's violent temper was putting her children in danger. Since then, she has focused on bringing up her children and, more recently, completed a university-degree course.

Olivia's children are now grown up and have both recently left home. This has left her with a mixture of emotions: emptiness and inertia now that her children have gone; hope and excitement at what may lie ahead in this new phase of her life; and a degree of anxiety about the way forwards and her ability to cope. Olivia came to CCL with the express intention of exploring her fears and anxieties with a view to understanding what lay behind them and finding a way to overcome them. She already had significant self-awareness but felt she needed the safety of the CCL environment to explore more rigorously what she was feeling and why. My role as listener was simply to help her engage with herself and find the answers which were already within. By the beginning of our second session, Olivia said she was feeling stronger and more grounded and, significantly, more able to connect with, and accept, her more vulnerable side. The next session was her last as Olivia felt she had got to the place she wanted to be and needed no more help from me.

Olivia came back to CCL with an entirely different issue about 6 months later. Again, she was very focused and knew exactly how she needed to use the CCL service. The security of the environment and safety of an open and accepting therapeutic relationship with a listener she trusted were vital elements in this process.

Brief reflections on the case studies

Alison and Olivia demonstrate something of the different ways in which CCL can be used, and the different issues which it can help address. Alison brought with her the raw, unstructured, chaotic pain of her life – a complex interweaving of social, emotional, psychological and spiritual issues – and sought some way of making sense of it and gaining strength to deal with it. Olivia brought a defined, but very important, part of her life to examine it and find ways of changing it. Both women, in their own ways, used the CCL service intentionally: Olivia, to explore some specific issues in a highly focused way with a view to making meaningful change; and Alison, as a means by which she could reconnect with her own energy and purpose, and sustain herself whilst living with her ongoing situation.

Conclusion

CCL is a new and innovative response to several different narratives running through healthcare in Scotland today. It brings these different threads together into a single offering which delivers to patients a spiritual care service which upholds some of the fundamental values of NHSScotland, namely a holistic and person-centred approach. It also embraces some of the more recent strategic emphases, such as the focus on identifying and fostering assets, and on the building of personal and community resilience. Though not emerging out of, or underpinned by, any particular religious or theological tradition, the approach has resonances with core values and themes found in mainstream faith and belief systems. Moreover, with its emphasis on the importance of being present, journeying with the patient, accompaniment and compassionate witnessing, it retains something of the 'otherness' characteristic of healthcare chaplaincy's pastoral theological heritage.

In the newly emerging healthcare environment in Scotland, CCL is assured a place. As an assets-based approach, empowering patients to self-manage their health and actively promoting wellbeing and resilience, CCL represents a positive and life-enhancing contribution to healthcare. It not only reflects the new strategic direction of travel but also exemplifies it. As spiritual care across Scotland finds its place in this new landscape, CCL is certain to be at the forefront of its developing and expanding profile.

References

Mowat, H. and Bunniss, S. (2011) *Full Report on the National Scottish Action Research Project, First Cycle: March 2010–March 2011.* Edinburgh: NHS Education for Scotland. Accessed on 23/03/2018 at www.nes.scot.nhs. uk/media/511533/ccl_1_final_report.pdf.

NES (awaiting publication) *Community Chaplaincy Scotland (CCL): National Handbook for Best Practice. Edinburgh:* NHS Education for Scotland.

Saunders, C. (1993) 'Introduction: History and Challenge.' In C. Saunders and N. Sykes (eds) *The Management of Terminal Malignant Disease.* London: Hodder and Stoughton.

Scottish Executive Health Department (2002) *Guidelines on Chaplaincy and Spiritual Care in the NHS in Scotland.* HDL 76. Edinburgh: Scottish Executive Health Department.

Scottish Government (2009a) *Shifting the Balance of Care.* Edinburgh: Scottish Government. Accessed on 23/03/2018 at www.shiftingthebalance.scot.nhs.uk/ downloads/1241609185-What%20is%20 SBC%20leaflet%20-%20May%202009.pdf.

Scottish Government (2009b) *Spiritual Care and Chaplaincy.* Edinburgh: Scottish Government. Accessed on 23/03/2018 at www.scotland.gov. uk/Resource/Doc/259076/0076811.pdf.

Scottish Government (2010) *The Healthcare Quality Strategy for NHSScotland.* Edinburgh: Scottish Government. Accessed on 23/03/2018 at www.scotland.gov.uk/Resource/ Doc/311667/0098354.pdf.

Scottish Government (2011) *Achieving Sustainable Quality in Scotland's Healthcare: A 20:20 Vision.* Edinburgh: Scottish Government. Accessed on 23/03/2018 at www.scotland.gov.uk/ Resource/0039/00398668.doc.

Scottish Government (2016) *Health and Social Care Delivery Plan.* Edinburgh: Scottish Government. Accessed on 23/03/2018 at www. gov.scot/Resource/0051/00511950.pdf.

Scottish Government (awaiting publication) *National Delivery Plan for Health and Social Care Chaplaincy and Spiritual Care Across Health and Social Care in Scotland.* Edinburgh: Scottish Government.

Chapter 18

From Person-Centred to People-Centred Spiritual Care

Jo Kennedy and Ian Stirling

Introduction

In Scotland, and in the UK generally, chaplains are funded by the National Health Service (NHS) and understand their role as fundamental in promoting spiritual health. Traditionally, they have exercised that role within hospital and hospice settings, often with people who identify themselves as being of a particular faith community.

In December 2011, Interfaith Scotland, in partnership with the NHS Education for Scotland (NES) Chaplaincy Training and Development Unit, appointed us to undertake a 10-month secondment to support NHS chaplains to promote spiritual health and wellbeing in community settings.

The secondment had several dimensions. It aimed to promote greater awareness, amongst those working within institutional settings in primary health and social care, of the potential of spiritual care to support health and wellbeing within communities. It also aimed to support the chaplaincy community to understand the issues facing those working in primary health and social care, the common challenges and the areas of shared interest.

Ultimately, we wanted to define the practice of promoting spiritual health in communities – who was doing it, how they did it and what it would take to support more of it to happen. Also, we were interested, of course, in finding out more about what difference it made.

We completed our secondment in 2013. Since then, there has been new legislation in Scotland on the integration of health and social care (Scottish Government 2016). This has entailed huge structural and cultural changes in the way care is provided by the state, working with independent and third (voluntary) sector providers. These changes have absorbed much of the attention of policymakers and practitioners at all levels, although it is too early to say how they are really impacting on those receiving services.

Concerns over the spiritual health and wellbeing of communities have not been allayed over this time. Health inequalities continue to widen in Scotland, and although the language has changed in the past few years, there is a continuing interest in how to support 'resilient communities'.

This chapter begins with the model we developed, to define what we mean by an 'assets-based approach to spiritual health'. It goes on to look at what it means in practice and it ends with an outline of what could be done to promote it. The 'assets-based approach' applies both to individuals and to communities and organizations. The role of chaplaincy within communities and organizations, moving from 'person- to people-centred spiritual care practice', provides a significant challenge to current chaplaincy practice in Scotland and is the core subject of this chapter.

Ian's own journey grounds our chapter in chaplaincy practice. Starting out as a healthcare chaplain working in a hospice setting, Ian's original understanding of his role was offering pastoral and spiritual care to patients, their families and staff. As the secondment progressed, he found himself broadening his reach to include the organization and the wider community. In time, he moved on from the hospice to become a parish minister and is deeply committed to a broad understanding of the development of the spiritual health and wellbeing of both his faith and surrounding geographical community, which involves him engaging with a range of local health and social care practitioners.

Context

Harry Burns, the chief medical officer in Scotland from 2005 to 2014, initiated a debate about assets-based approaches to health in his Annual Report of 2009 (Scottish Government 2010a). In this report he posited, quoting Jimmy Reid (a Scottish trade unionist) speaking in 1971, that many of Scotland's major health problems are caused by alienation, which comes from people lacking a sense of meaning and purpose in their lives. Instead of the deficit model, which drove most of our statutory service provision, he believed our healthcare system should focus on salutogenesis – the art of keeping healthy. This approach was already well established in the voluntary and community sector in Scotland. Based on Morgan and Ziglio (2007), at its core, salutogenesis asks:

- What aspects of the context in which we live influence our wellbeing and development?

- What factors make us more able to deal with the vagaries of life?

- What enables us to open to life's experiences?

- What contributes to overall levels of human flourishing?

Burns suggested that our approach to health improvement in Scotland needed to have at its base an effort to discover the assets within communities on which we can build health both individually and communally: 'An assets approach to health and development embraces a positive notion of health creation and in doing so encourages the full participation of local communities in the health development process' (Scottish Government 2010a, p.7). Assets approaches were not new in community-led healthcare practice but had had a limited impact on mainstream health interventions. The chief medical officer's interest sparked debate about how such approaches could change the way health improvement was conceived and delivered in Scotland.

The 'assets' movement ran alongside another movement which promoted a more person-centred approach to health and social care. This became one of the three ambitions of the *Healthcare Quality Strategy for NHSScotland* (Scottish Government 2010b). Since 2012, the emphasis on person-centredness has remained as a core part of national policy and is undoubtedly influencing practice. It has been built upon by the current chief medical officer in Scotland, Catherine Calderwood, into a focus on *Realistic Medicine* (Scottish Government 2015), which cites a good conversation between the patient and the practitioner at the centre of healthcare and attempts to address the problem of 'over-treating' – seen as both a budgetary issue and denying patients the right to influence their care.

The increasing longevity of the population in the industrialized world, and escalating associated rates of long-term conditions such as diabetes, depression and osteoarthritis, has given energy to the promotion of the practice of 'self-management', which is at heart a collaboration between patients and practitioners, and which should enable people to take more control of their health.

By 2011, the NES Chaplaincy Training and Development Unit believed that chaplaincy had far more to offer than one-to-one care within a system which focused on people's deficits or problems, and was actively engaging chaplains and wider healthcare practitioners in developing a vision for the future of healthcare chaplaincy in Scotland. The connection between Burns' ideas and the role of chaplaincy in promoting spiritual health within communities as an intrinsic part of overall health and wellbeing was made.

Chaplains already aspired to practise in a person-centred manner. As *Spiritual Care Matters* (NHS Education for Scotland 2009, p.6) states, 'Spiritual care begins with encouraging human contact in compassionate relationship and moves in whatever direction need requires.' Moreover, around that time

Scottish chaplains began to think of their role in developing spiritual health as more than responding to situations of spiritual 'dis-ease' or crisis. The consensus statement developed in 2010 by Scottish chaplains participating in a national conference organized by NES defined their primary responsibility as being 'to promote the spiritual wellbeing of healthcare communities and all who are part of them – patients, carers, staff and volunteers – 24 hours a day, 7 days a week' (Kelly 2012, p.471). However, the challenge in the assets-based approach began when chaplains were encouraged to apply that practice to whole communities rather than individuals.

Defining the approach

We quickly realized that we needed to be very clear about what we meant by an 'assets-based' approach and that this definition needed to be based both on the real experience, and on the aspirations of, chaplains themselves. In June 2012, we met with 12 Scottish healthcare chaplains to identify what their current practice was, what felt new and creative about what they were doing, and what more they could do to promote health and wellbeing. Their responses were grouped into three categories:

- work with individuals either in hospitals or in the community to promote individual resilience

- work with groups, mostly in the community, to promote community resilience

- work with organizations to promote organizational resilience.

We drew up models for each of the three categories. These models detail inputs, processes and short-, medium- and long-term outcomes (Table 18.1). The challenge inherent in the models is to demonstrate the 'theory of change' (i.e. that the activities undertaken by chaplains lead to the outcomes they identify). This chapter focuses on the second model – the one in which chaplains articulated how they were working with groups in the community to release their capacity to support one another spiritually.

One of the strengths of the model is that while it identifies inputs and processes, it does not specify the context in which spiritual care is delivered. This allows health and social care practitioners to locate it in their own setting whether that be, for example, mental health, palliative care, community care or bereavement care.

Table 18.1 Assets-based logic model

Inputs by	Processes	Short-term outcomes	Medium-term outcomes	Long-term outcomes
Chaplains	Community spirituality: mapping and developing community assets in relation to spiritual health Supporting community members/staff to deliver spiritual care Facilitating hope and recovery groups for people with mental health issues/ dementia Engaging with faith/ church groups Secular community rituals Mindfulness groups	Health practitioners and community members more confident in promoting resilience and a sense of coherence through addressing issues relating to spiritual health (e.g. hopelessness, isolation, loss, alienation) Faith groups more active in addressing issues of spiritual health in communities	Community resilience Community cohesion Sense of community and solidarity More people who experience inequality influencing decisions that affect their life or community	Stronger, safer and healthier communities Community influence and control

The model defines how chaplains promote the spiritual health of communities through working with community groups, health and social care practitioners within communities, and faith groups. The only inputs in our model are chaplains, although we understand there are many other health and social care practitioners working on the spiritual health of communities (Kennedy and McKenzie 2012).

The activities chaplains are undertaking, or would have liked to undertake, include:

- mapping and developing community assets or strengths in relation to spiritual health

- supporting community groups and health and social care practitioners working in communities to deliver spiritual care

- facilitating hope and recovery groups for people with mental health issues

- facilitating mindfulness groups

- engaging with faith groups and developing secular community rituals.

It is not an exhaustive list – we could have included many more activities – but these summed up the activities of the chaplains present. The immediate outcomes of these activities were, first, that health and social care practitioners and community members were more confident in promoting resilience and a sense of coherence through addressing issues relating to spiritual health (e.g. hopelessness, isolation, loss, alienation), and second, that faith groups were more active in addressing issues of spiritual health in communities.

The medium- and long-term outcomes were drawn from a model developed by the Edinburgh Health Inequalities Standing Group (2011). This group of professionals from across health and social care developed the toolkit to enable practitioners and projects to evaluate the difference they were making initially in relation to social capital and ultimately to health and wellbeing. It demonstrated how activities which promoted '"social capital" – the links, shared values and understandings in society that enable individuals and groups to trust each other and so work together' (Keely 2007, p.102) – related to the Scottish Government's National Outcomes (Scottish Government 2007). These links were important in demonstrating how the work of chaplains was ultimately aiming towards the same outcomes as the work of a whole range of other health and social care practitioners funded by the state. They also showed how spiritual health should be seen as a core part of community wellbeing and resilience.

We did not expect chaplains to demonstrate this themselves, but the *Social Capital, Health and Wellbeing Planning and Evaluation Toolkit* (Edinburgh Health Inequalities Standing Group 2011) cites a range of sources of evidence which show how activities which promote social capital in communities as a short-term outcome lead to the medium- and long-term outcomes cited above.

What does it look like in practice?

There were very few chaplains really engaging with the practice we describe in the model above; most were, and still are, focusing on person- rather than people-centred work. However, we did find some examples where chaplains were focused on the spiritual health of their whole organization or community rather than simply the people within them. Ian himself began to use the model as a way of understanding his role, and the story below illustrates his journey over the past 5 years – 3 years still as a healthcare chaplain in a hospice setting and the latter 2 years as a Church of Scotland parish minister.

In a hospice context

'I could never have anticipated the complexity.' With these words I introduced spiritual care at a meeting with the Ayrshire Hospice Board in late 2013. Arriving at the hospice in 2002, spiritual care had seemed so straightforward; it was all person-centred care. By 2013, I was excited about moving in a more 'people-centred direction'; excited because here was a chance to map the territory, sketch an outline of chaplaincy and perhaps even to lay the foundations for the future. I was keen to share the learning and insights I had gained from my secondment about a new model of chaplaincy that would meet the needs of communities rather than just individuals. That evening I was also quite nervous – aware that this might be the first and last chance to clearly convey, to disentangle, a decade or more of wrestling with the slippery concept of spiritual care in palliative care. *Seize the moment*, I thought. So, I did. Building on the social-capital-logic model I discovered on the secondment and informed by the work of Kellehear (2005) my message to the board was, 'the spiritual care strategy at the Ayrshire Hospice enjoys three levels of intervention':

1. one-to-one approaches to promote spiritual wellbeing and to ease spiritual distress; these interventions build resilience, coherence and capacity

2. organizational interventions to create the conditions for spiritual care: environment, ethos, character and values

3. community interventions to promote community resilience through compassionate communities – an approach to supporting people who are dying in the community.

These three levels of intervention are, I said, already being delivered on the ground within the hospice, by, for example:

1. one-to-one interventions

   This is Me (Alzheimer's Society and Royal College of Nursing) – a personal passport used widely within UK health and social care practice enabling patients to introduce themselves to the multidisciplinary team, ensuring that care is personalized and co-constructed.

2. organizational strategy

   • *Healthy Working Lives*, a Scottish Government (2018) sponsored programme to support a healthy workforce, led to a hospice health and wellbeing policy

- Values Based Reflective Practice (VBRP) supporting staff to reflect on and learn from their feelings and their experience (see Chapter 15)

- the creation of a labyrinth and garden room as spiritual spaces for patients, families and staff.

3. community interventions

This is because most of our living, dying and grieving is done in the community. The task, therefore, of the Ayrshire Hospice is to support dying and normalizing bereavement in community, as well as provide inpatient and outpatient care. I referred to emerging engagement with local schools and *To Absent Friends* (TAF) and my hope to engage with the Royal Scottish National Orchestra (RSNO) in a national project. TAF, a festival initiated by the Scottish Partnership for Palliative Care (2018) and held annually in November, encourages people to engage in courageous conversations about life, death and dying. It challenges death being a taboo subject and seeks to open conversations. The RSNO performed a concert in Glasgow Concert Hall to raise awareness of TAF, and the second year they went into schools to allow the children to tell stories, set them to music and performed them again in the same venue. The Ayrshire Hospice worked with schools in Ayrshire to produce lesson plans and assembly outlines, and enable children to be more open to issues around death, dying and grief. It included some training of teachers to empower them to hold these conversations themselves.

I went on to give a bit more of the policy-context background outlined at the beginning of this chapter, most of which was new to the board. My message was simple: It is all a matter of rebalancing the energy and the investments of time and resources, so that more time goes into community and organizational interventions alongside the one-to-one spiritual care of staff, patients and their relatives. In retrospect, I see that presentation being the moment my priority shifted from person-centred care to people-centred care.

I had embraced a broader vision than before. To gauge how far I had shifted, I tried out some of the evaluation tools developed by the Edinburgh Health Inequalities Standing Group (2011) to evidence and evaluate my new model. It is incredible how much of a change in my practice it shows. Stimulated by the secondment, I had re-calibrated the way I spend my time in the Ayrshire Hospice, allowing me to concentrate more on groupwork, organizational work and community engagement, as illustrated by the following figures: my weekly diary gradually shows a shift from 85% person-centred one-to-one care and 15% education of staff; through 60% person-centred one-to-one interactions, 30% support to other organizations and 10% community activity; to 30% individual care, 40% organizational and 30% community work. It really began to feel like I am a bridge builder between people and organizations and the community, rather than spending all my time supporting one person at a time.

Health and social care chaplaincy as parish ministry

Since leaving the Ayrshire Hospice and arriving in Carrick, Ayrshire (in southwest Scotland), I am working in a context which includes fishing villages and farmland – a new identity and a new role to promote spiritual health in the community. Although employed as a parish minister in the Church of Scotland, I see myself as a community chaplain: a bridge between the faith community and the local health and social care partnership.

In conversation with Dawn, the health and social care locality planning officer (a role bringing together local groups who share health concerns and to support them in addressing their concerns together) for Carrick, I said, 'Person-centred care is shifting to becoming people-centred care.' I am facing lots of challenges to hold the tension of self, church and community. I yearn for simple rituals bringing people together, such as sharing meals and cups of tea to support the bereaved and lonely in our area, music afternoons, mindfulness groups, and dog-walking meanders through the park. Some of this has already been implemented: a bereavement support group; a mindfulness group; and a music initiative which supports people with dementia.

The spiritual care strategy of my churches includes three levels of intervention from social-capital theory: *bonding social capital* – described as horizontal ties between individuals within the same social group; *bridging social capital* – ties between individuals which cross social divides or between social groups (Claridge 2004); and *linking or networking social capital* – co-constructed by a network or linkage in which people can form relationships built on trust and respect from otherwise disconnected silos informed by institutional and hierarchical power and authority (Burt 2001). These silos include:

1. one-to-one approaches (bonding) to promote spiritual wellbeing to enhance connection to the sacred other and to ease spiritual distress

2. organizational interventions (bridging and linking) to create conditions for spiritual care: liturgical/worship renewal, environment, ethos, character and values

3. community interventions (bridging and linking) to promote community resilience and spiritual health through compassionate
   communities.

These three levels of intervention are already being supported or envisioned
on the ground within Carrick and beyond. For example:

1. one-to-one intervention: Community Chaplaincy Listening (CCL)
   as described in Chapter 17, that is, local volunteers being recruited
   and trained to provide spiritual listening within local family doctor
   surgeries which support *bonding*

2. organizational strategy: to support staff to deliver spiritual care and
   maintain their resilience through VBRP (as described in Chapter 15)
   and monthly reflective afternoons to support health and social care
   practitioners – two interventions which also support *bonding*

3. community interventions: big sings with a local community choir;
   facilitating recovery groups for mental health; supporting *bridging*
   (for example, bridging local faith communities in Carrick to deliver
   a bereavement support service), that is, training volunteers to host
   Playlist for Life musical afternoons for people with dementia, and
   opening up low-level interventions, such as befriending the socially
   isolated for the whole of Carrick, and related to this, our churches
   becoming associated with annual remembrance (TAS) concerts;
   and *linking* – a conference for voluntary organizations which
   brings different organizations and people together with the aim of
   creating communities of kindness and compassion and linking local
   government strategies with those working on the ground.

Sitting with Dawn makes me realize that these are the early days in my new
role as a parish minister. She makes connections citing the spiritual care work
already happening through community development and mental health
practitioners. Previously she never thought of this as spiritual care. We then
envision the future:

• how to sustain a local listening culture, perhaps forming subgroups
  which could support family doctors, teachers in their classrooms,
  carers in their homes and the bereaved

• a culture of 'kindness afternoon' to support health and social care staff

• the creation of a 'compassionate Carrick' (an assets-based culture of
  supporting the dying in their own homes).

Creating a ripple effect of small acts of kindness and neighbourliness; changing behaviours and attitudes – through this, people would slow down and become more attentive to what is happening around them.

What do chaplains need to practise in this way?

Ian's story is an illustration of how taking a people- rather than person-centred approach has radically changed his practice. His hope is that by working through other people as well as directly with individuals, he will be able to address the spiritual health and wellbeing of the entire community, not just the individuals who live within it.

Ian's practice now involves: mapping assets; building capacity; creating opportunities; facilitating groups; facilitating secular rituals and gatherings; inspiring others; pushing boundaries; and engaging with faith communities. Most NHS chaplains are not trained to work like this. To do so would require training and support in community development practice, which includes mapping the community, identifying its strengths and empowering others. They would also need support to understand their leadership role in promoting spiritual health and wellbeing within their community, as well as be able to work with, inspire and be inspired by other health and social care practitioners.

What does it challenge?

Ian goes on to explain how he now understands his identity as a chaplain and as a minister:

Moving into the community invites me to reconfigure my identity and role as a chaplain and spiritual leader. I wonder whether the images of bridge builder, catalyst or enabler better captures chaplaincy's core identity. A chaplain's role is to imagine new ways of living which enhances spiritual health, builds bridges between secular and sacred communities who share a common goal of enhancing spiritual wellbeing, and enables people to utilize their gifts or assets to contribute to such. In doing so, people together may find shared meaning and purpose, and build communal resilience.

I still value the traditional pastoral model of spiritual care. I still seek to foster a personal spirituality which risks entering the depths and bears witness to trauma with no answers to hand; holds others in safe spaces and is moved with compassion; is really present. There are times when I am still working with individuals; yet, living now in the community demands something more. My new locus forces me to look deeper and wider, unsettling my identity of who I am and what my role is, and see how I am shaped by the voices from the community. To look wider means being aware of the connective webs that link individuals and organizations within a community so there is entanglement; to take the time to listen deeply to what is happening within me and around me; carving patterns and connections where previously there were none; and building new bridges. Reflection creates the breathing space for new conversations to happen, and sometimes with people, or organizations, whose paths previously I never crossed.

Working in the community discloses limitations of my time, energy and skills. Rather than being a burden, this invites me to rely more on others, to work collaboratively. I am inspired by the African philosophy of Ubuntu: 'A person is a person through others.' I could never have initiated the projects that I have over the past year on my own. Relying less on my own interventions, I now work with, and through, others to build spiritual health. This is a liberating and exciting state to find myself in, because I am surrounded by others' vision and energy. What I have learned is that the social and spiritual health and wellbeing of the community grows as I diminish self and focus on others and their inner resilience and innate assets. I encourage people to make it happen for themselves. A year on, it is great seeing the change, which is exemplified by the inner belief and confidence emerging in people who once were on the margins – ordinary voices saying 'I can sing' or 'I can spend time with the bereaved' or 'I care'.

Role of other health and social care practitioners in spiritual health

Ian describes his conversation with Dawn, the health and social care locality officer. These kinds of conversations are fundamental to chaplains practising in a new way. A new role for chaplaincy is as much of a challenge for these other practitioners as it is for chaplains themselves. During our secondment we arranged several training and networking sessions with other practitioners working in health and social care. They were surprised to find that chaplains were interested in the spiritual health of people who did not define themselves as having a faith, as well as those who did. Spirituality is as relevant for the non-religious as it is for the religious, because it is about the fundamental meaning of being human (Goldsmith 2011). They were also surprised to find that some of their own interventions supporting individuals to find meaning and purpose in their lives could be promoting spiritual health. Overall, they were keen to get more support from chaplains to promote the spiritual health of their organizations as well as of the communities in which they lived and worked.

What is the role of faith communities?

Ian is now living out his new approach to promoting spiritual health and wellbeing within communities as a parish minister. Many ministers, and those with similar leadership roles in other faith communities, would also see themselves as promoting the spiritual health of not only those belonging to their worshipping community but the wider geographic community also. What Ian brings is a confidence that he can perform that role more effectively by working with other practitioners, some of whom will have a faith base, and others of whom will not – all of whom, however, will have a shared purpose focused on building a sense of meaning and purpose in those 'alienated' communities which Jimmy Reid described so eloquently in 1971.

What do we recommend should happen next?

During our secondment, we found a lot of innovative spiritual care practice: some of it pioneered by chaplains, some by faith communities and some by health and social care practitioners. Some of it was called spiritual care and some of it was called person-centred, assets-based, holistic or compassionate care. Some of our interviewees in health and social care were excited by the idea of more integration between chaplaincy and health and social care practitioners to promote greater health and wellbeing; others struggled to disconnect spiritual from religious care, and that led to suspicion. Some chaplains saw the potential of solidifying the connections between their work and the health and wellbeing of individuals as well as communities; others felt anxious and bewildered. Much of what is needed in order to deliver real person-centred and holistic care is about getting out of our silos and working across boundaries.

At the time we made three recommendations, which were about integration, and we believe that they are as relevant today as they were then:

1. common frameworks

    Frameworks such as the assets-based approach to spiritual care (see Table 18.1) can help practitioners to understand each other's contribution to a set of common spiritual, health and wellbeing outcomes. Although the framework was devised in 2012 by chaplains themselves and has been used in practice, it has never been formally tested, revised and developed. We recommend that this take place.

2. joint training

    Joint locality-based training of chaplains and health and social care practitioners from across sectors on the meaning of spiritual care, the links with person-centred and assets-based approaches, and how it can be provided systemically, is likely to achieve a lot more than competency-based training within silos.

3. learning by doing and gathering stories

We know that developing the spiritual health of communities is the kind of work that goes unrecognized. Although people still benefit, lack of recognition and understanding of the approach means that we are not all able to learn from one another's practice. We recommend that there be a more focused attempt to learn by doing, and reflect on that learning, so that there are more opportunities for us to be inspired by one another.

References

Alzheimer's Society and Royal College of Nursing. *This is Me*. Accessed on 28/11/2018 at www.alzheimers.org.uk/sites/default/files/migrate/downloads/this_is_me.pdf.

Burt, R. (2001) 'Structural Holes Versus Network Closure as Social Capital.' In R. Burt (ed.) *Social Capital: Theory and Research*. New York, NY: Aldine de Gruyter. Accessed on 11/07/2018 at www.socialcapitalresearch.com/literature/conceptualisation/approaches/network.

Claridge, T. (2004) *Social Capital and Natural Resource Management: An Important Role for Social Capital?* Unpublished thesis, University of Queensland, Brisbane, Australia. Accessed on 11/07/2018 at www.socialcapitalresearch.com/literature/theory/types.

Edinburgh Health Inequalities Standing Group (2011) *Social Capital, Health and Wellbeing Planning and Evaluation Toolkit*. Accessed on 30/03/2018 at www.scdc.org.uk/media/resources/what-we-do/mtsc/Social%20Capital%20Health%20and%20Wellbeing%20toolkit.pdf.

Goldsmith, M. (2011) '"They Maintained the Fabric of This World": Spirituality and the Non-religious.' In A. Jewell (ed.) *Spirituality and Personhood in Dementia*. London: Jessica Kingsley Publishers.

Keely, B. (2007) *Human Capital: How What You Know Shapes Your Life. OECD Insights*. Paris: OECD Publications.

Kellehear, A. (2005) *Compassionate Cities: Public Health and End-of-Life Care*. London: Routledge.

Kelly, E. (2012) 'The development of healthcare chaplaincy.' *The Expository Times 123*, 10, 469–478.

Kennedy, J. and McKenzie, I. (2012) *The Search for Meaning and Purpose in Communities*. Edinburgh: NHS Education for Scotland.

Morgan, A. and Ziglio, E. (2007) 'Revitalizing the evidence base for public health: an assets model.' *Global Health Promotion 14*, 2, 17–22.

NHS Education for Scotland (2009) *Spiritual Care Matters: An Introductory Resource for all NHS Scotland Staff*. Edinburgh: NHS Education for Scotland.

Scottish Government (2007) *National Outcomes 2007*. Edinburgh: Scottish Government. Accessed on 25/03/2018 at www.gov.scot/About/Performance/scotPerforms/outcomes.

Scottish Government (2010a) *Health in Scotland 2009: Time for Change*. Annual Report of the Chief Medical Officer. Edinburgh: Scottish Government. Accessed on 02/09/19 at www.assetbasedconsulting.co.uk/uploads/publications/Health%20in%20Scotland%202009.pdf.

Scottish Government (2010b) *The Healthcare Quality Strategy of NHSScotland*. Edinburgh: Scottish Government. Accessed on 11/07/2018 at www.gov.scot/Publications/2010/05/10102307/0.

Scottish Government (2015) *Realistic Medicine*. Annual Report of the Chief Medical Officer. Edinburgh: Scottish Government.

Scottish Government (2016) *Health and Social Care Delivery Plan*. Edinburgh: Scottish Government. Accessed on 23/03/2018 at www.gov.scot/Resource/0051/00511950.pdf.

Scottish Government (2018) *Healthy Working Lives*. Accessed on 28/11/2018 at www.healthyworkinglives.scot/Pages/default.aspx.

Scottish Partnership for Palliative Care (2018) *To Absent Friends*. Accessed on 28/11/2018 at www.toabsentfriends.org.uk/content/ideas.

Chapter 19

Co-production and Promoting Spiritual Wellbeing in Mental Health

Julian Raffay and Don Bryant

Introduction

On a ward nursing-team away day, I (Julian) conducted a simple randomised controlled trial into the differences between service-user and nurse expectations of mental health wards. As trainers have done for years, I assigned the 24 staff into Group A and Group B. Group A wrote on sticky notes what they considered the priorities of their role. Group B recorded the things for which they would hope if admitted as patients. Despite the simplistic research design, the findings were dramatic: Group A listed processes and outcomes. Group B favoured compassion, showing little interest in systems and targets.

I was not the first to describe differences between nurse and service-user expectations (Forrest *et al.* 2000). Recognising such differences is, however, only the first step towards successfully balancing the art and science of nursing (and other disciplines). Our own research collaboration (Raffay, Wood and Todd 2016; Wood, Raffay and Todd 2016) reveals something of the effort within chaplaincy.

Beyond care

In his famous ode to love in 1 Corinthians 13, Paul's 'better way' is radically mutual. Just as the Mental Capacity Act (UK Department of Health 2013) encourages us to assume capacity, Seedhouse's (2008, p.149) 'autonomy flip' requires us only to do things 'to' people where their condition absolutely necessitates it. It may be time to move beyond 'care' with its unequal overtones to co-production (Carson and Lepping 2009; Slay and Stephens 2013). We begin this chapter by outlining the case for such an approach. We then share our own story and conclude by exploring the potential for chaplains to lead on a vision for services people want.

From sick role to co-production

Under this heading, we explore problems with evidence-based practice. We introduce recovery approaches and co-production and explain how valuing everyone's 'vital' contribution released us from anti-psychiatry and conflictual models. We next explore and evaluate the significance of co-production. We then ask whether we need to move from 'caring' to describing the therapeutic alliance in more egalitarian language. We offer some theological reflection on chaplaincy.

Evidence-based practice: the sick role's latest friend

Parsons (1951) proposed that 'being sick' is not simply a 'state of fact' or 'condition' but rather a specifically patterned social role. He later suggested that, in Western societies, a patient exchanges certain freedom for receiving care (Parsons 1975). Until recently, his work appeared increasingly dated; however, this is no longer the case with cost-pressure risks tipping the balance back from patient-centred approaches (Baxter, Mugglestone and Maher 2010) to evidence-based practice (Fernandez *et al.* 2015).

Evidence-based practice makes obvious sense until you enquire what is admitted as evidence and what is therefore excluded (and who decides). A dramatic example is where staff resuscitate a patient to a life they would not have chosen; another is where medication relieves a mental health service user of their voices but they consider the side effects more problematic. A hidden danger with evidence-based practice is that it reduces evidence to that which is measurable in an ever-decreasing, self-justifying circle (Salvador-Carulla, Lukersmith and Sullivan 2017). Compassion and spirituality are readily excluded with sometimes devastating effects (Delamothe 2013; Francis 2013).

In critiquing evidence-based approaches, we are not denying that such approaches have brought great strides to fields of medicine such as surgery; yet, even there, they are not the whole story. Evidence-based practice is not wrong but *insufficient*, at least as typically understood (Carson and Lepping 2009; Tsianakas *et al.* 2012). Mental health provision has been especially problematic, with the Schizophrenia Commission (2012, p.2) reporting a 'broken and demoralised system that does not deliver the quality of treatment that is needed for people to recover'. Positively for mental health chaplaincy, psychiatry is shifting from a primarily medical to a more recovery-focused perspective (South London and Maudsley NHS Foundation Trust and South West London and St George's Mental Health NHS Trust 2010).

Recovery approaches

In 1987, Deegan wrote a compelling article about her experience as a service user. She implicitly connected the word 'recovery' with Alcoholics Anonymous, making the backwards connection to the Quaker-inspired retreat at York, founded in 1792 (Kibria and Metcalfe 2016). This suggests that 'recovery' is a concept kindred to 'spirituality', possibly its secular equivalent (E. Wood, personal correspondence). Recovery approaches are transforming services (Rotheram and Raffay 2017; Shepherd, Boardman and Slade 2008) but can also be problematic (Slade *et al.* 2014). They mostly complement medical approaches, prioritising meaning and hope and aspiring to place the service user at the centre of service delivery (Bonney and Stickley 2008). Like conventional chaplaincy, recovery services can be very patient centred while avoiding critical engagement with organisational structures or deeper transformation of the service. When fighting an infection, 5 minutes with the general practitioner may be sufficient so long as the antibiotics work; however, when more invasive or extensive treatments are delivered, three studies illustrate how services can impact on people: Chambers *et al.* (2014) showed how listening to mental health service users could minimise the distress of compulsory detentions; The King's Fund (2011) demonstrated how experience-based co-design improved a breast cancer service; and McGregor, Repper and Brown (2014) suggested how a recovery college, where people are taught skills to manage their mental health, can be improved by insights from education and co-production.

Co-production

Whereas recovery focuses on the service user, co-production centres more on the healthcare system. Slay and Stephens (2013, p.3) define co-production as 'a relationship where professionals and citizens share power to plan and deliver support together, recognising that both partners have vital contributions to make in order to improve quality of life for people and communities'. However, co-production suffers weaknesses similar to Maslow's hierarchy when predicated on Arnstein's (1969) ladder of participation, begging the question of where service-user involvement will be most effective. Tritter and McCallum (2006, p.165) offer an altogether richer co-production 'mosaic' that considers organisational context (Handy 1993). Rose *et al.* (2014, p.37) recommend that involvement should 'relate to specific issues where there was an active consideration of the possible need for change and where action would follow'.

Co-production not only empowers but also challenges passivity, framing service users and carers as partners in health promotion and recovery. This is clearly a real benefit in managing chronic conditions, not least schizophrenia and dual diagnosis (mental health and substance misuse). Both recovery and co-production offer great opportunities to chaplains and remind us that 'chaplains, unless they understand their role as simply fishing for souls in a particular pool, are in a privileged position to understand the dynamics, possibilities and problems of a complex institution' (Forrester 2000, p.85). We can exercise leadership in promoting co-production and compassionate care to complement the best offerings of evidence-based practice. We might enquire where we would locate ourselves within Tritter and McCallum's (2006, p.165) 'mosaic'. The following scenario illustrates the significance of co-production.

The significance of co-production

At a recent National Health Service (NHS) chaplaincy symposium in Liverpool, I (Don) had the great pleasure of listening to Ewan Kelly talk on chaplaincy. He compared chaplains to dancers on the dance floor. He suggested that some should be on the balcony taking stock of events and opportunities. He mentioned that one of his great heroes was the late singer-songwriter Leonard Cohen. As a service user I would like to take this dance floor analogy a few steps further.

After deciding he would move to the balcony, Ewan decided he was missing something – appreciation of the outside world! He decided to stand by a window where he could see the comings and goings outside. While there, he saw a small group of young men stop and look at the hall. 'They are a funny lot in there,' said one of them, 'they think that "Hallelujah" was written by some guy called Leonard Cohen when everyone knows it was Jeff Buckley who also had a hit with it!' Almost incandescent, Ewan dashed downstairs. After forcing his way through the dancers, he arrived outside too late and the group had left.

I would like us to imagine that a few days later, one of the young men was talking to a girl called Jenny. He told her about 'Hallelujah' and that everyone was dancing to Leonard Cohen. This amused Jenny, who said that Jeff Buckley had not written the song and that she was determined to see how people could dance to Leonard Cohen. The next day, Jenny went to the dance hall and was seen by community chaplain Ken. They seemed to get on well together. Despite being unsure about whether to return, Jenny attended a few more sessions after much cajoling from Ken. At the fifth session Jenny suddenly became more animated and asked why they had changed the music. She could now hear Whitney Houston, her favourite artist, and hoped they would soon play 'Dancing Queen' – her all-time favourite Abba song. 'Ah!' said Ken. 'That's good; you are becoming much more positive and making your own mind up about what you want to hear.' 'We all hear different tunes,' Ken explained. 'The important thing is that you determine the tunes *you* want to hear both now and in the future.' Jenny thanked Ken but did not return!

A few weeks later, Ewan and Ken were talking, and the conversation turned to Jenny. They wondered:

- how Jenny was and where she was

- why she had not returned

- whether they could have done something differently

- why Jenny came at all

- why others were not engaging

- what Jenny and others are looking for

- if there are falsehoods or myths about the role of chaplains and other staff, and if so, how they can be rectified.

They decided to bring these matters up at the next national chaplaincy meeting to obtain other chaplains' opinions. Almost at the same moment, however, both Ewan and Ken thought, *No! What we really need is for Jenny and others like her to give us their opinions and involve them in what we do.* 'We'll do a survey,' said one of them. 'Yes,' said the other, 'and we'll produce a research project with questionnaires.' 'No!' they both agreed. 'We will involve service users from the very start, valuing and respecting their opinions. It will be revolutionary – we'll call it CO-PRODUCTION!'

At the same time, Jenny was reflecting on the past few weeks. She had felt so much better after the dancing and had decided to try to patch things up with her family, with whom she had not got on with previously. She immediately returned to Newcastle, where she was welcomed with open arms and slowly recovering from her turmoil. Jenny's thoughts included:

- grateful thanks to Ken for helping her through a difficult time

- regrets that she had not been in touch

- how she nearly did not return after the first few sessions

- how she had gone to the dancehall not knowing what to expect

- wishing that there was a community chaplain in her new area whom she could see from time to time, especially when feeling a bit low

- feeling that they were the experts – they knew what they were doing – so she could not contribute much

- some ideas about improvements at the dancehall but feeling she might be laughed at or her ideas dismissed out of hand

- wishing someone would contact her as she felt guilty in going back

- wanting to engage with other service users who had been through the same experiences

- a desire to help others in a similar situation to hers a few weeks ago

- feeling powerless because she did not know where to start in getting involved.

These are both sides of the coin, with the question being 'How do we get both parties to engage with each other?' Is it by sharing contact details or using social media? The answer is not simple and cannot be a one size fits all. Confidentiality and safeguarding must always be respected; however, support throughout service users' journeys must be maintained, especially when they are away from the dancehall.

A theology of chaplaincy

Christian readers may see resonance between co-production and Romans 1:12 where Paul shifts his emphasis from care to co-production. They may equally – regardless of denomination – find inspiration in the report *Setting God's People Free* (Archbishop's Council 2017).

A distinct challenge with sacred texts is our tendency to enjoy comforting passages while applying challenging ones to other people! Those who see chaplaincy purely as presence ministry may find the parable of the talents (Matthew 25:14–30) disturbingly supportive of evidence-based practice. Chaplains working in management and leadership roles in healthcare organisations earn more than many ward managers and should deliver commensurately. Leadership, vision and managing complexity are rightly expected at those levels, and we risk discrediting our profession if we do not deliver. Koestenbaum's *Leadership: The Inner Side of Greatness* (2002) contains relevant material for reflection.

To any chaplains who conceive of their role primarily in NHS management terms, Hosea 4:9 with its famous phrase 'like people, like priest' offers a prophetic challenge – literally. We recognise God calling some to NHS management roles. However, chaplains have a unique role (albeit alongside others) in championing compassion. Chaplains rightly challenge the institution when it becomes narrowly utilitarian or totalitarian, or both (Raffay 2016). It is easy to become lukewarm (Revelation 3:14–22).

As healthcare chaplains, we can easily suffer failure of nerve, finding comfort in presence ministry or management alone, whichever offers us the lesser line of resistance. However, favourable winds can help us navigate the less favourable ones. By developing our compassion and expertise – especially our weaker side – we maximise our impact, serving our employer, community and society. With this in mind, we share our story, not suggesting it is the right way, but hoping to inspire imaginative thinking.

Our adventure in spiritual wellbeing

Having introduced co-production, we now describe the highlights and disappointments of our experience in Liverpool. We further develop our co-produced understanding of the biopsychosocial-spiritual model. We then reflect on William Wilberforce's story of the challenges (and benefits) of introducing change. We end by considering mental wellbeing from a less individualistic perspective.

Our experience in Liverpool

If you have seen the film *Patch Adams* (Shadyac 1998), you will recall how the eponymous hero repeatedly creates transforming interactions with other service users. Engagement begins when he repairs an elderly man's leaking polystyrene cup. We identify with this account of trust and humanity as we learn together about co-production. Learning is the wrong word if it suggests nothing more than scholarly debate between members of our Lived Experience Advisory Panel. For ourselves, and the other members, it is an adventure where we reach into ever-deeper waters. Building on the principle that each of us has a vital contribution, we are making steady progress researching co-produced chaplaincy.

Though not for the fainthearted, this process has been hugely fulfilling. Over the past 3 years, our growing group has been meeting bimonthly – planning, developing and conducting research projects, step by step. We succeeded in the first phase of a quarter-million-pound National Institute for Health Research funding application, but they rejected our bid at the second. We successfully contested a Research Ethics Committee decision against allowing trained volunteer research assistants with lived experience from conducting interviews. We are currently testing the validity of outcome measures to evidence the impact of co-production on chaplaincy. We are also assessing recruitment and retention rates with 40 mental health service users over 6 months. The next phase will involve extensive work to operationalise co-produced chaplaincy and prepare for a randomised clinical trial. If successful, we hope to show that co-produced spiritual care is more effective than standard spiritual care. Beyond that, we anticipate our approach may be relevant to other disciplines.

A biopsychosocial-spiritual model

Our story, however, begins earlier. It brings together Mersey Care NHS Foundation Trust's strategic commitment to co-production under Michael Crilly, director of social inclusion and participation as well as my (Julian's) Sheffield research (Raffay 2014). We have moved beyond my earlier recommendation that 'our understanding of spiritual care should revolve around the perceptions of service users, carers and frontline staff, instead of predefined definitions sourced from textbooks' (Raffay 2012, p.68). To deepen our understanding, we formed a partnership with the Cardiff Centre for Chaplaincy Studies. We enlisted a researcher familiar with the field (Wood, Watson and Hayter 2011) and, as part one of our action research cycle, we conducted grounded theory and thematic analysis with 20 adult acute mental health service users in both our local and high secure divisions.

Two key points emerged. First, the grounded theory suggested that the heightened interest in spirituality might, in some measure, be in response to the biopsychosocial model's institutionalising tendencies. This understanding affirms, rather than denigrates, service-user religion or belief. As service users experience potentially alien environments, loss of their routines, their coping mechanisms – even their cigarettes – they search deeply for orientating resources. We believe that the impoverished and alien environment fuels sometimes excessive spiritual or religious practice. This led us to redefine our understanding of the spiritual and the biopsychosocial (Raffay et al. 2016). Rather than identify a fourth element, we perceive the spiritual as surrounding (and including) the three classic biopsychosocial elements. The Lived Experience Advisory Panel endorsed this interpretation.

Second, the mainly Christian participants, reflecting Liverpool's demographic, wanted chaplaincy to provide greater opportunity for worship and fellowship. They wished time with other Christians, enjoying what many churches offer. They sought to live their faith on the wards (with generally positive outcomes). They showed marked respect for people of other faiths but wanted to share their hope with atheists. Our findings silenced religious critics who saw co-production as a sellout to secularism.

The Royal College of Psychiatrists (South London and Maudsley NHS Foundation Trust and South West London and St George's Mental Health NHS Trust 2010, p.5) asserts that 'recovery is probably impossible without hope'. By co-producing our research, we have simply allowed our participants to tell us where they found hope. These findings suggest that chaplaincy can influence wider healthcare provision. Allowing service users and carers to set the agenda has delivered results that are counterintuitive to secular rhetoric.

William Wilberforce

Someone generously likened our task to that of Wilberforce. The compliment was flattering, but critically they stressed how his dogged determination over years eventually resulted in success. Our 'dream', quoting another reformer, is that one day people with mental health problems will be treated as equal to others. We invite you to live your dream as a National Health servant or servant in another agency.

Handy (1993, p.123) described organizations 'as the fine weave of influence patterns whereby individuals or groups seek to influence others to think or act in particular ways'. He also added that 'if we are to understand organizations, we must understand the nature of power and influence for they are the means by which the people of the organization are linked to its purpose'. We influence culture as much by leaving leadership to others as through our engagement.

Prevention, treatment and recovery

Cultural change, both within and beyond healthcare organisations, is central to addressing the stigma that Swinton (2000) sees as the greatest barrier for people with mental health problems. Why do so many find it unacceptable to deride people for a disability, their ethnicity or sexual orientation, yet regularly use language contemptuous of people with mental health problems?

As *Sustainability and Transformation Partnerships* (NHS England 2017) shift emphasis from treatment-based approaches to health promotion, will chaplains lag or show leadership? Health promotion emphasising prevention and recovery is highly amenable to co-production. Moreover, faith communities, with local infrastructure the NHS could only ever dream of, have much to offer. Creative partnerships could benefit both.

Community chaplains and chaplaincy volunteers, working alongside community development workers, have considerable expertise that could save the NHS both effort and money. Our experience in mental health is that 'fixing' individuals in isolation is rarely effective. When 'around 25% of girls and 10% of boys have been victims of sexual abuse' (Shooter 2012, p.1), stabilising people on psychiatric wards, only to return them to their original environment, is rarely a long-term solution.

We affirm 'being present' as a valid approach to chaplaincy but have attempted to show what can be achieved when chaplains think creatively rather than allow the institution to constrain them. One of the easiest ways to think creatively is by forming partnerships with like-minded people. Occupational therapists, dieticians and other professional disciplines are potential allies, but so too, at least if we take co-production seriously, are the people who use the services and the groups they form.

In the final part of this chapter, we build up to the idea of the chaplain as prophet, one who makes their distinct contribution to the whole.

Achieving spiritual wellbeing through strategic co-production

We now explore how we might use an assets-based approach to create environments where stakeholders can thrive. We explore brokenness and the often-times fractured institutions where service users aspire to recover and in which staff hope to keep their sanity. We discuss how faith communities, with chaplain-prophets at the interface, might collaborate with mental health services to promote a healthier society.

Co-production in the organisation

The NHS can harm staff as well as service users. Anyone who has seen over-busy staff and disheartened staff (or is one) will know. Indeed, I (Julian) was recently asked, 'How is someone who isn't motivated going to motivate someone who isn't motivated?' Co-production, in recognising everybody's 'vital' contribution, potentially addresses all stakeholders' concerns. For it to work, however, it must become based not just on welcoming 'vital contributions' but 'vital' people with whom one has 'vital' relationships of profound respect, forged through genuine enquiry. Tritter and McCallum (2006) show how some of the pitfalls of working in this area can be avoided. One such area regards the final say.

All too often, service users are offered pseudo-choices – like fast check-ins and chosen seats on flights – rather than any genuine influence over services. Rarely are their contributions proportionately remunerated (INVOLVE 2010). We see little recognition in services of the challenges which recovery approaches present staff. It is assumed that traditional staff–patient professional boundaries continue alongside a radically new model of interaction; however, this assumption leaves staff confused and potentially vulnerable. Co-producers need to recognise that different people have different levels of responsibility in a mental health service, but mature debate is always to be encouraged. This is more likely to happen in trusts with a healthy organisational spirituality. Chaplains are in a unique position to contribute, not least through their meetings with the chairs and chief executives of healthcare organisations (Raffay 2009).

The mechanisms of co-production

Meetings with senior leaders provide real opportunity. Staniszewska *et al.* (2012, p.138) observed:

> The outcomes of involvement seemed to be predominantly defined by the organizations involved rather than service users, so we know relatively little about the outcomes that service users wanted to achieve. Such difficulties challenge the notion of true partnership as certain groups dominate the ways in which methods, context or process are decided.

Anyone familiar with Freire's (1996) work will appreciate the issues. Recognising the differences between representation and co-production, Crepaz-Keay (2012, p.153) states that:

> expertise and experience are NOT the same thing. But, with support, and a methodical approach, experience can be transformed into expertise. With enough high quality effective involvement, services can be transformed into a powerful tool for positive mental health.

Clearly, achieving Crepaz-Keay's 'powerful tool for positive mental health' will involve both effort and some measure of confrontation. This infers an iterative process. Hickey *et al.* (2018) offer key principles and guidance to inform such a process (with respect to co-produced research design). This crucially involves the sharing of power – from which, they suggest, all other principles emerge.

Using assets to create healthy communities

Co-worked discussion may improve service delivery. Our own research identified participants' views on the qualities of a good chaplain (Raffay *et al.* 2016, p.6) but were inconclusive regarding pay bands. Weiner (1979, p.1129) reported on Pussin's work of 1793, recognising the benefits of employing service users and carers. We could perhaps turn austerity to advantage by recruiting chaplaincy support workers on suitable pay, delivering a service blended with chaplains' expertise. Indeed, Kara (2013, p.131) suggests that greater honesty about our own, sometimes indifferent, mental health could break down the dichotomies we may prefer to perpetuate.

Crawford (2005), Cahn (2000) and Ostrom (1996), among others, recognise the potential for co-production not only to benefit participating individuals but also to release insights and skills. Here we might strengthen Slay and Stephen's (2013) passing reference to 'vital' contributions to reach beyond involvement as extra hands to shaping services. A powerful example of this is a Doncaster food bank whose volunteers and board members experience chronic schizophrenia. By avoiding 'throwaway people' (Cahn 2000), they not only deliver better services but have moved from person-centred to people-centred care (see Chapter 18).

Co-production, like community development, requires trust, and here again many faith communities have much to offer. Whereas most professionals have shipped out to suburbia, faith leaders enjoy knowledge the NHS has long since lost. Collaboration, co-produced with residents and health promotion agencies, offers the best and possibly *only* way to create healthy communities; however, this calls for courage (Koestenbaum 2002, pp.136–168).

Chaplain-prophets

Seeking to deliver pastoral care across multiple sites, often significant distances apart, can be soul destroying. It can leave chaplains feeling isolated. Such effort, though praiseworthy, may be less fruitful – for the patients – than engaging other disciplines, reinforcing values or inspiring staff and managers. We refer readers who want to explore the 'avoidance of key questions about purpose and practice, role, and relationships' that readily erode confidence to Swift (2009, p.3).

Sentamu (2015, p.242), the Archbishop of York in England, invites churches to take a stand. His remarks could equally apply to chaplains or anyone of faith:

By showing fear and reluctance to act prophetically, the Church has failed to maintain a vision. By acting prophetically, I do not mean being a voice of a 'vested interest' among other interest groups, but instead a body which can stand back and be a voice for the powerless, the weak and the dispossessed. In my mind, it is more important than ever that churches of all denominations fulfil this role today.

Schön (1984, pp.3–20) described a crisis of confidence in the professions with people increasingly mistrusting of institutions. He argued that professional insights now find themselves – entirely appropriately – weighed in a marketplace of ideas where no one is considered to have divine revelation, neither chaplains nor doctors nor anyone else. Chaplains have a duty of candour to speak out; other professions have identical rights (Care Quality Commission 2015). Service users and carers have their own mechanisms but are typically more vulnerable.

From rhetoric to reality

Being a voice for the powerless undoubtedly involves both advocacy (Morgan 2016) and strategic leadership. Our experience reveals leadership to be neither easy nor about short-term fixes. Reality begins within our own chaplaincy teams when we ask a painful question: 'Are we delivering the services people want or that we enjoy delivering?' We have found the only morally acceptable answer involves learning to co-produce alongside people with lived experience (Carson and Lepping 2009). We need to admit our own mutable identities (Kara 2013) and sometimes variable mental health (Keyes 2002).

Authentic co-production may necessitate reconfiguring the staffing profile to discriminate positively towards people with necessary lived experience. Utilising co-produced service evaluation would be a good starting point. It may involve cooperation with likely and unlikely allies. We might begin with a co-produced provisional 5-year plan. It would undoubtedly need revising as trust deepens and co-production expands our horizons. Christian readers may see resonances with 1 Corinthians 12–13. Strategic co-production has the potential to improve both individual and organisational spiritual wellbeing. Chaplains are well placed to exercise leadership and encourage other disciplines to follow their example. Service users and carers, when they recognise integrity, will want to be involved.

Conclusion

Over the years, chaplaincy has supported several causes – counselling, spirituality, mindfulness – and we hope co-production is becoming one of them. We set out by outlining the disadvantages of traditional care approaches. We next described our personal journey into co-production. We then offered a vision of how chaplains might be of greater benefit through more strategic approaches. We believe that co-produced services are not only more effective but also more ethical. We dream of mental health (and other services) that reflect justice at every level, not least the strategic, and hope for chaplains to be able to exercise strategic leadership.

References

Archbishop's Council (2017) *Setting God's People Free*. London: Archbishop's Council.

Arnstein, S. (1969) 'A ladder of citizen participation.' *Journal of the American Institute of Planners 35*, 216–224.

Baxter, H., Mugglestone, M. and Maher, L. (2010) *The Experience Based Design Approach: Concepts and Case Studies*. Aldridge: NHS Institute for Innovation and Improvement.

Bonney, S. and Stickley, T. (2008) 'Recovery and mental health: a review of the British literature.' *Journal of Psychiatric and Mental Health Nursing 15*, 140–153.

Cahn, E. (2000) *No More Throw-Away People: The Co-Production Imperative*. Washington, DC: Essential Books.

Care Quality Commission (2015) *Regulation 20: Duty of Candour*. London: Care Quality Commission.

Carson, A.M. and Lepping, P. (2009) 'Ethical psychiatry in an uncertain world: conversations and parallel truths.' *Philosophy, Ethics, and Humanities in Medicine 4*, 7. Accessed on 27/12/2018 at doi.org/10.1186/1747-5341-4-7.

Chambers, M., Gallacher, A., Borschmann, R., Gillard, S. *et al.* (2014) 'The experiences of detained mental health service users: issues of dignity in care.' *BMC Medical Ethics 15*, 1–8.

Crawford, F. (2005) *Doing It Differently: An Asset-Based Approach to Wellbeing*. Glasgow: NHS Health Scotland and Scottish Council Foundation.

Crepaz-Keay, D. (2012) 'Evaluating Service-User Involvement in Mental Health Services.' In P. Ryan, S. Ramon and T. Graecen (eds) *Empowerment, Lifelong Learning and Recovery in Mental Health: Towards a New Paradigm*. Basingstoke: Palgrave Macmillan.

Deegan, P. (1987) *Recovery, Rehabilitation and the Conspiracy of Hope: A Keynote Address*. Accessed on 27/12/2018 at www.patdeegan.com/sites/default/files/files/conspiracy_of_hope.pdf.

Delamothe, T. (2013) 'Learning from Winterbourne View.' *British Medical Journal 346*, f433.

Fernandez, A., Sturmberg, J., Lukersmith, S., Madden, R. *et al.* (2015) 'Evidence-based medicine: is it a bridge too far?' *Health Research Policy and Systems 13*, 1–9.

Forrest, S., Risk, I., Masters, H. and Brown, N. (2000) 'Mental health service user involvement in nurse education: exploring the issues.' *Journal of Psychiatric and Mental Health Nursing 7*, 51–57.

Forrester, D.B. (2000) *Truthful Action: Explorations in Practical Theology*. Edinburgh: T. & T. Clark.

Francis, R. (2013) *Report of the Mid Staffordshire NHS Foundation Trust Public Inquiry: Executive Summary*. London: The Stationery Office.

Freire, P. (1996) *Pedagogy of the Oppressed*. London: Penguin.

Handy, C. (1993) *Understanding Organizations*. Oxford: Oxford University Press.

Hickey, G., Brearley, S., Coldham, T., Denegri, S. *et al.* (2018) *Guidance on Co-producing a Research Project*. Southampton: INVOLVE.

INVOLVE (2010) *Payment for Involvement: A Guide to Making Payments to Members of the Public*. Eastleigh: National Institute for Health Research. Accessed on 27/12/2018 at www.invo.org.uk/resource-centre/payment-and-recognition-for-public-involvement

Kara, H. (2013) 'Mental health service user involvement in research: where have we come from, where are we going?' *Journal of Public Mental Health 12*, 122–135.

Keyes, C. (2002) 'The mental health continuum: from languishing to flourishing in life.' *Journal of Health and Social Behaviour 43*, 207–222.

Kibria, A.A. and Metcalfe, N.H. (2016) 'A biography of William Tuke (1732–1822): founder of the modern mental asylum.' *Journal of Medical Biography 24*, 384–388.

Koestenbaum, P. (2002) *Leadership: The Inner Side of Greatness – A Philosophy for Leaders.* San Francisco, CA: Jossey-Bass.

McGregor, J., Repper, J. and Brown, H. (2014) '"The college is so different from anything I have done": a study of the characteristics of Nottingham Recovery College.' *The Journal of Mental Health Training, Education and Practice 9*, 3–15.

Morgan, G. (2016) *Independent Advocacy and Spiritual Care: Insights from Service Users, Advocates, Health Care Professionals and Chaplains.* London: Macmillan.

NHS England (2017) *Sustainability and Transformation Partnerships.* Leeds: NHS England. Accessed on 04/12/2018 at www.england.nhs.uk/stps.

Ostrom, E. (1996) 'Crossing the great divide: co-production, synergy, and development.' *World Development 24*, 1073–1087.

Parsons, T. (1951) *The Social System.* Glencoe, IL: The Free Press.

Parsons, T. (1975) 'The sick role and the role of the physician reconsidered.' *The Milbank Memorial Fund Quarterly. Health and Society 53*, 257–278.

Raffay, J. (2009) 'Checkmate for chaplains.' *Mental Health Chaplains' Newsletter*, summer edition.

Raffay, J. (2012) 'Are our mental health practices beyond HOPE?' *Journal of Health Care Chaplaincy 12*, 68–80.

Raffay, J. (2014) 'How staff and patient experience shapes our perception of spiritual care in a psychiatric setting.' *Journal of Nursing Management 22*, 940–950.

Raffay, J. (2016) 'The Francis Report (2013): Neo-Pharisaism in the National Health Service?' *Journal of Health and Social Care Chaplaincy 4.* doi: 10.1558/hscc.v4i1.29022.

Raffay, J., Wood, E. and Todd, A. (2016) 'Service user views of spiritual and pastoral care (chaplaincy) in NHS mental health services: a co-produced constructivist grounded theory investigation.' *BMC Psychiatry 16*, 200. Accessed on 28/12/2018 at doi.org/10.1186/s12888-016-0903-9.

Rose, D., Barnes, M., Crawford, M., Omeni, E., MacDonald, D. and Wilson, A. (2014) 'How do managers and leaders in the National Health Service and Social Care respond to service user

involvement in mental health services in both its traditional and emergent forms? The ENSUE study.' *Health Services and Delivery Research 2*, 10. doi: 10.3310/hsdr02100.

Rotheram, C. and Raffay, J. (2017) 'The life rooms: an innovative recovery approach.' *Journal of Recovery in Mental Health 1*, 35–41.

Salvador-Carulla, L., Lukersmith, S. and Sullivan, W. (2017) 'From the EBM pyramid to the Greek temple: a new conceptual approach to guidelines as implementation tools in mental health.' *Epidemiology and Psychiatric Sciences 26*, 105–114.

Schizophrenia Commission (2012) *The Abandoned Illness: A Report from the Schizophrenia Commission – Main Report.* London: Schizophrenia Commission.

Schön, D.A. (1984) *The Reflective Practitioner: How Professionals Think in Action.* New York, NY: Basic Books.

Seedhouse, D. (2008) *Ethics: The Heart of Health Care.* Chichester: Wiley. (Original work published 1988.)

Sentamu, J. (2015) *On Rock or Sand: Firm Foundations for Britain's Future.* London: SPCK.

Shadyac, T. (1998) *Patch Adams.* United States: Blue Wolf/Bungalow Productions/Farrell-Minoff.

Shepherd, G., Boardman, J. and Slade, M. (2008) *Making Recovery a Reality.* London: Sainsbury Centre for Mental Health.

Shooter, S. (2012) *How Survivors of Abuse Relate to God: The Authentic Spirituality of the Annihilated Soul.* Abingdon: Ashgate.

Slade, M., Amering, M., Farkas, M., Hamilton, B. *et al.* (2014) 'Uses and abuses of recovery: implementing recovery-oriented practices in mental health systems.' *World Psychiatry 13*, 12–20.

Slay, J. and Stephens, L. (2013) *Co-Production in Mental Health: A Literature Review.* London: New Economics Foundation.

South London and Maudsley NHS Foundation Trust and South West London and St George's Mental Health NHS Trust (2010) *Recovery Is for All: Hope, Agency and Opportunity in Psychiatry. A Position Statement by Consultant Psychiatrists.* London: SLAM/SWLSTG.

Staniszewska, S., Mockford, C., Gibson, A., Herron-Marx, S. and Putz, R. (2012) 'Moving Forward: Understanding the Negative Experiences and Impacts of Patient and Public Involvement in Health Service Planning, Development, and Evaluation.' In M. Barnes and P. Cotterell (eds) *Critical Perspectives on User Involvement*. Bristol: Policy.

Swift, C.A. (2009) *Hospital Chaplaincy in the Twenty-First Century: The Crisis of Spiritual Care on the NHS*. Farnham: Ashgate.

Swinton, J. (2000) *Resurrecting the Person: Friendship and the Care of People with Mental Health Problems*. Nashville, TN: Abingdon Press.

The King's Fund (2011) *The Patient-Centred Care Project: Evaluation Report*. London: The King's Fund.

Tritter, J. and McCallum, A. (2006) 'The snakes and ladders of user involvement: moving beyond Arnstein.' *Health Policy 76*, 156–168.

Tsianakas, V., Robert, G., Maben, J., Richardson, A. *et al.* (2012) 'Implementing patient-centred cancer care: using experience-based co-design to improve patient experience in breast and lung cancer services.' *Supportive Care in Cancer 20*, 2639–2647.

UK Department of Health (2013) *Code of Practice: Mental Capacity Act*. London: The Stationery Office.

Weiner, D.B. (1979) 'The apprenticeship of Philippe Pinel: a new document, "Observations of citizen Pussin on the insane".' *The American Journal of Psychiatry 136*, 1128–1134.

Wood, E., Watson, R. and Hayter, M. (2011) 'To what extent are the Christian clergy acting as frontline mental health workers? A study from the north of England.' *Mental Health, Religion and Culture 14*, 769–783.

Wood, E., Raffay, J. and Todd, A. (2016) 'How could co-production principles improve mental health spiritual and pastoral care (chaplaincy) services?' *Health and Social Care Chaplaincy 4*, 1, 51–56.

Part 7

Educating Chaplains

What Do Chaplains Need to Learn to Work in and Influence Twenty-First Century Healthcare Systems?

'Visiting Hour'[1]
In the pond of our new garden
Were five orange stains, under
inches of ice. Weeks since anyone
had been there. Already by far
the most severe winter for years.
You broke the ice with a hammer.
I watched the goldfish appear
blunt-nosed and delicately clear.

Since then so much has taken place
to distance us from where we were.
That it should come to this.
Unable to hide the horror
in my eyes, I stand helpless
by your bedside and can do no more
than wish it were simply a matter
of smashing ice and giving you air.

Formation is traditionally seen as a necessity to enable chaplains to accompany and hold, and inhabit systems, where helplessness in response to suffering and

---

1   Stewart Conn, *The Touch of Time: New & Selected Poems* (Bloodaxe Books, 2014; www. bloodaxebooks.com).

complexity is a norm. Part 7 of this book goes further. It explores formation as the essential foundation to promoting the transformative learning and leadership required to equip and empower chaplains to practise innovatively and effectively in the future at different levels of healthcare activity.

Collaborators who have already explored what the role of healthcare chaplains is, and potentially could be, in the future have encouraged readers to move beyond a model of presence and companionship. When chaplains *do* as well as be, it is imperative that chaplains act, as other healthcare professionals, with non-malevolence – indeed, beneficence. This implies competence as well as compassion.

How we ensure that chaplains be equipped to be and do whatever is needed – in new ways and new contexts – in a confident, creative and collaborative manner that meaningfully fulfils their sense of vocation, is the focus of Part 7.

The next two chapters seek to explore how chaplains may be best educated to maximize their input within twenty-first century health and social care systems in which they are employed to promote spiritual wellbeing. To recap, chaplains potentially practise at different levels of activity in healthcare – at an individual (*micro*) level, at team, departmental, locality or geographical area (*meso*) levels and across an organization, whole system, nation or international (*meta*) levels. How can chaplains be cultivated in order to empower them to practise in the contemporary milieu of rapid change in the planning and delivery of healthcare at any of these three levels? In tackling these issues, first, Ewan Kelly explores the importance of formation for chaplaincy practice. In Chapter 21, David W Fleenor and Ewan Kelly collaboratively consider how learning from different emphases in chaplaincy education in the US and the UK might enable the development of specialist chaplaincy education which equips chaplains to be spiritual agents of enablement and transformation in healthcare (based on Paterson and Clegg 2013). Together these pieces explore growing the capacity of chaplains to support the transformation of individuals, communities and systems. In doing so, this process affirms the strengths of persons in relationship to promote human flourishing – spiritually and, thus, holistically. It engages with questions of who chaplains need to be, what they need to know and do as well as how they might learn in order to embody and enact such a role to effect meaningful outcomes.

Chapter 20

Formation and the Intentional Use of Self

The Chaplain's Primary Resource

Ewan Kelly

Understanding our stories

'…everybody's got a sacred story, an organizing story, of who they are and what their place in the world is' (Barack Obama cited in Laskas 2018, p.10). Our stories are not formed in isolation but shaped by the families, communities, cultures and faith traditions (Bachelard 2015) or belief groups we inhabit. They inform not only who we are but the lens through which we see and interpret the world and our experience. Thus, an understanding of our stories is fundamental to our ability to form relationships and make space to listen to the individual and collective stories of others.

The intentional use of self is the primary tool a chaplain has in order to build relationships of trust and to practise in any context (Kelly 2012; Nolan 2013). Thus, effective chaplaincy requires a high degree of self-awareness. This is central to the process of chaplaincy formation – the developing vocational self-understanding of a person performing, or seeking to perform, the professional role of specialist spiritual care provider. Therefore, formation, as described in this chapter, must be of primary importance in the education for, and ongoing personal and professional development in, chaplaincy.

This chapter first provides some brief context and historical background to chaplaincy formation, particularly within the UK. It posits what relevant educational aims and approaches are required for formation in the twenty-first century. The concept of formation is explored at three different, but closely interlinked, dimensions: spiritual; psychological; and moral. In particular, its significance for laying the foundations for chaplains to work with practical wisdom is highlighted. Finally, the need to foster consistency in the rigorous formation of chaplains at a time of great stress and pressure in health and care services, particularly in the UK, is considered.

Context

Traditionally, those who have become chaplains in the industrialized world have been formed initially through their nesting in a faith community where they have actively absorbed not just a way of believing or speaking but a way of being (Gerkin 1997) and relating (Hauerwas and Wells 2004). Historically, within the UK formation for those who have entered healthcare, chaplaincy has been part of further ecclesial formation either in seminary and/or at theological college (i.e. developing a vocational understanding of self as clergyperson or church representative who then goes on to work as a chaplain) – an undergraduate theological education, in the main, equipping graduates with knowledge of their religious tradition (and potentially other traditions and cultures also); its stories, rituals and institutional history; and how it has shaped, and is shaped by, the world. The opportunity to participate in undergraduate pastoral theology classes which equip students to reflect on lived experience with heart and gut, not just head, or participate in practice-based learning, is increasingly limited in many centres of theological education.

Specific training and education for professional chaplaincy in the UK is a recent development (Swift 2015). A small number of postgraduate courses, uni- and multi-professional, which include, to varying degree, the fostering of pastoral formation as part of their curriculum for those already in healthcare chaplaincy settings, or who are interested in chaplaincy as a vocation, have developed in the UK. As Swift (2015, p.170) describes, the evolution of chaplaincy education in the UK has been 'sporadic and largely uncoordinated'. The creation of such courses is significant as they point not only to a perceived need but also a *real* need. Since 2009, these programmes have been structured or restructured to become more competency based (see Chapter 21) to align themselves with the UK Board of Healthcare Chaplains' (UKBHC) (2009) *Spiritual and Religious Care Capabilities and Competences for Healthcare Chaplains*. This framework was written specifically for mid-grade chaplains and revised in 2015 (UKBHC 2015) and 2017 (UKBHC 2017) for all grades. The formational content and aims of these postgraduate courses vary greatly from knowledge-based learning on how to theologically reflect to practice-based learning with qualified supervision and explicit learning outcomes which include heightening self-appropriation. Currently, there is also one foundational course for healthcare workers (formerly specifically for healthcare chaplains), including fledgling chaplains, which has some focus on formation. In Scotland, a postgraduate certificate in healthcare chaplaincy has been developed, designed as an entry qualification into the profession. It aims to enable graduates of the course to be fit for practice by evidencing the UKBHC's (2017) *Spiritual and Religious Care Capabilities and Competences for Healthcare Chaplains* and, thus, focuses on the knowledge and skills required for professional chaplaincy. Participants must be practising chaplains or be in a volunteer chaplaincy placement and mentored by a chaplain registered with the UKBHC (and may or may not have some supervisory training). In short, the depth and rigour of formation for healthcare chaplains entering the profession in the UK is piecemeal.

In addition, those who currently seek employment as chaplains, certainly in Scotland and in other northern European countries, are increasingly from a non-faith background. There is also a lack of experienced pastoral agents, ordained and non-ordained (with theological educations), applying for chaplaincy jobs in Scotland. Herein lies a crucial issue in the formation and training of chaplains. There is no longer a common meta-narrative which shapes and underpins the formation of chaplains. As one theological educator who took part in a review of Scottish chaplaincy education, training and formation (Paterson and Clegg 2013, p.28) put it, 'the gateway into chaplaincy is no longer ordination but education'. Hence, there is a movement towards chaplains being employed on account of their spiritual maturity and a relevant, significantly practice-based, education rather than on being in good standing with a faith community as well as having a theological education and some pastoral experience, as has been historically the case.

Historically and presently, formation for healthcare chaplains in North America, in several northern European countries, Australasia, Southeast Asia, South America and Africa is much more consistently rigorous than in the UK. This is due to the development of clinical pastoral education (CPE), which David expands on in Chapter 21. The CPE process seeks to deepen 'spiritual caregivers' emotional and spiritual self-awareness and professional identity formation' (Zollfrank and Garlid 2012, p.429). Overseeing accreditation bodies in different countries ensures that CPE programmes throughout the world have a structure similar to that of the Association for Clinical Pastoral Education.

Formation for what, why, how and by whom?
What and why?
Future chaplains must be formed to act as spiritual drivers or agents of change within healthcare organizations and systems to foster spiritual wellbeing at micro- and meso-levels, and potentially meta-levels also. The

aim is to form chaplains able to support individual and shared exploration and engagement with issues of meaning, purpose and hope, and to identify the assets available to promote such qualities. Several chapters in the second half of this book outline emerging models of chaplaincy, including the role of strategic leadership, which describe chaplains operating in this manner, creatively and collaboratively at meso- and meta-levels of healthcare activity. As much as working with individuals, engaging with teams, communities and committees requires self-awareness and personal and professional self-confidence to enable the spiritual dimension of health to be explored – self-awareness being increasingly recognized as being a core requirement to promote the development of transformational leadership in healthcare (Gilbert and Fulford 2010).

How? – the pedagogical approach

Formation is 'pedagogy for the whole person' (Carlin, Cole and Strobel 2012, p.447). It is education not just to promote intellectual or head knowledge (the focus of a traditional theological education, for example) but also an understanding of our feelings, morals, sexuality and spirituality within the context of our life history and present experience.

Practice-based learning is at the heart of chaplaincy formation and requires creating conditions where practitioners have permission to risk utilizing different aspects of their humanity, including their intuition as well as heart and head, whilst reflecting on practice in a one-to-one basis or group context. Without an element of risking of self, there can be no learning (Paterson 2013). Thus, a safe, non-judgemental facilitated space must be co-created where practitioners feel empowered to be vulnerable, open, innovative and seek to connect with others and self even in the midst of suffering, complexity and paradox. Individuals themselves are the experts. In such a 'liminal' (Kelcourse 2010, p.251) and 'authentic' (Waid 2015, p.702) space, wisdom is drawn out and practitioners are empowered to be curious and provisional, and in group settings to learn from one another. As chaplains or aspiring chaplains working in healthcare contexts, as we listen to the stories, pain, joy and questions of people, ultimately we face ourselves. We find mirrored in the experience of others resonances and dissonances with aspects of our own story. There is something challenging yet potentially profound and life changing in journeying with others into the unknown places (to us) of their lives and in doing so into *our* inner lives. This resonates with novelist Richard Flanagan's (2015) description of Australian prisoners of war being transported into the jungle to build the Burmese railway during the Second World War: 'They were like other young men, unknown to themselves. So much that lay within them they were now travelling to meet' (p.40). Those in chaplaincy formation do not travel alone. Hard though it may be at times, if we are open to reflection on practice and sharing with others where we have glimpsed something of ourselves whilst in practice, moments of deep learning about, and connection with, aspects of our inner self may occur. Stephen Muse (2007, p.183) beautifully sums up the ongoing developmental journey of formation as 'one of increasing capacity for embracing vulnerability'.

Who should provide personal and professional formation?

In Marilyn Robinson's (2014) novel *Lila*, John Ames, an elderly widow who, like his father before him, has ministered to the congregation and local community in the small American town of Gilead all his working life. Ames develops a deepening relationship with Lila, a younger itinerant woman, through a series of existential conversations – mainly prompted by Lila's probing questions as she searches for meaning in her life and multiple losses. Much of the time Ames sits, as they share a cup of coffee together, in silent accompaniment. During one such conversation, in her wondering aloud, Lila asks Ames why things seem to happen the way they do. The old minister permissively replies that he has been asking himself the same question most of his life. By briefly adding that there has been a share of sorrow in the house where they sit, he indicates he is no stranger to loss and transition. He concludes his brief intervention by saying that Lila's question is one 'I sort of live with' (p.30).

Much of chaplaincy formation is about learning to be honest, to own and live with such questions (those which Mark Stobert describes in Chapter 4); holding them, containing them and enabling others to verbalize them in their own way and own time. To enable this, chaplains like old John Ames need to be aware of their own stories, their own responses to suffering and loss, including their own lack of answers and understanding, and be able to live with that, to make space for the stories and struggles of others. In short, (fledgling) chaplains not only need to be able to live with mystery and the unfathomable but also need to regularly retreat, during their ongoing vocational journey, to a safe place with a trusted wise other to articulate their own existential angst and struggles. In other words, chaplains need their own John Ames to accompany and hold a space for them, thus enabling initial and ongoing (re)formation and living with questions – their own, including those that relate to vocational satisfaction (Jones and Pendleton Jones 2008), and those of others.

Spiritually and psychologically mature chaplaincy educators of character, like John Ames, are required to facilitate the specialist formation of chaplains – people who have abilities similar to those of Ames and have integrated their reflected experience into their practice. Necessary supervisory training and ongoing supervision also are required for those who offer accompaniment.

Formation as a foundation for creativity and transformation

Chaplains not only need an education (the acquisition of relevant knowledge), and training (the development and honing of certain skills in order to perform core tasks), but crucially require specialist and rigorous formation (an understanding of their being). Formation involves a person intentionally turning away from the routine and busyness of life to reflect on who they have been and who they are, and be open to who they are becoming. Self-knowledge, like any form of knowledge, being provisional, contextual and fragile, requires ongoing attention to remain relevant and rigorous. It is a process which promotes the deepening of a person's understanding of their whole self in a vocational role (Heitink 1993).

Enabling chaplains to become self-aware, reflexive practitioners (who can reflect not just *on* past practice but *in* the moment of practice) necessitates an ontological emphasis not only in cultivating effective chaplains but throughout a chaplain's career. It is the ongoing process of (re)formation through reflecting on past practice to deepen an understanding of self which provides the basis for reflexivity in future practice. This requires habitual time, attention and commitment.

Reflexivity is a key component in the development of *phronesis* or practical wisdom – the ability to make or discern good judgements or decisions in the immediacy of practice informed by reflection on accumulated experience and the moral character of the practitioner (see below). Making normative such habitual practice of reflection on individual and communal human experience helps provide the foundation for fostering practical wisdom – reflexive ability evolving from a reflective attitude.

Moving from being reflective to reflexive is an example of transformational learning which, in turn, can potentially lead to transforming practice. (See Ken Donaldson's case study in Chapter 15 for an illustration of this.) This only can occur with a significant degree of intentional self-appropriation already having taken place. In other words, formation is the basis for the possibility of enabling transformation of self and personal practice. This then affords the opportunity to help facilitate transformation in others' lives (individually or corporately) and in the cultures and systems chaplains inhabit. Fundamentally, without formation there can be no real transformation.

Key aspects of human personhood in chaplaincy formation

Three aspects of personhood that crucially must be explored during chaplaincy formation will now be considered: a person's spirituality; their psychological development; and the moral dimension to their living (i.e. their character). The significance of these dimensions has been previously emphasized by Australian pastoral theologian Neil Pembroke (2007) and in outlining recent proposed research into the 'holistic' formation of church members enabled by local pastors (Pembroke *et al.* 2018) based on Pembroke's previous seminary-based work in ministerial formation. I particularly want to focus on the spiritual and moral dimensions in relation to vocational fulfilment and the role of formation in helping to lay the foundations for a practitioner's capacity to work with practical wisdom. However, it is important to state, like Pembroke (2007) and Pembroke *et al.* (2018), that though we may seek to describe these three different aspects of human makeup, they each are far from distinct as they interweave and influence one another as part of a complex whole.

Spiritual dimension

The spiritual dimension is that which seeks meaning, purpose and hope in life and living. A significant contribution to a person's sense of meaningful self or identity is their embodiment of a vocational role. It is what makes them 'fly' or feel alive in their work – satisfaction at work not just being a response to the world's need. For many fledgling chaplains, the Judeo-Christian narrative will be significant in underpinning what gives meaning and purpose and hope to their personal life and vocational practice. Formation is an inherent part of Judeo-Christian tradition, an activity of God, what God does to mould and shape God's people in order to enable them to share love and justice in the world.

> I the Lord called you with righteous purpose
> And have taken you by the hand;
> I have formed you, and destined you to be a light for peoples,
> A lamp for nations.
> (Isaiah 42:6)

God has given his people gifts and abilities and a vocational role to perform. Within the Judeo-Christian tradition, using such gifts and discerning the appropriate role which God intends for a person will enable the possibility of a meaningful working life. However, as already described, the underlying motivation for an increasing number of chaplains is more broadly spiritual than theological. Whatever a fledgling chaplain's beliefs, values and worldview, part of the process of formation is facilitating the exploration of what informs their vocational desire. This is not just to help enable them to test whether they can thrive in a chaplaincy role (Heitink 1993). Formation is also about helping practitioners identify what envisions and enlivens their practice; connecting them with their passion or 'great gladness' (Buechner, as cited by Muse 2007, p.187). Identifying what shapes and informs a person's vocation near the beginning of their career gives them a benchmark to revisit during ongoing reflective practice and supervision in years to come.

One way to facilitate such reflection is to ask chaplains in training to outline their vocational canon – the stories, myths, poems, lyrics, music and art which the practitioner considers sacred and which inform their vision of chaplaincy and spiritual care. This may include, but is not limited to, religious texts, and may be written, oral or living (the example or modelling of a significant other) stories or otherwise. More than that, such a sacred canon helps shape a person's understanding of self as a chaplain that evolves in the correlation between a practitioner's vocational canon and ongoing reflection on practice. This enables a student chaplain to both deepen their self-knowledge as a person and as self in the role of specialist spiritual care practitioner in an ongoing way. Reflection on practice stimulated by exposure to the vast array of their unique responses to the worst and best of human experiences and the dynamics of complex human interaction may shed new light on, or challenge, the relevance of familiar texts. So, too, may reflection on the impact of working within different contexts and the structures and systems of healthcare organizations. Reflection on an article describing a piece of relevant research or the experience of involvement in audit or research may also provide an experiential focus for such theological or spiritual reflection prior to seeking to translate the research or audit into practice. Aspects of a practitioner's sacred canon may be affirmed as important, reinterpreted or discarded for alternative, more relevant narratives which may be discovered during group reflective practice or individual supervision through exposure to other texts from a variety of sources. In turn, such spiritual – or for many theological – reflection potentially may enliven or change future practice.

An important aspect in the spiritual formation of fledgling chaplains is encouraging and supporting them in their own spiritual practices (see 'Moral aspect' below) – activities which offer meaning, purpose, hope and the possibility of transcendence in their lives as persons. This includes, but is more than, prayer and worship, or contemplation and meditation (Bachelard 2015) or mindfulness. It also means making time and having energy for fostering relationships in which practitioners receive as well as give love, for playing and for the enjoyment of nature. If chaplains are to empower others to (re)discover or (re)connect with the assets in their lives – within, between, around and beyond them – which foster spiritual wellbeing, then they need to be able to do the same for themselves over the long haul.

Psychological aspect

Here I highlight three significant dimensions of a carer's psychological makeup for spiritual care practice:

1. The danger of codependency. Professionalization in chaplaincy, as well as in other caring professions, may lead to the cared-for person becoming dependent. As Heitink (1993, p.318) puts it: 'Assistance creates need and makes people dependent.' In principle, chaplains seek to enable a person's autonomy and self-management, not to direct or create dependence; however, caring professions, such as chaplaincy, attract 'self-sacrificing, generous, other-directed and idealistic people' (Au and Cannon 1995, p.46) who often carry significant wounds from their childhood (Muse 2000). Such altruistic qualities may be positive in appropriate measure, but codependency develops when practitioners have a need to compulsively care, driven by a desire to find worth, value and affirmation in caring. Such behaviour has its origins in conditions of worth experienced as a child – not being loved for simply being a unique person and finding affirmation only received in response to doing or achieving. Codependency potentially leads to practitioner exhaustion, burn out, disillusionment and depression in the long term. This links closely with the second point.

2. Our past informs our present. In particular, our early upbringing and the relationships we had with authority figures in our childhood can impact on the way we relate within relationships in the present. It is important that we be aware that we can act out those relationships in the present when we bump into behaviours or characteristics in others that may subconsciously reconnect us with those figures from the past and their attitudes and actions towards us. The formational process with relevant supervision may afford the opportunity for practitioners to become more self-aware about interpersonal childhood dynamics

and to develop new patterns of relating, replacing old, repeated, unhealthy ones (Livingstone *et al.* 2009).

3. That which any of us, due to societal and familial conditioning, considers socially unacceptable and is suppressed within our subconscious may leak out, despite our best conscious efforts, and find expression, or projection, in our interactions with others and systems and structures. We may learn at an early age that expressing certain feelings, such as anger, sadness or frustration, is not socially appropriate; similarly, expressing or exploring our sexual desires, ambition or creativity. Hence, for example, 'We stigmatise others in order to distance ourselves from that which we most fear in ourselves' (Hickox 2015, p.26). There can be a fear that in making such aspects of our 'shadow' conscious we will act them out; however, going contrary to this consciousness gives us choice and the opportunity to decide, according to our character and sense of responsibility, whether to act or not (Au and Cannon 1995). Well-supervised regular reflection on practice affords opportunity for such consciousness raising to occur.

Moral aspect

Finally, the significance of the development of a trainee chaplain's character or values base as part of formation is considered now. This includes the self-understanding of the role of their sense of responsibility on their way of being, relating and choosing in practice (i.e. on the development of practical wisdom). Becoming professional or part of a certain profession is often equated with a list of dos and don'ts – indoctrination or enculturation into a certain way of behaving or often a way of *not* behaving or else risking expulsion (Carlin *et al.* 2012). However, I want to suggest, like William Willimon (2000), in terms of making choices within the complexity of spiritual care practice, that what goes on in terms of formation of character is more important than being guided by rules and procedures. According to Wells and Quash (2010, p.196), 'Character is formed by the regular and disciplined performances of practices that after long exercise emerge as *habits*.' Such habits in the development of a fledgling's chaplain's character critically include regular and intentional reflection on practice, being committed to learning in community as part of formation and ongoing (re)formation as a chaplain. Hence, for example, involvement in making explicit expectations and assumptions about individual and group behaviour and (re)clarifying group ground rules and values within a community of learning are important if, in such an environment, character is to be (re)formed.

Colleen Griffith (2014, p.59), reflecting on Pierre Bourdieu's understanding of *habitus*, considers his interpretation of the concept to be 'referent for acquired ways of thinking and acting that individuals and groups develop in response to absorbed conditions of social structures'. She goes on to quote fellow practical theologian Elaine Graham (2002, pp.102–103), who further expands on *habitus* functioning as 'the residuum of past actions, a deposit of past knowledge and practice, but which is always available as the raw material for creative agency, or "regulated improvisation"'.

Such innovative practice is informed and honed by the learned habit of reflection on past practice which has helped build up, over time, a foundational repository of knowledge, insights and comparisons from past experience. Such a 'storehouse' (Cahalan 2016, p.276) becomes closely intertwined with a practitioner's personhood and can be drawn on as she begins to learn to be a spiritual-change agent acting with *phronesis*. Dunne (2011, p.19) puts it this way: 'the springs of [such] judgement are deeply recessed in one's mind, character and being, and therefore are expressive of the kind of person – as well as, or rather, in and through, the kind of practitioner – that one has become.'

Over time chaplains 'develop good judgements as they learn the practice' (Tilley 2014, p.97). Tilley (2014) and Newitt (2016) also suggest that we learn how to make good judgements from exemplary practitioners (such as John Ames). Thus, a supervisor who models choices taken in the moment of facilitation which, for example, empower individual and group learning may influence the promotion of chaplaincy character development.

Much has been written about the importance of engaging regularly in spiritual practices for the moral, as well as spiritual, formation of Christians. For example, Wells and Quash (2010, p.197) write of the 'significance of worship in honing the habits and moral imagination of Christians'. Cahalan (2016) describes that a rediscovery of the prayer life of the desert fathers, with an emphasis on praying with the scriptures, promotes a way of knowing wisdom and making choices that is not purely rational. Different approaches to contemplation and meditation from other belief systems and traditions also may enable chaplains to orientate their lives and professional practice towards making wise decisions based, for example, on compassion and love.

Conclusion: promoting consistent formation for chaplaincy

A lack of consistency in the formational content within educational programmes preparing participants for entry into the chaplaincy profession in the UK means fledgling chaplains complete curricula which promote or value personal formation to varying degrees. Such piecemeal formational opportunities leave some chaplains ill equipped and vulnerable in dealing with the complexity of human relationships and rapidly changing, cost-driven twenty-first century healthcare. In a Scottish context, Paterson (2014, p.171) observes that during the process of supervision some chaplains lack the 'inner spiritual or psychological resilience' to receive feedback and not to perceive it as criticism or feel responsible for the impact a piece of practice they have shared has had on others. Lack of personal confidence impacts on the individual and corporate professional identity of chaplains. This, in part, may have contributed historically to chaplains' reticence to promote their services, fully integrate into multidisciplinary teams and strategically engage with healthcare managers and leaders (see Chapter 22 for further discussion). Burnard (2002), writing for nurses and healthcare professionals in general, states that as we become more self-aware, we can start to act more purposively with intent rather than be passive recipients of others' actions and decisions.

There is urgent need throughout the UK to develop a standardized, specialized formational education programme which focuses on psychospiritual and character development as a minimum requirement for aspiring chaplains. This need not be CPE (see Chapter 8 for the influence of CPE on two English centres), but it requires similar rigour and consistency of formational content and form. Its theoretical underpinning must be spirituality, psychology, ethics, educational theory and group dynamics. Considerable practice-based learning with trained supervisors in communities of learning and shadowing of experienced mentors (Newitt 2016) which foster personal and professional identity, self-esteem and confidence are a necessity. Cultivating new chaplains who are self-aware and comfortable and confident in their own skins will enhance their ability to creatively collaborate as well as intentionally evidence and present their worth, adapt innovatively to working in different contexts and enact new models of chaplaincy.

References

Au, W. and Cannon, N. (1995) *Urgings of the Heart: A Spirituality of Integration*. New York, NY: Paulist Press.

Bachelard, S. (2015) 'The transforming ground of our being: a personal reflection.' *Health and Social Care Chaplaincy 3*, 2, 129–141.

Burnard, P. (2002) *Learning Human Skills: An Experiential and Reflective Guide for Nurses and Health Care Professionals*. Oxford: Butterworth-Heinemann.

Cahalan, K. (2016) 'Spiritual Practices and the Search for a Wisdom Epistemology.' In D. Bass, K. Cahalan, B. Miller-McLemore, J. Nieman and C. Scharen (eds) *Christian Practical Wisdom: What It Is. Why It Matters*. Grand Rapids, MI: Eerdmans Publishing.

Carlin, N., Cole, T. and Strobel, H. (2012) 'Guidance from the Humanities for Professional Formation.' In M. Cobb, C. Puchalski and B. Rumbold (eds) *Oxford Textbook of Spirituality in Healthcare*. Oxford: Oxford University Press.

Dunne, J. (2011) 'Professional Wisdom in Practice.' In L. Bondi, D. Carr, C. Clark and C. Clegg (eds) *Towards Professional Wisdom*. Farnham: Ashgate.

Flanagan, R. (2015) *The Narrow Road to the Deep North*. London: Vintage.

Gerkin, C. (1997) *An Introduction to Pastoral Care*. Nashville, TN: Abingdon Press.

Gilbert, P. and Fulford, K.W.M. (2010) 'Bringing the spirit and values back into public services.' *The International Journal of Leadership in Public Services 6*, 2, 6–19.

Graham, E. (2002) *Transforming Practice: Practical Theology in an Age of Uncertainty*. Eugene, OR: Wipf and Stock.

Griffith, C. (2014) 'Practice as Embodied Knowing: Epistemological and Theological Considerations.' In C. Wolfteich (ed.) *Invitation to Practical Theology: Catholic Voices and Visions*. New York, NY: Paulist Press.

Hauerwas, S. and Wells, S. (2004) 'The Gift of the Church and the Gifts God Gives it.' In S. Hauerwas and S. Wells (eds) *The Blackwell Companion to Christian Ethics*. Oxford: Blackwell Publishing.

Heitink, G. (1993) *Practical Theology: History, Theory, Action Domains*. Grand Rapids, MI: Eerdmans Publishing.

Hickox, A. (2015) 'Charles Kennedy's battle with the bottle.' *The Guardian*, 8 June 2015, p.26.

Jones, G. and Pendleton Jones, S. (2008) 'Leadership, Pastoral Identity, and Friendship: Navigating the Transition from Seminary to the Parish.' In A. Cole (ed.) *From Midterms to Ministry: Practical Theologians on Pastoral Beginnings*. Grand Rapids, MI: Eerdmans.

Kelcourse, F. (2010) 'Intersubjective and Theological Contexts of Pastoral Counselling Supervision.' In W. DeLong (ed.) *Courageous Conversations: The Teaching and Learning of Pastoral Supervision*. Lanham, MD: University Press of America.

Kelly, E. (2012) *Personhood and Presence: Self as a Resource for Spiritual and Pastoral Care*. London: T. & T. Clark International.

Laskas, J.M. (2018) 'Dear Obama.' *The Guardian Review*, 18 August 2018, pp.6–11.

Livingstone, B., Mills Myers, K., Jordan, M., Scott Jelinek, B. and Plumley, A. (2009) 'Pastoral formational process for seminarians: a new model for developing psychologically healthy pastors.' *Journal of Pastoral Care and Counseling 63*, 3–4, 1–7.

Muse, S. (2000) 'Keeping the wellsprings of ministry clear.' *Journal of Pastoral Care 54*, 3, 253–262.

Muse, S. (2007) 'Clergy in crisis: when human power isn't enough.' *The Journal of Pastoral Care and Counseling 61*, 3, 183–195.

Newitt, M. (2016) 'Healthcare chaplains among the virtues.' *Practical Theology 9*, 1, 16–28.

Nolan S. (2013) 'Re-evaluating chaplaincy: to be or not…' *Health and Social Care Chaplaincy 1*, 1, 49–60.

Paterson, M. (2013) 'Mirror, mirror on the wall: from reflective practice to transformative practice.' *Health and Social Care Chaplaincy 1*, 1, 67–74.

Paterson, M. (2014) 'Healthcare Chaplaincy: From Clinical Supervision to Transformative Storytelling within the NHS.' In M. Paterson and J. Rose (eds) *Enriching Ministry: Pastoral Supervision in Practice*. London: SCM Press.

Paterson, M. and Clegg, C. (2013) *Education, Training and Formation for Healthcare Chaplains: Report of an NHS Review*. Edinburgh: NHS Education for Scotland.

Pembroke, N. (2007) *Moving Toward Spiritual Maturity: Psychological, Contemplative and Moral Challenges for Christian Living*. New York, NY: Haworth Pastoral Press.

Pembroke, N., Coyle, S., Gear, J., Gubi, P. *et al.* (2018) 'Toward a structured, tri-domain model of companioning in Christian formation by pastoral agents in a congregational setting: a preliminary report on an initial research project.' *Journal of Pastoral Care and Counseling* 72, 2, 104–115.

Robinson, M. (2014) *Lila*. London: Virago Press.

Swift, C. (2015) 'Healthcare Chaplaincy.' In C. Swift, M. Cobb and A. Todd (eds) *A Handbook of Chaplaincy Studies*. Farnham: Ashgate.

Tilley, T. (2014) 'Practicing the Faith: Tradition in Practical Theology.' In C. Wolfteich (ed.) *Invitation to Practical Theology: Catholic Voices and Visions*. New York, NY: Paulist Press.

UK Board of Healthcare Chaplains (2009) *Spiritual and Religious Care Capabilities and Competences for Healthcare Chaplains*. Cambridge: UK Board of Healthcare Chaplains. Accessed on 19/09/2018 at www.ukbhc.org.uk/chaplains/compentencies.

UK Board of Healthcare Chaplaincy (2015) *Spiritual and Religious Care Capabilities and Competences for Healthcare Chaplains Bands 5, 6, 7 and 8*. Cambridge: UK Board of Healthcare Chaplaincy. Accessed on 06/04/2017 at www.ukbhc.org.uk/sites/default/files/ukbhc_spiritual_and_religious_capabilities_and_competences_bands_5_-_8_2015.pdf.

UK Board of Healthcare Chaplaincy (2017) *Spiritual and Religious Care Capabilities and Competences for Healthcare Chaplains Bands 5, 6, 7 and 8*. Cambridge: UK Board of Healthcare Chaplaincy. Accessed on 10/09/2018 at www.ukbhc.org.uk/sites/default/files/ukbhc_spiritual_and_religious_capabilities_and_competences_bands_5_-_8_2017.pdf.

Waid, H. (2015) 'Professional identity (trans) formation in medical education: Reflection, relationship, resilience.' *Academic Medicine 90*, 6, 701–706.

Wells, S. and Quash, B. (2010) *Introducing Christian Ethics*. Chichester: Wiley-Blackwell.

Willimon, W. (2000) *Calling and Character: Virtues of the Ordained Life*. Nashville, TN: Abingdon Press.

Zollfrank, A. and Garlid, C. (2012) 'Curriculum Development. Part II: Clinical Pastoral Education.' In M. Cobb, C. Puchalski and B. Rumbold (eds) *Oxford Textbook of Spirituality in Healthcare*. Oxford: Oxford University Press.

Chapter 21

Educating and Equipping Chaplains to Practise in New Paradigms

David W Fleenor and Ewan Kelly

Introduction

We have begun to consider the significance of formation in chaplaincy education and in promoting good practice through the intentional use of self. This chapter seeks to build on this foundation. We shall now further explore how chaplains may be best cultivated to equip them to work with practical wisdom and as competent agents of change to foster individual and corporate spiritual wellbeing within shifting paradigms of health and care planning and delivery. Others have previously expressed the need for transformation of chaplaincy education and training in relation to changing contexts in healthcare, particularly with reference to clinical pastoral education (CPE) in the US (e.g. Massey 2014; Tartaglia 2015).

(The paradigm shifts we have identified are given in Table I.1 of this book's Introduction.)

Another paradigm shift currently gathering momentum within the global chaplaincy community is a movement away from a strongly Rogerian psychotherapeutic approach to an evidence-based, outcomes-focused approach. Such an advance is part of the overall professionalization of chaplaincy and the need to promote best practice, which enhances quality of life in a person-centred manner.

Within such a context this chapter asks: What kinds of education and training are required to optimally prepare chaplains to operate as spiritual agents of transformation in times of rapid transition and complexity? What kind of educational models effectively equip chaplains to work as agile spiritual drivers or enablers at *micro* (with individuals), *meso* (with teams, departments and local communities/institutions in particular localities or areas) and *meta* (across organizations, systems, countries and internationally) levels within healthcare systems and communities, in collaboration with other health and care disciplines and agencies, including faith communities, to promote spiritual wellbeing?

Several educational models for chaplains exist across the globe. Each model has strengths, but none in their current iterations are optimal for the challenges faced by twenty-first century chaplains. The answers to the questions posed here may be found by the synthesis of the strengths of two prevalent educational approaches within chaplaincy: the consistency and rigour of the process model found in the US; and the competencies-based model in the UK. Drawing upon the assets of each model may quite possibly help in cultivating chaplains fit for purpose to meet the demands of providing entrepreneurial spiritual care in ever-changing global healthcare systems. Herein we outline emerging indicative aspects of chaplaincy education required for entry into the profession and then describe similar aspects for ongoing personal and professional transformational learning.

An assets-based approach to writing collaboratively

In line with the temper of this book, we sought to write this chapter collaboratively, intentionally utilizing our assets as a starting place to inform not just its content, but also the way it was co-constructed. Our collaboration emerged out of a developing relationship of trust and mutual respect through initial meetings at conferences. Over several meals we discussed the similarities and differences, as we saw them, in professional chaplaincy in the UK and the US. These conversations excited us. We decided we would begin video-conferencing with one another to outline the chapter. A series of recorded reflective and exploratory conversations ensued, enabling not only a deepening understanding of each other's cultural contexts and approaches to chaplaincy education and training in those contexts, but also transformational learning. What emerged was a modelling of the pedagogical method we sought to articulate – risking taking a creative and collaborative approach to writing that opened new horizons and possibilities for us and changed our writing practice.

David's assets

I am David Fleenor, a 43-year-old American, who began his spiritual journey in the Southern Baptist Church as a teenager. That is where I first encountered God and experienced a sense of calling to the ministry. My theological questions and a search for a more intense encounter with the Holy Spirit, however, led me to Pentecostal Christianity. I was educated at both a Pentecostal college and a Pentecostal seminary before leaving that tradition to become an Episcopalian. The inflexion point for my decision to leave Pentecostalism occurred during my first unit of CPE in my middle year of my Master of Divinity degree programme at the Pentecostal Theological Seminary. The curriculum required that I take a unit of CPE, so I dutifully applied and was accepted into the nearest programme.

CPE was my first experience of serving and learning in an ecumenical and multifaith environment. In terms of learning, I found myself surrounded by peers and supervisors from various Christian traditions who held views and pastoral approaches that differed from mine, which was often disorienting. For example, one of my Christian peers did not believe in the divinity of Christ. That had always been a fundamental belief of mine and I couldn't understand how one could identify as a Christian, particularly a Christian minister, without maintaining such a belief. This disoriented me and caused me to deeply reflect on my own faith and what it meant to be a Christian minister. My supervisors and peers guided me through those much-needed periods of disorientation, which led to fruitful, albeit painful, periods of reorientation. It was through that process – of orientation, disorientation and reorientation – that a significant shift in my identity took place. I began to realize two important things: I was no longer Pentecostal; and I wanted to be a hospital chaplain rather than a minister in a congregation.

CPE led to a significant transformation in the way I viewed the world, which changed how I thought, related and understood myself. Later, I went on to become an Episcopal priest, a board-certified chaplain and a certified clinical pastoral supervisor. I am now the director of education at the Center for Spirituality and Health and the Icahn School of Medicine at Mount Sinai in New York City, where I teach medical students generalist spiritual care and chaplaincy students specialist spiritual care.

My experience of CPE, and the transformation I personally experienced as a result of it, is one of the assets I bring to this work. I know firsthand how formative and transformative CPE can be. I am also aware of how it can go awry. CPE's strength is its weakness: CPE honours the messy processes inherent in the formation, development and transformation of spiritual caregivers. The CPE supervisor's ability to live, move and have her being in those subjective and untidy processes helps to give birth to new self-understanding, to facilitate the maturational processes of both human and professional development. The weakness is that CPE may not always teach the knowledge and skills necessary to become a competent healthcare chaplain. I believe CPE needs to retain the subjective process-oriented elements that promote self-awareness and incorporate a competency-based approach that helps to ensure that chaplains have mastery of a common knowledge base and skill set.

Ewan's assets

I am Ewan Kelly, a 53-year-old Scot who started vocational life as a junior doctor. It was not until beginning work as a chaplain several years later in an acute hospital, with the support of pastoral supervision, that I began to realize I needed to *unlearn* much to work in such a role. I had not appreciated as a medical student, in the 1980s, the extent to which I had been enculturated into a role, and healthcare system, which was so task orientated. The focus was on curing or fixing (accentuating my personal human need to do so!) – often doing *to* rather than doing *with* patients (not people) – the medical curriculum I was educated in being competency based. Such an education helped me as a fledgling chaplain to feel comfortable inhabiting an acute hospital system. It gave me insight into its culture, priorities and concerns in relation to procedures and processes with an emphasis on safety, measured replication of tasks and effectiveness. However, such a competency-focused education did not prepare me for being with others and myself as a chaplain. Even after undertaking formation as a Church of Scotland minister in training with practice-based learning experiences and reflective practice opportunities, as well as choosing a pastorally orientated path through my theological education, I still felt unskilled and helpless in the face of others' suffering as I transitioned from doctor to chaplain. My formation as a chaplain was of the pick-and-mix variety. With guidance I intentionally sought pastoral supervision, spiritual direction and therapy, not just to seek to deliver good practice but to help me grow and keep well. This experience informed my determination whilst in a leadership role within Scottish chaplaincy to seek to promote the normalization of ongoing formational and transformational learning to complement previous work colleagues had done to develop competencies and capabilities to inform chaplaincy practice and education (NHS Education for Scotland 2008).

Through our conversations together, we each recognized the strengths of the type of chaplaincy education broadly provided in our countries but simultaneously struggled with the ways in which both are incomplete and fail to prepare chaplains for the realities faced. By beginning to understand how chaplaincy education worked in the other's context, we came to see that the other had what the other was lacking. In the US, CPE is the predominant form of chaplaincy education. It is rooted in a process model of education that dates to the early twentieth century. In the UK, specialist chaplaincy education is relatively new and has become increasingly competency based. The strength of the process-based model in the US is that it very successfully forms and shapes chaplains to practise in self-reflexive ways, but it lacks a standard body of knowledge and clear sets of skills to master. The strength of the competency-based model in the UK is that the knowledge and skills are clear and targeted, but nationally there is a lack of consistency in the depth and approach to the formation of the person as practitioner (as outlined in Chapter 20). What is needed is an educational programme that brings together the strengths of both approaches and makes up for the other's weaknesses.

Two models of chaplaincy education

To better understand what a synthesized educational model for those seeking to become chaplains could look like, it is important to describe the individual models first. This section will describe the process model of chaplaincy education in the US and the competency-based model employed in the UK, as well as their strengths and weaknesses.

The process model of education in the US

In the US, chaplains are trained primarily through CPE, a process model of education that focuses heavily on the development of self-awareness and the integration of one's own human story with one's professional practice. The founders of CPE, in the early twentieth century, believed that theological students had enough conceptual knowledge, maybe even too much of it. They sought to reform theological education by putting students in contact with suffering people to promote the integration of conceptual knowledge into the practice of their ministries. To do so, CPE 'stressed emotional and personal authenticity in a pastoral role' (King 2007, pp.149–150).

As King (2007) points out, different leaders emerged within the developing CPE movement who emphasized different learning foci. One group (Boisen, Keller and Hiltner) emphasized knowledge acquisition and another (Cabot, Dicks and Guiles) stressed skill building. Others (e.g. Johnson) centred on dynamic interpersonalism, that is, the formation and transformation of the practitioner's personality. Frederick Kuether (1958) summed up the history (until then) of CPE in terms of its focus of enabling chaplains to:

1. do appropriate things to be of help (1920s)

2. know appropriate things to be of help (1930s)

3. say appropriate things to be of help (1940s)

4. be appropriately to be of help (1950s) (King 2007, p.23).

It is this final question with its focus on what the practitioner must *be* that has remained the central focus of CPE. King (2007, p.48) writes: 'The interpersonalist theme has endured and developed through time, continuing through the present as a dominant focus of clinical pastoral education. This focus is a profound strength, but also a weakness of CPE.'

It is a strength because students often complete CPE with profound abilities to understand how their personal histories affect their ministry practice, how their embedded theologies may not match up with their deliberative ones and how others – peers, educators and patients – see and experience them in relationship. This is, of course, not an exhaustive list of outcomes but very common ones. All of this makes for highly self-reflexive practitioners capable of empathy, connection and ethical practice. The intense focus on the development of the personhood of the practitioner is what enables chaplains to be drivers of change because of their ability to reflect *on* practice (reflection) as well as to reflect *in* practice (reflexivity). This enables their potential to be nimble and agile persons and professionals. Most chaplains demonstrate this daily at micro- and meso-levels as they provide spiritual support to patients, families and staff in health and care systems.

CPE runs the risk, however, of devolving into navel gazing which seeks to facilitate the healing of the practitioner more than the healing of others. In fact, for decades clinical pastoral educators have debated whether CPE is therapy or education. This is understandable given that many, if not most, clinical pastoral educators draw upon psychotherapeutic theories (for example, those of Irvin Yalom and Donald Winnicott) to inform their educational practices. Most of them have concluded that, as the name would indicate, CPE is education, not therapy, but the line is often blurred. This is the primary liability of the process model of CPE. It is an educational model that can focus too much on the personhood of the practitioner who inhabits the professional role. The flaw of this approach is that students may end CPE unable to understand or explain how they will provide competent spiritual care. This decreases their self-confidence and limits their abilities to advocate for themselves within the healthcare context. This stems from the absence of a formally agreed upon standardized body of knowledge that chaplains need to master, and a lack of clarity as to what chaplains need to do to perform their role consistently, safely and competently (Wintz and Hughes 2018). These two deficiencies are precisely what the competency-based model of the UK addresses.

The UK competency-based model of chaplaincy education

Competency-based healthcare training was influenced by its evolution within technological and vocational training in the industrialized world, which sought to make national workforces more productive and efficient. In order to construct competencies for a role, each task is systematically broken down into its constituent parts. Competencies focus on what the person needs to be able to do, as well as what they must know and understand to perform tasks effectively (Skills for Health 2017). When tasks are performed according to the competencies developed, measurable outcomes for each one can be identified. Competency frameworks lay out such information and inform the training for the set of tasks carried out in a certain role. According to Kelly (2012), this enables educators and trainers to:

- construct curricula that are grounded in students and practitioners' real needs

- create clear learning aims and outcomes for courses delivered

- assess what they deliver in terms of relevance to, and impact on, practice.

Competency-based training and practice has enabled healthcare providers to evidence quality assurance and clinical governance as service users', organizations' and governments' demands for safe, competent and accountable care has increased.

Competencies for chaplains began to be developed in the UK early in the twenty-first century (Gordon and Mitchell 2004; NHS Education for Scotland 2008). These competencies were driven by the perceived need for increased professionalism and the integration of chaplaincy into healthcare. Since 2009, with the publication of the UK Board of Healthcare Chaplains' (UKBHC) *Spiritual and Religious Care Capabilities and Competences for Healthcare Chaplains* (revised in 2015 and 2017) (UKBHC 2009, 2015, 2017), specialist training for UK chaplains has become increasingly competency based (see also Chapter 8).

Such specificity and focus in articulating the different activities chaplains perform, and in the education and training required to enable them to do so, not only equips chaplains for the job they are employed to do but also fosters confidence in their ability to do so competently. The development of competency frameworks has helped clarify thinking and communication about a chaplain's role. In addition, competencies have not only enabled a standardization of the tasks performed by chaplains operating at different grades but also a common agreement of the outcomes required to demonstrate proficiency in the performance of each task (UKBHC 2017).

More recently, chaplaincy professional associations and bodies globally have published similar chaplaincy competencies: in Australia, a competency-based framework (Spiritual Health Victoria 2016); and in North America, a scope of practice (HealthCare Chaplaincy Network 2016) and common qualifications and competencies (Board of Chaplaincy Certification 2016–2017) with a view to promoting professional practice. Such competency documents globally are significant steps in the right direction, but they remain incomplete as a basis for chaplaincy training and education.

Their primary weakness in informing professional practice or educational programmes is that they take no account of the person who inhabits the professional role. Competencies do not take into consideration how aware a practitioner may be of the extent to which their particular human story influences their practice. There remains a need to ensure the integration of a practitioner's personal history, beliefs and values as a fundamental aspect of their education and practice-based training (HealthCare Chaplaincy Network 2016).

Second, the competency frameworks currently available are written to equip chaplains to work in paradigms that primarily focus on spiritual 'disease', not promoting wellbeing, in institutional contexts. They reinforce a deficits-focused system, which promotes dependency on professionals.

In order to respect and give credence to the complexity of spiritual care practice, groups of competencies have been placed within capability domains (NES 2008) and latterly within groups of capabilities (UKBHC 2015, 2017) to create capability and competency frameworks. Capabilities 'describe the extent to which an individual can apply, adapt and synthesise new knowledge from experience and continue to improve his or her performance' (UKBHC 2017, p.2). They also describe the attitudes and behaviours expected of practitioners as they advance through levels or grades within a profession (Spiritual Health Victoria 2016, p.38). According to the UKBHC (p.2), capability and competency frameworks focus on:

- realizing people's full potential
- developing the ability to adapt and apply knowledge and skills
- learning from experience
- envisaging the future and making it happen.

Such aspirations are at the heart of any continuing professional development programme enabling lifelong learning and are significant in the growth of future chaplains as well as those already practising at whatever grade.

Synthesis of the two models

For chaplains to be able to maximize their input within ever-changing twenty-first century health and care systems, an approach to educating chaplains is needed that brings forward critical elements of the competency-based approach used in the UK and the process model of CPE used in the US.

To help conceptualize the elements that need to be synthesized, let us first define the broad learning domains of chaplaincy education. They may be summed up as learning to know, to do and to be. The strengths of the UK's approach are in *knowing* and *doing*, whereas the strength of the US's approach is in *being*. *Knowing* is the domain concerned with acquiring new knowledge with the purpose of promoting individual and communal spiritual wellbeing. *Doing* is the domain focused on the acquisition of skills and the practice of spiritual care. The *being* domain focuses on the development of the personhood of the practitioner.

Knowing and doing

It is beyond the scope of this chapter to list the current knowledge and skills described in any chaplaincy competency framework. (See Chapter 8 for a broad outline of those in the UKBHC's 2017 framework.) Instead, we want indicatively to outline new knowledge and skills required to equip chaplains entering the profession to work as spiritual enablers or leaders of transformation within emerging new paradigms in healthcare. We also want to emphasize some key knowing and doing which have recently begun to emerge as important within chaplaincy education and training to support key tasks which chaplains are increasingly required to perform (mirroring developments in the education and training of other healthcare professionals).

Significantly, we want to highlight the following *knowledge* required:

- Strategic literacy – an understanding of significant national and organizational healthcare policies and strategic thinking (see also Chapter 22). This will, for example, aid chaplains to understand where spiritual care promotes or may help enable delivery of key healthcare objectives and to support the development of chaplaincy strategy to do so. In addition, such learning will provide a foundation for further training for those chaplains taking up strategic posts. Introducing strategic issues at an early stage in chaplaincy professional development is important for succession planning and career progression. In addition, such literacy will also help chaplains contribute to the necessary planning and development of spiritual care services which bridge acute, palliative and community settings.

- Transformational leadership theory – enabling any chaplain to take on the task of leadership (see Chapter 22) and facilitate change in a variety of contexts.

- Research literacy – increasingly recognized as a key component of chaplaincy education, particularly promoted globally by the innovative and collaborative work of Transforming Chaplaincy (2019) (see also Chapter 12).

- Educating and resourcing others – chaplains, as part of maximizing their impact within a healthcare system, are prioritizing enabling other health and care professionals to deliver sensitive spiritual and cultural care, as part of their role. Thus, equipping aspiring chaplains with some basic educational theory, including understanding learning styles, has become highly relevant.

It is noteworthy that in medicine (Moberly 2016) as within chaplaincy, leadership and research are being proposed to play some part in every practitioner's career to enhance care.

To enable fledgling chaplains to be fit for purpose to work in a variety of contexts, some new and emerging *skills* are required, such as the following:

- Contextual analysis – equipping chaplains to interpret, and orientate themselves within, the communities and organizations they are inhabiting as a key step in prioritizing and informing the model(s) or aspects of chaplaincy they wish to embody and enact in a particular context.

- Asset mapping (see Chapter 18) – intentionally identifying (by, not limited to but importantly including, building networks of relationships) the strengths in a community or organization which help to promote spiritual wellbeing.

- Stakeholder mapping – intentional discovery and mapping out of who the key individuals and groups (from the powerful to the disempowered) are, within an organization or community, with whom to engage and build relationships in order to enable the co-production of spiritual wellbeing.

- (Personalized) outcomes planning (see Joint Improvement Team 2012 for an example of one approach) – promoting co-production (see Chapter 19) by aiding chaplains to work with individuals, families and communities to name and work towards the outcomes they desire which enhance their spiritual wellbeing. Here the story of

Jesus and blind Bartimaeus sets a healthy precedent: Jesus, before he acts to help blind Bartimaeus, gives him the opportunity to name the particular outcome he desires (Mark 10:46–52).

- Leadership – translating transformative leadership theory into practice by, for example, leading a small supervised project seeking to effect change within a team or group.

- Research – translating research literacy into practice by undertaking a small supervised piece of audit or research; building on Tartaglia's (2015) proposal that trainee chaplains need to move towards participation in research; and in addition, being supported to disseminate the findings through oral presentations and publishing (such training may be best undertaken once in a chaplaincy post for those interested in research, but there may well be motivated students for whom this may be a transformative option).

Being

Using the clinical method of learning, often informed by Mezirow's transformational learning theory (Mezirow 1997), CPE focuses on the development of the person of the practitioner. Within CPE this occurs in a peer group supervised by a certified clinical pastoral educator who teaches chaplaincy students a reflective process aimed at facilitating their personal and professional development. This reflective process includes activities that help students to:

- excavate their autobiographies by exploring the positive and negative effects their families of origin, cultural and social environments and significant and influential relationships have on them

- identify and reflect on their embedded and deliberative theologies and worldview

- receive and give feedback about the relational dynamics they exhibit and observe as a peer group

- identify and reflect on their personal and professional strengths and weaknesses (Association for Clinical Pastoral Education 2016).

Chaplaincy is an improvisational art. It is through the *being* domain of chaplaincy education that chaplains learn to show up in any situation, meet any patient and, in that moment, assess and address their spiritual distress (i.e. such formational and transformational learning promotes the growth of practical wisdom). There is no script for this kind of work. It requires that the practitioner be ready to read and respond to the situation in the moment.

For the fostering of practical wisdom to be maximized within this synthesized model, the exploration of the moral development of a student (i.e. their character) as an inherent part of promoting reflexivity in decision-making would need to be a core explicit aspect of the *being* domain.

To equip fledgling chaplains to work in a variety of contexts, practice-based learning placements must be undertaken in a variety of outpatient and community contexts as well as in acute and palliative settings, including with voluntary organizations and faith communities promoting health and wellbeing.

Furthermore, to help enhance interdisciplinary collaboration and break down the silo mentality that exists in healthcare, some appropriate knowledge and skills-based learning may be taught in an interdisciplinary and inter-agency manner (Scottish Government 2011). In addition, promoting practical wisdom can be enjoyed similarly as appropriate, for example the Values Based Reflective Practice model utilized with inter-professional groups in Scotland (see Chapter 15).

Transformational learning: chaplains as drivers of change

The aim of specialist chaplaincy education in the early stages of a practitioner's vocational journey, prior to and as they enter the profession, is not to cultivate individuated chaplains; rather, its purpose is to encourage and equip fledgling chaplains to engage meaningfully in a lifelong personal and professional journey of self-discovery, (re)formation and learning which nurtures and ignites (Kline 2009) transformation. As C.S. Lewis (cited by Strang 2017, p.132) states: 'Nothing yet is in its true form.'

Such a foundational education aims, as Mary Oliver (2007) alludes to in her poem 'Messenger', to promote an attitude of openness and receptivity to cultivating astonishment along the way – reflecting on, and enjoying in the moment, opportunities for illumination and enlivening. This is not just about offering students or trainees tools and resources to support such things but also about infusing a habit and commitment to ongoing reflection on practice and vocational motivation as well as personal spiritual practices, as described in Chapter 20.

Transformational education seeks to support chaplains working at different levels of healthcare activity to thrive in their work rather than merely survive. It is to empower chaplains to take responsibility for their own learning rather than to act as apprentices relying on a supervisor to direct it. Transformational learning seeks to enable them to draw sustenance from their own spiritual wisdom by offering spaces to (re)connect with (and reinterpret) the fire in their belly (Michael Paterson, oral presentation as part of *Diploma on Pastoral Supervision and Reflective Practice*, 2017) – their vocational canon (see Chapter 20). It is to offer opportunities along the way to further develop chaplains' knowing and doing appropriate to their grade and experience and, crucially, to continually support the fostering of the quality of their being, relating and deciding (i.e. active and ongoing self-appropriation). As Goldie (2012, cited by Waid 2015, p.701) puts it: 'Education [of chaplains] in its broadest sense is about the transformation of the self into new ways of thinking and acting.' And yet it is more. It is to continue to equip and support chaplains to work innovatively and collaboratively in a variety of contexts, whatever their experience and grade. It is to enable over time and with reflected experience 'judgements and decisions [to be] made in the manner of a virtuoso social and political actor' (Poole 2008, p.586). In other words, core to continual personal and professional development for chaplains is to support them to work towards practising consistently with *practical wisdom* with confidence and flair as specialist spiritual care practitioners. For a chaplain to remain open to that which she is becoming over the long haul is undoubtedly a challenge; however, with regular reflection on the lived experience of practice, not only can practical wisdom be fostered but also the chaplain's sense of vocation retained (Bunniss 2014; Kelly 2013).

Indicative suggestions for ongoing transformative learning

The suggestions include the following:

1. Specific knowledge and skills training to equip chaplains to perform their contextual role competently, relevant to their grade and level of experience.

2. Pastoral supervision (individual and group) where spiritual and theological reflective practice enables participants to regularly and intentionally correlate practice with their vocational canon. This is vital to continue to foster the ongoing unique professional identity of chaplains. Supervision seeks to help chaplains 'feel a firm persuasion in our work – to feel that which we do is right for ourselves and for the good of the world' (Whyte 2003, p.4) – thus keeping us well and alive in our work.

3. Reflection groups involving those with shared interests in particular aspects of chaplaincy work. (Use of digital technology is helpful here.)

4. Counselling or therapy – with a focus on the chaplain as a person.

5. Spiritual direction (as appropriate) with a focus on the chaplain's relationship with God or spiritual guidance relevant to the chaplain's faith or beliefs.

6. Reflective writing, for example journalling, and engagement in, and with, other creative forms such as poetry, music and art.

7. Mentorship for chaplains (especially in the first 3 years of practice) – mentors having relevant experience, reflected wisdom and training; specialist mentorship for those with specialist interests or roles, for example for new researchers (as being developed by Transforming Chaplaincy 2019) and strategic leaders.

8. Coaching – many in strategic leadership posts outwith chaplaincy, particularly operating at meta-levels of healthcare, receive ongoing coaching due to the complexity of strategic leadership roles.

To optimize transformative learning, chaplaincy leadership is required (within international and national bodies, healthcare organizations and local teams) which fosters learning-orientated cultures where the spirit of critical companionship is cultivated. This includes chaplains maintaining a record of their continuing professional and personal development which demonstrates 'reflection, improvement and positive impact' (Fraser 2013, p.30).

Conclusion

As British statesman Benjamin Disraeli once said, 'Change is inevitable. Change is constant.' Nowhere is that truer than in healthcare in the twenty-first century. Chaplains, like those of our interdisciplinary colleagues, can resist change or help to drive it. Once we decide to drive it, we may draw upon the assets inherent within the formation processes of chaplaincy education to aid the transformation of healthcare. In so doing, we will prove ourselves to be valuable resources to the healthcare institutions and communities with whom we work.

A formational and transformative educational programme for chaplains delivered consistently across each country that brings together a standardized body of knowledge (knowing), a comprehensive set of relevant skills (doing) and an agreed process for enhancing self-understanding (being) would more rigorously enable chaplains to be fit-for-purpose drivers of spiritual transformation at micro-, meso- and meta-levels of healthcare activity. These programmes would grow more competent and confident chaplains to help collaboratively shape and influence the development of healthcare services to become more person centred, co-produced, equitable and just. Collaboration worldwide to work towards the development of a framework to underpin such programmes, informed by recent research on religion and spirituality (Ragsdale 2018), which were adjusted to suit particular cultures, would enable shared educational learning and globally promote the professionalization of chaplaincy.

References

Association for Clinical Pastoral Education (2016) *ACPE Standards and Manual*. Decatur, GA: Association for Clinical Pastoral Education. Accessed on 29/07/2017 at www.manula.com/manuals/acpe/acpe-manuals/2016/en/topic/cover-page.

Board of Chaplaincy Certification (2016–2017) *Common Qualifications and Competencies for Professional Chaplains*. Hoffman Estates, IL: Board of Chaplaincy Certification Inc. Accessed on 09/05/2017 at www.professionalchaplains.org/files/2017%20Common%20Qualifications%20and%20Competencies%20for%20Professional%20Chaplains.pdf.

Bunniss, S. (2014) *Values Based Reflective Practice Evaluation Report*. Glasgow: Firecloud Research. (Unpublished.)

Fraser, D. (2013) 'CPD – an essential component of healthcare chaplaincy.' *Health and Social Care Chaplaincy 1*, 1, 22–34.

Goldie, J. (2012) 'The formation of professional identity in medical students: considerations for educators.' *Medical Teaching 34*, 641–648.

Gordon, T. and Mitchell, D. (2004) 'A competency model for the assessment and delivery of spiritual care.' *Palliative Medicine 18*, 7, 646–651.

HealthCare Chaplaincy Network (2016) *Scope of Practice*. New York, NY: HealthCare Chaplaincy Network. Accessed on 04/04/2017 at www.healthcarechaplaincy.org/docs/research/scope_of_practice_final_2016_03_16.pdf.

Joint Improvement Team (2012) *Talking Points: Personal Outcomes Approach Practical Guide*. Edinburgh: Joint Improvement Team.

Kelly, E. (2012) 'Competences in Spiritual Care Education and Training.' In M. Cobb,

C. Puchalski and B. Rumbold (eds) *Oxford Textbook of Spirituality in Healthcare*. Oxford: Oxford University Press.

Kelly, E. (2013) 'Translating theological reflective practice into values-based reflection: a report from Scotland.' *Reflective Practice 33*, 245–256.

King, S.D. (2007) *Trust the Process: A History of Clinical Pastoral Education as Theological Education*. Lanham, MD: University Press of America.

Kline, N. (1999) *Time to Think: Listening to Ignite the Human Mind*. London: Cassell Illustrated.

Kuether, F. (1958) 'The Council for Clinical Training: the core of clinical training is "learning by doing".' *Pastoral Psychology 4*, 17–20.

Massey, K. (2014) 'Surfing through a sea-change: the coming transformation of chaplaincy training.' *Reflective Practice 34*, 144–152.

Mezirow, J. (1997) 'Transformative learning: theory to practice.' *New Directions for Adult and Continuing Education 74*, 5–12.

Moberly, T. (2016) 'Looking ahead.' *British Medical Journal 352*, 8046, 331.

NHS Education for Scotland (2008) *Spiritual and Religious Care Competences and Capabilities for Healthcare Chaplains*. Edinburgh: NHS Education for Scotland. Accessed on 06/04/2017 at www.nes.scot.nhs.uk/media/206594/010308capabilities_and_competences_for_healthcare_chaplains.pdf.

Oliver, M. (2007) 'Messenger.' In *Thirst*. Tarset: Bloodaxe Books.

Poole, E. (2008) 'Organizational spirituality: a literature review.' *Journal of Business Ethics 84*, 577–588.

Ragsdale, J. (2018) 'Transforming chaplaincy requires transforming Clinical Pastoral Education.' *Journal of Pastoral Care and Counseling* 72, 1, 58–62. Accessed on 26/11/2018 at doi.org/10.1177/1542305018762133.

Scottish Government (2011) *Commission on the Future Delivery of Public Services*. Edinburgh: Scottish Government. Accessed on 02/10/2018 at www.gov.scot/Resource/Doc/352649/0118638.pdf.

Skills for Health (2017) *Statements of Competency*. Bristol: Skills for Health. Accessed on 05/04/2017 at www.skillsforhealth.org.uk/standards/item/215-national-occupational-standards.

Spiritual Health Victoria (2016) *Capability Framework for Spiritual Care Practitioners in Health Care Services*. Victoria: Spiritual Health Victoria. Accessed on 06/04/2017 at www.spiritualhealthvictoria.org.au/standards-and-frameworks.

Strang, E. (2017) 'Bird-Woman.' In *The Forward Book of Poetry*. London: Forward Worldwide.

Tartaglia, A. (2015) 'Reflections on the development and future of chaplaincy education.' *Reflective Practice* 35, 116–133.

Transforming Chaplaincy (2019) Accessed on 06/08/2019 at www.transformchaplaincy.org.

UK Board of Healthcare Chaplaincy (2009) *Spiritual and Religious Care Capabilities and Competences for Healthcare Chaplains*. Cambridge: UK Board of Healthcare Chaplaincy. Accessed on 19/09/2018 at www.ukbhc.org.uk/chaplains/compentencies.

UK Board of Healthcare Chaplaincy (2015) *Spiritual and Religious Care Capabilities and Competences for Healthcare Chaplains Bands 5, 6, 7 and 8*. Cambridge: UK Board of Healthcare Chaplaincy. Accessed on 06/04/2017 at www.ukbhc.org.uk/sites/default/files/ukbhc_spiritual_and_religious_capabilities_and_competences_bands_5_-_8_2015.pdf.

UK Board of Healthcare Chaplaincy (2017) *Spiritual and Religious Care Capabilities and Competences for Healthcare Chaplains Bands 5, 6, 7 and 8*. Cambridge: UK Board of Healthcare Chaplaincy. Accessed on 19/09/2018 at www.ukbhc.org.uk/sites/default/files/ukbhc_spiritual_and_religious_capabilities_and_competences_bands_5_-_8_2017.pdf.

Waid, H. (2015) 'Professional identity (trans) formation in medical education: reflection, relationship, resilience.' *Academic Medicine* 90, 6, 701–706.

Whyte, D. (2003) *Crossing the Unknown Sea*. New York, NY: Riverhead Books.

Wintz, S. and Hughes, B. (2018) 'Standardized methods of education within clinical training for chaplaincy.' *PlainViews* 15, 1. Accessed on 23/11/2018 at www.researchgate.net/publication/322808014_Standardized_Methods_of_Education_within_Clinical_Training_for_Chaplaincy/citations.

Part 8

Shaping the Future

Part 8 is an exploration of the urgent need, in a complex and rapidly changing global healthcare landscape, for chaplaincy as a profession to be more strategically mindful. In such a context, it is argued that chaplaincy must take the meaningful risk of increasingly intentionally stepping away from, or rather above, the coalface of operational provision; taking time to observe, analyse and reflect on the terrain and cultures which chaplains inhabit and collaboratively exploring possible strategic ways forward; then, enacting relevant innovative and entrepreneurial approaches or models which are not only fit for purpose in ever-evolving systems and communities but crucially are a collaborative part of their ongoing transformation.

Fostering (spiritual) wellbeing in complex post-industrial milieus where the causes of ill health and disease are multi-factorial and linked as much with social and economic issues as physical or psychological pathology is challenging. However, voices not representing chaplaincy and faith communities are becoming increasingly vocal regarding the significance of the spiritual dimension in promoting public health. In her book *Tears that Made the Clyde*, Carol Craig (2010) looks to spirituality as a key factor in improving wellbeing in Scotland's largest (and an increasingly secular) city, Glasgow – infamous for health inequalities and poor life expectancy within deprived communities. In order to help enhance the quality of life for Glaswegians, she urges a 'move from materialism to values which stress the importance of beauty, nature, meaning and transcendence… Spirituality matters and as individuals (and communities) we would benefit from giving it a place in our lives' (pp.376–377). Kevin Franz and contributors to the previous section point the way ahead as to how chaplains in Glasgow and across the post-industrialized world innovatively and collaboratively respond to such insight and opportunity. The auditor general of the National Health Service in Scotland (2018) suggests leadership is key to the future development of effective health and care provision. Within the chaplaincy community, how can transformative leadership enable the enactment and embedding of new models of chaplaincy? How can such leadership, at meta- and meso-levels of healthcare activity, foster a culture within chaplaincy of transformative learning to support such transitioning and innovation? How can such leadership concurrently ensure the continuing integration of chaplaincy as a recognised profession within health and care systems and, thus, enhance its ability to influence and enable transformation of cultures, organisations and systems?

References

Auditor General (2018) *NHS in Scotland 2018.* Edinburgh: Audit Scotland.

Craig, C. (2010) *Tears that Made the Clyde: Wellbeing in Glasgow.* Glendaruel: Argyll Publishing.

Chapter 22

Strategic Leadership in Healthcare Chaplaincy

Cheryl Holmes and Ewan Kelly

Introduction

This chapter seeks to help the reader reflect on the significance of strategic leadership, and in particular transformative approaches, within contemporary healthcare chaplaincy. It focuses on chaplaincy leadership operating at meso-levels (with teams and departments, within localities or communities or in specified aspects/areas of an organization) and meta-levels (across entire systems, organizations, nations and globally) of healthcare activity. Cheryl Holmes, chief executive officer for Spiritual Health Victoria (SHV), presents a case study from an Australian context, and Ewan Kelly, former programme director for Healthcare Chaplaincy and Spiritual Care in NHS Education for Scotland (NES), presents a case study from a Scottish context.

Cheryl describes the elements of strategic leadership demonstrated by SHV in the move towards professional recognition of spiritual care practitioners as an allied health discipline and the opportunities arising from that change. Ewan outlines the development of strategic leadership within Scottish chaplaincy and reflects on its impact on Scottish healthcare as well as chaplaincy in particular. This includes reflections on his leadership journey and learnings from it.

Cheryl and Ewan first met at a conference in Glasgow in 2012. Subsequent conversations about their shared interest in strategic leadership has been fostered by opportunities to participate in spiritual care learning events in different parts of the world.

In setting the scene for these case studies, a brief background and description of what strategic leadership might look like is offered. In addition, the increasing importance of such a role within specialist spiritual care in the complex healthcare and societal landscapes in which chaplains currently work is discussed.

A newly emergent aspect

Historically, chaplains have primarily focused on the urgent and immediate needs in their practice in institutional contexts (Kelly 2013). Until recently, proactively taking time out to reflect on the future of their service, what might be of importance or priority for it and its potential influence on healthcare policy and modes of provision has not been a normative activity. All chaplains, whatever level they are practising at, have the ability to initiate acts of leadership (Hospital/Healthcare Chaplaincy Joint Training Office 2006), for example at a micro-level taking the lead on a particular initiative within a ward or chaplaincy team setting. As Sharon Allen (2016, p.36), the chief executive of Skills for Care (a UK-based care sector workforce development agency), puts it, the act of 'leadership is not about the specific role you are in. In the end it's about the way you apply yourself.'

A strategic chaplaincy leadership role intentionally looks to envision and transform the future of specialist spiritual care, including research and education, with the aim of enhancing the spiritual wellbeing of those within their geographical or organizational remit. Strategic leaders may also seek to enable chaplaincy to influence aspects of local, national or global healthcare policy and how people-centred (both staff and service users) services are designed and delivered.

However, as outlined in Chapter 21, strategy belongs not just in the realm of those who inhabit such leadership posts. There is a need for all chaplains to be strategically literate – to understand the significance of strategic engagement and be familiar with policies and priorities which chaplaincy may help to deliver, or to transform, for the promotion of spiritual wellbeing and flourishing. Moreover, any number of chaplains in an organization, region or country may actively support appointed strategic leaders in any envisioning process, or act as collaborators and sounding boards in the creation or critique of policy and future planning.

The increased realization of the significance of strategic leadership is reflected in its place within recently developed capability frameworks for specialist spiritual care practice in Australia (Spiritual Health Victoria 2016a) and in the UK (UK Board of Healthcare Chaplaincy 2017). In North America common qualifications and competencies for chaplains have been created which also point towards strategic leadership as a key function in engagement with organizational systems and processes (Board of Chaplaincy Certification 2016–2017).

Chaplains who lead spiritual care teams (strategic leaders working at a meso-level) have management responsibilities as well as strategic ones. Management focuses on prioritizing and utilizing resources (human, financial and practical) in the present. Leadership, on the other hand, is about envisioning and enabling the development of plans and strategy and influencing organizational policymaking and service design for the future. Historically, lead chaplains, like others in equivalent roles in health and social care, have got caught up in the pressures of managing the immediate needs. Rob Grieg (National Development Team for Inclusion 2017) blogs about reflections from those who participated in a leadership programme run by his organization (a not-for-profit one working to enable people at risk of exclusion, due to age or disability, to live the life they choose). One of the four most common themes identified by participants was 'the realization that work pressures cause leaders to focus almost exclusively on day to day management not leadership'. Moreover, in the past, little or no training was offered in strategic leadership within chaplaincy (Hospital/Healthcare Chaplaincy Joint Training Office 2006). It is only recently that this issue has begun to be addressed. For example, in Scotland, following the development of a national strategic leadership group for healthcare chaplains in 2010, the first national training programme for strategic leads was delivered in 2012, supported by facilitated action-learning sets to enable group reflection on leadership practice. In 2017, the Association for Clinical Pastoral Education in North America first hosted a webinar series entitled 'Advancing Chaplaincy: Learning to Think and Act Strategically' (Association for Clinical Pastoral Education 2017). This series was sponsored and marketed by Transforming Chaplaincy and made use of technology to reach a larger audience. The popularity of the programme has meant further strategic leadership webinars being offered.

Strategic leadership in the current context

As has been outlined in this book's Introduction, our present health and care environments are informed by challenges such as demographic changes, increasing comorbidity, financial limitations and people's increased expectations of good quality of life for longer. To recap, this has prompted paradigm shifts in the philosophical underpinning of health and care theory, planning and delivery, as summarized in Table I.1 of this book's Introduction.

Alongside these shifts has been a growing focus on the broad realm of patient experience rather than the narrower measures associated with patient satisfaction. Such a change in context and approach to healthcare requires new vision for promoting health and wellbeing. This therefore necessitates innovative and relevant ways of working and models of practice to be developed by healthcare professionals working within and across professions as well as in partnership with service users and agencies from other sectors. Alternative, creative ways of practising chaplaincy, including education and research that informs it, are required which many collaborators thus far have described. To promote and enable change and innovation, the style of strategic leadership within healthcare has also transitioned from a heroic and authoritative approach to a more transformative and collaborative one (Bevan and Fairman 2014; Till and McKimm 2016). Whilst intentional strategic leadership may be a new phenomenon for chaplains, it is interesting that many of the traits or abilities described as important for transformative leadership are ones with which healthcare chaplains would resonate. Such leaders are described as self-aware (Gilbert and Fulford 2010), reflective and reflexive (Reave 2005), work from a strong values base (Alimo-Metcalfe *et al.* 2008), understand the strength in vulnerability (Brown 2012) and seek to create shared meaning (Alimo-Metcalfe and Sondhi 2010; Gilbert and Fulford 2010).

In addition, strategic leaders who seek to engage with others to transform services need to:

- inspire them with passion and a high level of engagement

- enable shared or co-created envisioning

- utilize power and role authority to empower and enable

- encourage questioning and critical and strategic thinking. (Alimo-Metcalfe *et al.* 2008)

Such a style of leadership does not pretend to have all the answers to the increasing challenges in an ever-complex terrain and is not afraid to ask questions, often difficult ones, for colleagues and collaborators to wrestle with and corporately seek a way forwards. As never before, health and care systems struggle to find new, meaningful, people-centred and effective ways to promote wellbeing and contribute to human flourishing in uncharted and uncertain times. Through its strategic leadership, chaplaincy can respond to these opportunities to influence how such local, organizational, state or regional and national systems evolve and help shape what they may look like in the future.

The following two case studies from different parts of the globe illustrate the impact strategic leadership within the field of specialist spiritual care can make in transformative and different ways.

Case studies

From Spiritual Health Victoria, Australia

Introduction

This case study covers a period of approximately 7 years (2009–2016) and describes the path towards the recognition of spiritual care as an allied health profession by the Department of Health and Human Services in Victoria. The story could be traced even further back, as there are many building blocks (and leaders) that lay the foundations for transformational change. However, for the purposes of this chapter, there is room for only part of the story. This in itself illustrates something about what it takes for transformational change. It is a process, it needs many people to contribute and it is continual. Strategic leadership works consistently in this uncertain environment with curiosity and openness to the opportunities that change makes possible.

Context

Spiritual Health Victoria (SHV) is the peak body for the development and promotion of quality spiritual care in all health services in Victoria, Australia. Victoria is one of six states with two territories in Australia and has a population of 6.2 million (out of a total Australian population of 24.1 million). Australia has a mixture of public and private health systems with a mixed funding model, shared between the federal government (the largest funder), states, territories and the non-government sector. SHV is funded by the Victorian State Government and works with faith communities, health services, spiritual care practitioners, the government and other agencies to enable quality spiritual care in all Victorian health services. SHV currently has eight staff (5.4 FTE) to enable this work with a focus on education, research, support and development. A significant portion of the government funding received by SHV is disbursed to the 15 faith communities who are members of SHV for the development and provision of spiritual care in hospitals. As in other contexts, the provision of spiritual care services has changed in Australia, and especially in Victoria, which leads the way nationally in the public sector towards a professional model of spiritual care. Increasingly, spiritual care practitioners are directly employed and funded by the health services, a move away from the traditional model of chaplains (usually clergy) employed, funded and appointed to hospital positions by the churches (although a number of these positions continue). This shift parallels the changes seen in Australian demographics. Increasingly, the Australian Bureau of Statistics census data demonstrate reduced numbers of people identifying as Christian (52.2%), increasing numbers of people identifying with other faith traditions (8.2%) and more people nominating 'no religion' (Australian Bureau of Statistics 2016). (At 30.1%, this was higher than any other single Christian denomination for the first time.) The shifts also correspond with the growing literature and research that highlight changes in the breadth of understanding about spirituality, spiritual needs and the contribution that spiritual care can make to health outcomes and patient wellbeing.

Increasingly, in healthcare today, spiritual care practitioners are expected to work as part of the multidisciplinary team and to adhere to, and contribute to, health service policies and strategic priorities. However, the status of spiritual care practitioners has, in many health services, remained somewhat ambiguous, as has their place within the organizational structure. This has often led spiritual care to be relegated to the periphery of the organization. In order to be influencers of change, spiritual care practitioners need to be at the table where priorities and directions for the future are discussed. As strategic leaders, the staff of SHV identified this as an issue that needed to be addressed and began the process of moving spiritual care towards recognition as an allied health profession.

Towards professional recognition

How do strategic leaders identify issues and create opportunities? Relationships, connections and conversations are key, not only in the initial identification of an issue but also in continuing to work with that issue. SHV facilitates a Spiritual Care Management Network that provides an opportunity for spiritual care practitioners in leadership and management positions to meet with senior staff from SHV on a regular basis (three to four times per year). These meetings provide opportunity for the sharing and exchange of information, progress, issues and current challenges, and enable SHV to be connected with the experience of practitioners on the ground. These meetings were one of the places where discrepancies between the status of spiritual care and its place within the organizational structures of the health services first began to emerge. It also became evident that spiritual care practitioners were more often given a voice around the table for significant strategic conversations when they were recognized as part of the multidisciplinary team. SHV staff identified that frequently this coincided with spiritual care organized under allied health in organizational structures.

Recognizing that in Australia there had been little work done to identify and publish the capabilities and competencies required of professional spiritual care practitioners, SHV produced the first Capabilities Framework for Pastoral Care in 2009 (Healthcare Chaplaincy Council of Victoria). Based on international capabilities and competencies work in the US and the UK, and co-created with a team of practitioners, this document provided the basis for SHV to have further conversations with the Australian government towards recognition of spiritual care. The Capabilities Framework was then revised in 2011 (Healthcare Chaplaincy Council of Victoria), again in consultation with spiritual care practitioners, and became a significant document in the development of the National Professional Standards of Practice produced by Spiritual Care Australia (SCA) in 2013.

During this period conversations continued at a number of levels. This was important as a way to constantly check and monitor assumptions about the directions. There were a small number of voices expressing concern at the directions taken towards professionalization. These voices represented practitioners and religious representatives, both in Victoria and across Australia, concerned at what might be lost should spiritual care become so embedded in the system. It was important to listen deeply to these concerns and to engage in honest conversations. One of the consequences of any change is that it involves loss. This may be the loss of how things have always been and, perhaps, the loss of control. Acknowledging the pain and grief felt and enabling that to be spoken and shared is a significant aspect of leadership (and spiritual care). In this case, it was necessary to hold the tensions and conflict this created.

For some practitioners, their place in the organizational structure was already working well for their department, and to enforce a new place within the structure might jeopardize this established relationship. In such instances we became clear that the objective of any change was to support those spiritual care practitioners struggling at the meso-level to find a credible place within their organizational system. There was no expectation that all hospitals should implement organizational restructuring based on this change. This recognized the local differences already *in situ* in a range of ways in any comparison between hospitals. It was obvious that the organizational structures of large metropolitan hospitals were different to those of smaller regional hospitals. The principle of professional recognition still applied, but there needed to be room for implementation that worked at the local level.

For religious representatives this change represented a shift in the locus of control and recognized the increasing responsibility of the health service as a primary provider of spiritual care. Furthermore, this change would bring recognition of spiritual care at a meta-level that could enable models for the provision and funding of spiritual care to be embedded as an integral part of Victorian health services. There were a number of potential losses facing the faith communities, for example the loss of control as the recognized primary voice and provider for spiritual care, and the loss of funding should the models change. For the Christian Churches especially, with a long history of providing chaplaincy services to Victorian public hospitals, these were confrontational prospects. Working with resistance to change can be a significant part of strategic leadership. Often, as in this case, knowing where resistance is likely to come from enables early groundwork to prepare the way for change. Communication is key here. There is a need to constantly monitor the environment and to keep all stakeholders abreast of the information they need to inform their decisions. SHV leaders prepared papers and met two or three times per year with faith community members to ensure they had all of the pertinent information about the context of change. In this case the Royal Commission into Child Sexual Abuse brought about increasing disenfranchisement for the churches in the wider society at large. SHV was asked by the government to provide some assurance about the quality of the people appointed by faith communities to provide spiritual care. This led to the development of the Spiritual Care Providers (Faith Community Appointed) Credentialling Framework and the undertaking of faith communities to develop and implement a credentialling process (Spiritual Health Victoria 2015). SHV leaders used every opportunity to inform faith community members of the shifts occurring in society and in the health context. This included the changes in demographics (as described above), the changes in language and understanding about spirituality and spiritual care, and the international literature and research about spiritual care in health. Some flagship models of spiritual care provision in a number of Victorian hospitals demonstrated the opportunities created for spiritual care provision, with the faith communities as partners. This enabled the faith communities to see the possibilities and shape for their continuing role and to recognize that working towards the professionalization of spiritual care practitioners could enhance and enable their role rather than diminish and exclude them.

In all of this, it is important for those who are challenged and confronted by change to understand that the end goal has not already been decided. In this case, while SHV worked towards the professionalization of spiritual care practitioners, the complete picture of what that might look like in terms of models for spiritual care provision going forwards was still unknown. Consultation is empty and meaningless if the decision has already been made and there is no room for other ideas. Questions and concerns raised in the process must be taken seriously. Strategic leaders need a good dose of humility, and courage, knowing that the way forwards often emerges in the crucible of tension.

During this period SHV went through some considerable shifts as an organization. Once again informed by international research, wider society and changes within the Australian health context, a facilitated process for the SHV board led to a new vision, mission and name for the organization (which until 2014 was known as the Healthcare Chaplaincy Council of Victoria).

In parallel with the above, SHV leaders continued to identify areas that needed to be addressed in the context of professional spiritual care. Data collection was a significant area of inconsistency across hospitals. SHV leaders established a working group of spiritual care managers, leading to the development of the Spiritual Care Minimum Data Set Framework (Spiritual Health Victoria 2016c). Alongside this work, SHV leaders commenced the development of spiritual care guidelines, initially basing this on NHS Chaplaincy Guidelines (Swift 2015). Reference was then made to the National Health Standards and other national and Victorian policy statements. This collaborative work resulted in the Spiritual Care in Victorian Health Services: Towards Best Practice Framework (Spiritual Health Victoria 2016b).

The final major project undertaken was the revision of the 2011 Capabilities Framework. A major rewrite was undertaken, and a new framework was strategically aligned with two Australian source documents: the National Common Health Capability Resource (Health Workforce Australia 2013) and the Victorian Allied Health: Credentialling, Competency and Capability Framework (Victorian Government 2014). The new SHV capability framework was written in collaboration with senior practitioners in the field and reviewed by senior practitioners, SCA and senior allied health managers, resulting in the Capability Framework for Spiritual Care Practitioners in Health Services (Spiritual Health Victoria 2016a).

These documents are mentioned as they proved to be the catalyst needed in the move towards recognition as an allied health profession. The frameworks were sent to the Victorian chief allied health advisor, and a number of meetings ensued. The frameworks, along with the SCA National Standards of Practice (2013), demonstrated the professional level at which spiritual care practitioners were already working across health services. At the end of 2016, the chief allied health advisor agreed that spiritual care should be recognized as an allied health profession.

This could be the end of the story, but things are never quite so clear-cut. SHV continues to work with the Victorian state government, health services and spiritual care practitioners on the implications of this recognition.

Change is often seen in small, incremental steps. At the meso-level, this professional recognition has enabled several spiritual care practitioners to negotiate a credible place within hospitals' organizational structures reporting directly to the director or manager of allied health. It has also led to the renaming of a number of departments from chaplaincy or pastoral care to spiritual care, ensuring consistency of language.

At the meta-level this professional recognition has given SHV staff a voice in a number of strategic meetings. SHV has attended the Victorian Allied Health Leadership Council currently addressing a number of issues that align with key strategic concerns for spiritual care, for example the need for research capabilities and capacity to be developed across allied health disciplines. SHV has become involved in strategic conversations about health informatics and data collection, ensuring that spiritual care is integrated in any future developments in this area. SHV was also able to negotiate direct involvement with the Victorian Department of Health in a project initiated to enable a number of allied health disciplines to address issues of credentialling or registration and professional identity. There is a long way to go and this has only happened in Victoria. Working towards national consistency has been another step along the path, with a national consensus conference held in June 2017 to continue that process. Just as change is continual, so is the need for strategic leadership at every level. As health services increasingly focus on safety and quality, alongside person-centred care and patient experience, it is incumbent on strategic leaders in spiritual care to continually look for, and make the connections between, what matters in health and the ways spiritual care can contribute and lead.

Reflections

This case study from SHV has demonstrated some of the key aspects of strategic leadership: awareness of the environment; connecting with people and co-creating vision; listening deeply to as many stakeholders as possible; taking questions and concerns seriously; being humble (vulnerable); having courage; and taking time for reflection and discernment. Spiritual care practitioners have much to contribute as strategic leaders in healthcare.

From NHSScotland

Introduction

This case study reflects on the role of strategic leadership in the transformational change Scottish chaplaincy has been in the process of undergoing in recent years. What is described is the strategic collaborative work done within the Scottish chaplaincy community between 2009 and 2015 to raise its profile within Scottish healthcare and to influence and enhance the national delivery of the Scottish government's:

- person-centred care work streams within its Healthcare Quality Strategy of NHSScotland (Scottish Government 2010)

- Achieving Sustainable Quality in Scotland's Healthcare: A '20:20' Vision (Scottish Government 2011a) to further develop the care and wellbeing of people in community settings (Scottish Government 2011b).

Broad context

Scotland is a small country of 5.4 million people (National Records for Scotland 2017) with a publicly funded health service. Fourteen territorial health boards across Scotland utilize allocated monies to deliver healthcare as outlined in national policy. The health boards have autonomy in financial allocation to enable service provision in order to meet government targets and enact policy in their geographical area. How much funding is afforded to spiritual care in each health board varies according to population and each board's priorities and perceptions. Spiritual care delivery in every locality is informed by national guidelines (there are no statutory requirements) published in 2002 by the then Scottish Executive's Health Department and later revised in 2009 by the Scottish government. At the time of writing, guidelines are being sought to be replaced by the first National Delivery Plan for Health and Social Care Chaplaincy and Spiritual Care Across Health and Social Care in Scotland (currently in draft form).

As Derek Fraser describes in Chapter 8, by 2009 chaplains were no longer employed by the national church in Scotland but directly by health boards to work generically, in the main, to provide spiritual care for those inhabiting healthcare contexts. Those with specific religious needs are often, with consent, referred to a representative of the person's own faith community. Scotland, though, is an increasingly secular country with limited ethnic and religious diversity – 58% of the population having no religious affiliation and only 2% of the population being associated with a non-Christian faith community (Scottish Social Attitudes Survey 2017).

By 2009, much collaborative work (involving chaplains, faith and belief groups, and other healthcare disciplines) had been done in Scotland to begin to professionalize chaplaincy (as outlined in Chapter 8) and the fruit of its labour lay the foundation for further transformation. The Spiritual Care and Chaplaincy Guidelines (Scottish Government 2009) pointed to the need for the development of a strong evidence base for Scottish chaplaincy and the merits of exploring further the delivery of spiritual care outwith institutions, particularly in family-doctor surgeries. A lot of intentional effort had been put into fostering and promoting positive relationships and clear lines of communication with the Scottish government. Also, in this period, a standalone training and development post, which was funded by the Scottish government, became integrated into NHS Education for Scotland (NES) – the body responsible for the education and training of all healthcare professionals. The role was regraded and retitled as 'programme director for healthcare chaplaincy and spiritual care in Scotland' and evolved into a more strategic one. This afforded increased opportunity for creativity and collaboration with other health professions in education and training as well as opportunities for networking and influencing.

However, in 2009, the integration of Scottish chaplains into health board services and local multidisciplinary teams remained piecemeal across the country. The profile of chaplaincy was dependent on personality, local interest and relationships rather than on integration into policy and national standing. Chaplains tended to work under the radar of regional and national healthcare leadership. This meant chaplains could work with relative autonomy but had scarce strategic influence. Scottish chaplaincy at this time had little evidence base, cohesion or coordinated strategic planning.

Then, global financial austerity hit. This changed the healthcare landscape worldwide, particularly for those health services that were funded publicly. Within this context I was appointed to the programme director's post – expecting to be an educator, resourcer and supporter of chaplains, I found myself needing to rapidly learn about strategic leadership, for it seemed that very quickly chaplaincy would become a soft target for the inevitable cost-cutting that would follow. Chaplaincy was not around the table of influence consistently locally or nationally and, thus, was susceptible to being taken off the menu. More than that, I believed, if the small chaplaincy community (approximately 130 in all – 50% of them being full-time) was to maximize its potential contribution to the wellbeing of people and healthcare services of Scotland, we needed to be more strategic and cohesive in our approach.

Some reflections on the strategic leadership journey within the Scottish chaplaincy community between 2009 and 2015 are now offered under headings which represent different aspects of leadership which seek to foster transformational change:

• promoting strategic thinking

- engagement

- cultivating innovation and creativity

- promoting a culture of learning and reflection.

These dimensions are not exhaustive, but the intention is to give a flavour of the culture which was sought to be co-created. At the beginning of my involvement in 2009, much of what I was doing was instinctive and based on learning from leading local spiritual care teams in the past. It was only after participating in a Scottish government-sponsored national transformational leadership programme (in 2010–2011) with strategic leaders from a variety of healthcare disciplines that I could begin to articulate more clearly what underpinned my approach and vision.

Promoting strategic thinking

Despite the challenges, and the fact that chaplains felt they had little voice or influence within Scottish healthcare, there was strong belief within the chaplaincy community that our role was a significant aspect of holistic care. Many also felt chaplains had an important contribution to make in shaping healthcare culture. This helped inform my motivation as a strategic leader to cultivate and enable a culture of strategic thinking (Senge 1990) within the Scottish chaplaincy community – the aim being to become a more cohesive, influential and effective body; in other words, to help chaplains understand the importance of taking protected time away from the dance floor of spiritual care delivery – where chaplains are skilled at responding in the immediacy to the intricacies of the rhythm of, and steps in, another's dance – to risk climbing to the balcony above. In doing so there was the opportunity to see the bigger healthcare picture – to look at recurrent patterns and behaviours on the *whole* dance floor; in addition, to notice and wonder about what chaplains currently did, and might do differently in the future, to maximize the impact of chaplaincy practice on the wellbeing of the people of Scotland and enable the future flourishing of Scottish chaplaincy.

In short, I believed chaplaincy needed to move from a default responsive operational outlook to a more proactive and intentional strategically informed one. This, however, was a countercultural approach that mystified many chaplaincy colleagues when I first took up post. 'So, you're leaving real chaplaincy for the dark side of management,' as one colleague summed up many people's thoughts when I left a hospice chaplain's job to take up the national leadership role.

I realized I was going to be involved in promoting a huge cultural shift. Not only was much learning required by me to understand more fully what the issues were for chaplains in relation to their roles and how they saw the future of chaplaincy, I also saw this as a chance for chaplains to see the opportunities a more strategically informed chaplaincy community might afford. I realized I could not do this alone. Such an ambition required engagement and collaboration. As Hacker (2015, p.15) puts it, 'It requires many to change mindsets and behaviours.' However, the first aspect of engagement required for transformation, prior to people, is with context.

Engagement

Engagement with healthcare culture and policy context

In order to enable chaplaincy to maximize its impact in promoting spiritual wellbeing for the people of Scotland in a relevant and meaningful way, the *meta* context in which we sought to do so needed to be understood. To do so with significant intention, investment of time and energy was counterintuitive to the majority of chaplains. However, when we did so, we noticed paradoxically – amidst the risk-averse, acute-care-focused and target-driven culture of NHSScotland (where the *what* and the *when* were the predominant strategic questions asked) – that government-policy documents also started to talk of promoting innovation (Scottish Government 2011b) as well as person-centred care in seeking to keep people well in community settings (Scottish Government 2011a). The Scottish government began publicly stating that in order to change the way health and social care was delivered required informed and meaningful risk-taking to test new approaches. Thus, *how* healthcare was delivered and *why* began to receive more attention in strategic arenas as part of the increased interest in person-centred, co-produced and outcomes-focused care. There was a political milieu emerging in which chaplains could connect with issues driving policy initiatives and find levers to not only influence funding opportunities but also service delivery and organizational culture.

Engagement with chaplains

Initial engagement with chaplaincy teams during the process of transformation was done through visits to each territorial board and in an ongoing way through inviting chaplains to learning events. Importantly, these continual professional development (CPD) sessions had a strategic element, especially initially in relation to the political and policy context. Listening and responding to an individual chaplain's concerns and anxieties was a significant aspect of leadership, especially during the early stages.

Priority was given to the development and circulation of a regular newsletter to all chaplains two or three times a year, to keep them informed of activity, CPD opportunities and suggested reading with the aim not just of promoting communication but also a strategically informed learning community.

Fostering chaplaincy cohesion

Before we could seriously begin to engage in strategic thinking nationally, Scottish chaplains needed to feel part of a more coherent body in which they could relate meaningfully with each other about their role. In order to further promote such an enhanced sense of belonging within the national chaplaincy community and to enable a sense of ownership of what Scottish chaplaincy's shared identity might be, NES organized a series of regional consultation days followed by a national consensus conference for chaplains. The aim was to create a single consensus statement articulating chaplaincy's specialist role within NHSScotland (Kelly 2012). This enabled individual chaplains to contribute, have some ownership of their role description and explore with each other the significance of role consistency within Scottish chaplaincy. In addition, it was also an opportunity for those in leadership roles to listen to chaplains' professional self-understanding and hear more about the impact of change and transition.

Engagement with chaplaincy leadership

Each geographical health board in Scotland has an appointed chaplaincy or spiritual care service lead, and up till 2009 those leads met infrequently to network and share experiences. Attendance and intention varied. In November 2010, at the invitation of NES, all the lead chaplains in Scotland gathered for 5 days to participate in a *Reflective Leadership* residential programme. It marked the beginning of collaborative strategic thinking and leadership training in Scotland. The aim was to enable leadership to be developed within a community of ongoing learning (Kerr 2013) where no one has all the answers but all could potentially contribute to the development of strategic thinking.

The leadership group was a disparate one: members had different ideas of what chaplaincy might be; had different priorities within their particular contexts; and had little or no leadership training (most having been appointed for their length of service and management ability). The gathering enabled lead chaplains to spend time together, deepen relationships and share their aspirations and concerns about the future of Scottish chaplaincy. During this gathering six strategic priority workstreams emerged to be led by different lead chaplains:

- service development

- developing an evidence base

- engaging in shaping healthcare policy

- professional development for lead chaplains

- developing reflective practice

- communications.

Whilst some of this work was aspirational, it formed the future basis of the strategic thinking and a platform for ongoing engagement. This gathering was the genesis of the Strategic Leadership Group (SLG) for Scottish health and social care chaplaincy which acted as a conduit for transformational change within the chaplaincy community. External facilitation during the group's formative period enabled exploration of the challenge of change and group dynamics; facilitating expression of feelings, deeper listening and promotion of collaboration.

After discerning that the Healthcare Quality Strategy of NHSScotland (Scottish Government 2010) and the '20:20' Vision for Health and Social Care (Scottish Government 2011b) were the right policy and funding waves to ride on to enable maximization of chaplaincy's strategic profile and impact, the SLG utilized such policy momentum and the energy created at local health board delivery level to its advantage. Three national programmes of innovative chaplaincy work (the genesis and evolution of these programmes are described in Chapters 13, 15 and 17) were aligned to three of the four workstreams of the Scottish government's person-centred care approach (Table 22.1) (Scottish Government 2010).

Table 22.1 Scottish chaplaincy's national programmes of work

Workstream of the Scottish government's person-centred approach	Scottish chaplaincy's national programme of work
Co-production (supporting self-management)	Community Chaplaincy Listening
Care experience	Spiritual care Patient Related Outcome Measure
Staff experience	Values Based Reflective Practice

These innovative approaches sought to utilize chaplains' natural abilities and build on their strengths of self-awareness, relationality, listening and curiosity. Every lead chaplain across Scotland agreed to begin to integrate these programmes into the work of their board chaplaincy teams, the aim being to help the Scottish government and local health boards to deliver and evidence person-centred care across Scotland. The uptake at first was sluggish in some health boards, with interest in one or two of the programmes, and others immediately embraced all three. Likewise, some chaplains resisted involvement initially and felt ill equipped to become involved. Scottish government funding was given to help embed and sustain these programmes of work, including – importantly – to train, support and supervise chaplains in the utilization of these approaches in their practice.

Engagement outside chaplaincy

Much engagement and networking was done with national and regional strategic leaders from other healthcare disciplines, as well as outwith healthcare, for example in the voluntary sector. Intentional engagement was sought upwards with civil servants and government, for example with the chief medical and nursing officers and government lead for allied health professionals in Scotland. Accepting and creating opportunities to speak at national conferences and events, organized by government and other healthcare disciplines, on spiritual care and how chaplaincy can promote person-centred (including staff) care were prioritized. Funding was sought to travel abroad to network and learn from other strategic leaders globally and those health and social care leaders and academics interested in promoting communal wellbeing.

Engagement with national and regional healthcare leaders also involved inviting them to chair, speak at or participate in conferences and learning events. These events, strategically named, involved the sharing of innovative chaplaincy practice and research, particularly focused on quality and promoting wellbeing. This also meant engaging with government to fund such gatherings. Two examples were held in the same week in 2012: a national event entitled 'Enhancing Wellbeing and Saving Money: An Evidence Based Approach' was chaired by the deputy chief nursing officer for Scotland; in addition, an international conference entitled 'Spirituality and Health: Improving Outcome and Enhancing Wellbeing' was opened by the Scottish minister for public health and included the chief medical officer for Scotland as a keynote speaker. These events contained particular sessions on Community Chaplaincy Listening (CCL), Values Based Reflective Practice (VBRP) and the Patient Related Outcome Measure (PROM) in their various iterations and any findings or evaluations performed. They aimed to showcase chaplaincy activity, build strategic relationships, reveal the added value and value for money of chaplaincy, as well as promote shared learning.

Cultivating innovation and creativity

As well as seeking to model an innovative and creative approach to chaplaincy development and delivery, there was an intention to foster a culture of seeking new ways to envision and practise specialist spiritual care in twenty-first century health and social care within Scottish chaplaincy. Previous innovative projects were built on, for example the development of Spiritual Care Matters (NHS Education for Scotland 2009) – a creative resource to promote spiritual care education and training across healthcare disciplines which was well used in clinical and university settings. Government funding was sourced to promote innovative approaches to the utilization of this educational tool through the award of small grants to chaplains working with multidisciplinary colleagues in a variety of contexts. A national learning event for all those working in healthcare and educational contexts entitled 'Innovative Spiritual Care Education, Practice and Research in Scotland' was held in 2011 to share the approaches developed and their evaluated impact on the learning and practice of students and practitioners with health and social care. Grant recipients were also encouraged to disseminate their work and findings through publication (for example, McTaggart *et al.* 2013). Fostering such local innovation and the creative vocational energy this initiative generated laid the foundation for some chaplains' initial engagement with the CCL, VBRP and PROM national programmes of work. Moreover, the collaboration chaplains enacted with respect to Spiritual Care Matters (NHS Education for Scotland 2009) and its creative application also helped the SLG to consider strategically new models of chaplaincy with a focus on resourcing, enabling and supporting healthcare staff to deliver spiritual care, rather than chaplains being seen primarily as the deliverers themselves. Further CPD events, such as one held in 2013 during which health board teams were invited to present to their colleagues from around Scotland a piece of innovative practice of which they were proud, were organized with the intention of promoting local, as well as national, creativity and innovation in chaplaincy.

Promoting a culture of learning and reflection

Work done to encourage learning with respect to strategic thinking and transformational leadership was set in a broader context of intentionally promoting a culture of reflective and reflexive practice within Scottish chaplaincy. Group reflective practice and individual pastoral supervision became increasingly normative for chaplains practising at all levels during the period this chapter describes, including those in leadership roles, with training for facilitators and supervisors funded by the government.

A review of education, training and formation for Scottish chaplains (Paterson and Clegg 2013) highlighted the need at a time of transition to further train, equip and support chaplains to work in the new paradigms emerging in health and social care. However, its most significant finding pointed to the fact that for chaplains to be involved in fostering transformation in an increasingly complex health and social care terrain, all who enter the profession need to have completed the same rigorous formational programme – self-awareness (see Chapters 20 and 21) being the primary tool a chaplain has to engage meaningfully and creatively with persons, systems and structures as a basis for transformation. Moreover, the review recommended that such a formational curriculum must contain a leadership and empowerment component.

Creating learning opportunities as a strategic leader
I discovered very early in my leadership journey that I needed to be intentional about creating learning opportunities. I was fortunate to be able to apply for, and be accepted into, a multidisciplinary leadership programme which enabled me to have one-to-one coaching as well as reflecting on leadership practice regularly with peers in medicine, nursing, pharmacy and laboratory services as part of an action-learning set. Once the 18-month programme ended, the action-learning set still met and I also sought regular supervision with a specific focus on transformational leadership. These opportunities for reflection and ongoing learning were not only restorative but also transformative for me as a person as well as a strategic leader. Moreover, they enabled me to gain confidence in my leadership role and reduced feelings of loneliness and isolation, as a strategic leader, which I discovered were shared experiences with my multidisciplinary colleagues.

Reflections

This was not an easy journey for the Scottish chaplaincy community as it meant radical challenge and change to the way chaplaincy was previously understood and delivered by many Scottish chaplains. The transformative leadership style utilized, though seeking to be collaborative, was, on reflection, disruptive. Routines and norms were not just questioned but thrown up in the air. Risks, however meaningful they were thought to be in order to seek to enable chaplaincy not just to survive but to flourish, albeit differently, in an increasingly complex and ever-changing context, were encouraged to be taken. This brought anxiety for some, energized others and brought learning for all who engaged. Such a leadership approach resulted in the consultative, collaborative development of a draft, 'National

Delivery Plan for Health and Social Care Chaplaincy and Spiritual Care Across Health and Social Care in Scotland', which aims to bring further strategic consistency to health and social care chaplaincy practice in the promotion of individual and communal spiritual wellbeing. At the delivery plan's heart is the continuation of the embedding of CCL, VBRP and PROM research as norms for chaplaincy practice. These three national programmes of work have not only raised chaplaincy's profile in Scotland with strategic healthcare leaders at government and territorial board level, they have also helped to shape and enhance the delivery, and evidence the significance, of person-centred care in Scotland.

Conclusion

Not only in Australia and Scotland, but also within the healthcare chaplaincy community globally, there is a growing and shared interest in the development of strategic leadership and thinking. Whilst strategic leadership is always contextual, it would seem that creating a forum or network for the fostering of strategic leadership and thinking worldwide would be advantageous for the development of the profession. In this endeavour, the work undertaken in the strategic development of chaplaincy research could provide a model (for example, a network for research was established through the auspices of the Joint Research Council of the Association of Professional Chaplains in the US). Learning and supportive opportunities could be further developed through mentoring, webinars and online educational material. Such a global community of learning would not only promote innovation, collaboration and engagement – it could potentially encourage shared thinking about promoting strategic literacy, research and succession planning with respect to strategic leadership. Strategic leadership requires 'big picture' thinking and envisioning – the health and social care world globally is chaplaincy's oyster. Chaplaincy leaders from across the world, sharing together and learning from one another in an intentional and regular way, could enhance the strategic influence of chaplaincy for the promotion of spiritual wellbeing of local and more global populations. In today's world, spirituality that leads us back to our common humanity and to each other in community is needed more than ever. Chaplaincy could lead the way towards this vision.

References

Alimo-Metcalfe, B. and Sondhi, R. (2010) 'Should NHS leaders be accountable to staff?' *Health Service Journal*, 18 March, 18–19.

Alimo-Metcalfe, B., Alban-Metcalfe, J., Bradeley, M., Mariathasan, J. and Samele, C. (2008)

'The impact of engaging leadership on performance attitudes to work and wellbeing at work: a longitudinal study.' *Journal of Health Organisation and Management 22*, 6, 586–598.

Allen, S. (2016) 'Tackling social care's leadership problem.' *The Guardian*, 9 March 2016, p.36.

Association for Clinical Pastoral Education (2017) *Advancing Chaplaincy: Learning to Think and Act Strategically.* Accessed on 14/04/2018 at www.transformchaplaincy.org/grants-training/webinars.

Australian Bureau of Statistics (2016) *Census Data: Religion.* Accessed on 09/01/2018 at www.abs.gov.au/AUSSTATS/abs@.nsf/mediareleasesby ReleaseDate/7E65A144540551D7CA2581 48000E2B85?OpenDocument.

Bevan, H. and Fairman, S. (2014) *The New Era of Thinking and Practice in Change and Transformation: A Call to Action for Leaders of Health and Care.* Accessed on 27/12/2017 at http://aace.org.uk/wp-content/uploads/2014/08/nhsiq_white_paper.pdf.

Board of Chaplaincy Certification (2016–2017) *Common Qualifications and Competencies for Professional Chaplains.* Accessed on 09/05/2017 at www.professionalchaplains.org/files/2017%20Common%20Qualifications%20 and%20Competencies%20for%20 Professional%20Chaplains.pdf.

Brown, B. (2012) *Daring Greatly: How the Courage to Be Vulnerable Transforms the Way We Live, Love, Parent and Lead.* New York, NY: Penguin Group (USA).

Gilbert, P. and Fulford, K.W.M. (2010) 'Bringing the spirit and values back into public services.' *The International Journal of Leadership in Public Services* 6, 2, 6–19.

Grieg, R. (2017) 'Four lessons in leadership.' *National Development Team for Inclusion Blog*, 24 April 2017. Accessed on 28/11/2017 at www.ndti.org.uk/blog/four-lessons-in-leadership.

Hacker, S.K. (2015) 'Leading cultural transformation.' *The Journal for Quality and Participation*, January, 13–16. Accessed on 03/04/2018 at http://stephenhacker.com/wp-content/uploads/2015/01/leading-cultural-transformation_jan2015.pdf.

Healthcare Chaplaincy Council of Victoria (2009) *Capabilities Framework for Pastoral Care and Chaplaincy.* Melbourne,Victoria: Healthcare Chaplaincy Council of Victoria Inc.

Healthcare Chaplaincy Council of Victoria (2011) *Capabilities Framework for Pastoral Care and Chaplaincy.* Melbourne, Victoria: Healthcare Chaplaincy Council of Victoria Inc.

Health Workforce Australia (2013) *National Common Health Capability Resource: Shared Activities and Behaviours in the Australian Health Workforce.* Adelaide: Health Workforce Australia.

Hospital/Healthcare Chaplaincy Joint Training Office (2006) *The Mirfield Report: Report of the Workshop on Chaplaincy Leadership.* London: Hospital/Healthcare Chaplaincy Joint Training Office.

Kelly, E. (2012) 'The development of healthcare chaplaincy.' *The Expository Times 123*, 10, 469–470.

Kelly, E. (2013) 'Policy, practice and strategic priorities and healthcare chaplaincy.' *Scottish Journal of Healthcare Chaplaincy* 16, 53–59.

Kerr, J. (2013) *Legacy: What the All Blacks can Teach Us about the Business of Life.* London: Constable.

McTaggart, I., Munro, G., Rogerson, E. and Martingale, L. (2013) 'Learning about spiritual care: it matters!' *Scottish Journal of Healthcare Chaplaincy* 15, 1, 16–20.

National Records for Scotland (2017) Population of Scotland. Accessed on 28/06/2019 at https://www.nrscotland.gov.uk/statistics-and-data/statistics/scotlands-facts/population-of-scotland.

NHS Education for Scotland (2009) *Spiritual Care Matters: An Introductory Resource for all NHSScotland Staff.* Edinburgh: NHS Education for Scotland.

Paterson, M. and Clegg, C. (2013) *Education, Training and Formation for Healthcare Chaplains: Report of an NHS Review.* Edinburgh: NHS Education for Scotland.

Reave, L. (2005) 'Spiritual values and practices related to leadership effectiveness.' *The Leadership Quarterly* 16, 655–687.

Scottish Government (2009) *Spiritual Care and Chaplaincy.* Edinburgh: Scottish Government. Accessed on 03/08/19 at www.gov.scot/publications/spiritual-care-chaplaincy.

Scottish Government (2010) *The Healthcare Quality Strategy of NHSScotland.* Edinburgh: Scottish Government. Accessed on 03/04/2018 at www.gov.scot/Publications/2010/05/10102307/0.

Scottish Government (2011a) *Achieving Sustainable Quality in Scotland's Healthcare: A '20:20' Vision.* Edinburgh: Scottish Government. Accessed on 03/04/2018 at www.gov.scot/Topics/Health/Policy/2020-Vision/Strategic-Narrative.

Scottish Government (2011b) *A Routemap to the 2020 Vision for Health and Social Care.* Edinburgh: Scottish Government. Accessed on 3/3/2018 at www.gov.scot/Resource/0042/00423188.pdf.

Scottish Social Attitudes Survey (2017) *Scots with No Religion at Record Level*. Accessed on 03/04/2018 at www.scotcen.org.uk/ news-media/press-releases/2017/july/ scots-with-no-religion-at-record-level/?_ ga=2.210933461.1711967086.1522758939- 960747545.1522758939.

Senge, P. (1990) *The Fifth Discipline: The Art and Practices of Organizational Learning*. New York, NY: Doubleday.

Spiritual Care Australia (2013) *National Standards of Practice*. Accessed on 29/11/2017 at www. spiritualcareaustralia.org.au/SCA/About_Us/ Standards_Policies/SCA/Standards_and_ Policies.aspx?hkey=a9ff6708-6bf9-4577-a908- d58f7d2ba953.

Spiritual Health Victoria (2015) *Spiritual Care Providers (Faith Community Appointed) Credentialling Framework*. Melbourne, Victoria: Spiritual Health Victoria. Accessed on 29/11/2017 at www.spiritualhealthvictoria.org. au/standards-and-frameworks.

Spiritual Health Victoria (2016a) *Capability Framework for Spiritual Care Practitioners in Health Services*. Melbourne, Victoria: Spiritual Health Victoria. Accessed on 29/11/2017 at www.spiritualhealthvictoria.org.au/standards- and-frameworks.

Spiritual Health Victoria (2016b) *Spiritual Care in Victorian Health Services: Towards Best Practice Framework*. Melbourne, Victoria: Spiritual Health Victoria. Accessed on 28/11/2017 at www.spiritualhealthvictoria.org.au/standards- and-frameworks.

Spiritual Health Victoria (2016c) *Spiritual Care Minimum Data Set Framework*. Melbourne, Victoria: Spiritual Health Victoria. Accessed on 28/11/2017 at www.spiritualhealthvictoria.org. au/standards-and-frameworks.

Swift, C. (2015) *NHS Chaplaincy Guidelines 2015: Promoting Excellence in Pastoral, Spiritual and Religious Care*. London: NHS England. Accessed on 28/12/2017 at www.england. nhs.uk/wp-content/uploads/2015/03/nhs- chaplaincy-guidelines-2015.pdf.

Till, A. and McKimm, J. (2016) 'Leading from the frontline.' *British Medical Journal 353*, 56–57.

UK Board of Healthcare Chaplaincy (2017) *Spiritual and Religious Care Capabilities and Competences for Healthcare Chaplains Bands (or Levels) 5, 6, 7 and 8*. Accessed on 29/11/2017 at www.ukbhc.org.uk/sites/default/files/ ukbhc_spiritual_and_religious_capabilities_ and_competences_bands_5_-_8_2017.pdf.

Victorian Government (2014) *Allied Health: Credentialling, Competency and Capability Framework – Driving Effective Workforce Practice in a Changing Health Environment*. Accessed on 21/04/2018 at www2.health. vic.gov.au/health-workforce/allied-health- workforce/allied-health-ccc-framework.

Chapter 23

Future Directions

Posing and Living with Questions

Ewan Kelly and John Swinton

Introduction

In our concluding chapter, emerging from the contributions to this collaborative work, we offer readers some strategic questions to consider about the future of healthcare chaplaincy operating at three levels of healthcare activity:

- *micro* (individual) level

- *meso* (team, departmental, community or locality/institution within a healthcare system or organization) level

- *meta* (organizational, systems, national or international) level.

We do so believing chaplaincy has a key role in modelling a holistic approach to practice, which is at the core of people-centred health and social care. We also feel that transformative strategic leadership globally has a pivotal role to play in the future development of the chaplaincy profession and how chaplaincy potentially influences, and works within, rapidly evolving healthcare systems and cultures. Crucially, in such complex and transitional times, transformative leadership is not about having all the answers and applying them; rather, it is to understand context and listen to the wisdom and learnings from the initiatives of others. Importantly, it is then asking appropriate questions to enable colleagues to explore identified issues and find ways forward together. Such a collegial approach requires collaboration, communication and the building of relationships of trust to enable the taking of discerned meaningful risks (see below) to find contextual and prophetic ways forward.

We do not seek to proscribe what form chaplaincy practice will take in particular contexts in the future. We do, however, want to endorse a model of chaplaincy which might underpin practice at different levels of healthcare activity in those contexts. In doing so we have the development of the chaplaincy profession in mind; however, primarily, the approach proposed is made with what we feel is the *telos* of chaplaincy in the twenty-first century – the fostering of the spiritual wellbeing of people – at the forefront of consideration.

Such questions and the model proposed are significantly informed by the current context in which chaplains practise. The following is a brief reminder of what we consider are increasingly major contributors to spiritual 'dis-ease' (and financial cost in health and social care) in the post-industrial world:

- rapid demographic changes and the related increasing number of people living with one or more long-term conditions (and the associated losses of function, role and identity)

  Long-term, incurable conditions (such as diabetes, dementia, chronic obstructive airway disease and osteoarthritis) are more prevalent in older people; for example, in England, 58% of people over 60 years of age compared with 14% of people under 40 years (UK Department of Health 2012). People living with long-term conditions account for about 50% of all family doctor appointments, 64% of all outpatient appointments and over 70% of all inpatient bed days (UK Department of Health 2012). Treatment and care for people with long-term conditions is estimated to take up around £7 in every £10 of total health and social care expenditure in England (UK Department of Health 2012).

- health inequalities and poverty

  For example, people in the poorest social class in England have a 60% higher prevalence of living with long-term conditions than those in the richest social class, and 30% more severity of disease (UK Department of Health 2012).

- societal loneliness and isolation

  Within a US context, one in four people regularly feel lonely, and such chronic loneliness increases the odds of an early death by 20% – a similar impact on morbidity as obesity (Adams 2016).

- staff (in health and social care) and care provider (family members, friends and neighbours) stress

- increased expectations of quality and quantity of life by the general population (and the impact when people feel these expectations are not met)

Pausing to reflect before looking forward

As practical theologians, following engagement with practice (in the form of contributions to this book), we want to refer to some theological and spiritual reflection before offering questions for readers to consider contextually in order to envision the way forward for future chaplaincy practice at different levels of healthcare activity. We want to refer to:

- Jesus's encounter with blind Bartimaeus (Mark 10:46–52) – a story involving courage, choosing to risk being open to transformation, leaving behind a well-defined identity and journeying forward

- the parable of the talents (Matthew 25:14–30) – a story which challenges the hearer to risk using her abilities entrepreneurially, with the possibility of failure, in order to enable positive outcomes which are subject to accountability

- the Nazareth manifesto of Jesus (Luke 4:18–19) – recognizing inequality and its impact on wellbeing and choosing a preference for the poor and the marginalized.

This is a significant part of what makes chaplaincy unique amongst the healthcare professions – envisioning and future practice being informed not just by research and the external pressures and narratives of health and care culture, important as they both are. Therefore, it is important that a vision for chaplaincy, and its enactment at micro-, meso- and meta-levels of healthcare activity, be shaped also by intentional spiritual or theological reflection according to a chaplain's vocational canon – the spiritual basis for a person's understanding of their role. A challenge being, however, in our postmodern context, that there is no one single meta-narrative which informs such understanding.

An important principle which informed the process by which this book was co-constructed resonates with a central theme in all three aforementioned biblical narratives: to enact an ongoing transformational personal and professional, and thus fulfilling, life is to take *meaningful risks*. The process by which this edited book was co-created is as important to us as the product itself, for we hope the approach to its co-construction models an intent which we believe is important for the future development and professionalization of chaplaincy as well as the spiritual wellbeing of the people with whom chaplains work. Such *meaningful risk-taking* involves the active fostering and support of activities which are discerned to potentially, but are not necessarily guaranteed to, promote transformation and enhance wellbeing. In relation to this book, this involved, and for the future of healthcare chaplaincy (at different levels of healthcare activity) will mean:

- collaboration based on relationships of trust

- innovation and creativity

- promoting a learning culture which enables:

  - fostering public storytelling and dissemination of new approaches and initiatives, and the learnings from such activity (by the well-known and established chaplains as well as those doing it for the first time)

  - influencing of future practice which is people-centred and contextually relevant.

Further reflections on the significance of *meaningful risk* and what it may involve to enable the promotion of transformation are threaded through this concluding chapter. In order to facilitate readers' engagement with issues and questions regarding the future of healthcare chaplaincy, contributors have helped enable the processes given below.

Looking back

This book has outlined the evolution of chaplaincy from a fledgling to a maturing healthcare profession with contributions from across the world. Different chapters have reflected on that growing professional identity and, with it, an understanding of necessary educational requirements and strengthening evidence base to enhance professional confidence and practice. Moreover, collaborators have shared their reflective insights and innovative practice, which celebrate the profession's creativity, engagement in collaboration and impact up to the present day. Such looking back sets a foundation for looking forward, particularly with strategic intent and vision (Cadge 2018).

Looking in

The argument has been made for the need for rigorous and consistent formation as a basis, not just for ongoing transformative learning and practice, but also for developing personal and professional confidence. This in turn promotes relationship building, envisioning and innovation at micro-, meso- and meta-levels of healthcare activity – key requirements for chaplaincy practice in the twenty-first century. Furthermore, the importance of ongoing support for each chaplain's inner journey and, thus, their continual deepening self-awareness has been emphasized, for such is a key ingredient of transformative leadership as much as when accompanying individuals. In addition, it is fundamental to helping sustain and nurture chaplains throughout their vocational journeys.

Looking around

The case has been made that, to enable relevant practice, chaplains need to be able to analyse and understand the context they are working in – locally, organizationally, nationally and globally. This necessitates appropriate knowledge and skills being acquired and time and support being given for contextual analysis to be performed. An integral part of such activity is the development of strategic literacy for all chaplains. The aim of such literacy is to enable chaplaincy practice, at whatever level of healthcare activity, to be fit for purpose and to support organizations and systems in the delivery of policies which promote spiritual wellbeing. The liminal health and care landscape described in this book also affords opportunities for chaplaincy to influence future just, inclusive and people-centred strategic planning of health and care services at meso- and meta-levels. This requires that chaplains understand and can navigate systems' complexities.

Looking within the profession

Chaplains are not only living with, and are in, liminality, but the profession as a whole is in liminality – a betwixt and between place – a place of transition and flux. Perhaps it has always been this way; however, the complexity, uncertainty and speed of change in healthcare and wider society is like never before. The profession is on the threshold of new models of practice – new ways of being, influencing and connecting.

In such a time of transition, all that is established and all that is emerging sit alongside each other – often in tension. This book has sought to enable such creative tension to be – and to be an offering with which to engage. We hope this reflects some of the conversations that are current within the chaplaincy profession globally, for example discussion about the role of outcomes, the place of an evidence base (and of what sort), chaplaincy as art or science and chaplaincy as fundamentally a profession which accompanies individuals in crisis in institutional settings or as one which majors in promoting communal spiritual wellbeing.

Looking beside

Cadge (2018) describes chaplaincy as a 'companion' profession. Chaplains certainly learn much from those we accompany (Casement 1985) and those who accompany *us* – academics, researchers, educators, healthcare managers as well as leaders and practitioners from other health and care disciplines. This book has sought to offer insights and reflections by representatives from both groupings from whom chaplains can learn and by whom they are affirmed and asked questions. Co-production takes such learning to the next logical step by inviting chaplains not just to learn from those we work with but also to risk co-producing health, including spiritual health, care services and the research that evaluates such things.

Looking forward

Looking forward requires the courage that Bartimaeus showed. He was blind. This afforded him a certain identity and role which was profoundly negative. However, he wanted, and was energized by, the possibility of something more meaningful. He chose to cast aside the security of the status quo and risked opening himself to transformation – not remaining stationary but actively taking a new direction. The global context within which chaplains are currently working provides opportunities for transformation (and to help transform) as well as challenges for chaplaincy. Whilst inhabiting a place which is betwixt and between, chaplaincy is on the threshold. Are chaplains brave enough, equipped well enough and personally and professionally confident enough to step forward through this threshold into a land of new possibilities and opportunities? Before we do so – or even more frightening or exhilarating (depending on your perspective), *as we do so*, such is the gathering pace of change – we need to ask ourselves some searching and significant questions in order to inform our envisioning for now and the future.

Future directions

Questions

As current models of healthcare in the post-industrial era are no longer sustainable, change is inevitable. Change is already happening, and the speed at which it takes place will only quicken. This necessitates, within the current conditions of flux, that chaplaincy as a profession, as with other health and care disciplines, has honest and bold intra-professional conversations about our professional role, our priorities and our models of working for the future.

Such conversations can pave the way for interdisciplinary engagement and with policymakers and politicians.

From experience, strategically orientated questions are only heard and considered seriously when there are relationships of trust between those who ask the questions and those to whom the questions are directed. Moreover, those who ask the questions need to be perceived as having professional credibility by those who are invited to receive and explore them. This has significant implications for chaplains operating in strategic leadership roles at meso- and meta-levels of healthcare activity. We invite readers to consider the following in relation to the future envisioning of healthcare chaplaincy and encourage reference to relevant contributions within the book to deepen engagement:

1. Whose need is being met by current prevalent chaplaincy models and foci of working?

2. Most of healthcare is delivered outwith institutional contexts in community or outpatient contexts. Why then does the vast majority of chaplaincy work still occur in institutional settings which focus on fixing deficit?

3. How can we work differently, utilizing our abilities, knowledge and skills, to maximize our impact on the spiritual wellbeing, not just health, of individuals, local communities, organizations and systems? Locally, nationally and internationally?

4. What might it feel like for chaplains to work collaboratively and creatively with faith communities, voluntary organizations and community members, as well as other health and care professionals in local communities, to co-produce individual and communal spiritual wellbeing (perhaps with, for example, a focus on reducing isolation and loneliness in the frail elderly)?

5. How might chaplaincy resources, human and financial, be redistributed for priority use in materially disadvantaged communities?

6. What might it be like to continue to work in institutions accompanying individuals in distress part-time *and* be involved in new ways of working in community contexts?

7. What might it be like to not meet certain people's or organizational perceived needs if chaplaincy was envisioned and delivered differently?

8. How might chaplaincy potentially influence the co-produced redesign of health and care services which actively involves service users to promote wellbeing?

9. How might it feel to be part of that which influences such an approach, where spirituality is central rather than peripheral, and/or be involved in its delivery locally?

10. What would it be like to be part of collaboratively and intentionally helping to deliver aspirational policies which are informed by a salutogenic (Antonovsky 1987) or assets-based vision?

   For example, the Scottish Government's (2011a) 'Achieving Sustainable Quality in Scotland's Healthcare: A 20:20 Vision' which seeks to enable 'by 2020 everyone…to live longer healthier lives at home, or in a homely setting'. This involves having 'a healthcare system where we have integrated health and social care, a focus on prevention, anticipation and supported self-management'(p.2).

   What would it feel like to step forward at meso- and meta-levels of healthcare activity and say to organizational and political leaders, 'Chaplains can help you deliver such person- and people-centred policies'?

   And to say, 'This is how we will do it. This is the gathered evidence or developing evidence base which shows we can do it and how it impacts positively on the wellbeing of people.'

11. How do the above questions relate to your vocational canon – those spiritual resources which inform the values and attitudes which underpin your practice?

We hope many other questions will have emerged for readers whilst reading the varied contributions which will provoke conversations about the strategic development of chaplaincy globally and more locally.

Toward envisioning the future for healthcare chaplaincy

In order to further maximize chaplaincy's impact on the spiritual wellbeing of the people with whom chaplains work, we endorse the model of chaplains acting as *spiritual drivers or agents of transformation* (based on Paterson and Clegg 2013) working at micro-, meso- and meta-levels of healthcare activity. Embracing such a model chaplaincy requires changing its current emphasis in key aspects of its approach to work effectively and creatively in our liminal and financially challenged twenty-first-century context (appreciating that there are variations in different contexts). Table 23.1 summarizes the shifts in chaplaincy practice which may be required to enable such a model to maximize its impact on spiritual wellbeing.

Table 23.1 Summary of proposed shifts of foci for
the future of healthcare chaplaincy

Current focus of chaplaincy practice	Moving toward
Person centred	People centred
Ill health	Promoting wellbeing
Institutional	More community based
Micro-level of healthcare activity	Meso- and meta-levels of healthcare activity
Management of chaplaincy services	Transformative strategic leadership
Chaplaincy collaboration piecemeal	Chaplaincy collaboration strategically planned
Local, piecemeal innovation	Creating intentional culture(s) of innovation and learning

The proposed shifts in the foci of chaplaincy's priorities has wide-reaching implications for the future of the chaplaincy profession.

Intra-professional implications

In this section we will explore some of the *intra-professional* implications under the following headings:

- strategic and dispersed transformational leadership and collaboration
- education and training
- innovation
- research, audit and improvement.

Strategic and dispersed transformational leadership and collaboration

It is only recently that chaplaincy globally has begun to understand the necessity and benefit of developing strategic leadership and not just working to a management model within the profession. Strategic leadership operating at meso- and meta-levels of healthcare activity, as spiritual enablement of transformation, is imperative if chaplaincy is to be fit for purpose within emerging health and care systems, the goal of which is promoting individual and communal wellbeing and not just seeking to cure, fix or fill deficits. Chaplaincy leaders in localities, organizations and networks, as well as of associations and national services, need to take meaningful risks in seeking to bring about cultural change in chaplaincy globally. This includes promoting a culture in chaplaincy in which new approaches can be tried, evaluated, reflected upon, learned from and, as appropriate, embedded and normalized. This requires courageous and transformative leadership which not only envisions in liminal spaces but promotes the co-creation of permissive innovative and learning cultures.

Alongside this is the need to foster greater collaboration, communication and knowledge exchange within the global chaplaincy community. This is not just about research as, for example, is already established through organizations such as Transforming Chaplaincy, the European Research Institute for Chaplains in Healthcare (ERICH) and the Joint Research Council (an initiative of the Association of Professional Chaplaincy in the US), but also in relation to:

- formation, education and training
- developing and supporting strategic leadership and envisioning
- knowledge exchange of best practice
- promotion of innovation and creativity.

Such a culture of collaboration can be only developed through an intentional commitment to the time and energy required to build relationships of trust at meta-levels of healthcare activity between strategic chaplaincy leaders of organizations, healthcare systems, professional associations and in different areas of professional interest worldwide. We hope that collaborative contributions in this book model the benefits and learnings from international relationships, interaction and exchange.

Education and training

We believe, as introduced in Chapter 21, there is merit in seeking to co-produce a global common framework to underpin the formational and educational development of chaplains to be fit for purpose to work as spiritual agents of transformation in twenty-first-century healthcare. This would require much prior relationship building and collaboration by chaplaincy educationalists from a range of cultures and contexts who prioritize different models of chaplaincy and, thus, educational emphases. Prior to such a piece of work, the development of competencies and capabilities relevant to new emergent models of healthcare chaplaincy would need to be created in turn to inform any educational frameworks developed. As above, the process of such enterprises would be as significant, if not more so, than any end products which might be produced. Deepening understanding of contexts and chaplaincy models, building relationships and sharing educational initiatives would be beneficial for the ongoing professionalization of chaplaincy and how it promotes spiritual wellbeing globally and locally.

Innovation

Strategically fostering and supporting innovation internationally, nationally and within organizations and systems would be significant for the development of chaplaincy and how it seeks to maximize its impact on the wellbeing of people individually and communally. This is not to say that innovation and creativity in practice, education, research and leadership is not alive and thriving within chaplaincy, but rather that, predominantly, it happens in a piecemeal way. It would be a very different thing for innovation to be strategically planned for, and supported as, integral aspects of organizational or national programmes of work or delivery plans. Again, the research agenda within global chaplaincy leads the way. For example, ERICH has developed an Innovation and Development Forum made up of chaplaincy researchers and academics across Europe. Why is innovation so significant in the current liminal global context?

Working out of a place of *habitus*, performing tasks in healthcare (including chaplaincy) consistently safely and effectively, informed by relevant competencies and standards, is important. It ensures the safety of people and clarity of role. The impact of well-defined tasks performed can be quantitatively measured and disseminated to prove value. Relevant educational programmes can be developed with clear learning outcomes and curricula. Such an approach to work emerges from a modernist or positivist epistemology and predominates current healthcare culture. With the combination of financial pressures and such a competency-based approach, a risk-averse environment which is heavily governanced may be precipitated. At its extreme, a 'command and control' culture develops where an industry is made out of producing quantitative data to enable comparisons against objective 'targets' to be made in order to scrutinize departmental and organizational 'performance'. Such performance targets have their place, but when they predominate over other measures (such as patient stories or indicators of wellbeing) to communicate how well a healthcare organization is functioning, a culture is created which pressurizes staff and management alike. Such a risk-averse approach to healthcare is not only limited and stifling in terms of creativity and innovation; it also is unsustainable due to current financial austerity and rapid changes in demographic and comorbidity patterns (Auditor General 2018). New approaches are required.

There is a need to balance, and indeed perhaps counter, such habitual intention with *phronesis* (i.e. working at any level of healthcare activity from a place of professional wisdom where decision-making is informed by reflection and reflexivity based on information from head, heart and gut, and underpinned by character). Whilst valuing safety and competency, a culture of meaningful risk to promote innovation also needs to be promoted in chaplaincy. This, we believe, is crucial for the continuing development of chaplaincy and, indeed, for maximizing its impact on the spiritual wellbeing of people, communities and organizational cultures. It is important in such an environment that when initiatives do not work out as hoped, they are not considered as mistakes or errors but as opportunities for learning and development. Innovation and creativity, thus, can flourish within a permissive learning culture.

Despite the increasingly performance-targeted and safety-oriented emphasis in Scottish healthcare culture at present, there remains within aspirational policies something else. For example, within the Scottish Government's (2011b) *A Route Map to 2020 Vision for Health and Social Care* – a resource document pointing toward how the transformation of Scottish health and social care may be achieved as outlined in the Scottish Government's (2011a) *Achieving Sustainable Quality in Scotland's Healthcare: A 20:20 Vision* – there are outlined 12 priority areas for improvement to support the policy's delivery. Of these priority areas, sitting alongside the need to improve efficiency and productivity is the need to innovate in order to deliver effective quality, sustainable and value-for-money healthcare. As described in Chapters 13, 15 and 17, Scottish chaplains took meaningful risks at all three levels of healthcare activity as they sought to innovate and take advantage of specified Scottish Government funding streams. Such innovation has promoted individual and communal spiritual wellbeing and enabled the enactment of government policy. Moreover, it has changed the shape of Scottish chaplaincy and helped maximize and measure its impact on the spiritual wellbeing of the people of Scotland. It has also reinforced learning, as in the parable of the talents, that when finance is offered in trust, responding to governance and accountability is both morally right and an opportunity to build (in this case professional) credibility and trust. In addition, the realization of the significance of finding ways to measure and disseminate the impact of innovation and practice was reinforced.

Research, audit and improvement

There will continue to be a need to develop a relevant evidence base for chaplaincy which speaks to, and is heard, within an empirically informed culture which focuses on the healthcare needs of individuals within institutions. The recent strategic momentum gathered globally within chaplaincy research, based on many years of hard work and envisioning, is to be greatly commended. Chaplains, in the words of George F Handzo (see Chapter 7), need to be pragmatic in their approach to research methodology. Current prevalent research work involving case studies and patient-related outcome measures, for example, has enabled many chaplains to participate in research for the first time. Research literacy is quickly becoming understood as a fundamental aspect of chaplaincy education, and this needs to be built on for the ongoing professionalization of chaplaincy.

However, in the future there will be the need for a parallel move within chaplaincy research in alignment with a change in chaplaincy practice focus from individual care and outcomes to communal engagement and shared outcomes; thus, a need for case studies which reveal how chaplains engage and relate whilst seeking to promote communal spiritual wellbeing to understand more deeply what it is about such chaplaincy practice that may uniquely affect such things. There will be a need for research into how communal, not just individual, spiritual needs may be best assessed and to what extent chaplaincy involvement impacts on communal spiritual wellbeing through outcomes-focused research.

There is no doubt, as systems remain under financial strain, even if gradually transitioning to systems more focused on wellbeing, that the need for monitoring of performance as part of governance and accountability will continue. Chaplains, therefore, will increasingly be required to creatively utilize measurements designed to capture the outcomes and experience of people they work with as part of quality improvement in a variety of contexts. For example, in Scotland a core suite of indicators has been developed within a National Health and Wellbeing Outcomes framework for working with people living with comorbidities (The Health and Social Care Alliance Scotland n.d., p.17). Being able to show, for example, that chaplains have been able to enhance the engagement of staff in their work (one indicator in the framework) through the facilitation of Values Based Reflective Practice (VBRP) (see Chapter 15) enables chaplains to evidence their added value and value for money.

New chaplaincy standards (see Chapter 8) which enable the auditing of chaplaincy services will need to be developed which relate to chaplaincy involvement in the promotion of corporate spiritual wellbeing within different contexts – standards which enable the auditing of spiritual care services working in community contexts, not just in healthcare institutions.

Facilitation of the co-production (see Chapter 19) of research design involving service users is another creative way chaplains can act as spiritual agents of transformation within organizations and systems to promote a people-centred approach to health and wellbeing.

Chaplains as spiritual enablers or drivers of transformation

The move from shifting the focus of chaplaincy work from persons to people, from institutions to community settings and increasing engagement at meso- and meta-levels of healthcare activity resonate with the shift in the world of pastoral theology from a focus on living human documents to living human webs. With this shift is a recognition that there is 'a social web of systems, structures and policies that individuals are tangled up with' (Pembroke 2017, p.134). This can have a considerable impact on the spiritual wellbeing of individuals, teams, institutions and local communities. Maximizing a chaplain's contribution to promoting wellbeing in an organization or community using relational, reflective and reflexive gifts might mean at a meso-level facilitating VBRP (see Chapter 15) with a group of managers and leaders from healthcare and/or community groups. It could also mean investing time to build supportive relationships with strategic leaders or members of groups which represent staff interests. Such relationships may lead to mutual understanding of each other's roles and invitations to sit on policymaking or advocacy groups. At meta-levels, Anne Vandenhoeck articulately describes the importance of forging similar relationships with politicians, faith and belief leaders, and national or international figures who have a wellbeing agenda (see Chapter 9). In short, central to acting as a spiritual enabler of transformation at meso- and meta-levels of healthcare activity is intentionally forging relationships or alliances to enable collaborative working and influencing. This fosters collaboration with others who are interested in reducing the causes as well as the symptoms of ill health and lack of wellbeing, such as health inequalities and staff stress.

There are many like-minded citizens who staff and utilize health and care services who have similar concerns, whether they would call them spiritual or not, who would wish practice to be holistic and people-centred, and the design of services to be co-produced. For example, a group of family doctors and academics concerned with making clinical guidelines less systems focused stated, 'Good care involves a partnership between patients and healthcare professionals where people matter more than their separate health conditions' (McCartney *et al.* 2016, p.361).

Developing relationships with medical leaders such as Ken Donaldson (Chapter 15), and others who have influence, passion and share similar values, may help chaplains to play a significant role in cultural transformation, for example in re-humanizing healthcare – thereby contributing to transforming services such that they become less 'soulless, anonymous, wasteful and inefficient' (Porter 2002, cited by Goodrich and Cornwall 2008, p.2).

In a real sense, to act as spiritual enablers of transformation in health and care systems and communities requires all chaplains to enact a leadership role. To promote such dispersed leadership has implications not only for formation, education and training; it has implications also for the *style* of strategic leadership utilized. It requires one of empowerment, acting with practical wisdom and being prepared to take meaningful risks in people, and with people, for the people they seek to empower, with the aim of promoting meaning and wellbeing for both.

Final comments

Dag Hammarskjold was a secretary general to the United Nations in the post-war era. Professionally, as a diplomat, he sought wholeness for, and re-connection between, different parts of a fractured global community. Personally, he was a starkly honest spiritual diarist. Hammarskjold found meaning and purpose in his values-based struggles to promote shared human flourishing through transformative leadership involving self-awareness, much intentional reflection, relationship building, collaboration and envisioning. May the global healthcare chaplaincy community, in risking to 'advance' the soul of healthcare for the future, whilst not losing touch with our profession's evolution, resonate with Hammarskjold's (1966) approach to life, even in the most uncertain of times – giving thanks for what has been and saying *yes* to all that will emerge!

References

Adams, T. (2016) 'John Cacioppo: loneliness is like an iceberg – it goes deeper than we can see.' *The Guardian*, 28 February, pp.12–13. Accessed on 01/07/2019 at www.theguardian.com/science/2016/feb/28/loneliness-is-like-an-iceberg-john-cacioppo-social-neuroscience-interview.

Antonovsky, A. (1987) *Unraveling the Mystery of Health: How People Manage Stress and Stay Well.* San Francisco, CA: Jossey-Bass.

Auditor General (2018) *NHS in Scotland 2018.* Edinburgh: Audit Scotland.

Cadge, W. (2018) 'Healthcare chaplaincy as a companion profession: historical developments.'

Journal of Healthcare Chaplaincy, 13 August, 1–16. doi: 10.1080/08854726.2018.1463617.

Casement, P. (1985) *On Learning from the Patient.* London: Tavistock Publications.

Goodrich, J. and Cornwall, J. (2008) *Seeing the Person.* London: King's Fund.

Hammarskjold, D. (1966) *Markings.* (Translated by W.H. Auden and L. Sjoberg.) London: Faber and Faber Limited. (Original work published 1964.)

McCartney, M., Treadwell, J., Maskrey, N. and Lehman, R. (2016) 'Guideline driven care: time to get personal.' *British Medical Journal 353,* i2452, 360–361.

Paterson, M. and Clegg, C. (2013) *Education, Training and Formation for Healthcare Chaplains: Report of an NHS Review.* Edinburgh: NHS Education for Scotland.

Pembroke, N. (2017) *Foundations of Pastoral Counselling.* London: SCM Press.

Scottish Government (2011a) *Achieving Sustainable Quality in Scotland's Healthcare: A 20:20 Vision.* Edinburgh: Scottish Government.

Accessed on 23/03/2018 at www.scotland.gov. uk/Resource/0039/00398668.doc.

Scottish Government (2011b) *A Route Map to 2020 Vision for Health and Social Care.* Edinburgh: NHS Scotland. Accessed on 16/12/2018 at www2.gov.scot/Resource/0042/00423188.pdf.

The Health and Social Care Alliance Scotland (n.d.) *Many Conditions, One Life: Living Well with Multiple Conditions.* Glasgow: The Health and Social Care Alliance Scotland.

UK Department of Health (2012) *Report: Long-term Conditions Compendium of Information* (3rd edition). London: Department of Health. Accessed on 19/12/2018 at https://assets. publishing.service.gov.uk/government/ uploads/system/uploads/attachment_data/ file/216528/dh_134486.pdf.

Subject Index

Sub-headings in *italics* indicate tables and figures.

Author Index